CLASSIC CARS AND
AUTOMOBILE
ENGINEERING

Volume 1

BALLOON TIRE—REAR WHEEL

ENGINE, PRINCIPLES, CYLINDERS, CRANKSHAFTS, CARBURETORS, CLUTCHES

Classic Cars and Automobile Engineering:
Volume 1

Engine, Principles, Cylinders, Crankshafts, Carburetors, Clutches

Restored by Mark Bussler

More books at
CGRpublishing.com

The Complete Ford Model T
Guide: Enlarged Illustrated
Special Edition

The American Railway:
The Trains, Railroads, and People
Who Ran the Rails

Antique Cars and Motor Vehicles:
Illustrated Guide to Operation,
Maintenance, and Repair

Automobile Engineering

A General Reference Work

FOR REPAIR MEN, CHAUFFEURS, AND OWNERS; COVERING THE CONSTRUCTION, CARE, AND REPAIR OF PLEASURE CARS, COMMERCIAL CARS, AND MOTORCYCLES, WITH SPECIAL ATTENTION TO IGNITION, START-ING, AND LIGHTING SYSTEMS, GARAGE EQUIPMENT, WELDING, FORD CONSTRUCTION AND REPAIR, AND OTHER REPAIR METHODS

Prepared by a Staff of

AUTOMOBILE EXPERTS, CONSULTING ENGINEERS, AND DESIGNERS OF THE HIGHEST PROFESSIONAL STANDING

Illustrated with over Fifteen Hundred Engravings

FIVE VOLUMES

CHRYSLER CROWN IMPERIAL, 1925

Table of Contents

VOLUME I

Gasoline Automobiles

By Morris A. Hall   *Revised by Tom C. Plumridge*

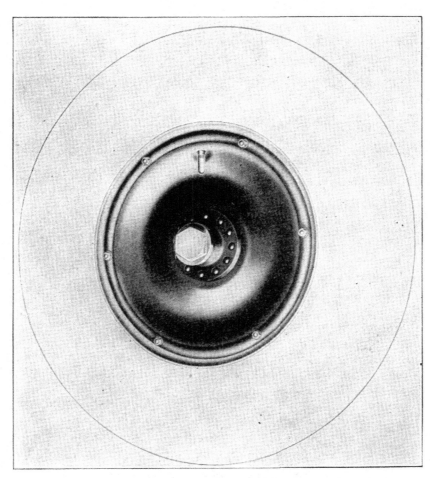

CURVED DISC WHEEL
Courtesy of Motor Wheel Corporation

Foreword

THE period of evolution of the automobile does not span many years, but the evolution has been none the less spectacular and complete. From a creature of sudden caprices and uncertain behavior, it has become today a well-behaved thoroughbred of known habits and perfect reliability. The driver no longer needs to carry war clothes in momentary expectation of a call to the front. He sits in his seat, starts his motor by pressing a button with his hand or foot, and probably for weeks on end will not need to do anything more serious than feed his animal gasoline or oil, screw up a few grease cups, and pump up a tire or two.

And yet, the traveling along this road of reliability and mechanical perfection has not been easy, and the grades have not been negotiated or the heights reached without many trials and failures. The application of the internal-combustion motor, the electric motor, the storage battery, and the steam engine to the development of the modern types of mechanically propelled road carriages has been a far-reaching engineering problem of great difficulty. Nevertheless, through the aid of the best scientific and mechanical minds in this and other countries, every detail has received the amount of attention necessary to make it as perfect as possible. Road troubles, except in connection with tires, have become almost negligible and even the inexperienced driver, who knows barely enough to keep to the road and shift gears properly, can venture on long touring trips without fear of getting stranded. The refinements in the ignition, starting, and lighting systems have added greatly to the pleasure in running the car. Altogether, the automobile as a whole has become standardized, and unless some unforeseen developments are brought about, future changes in either the gasoline or the electric automobile will be merely along the line of greater refinement of the mechanical and electrical devices used.

⬤ Notwithstanding the high degree of reliability already spoken of, the cars, as they get older, will need the attention of the repair man. This is particularly true of the cars two and three seasons old. A special effort, therefore, has been made to furnish information which will be of value to the men whose duty it is to revive the faltering action of the motor and to take care of the other internal troubles in the machine.

⬤ Special effort has been made to emphasize the treatment of the Electrical Equipment of Gasoline Cars, not only because it is in this direction that most of the improvements have lately taken place but also because this department of automobile construction is least familiar to the repair men and others interested in the details of the automobile. A multitude of diagrams have been supplied showing the constructive features and wiring circuits of the majority of the systems. In addition to this instructive section, particular attention is called to the articles on Welding, Shop Information, Electrical Repairs, and Ford Construction and Repair.

OUTLINE OF AUTOMOBILE CONSTRUCTION

Of all the applications of the internal-combustion motor, it is safe to say that none is more important than that applied to the propulsion of the modern motor vehicle—the automobile—which nowadays throngs the roads and streets of nearly every country in the world, and serves a myriad of utilities as they never have been and never could be served by animal transportation.

Standardized, inexpensive to buy, and inexpensive to operate, almost unfailingly reliable, and proved capable of use in the hands of even the most unmechanical of operators, the automobile is at last coming fully into its own. Its design has become recognized as a branch of engineering by itself, its manufacture constitutes one of the greatest of the mechanical industries, and its use is a common necessity.

Naturally, in so tremendous a development, there is sustained by the general public every possible sort of relationship with the automobile, from that of the merely casual observer and occasional user, to the more interested owner; and thence on, in ever closer touch with the full significances of this field of engineering, to the high-skilled and well-paid drivers of cars, the experts who repair them, the shopmen who build them, and the engineers and draftsmen who design them.

All along this line there is an increasing need for knowledge—a demand for definite, specific, usable information concerning the science upon which the motor vehicle is based, and the practice upon which its construction and performance are founded.

In no other important field of engineering is there such a lack of correct and authoritative literature as in the automobile field.

This undoubtedly is due to two conditions that have been involved in the rapid growth of the automobile from a mere experiment to an achieved and commercial fact. The first condition is the circumstance that the men who have deeply studied the automobile from an engineering standpoint, and who are best informed about it, have not had the time to place upon paper the facts with which they are acquainted. The second condition—resulting from the rapid development of automobile design and engineering practice has left no time for the establishment of a formulated science, upon which textbooks of a genuine and permanent authority may be based.

What follows will be an advanced and comprehensive treatment of the very latest devices applied in automobile engineering. All are carefully described, their essentials fully analyzed, and their important details fully illustrated.

Historical material of any kind is useless in a work of this sort, which is intended primarily for the man in the shop, who does the actual work of completing the car in the first place, and the man in the garage who keeps it in running order thereafter. It will suffice to say that while most of the worthy efforts and early progress in the development of the explosion motor and the automobile were made abroad, American designers and American workmen have since shown the way in this field to the whole world, so that today we import a negligible number of motors and cars, while we export to every other country of the world.

GENERAL OUTLINE OF MOTOR-CAR CONSTRUCTION

In general, all motor cars follow along the same broad lines. So much has this become the case in the last few years that a large number of the parts, units, and accessories entering into the construction of the car have become standardized and may, to a certain extent, be taken off one car and placed on another without extensive alteration. This has been done, too, without interfering in any way with the initiative of the various designers.

Groups and Parts. Practically all modern gasoline motor cars may be divided, in a mechanical sense, into six groups of parts or units. These are: (1) the engine, or power-producing group; (2) the clutch group, needed, as will be explained later on, with all forms of explosion motor; (3) the transmission, or gearset, for producing the various car speeds and different powers, while the engine gives a practically constant speed and power output; (4) the final drive group, which connects the speed variator or transmission with

SPRAGUE ELECTRIC DYNAMOMETER EQUIPMENT AT THE PLANT OF WEIDLEY MOTORS COMPANY, INDIANAPOLIS, INDIANA

the rear wheels, and thus propels the car. Of necessity, this includes the rear axle, while the front axle is usually grouped with the rear; (5) the steering device, for controlling the direction of motion; and (6) the frame, upon which all these and their various accessories are hung, with the springs for suspending the frame upon the axles of the car. There is, of course, a seventh group, the body, but that need not be discussed here, since reference is now made only to the mechanical parts.

Chassis Assembly. In the plan view of a modern motor car, page 4, the relative positions of the various units are clearly shown. In this, note that the engine is placed at the front of the outfit. This is now the position all the modern motor-car manufacturers use. The engine is to generate the power by drawing in, compressing, and exploding gas from gasoline.

Cylinder and Crankshaft Sub-Group. All this work is actually done within the *cylinder*, which really forms the basic working medium of the engine. The actual drawing-in of the gas, its compression and power are accomplished by the movements of the *piston* up and down in the cylinder bore. The piston is moved upward and downward by the rotation of the *crankshaft* except when the explosion reverses the situation, and the piston moves the crankshaft, to which it is attached by means of the *connecting rod.* The piston is made to fit tightly in the cylinder by means of *piston rings*, which are compressed into slots formed in the outside of the piston for this purpose. The connecting rod is forced to rotate by its attachment at the lower end to one of the *crankpins* of the crankshaft, which is held in the *crankshaft bearings* fastened in the *crankcase.* It is enabled to turn slightly at the upper, or piston, end by being pivoted on the *piston pin* or *wrist pin.* For convenience the crankcase is usually made in two parts, called the upper and lower *halves.* The cylinders are usually made with a removable *cylinder head* or a smaller removable *cylinder cover.*

Carburetion Sub-Group. The production of the gas necessitates what is called a *carburetor*, a good-sized *fuel tank*, and piping to connect the two. The fuel is not always pure and must be filtered through a *strainer.* There is a cock in the piping for turning gasoline from the tank to the carburetor on and off, while the gas produced is taken into the engine through an *inlet*

GASOLINE AUTOMOBILES

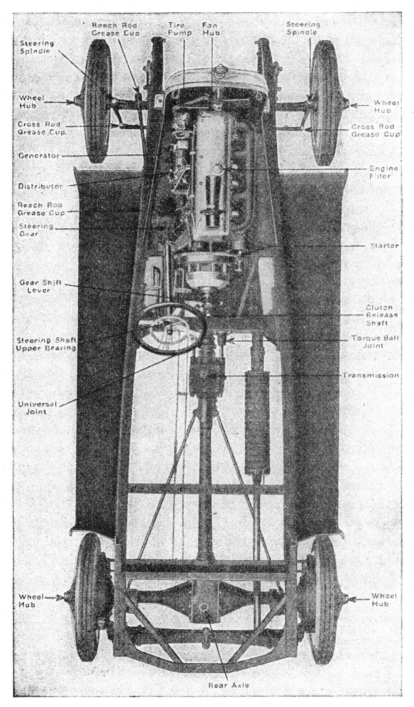

Plan View of the Marmon Chassis

manifold. These and other parts, the functions and construction of which will be explained in full later on, constitute the carburetion sub-group.

Inlet and Exhaust Valves. In order to get the gas, which is produced by the carburetion group, into the motor cylinders at the proper time and in the proper quantity, *inlet valves* are necessary. These valves are operated by *cams* on a *camshaft*. The camshaft, which will be explained in detail later, is driven from the *crankshaft* of the engine. After the gas has been admitted into the cylinders, compressed, and exploded, it is of no further use and must be removed from the cylinders. As this must be done at the proper time, and as the proper quantity must be removed, additional valves known as the *exhaust valves* are necessary. These are also operated by cams on a camshaft, driven from the crankshaft.

Exhaust System. The exhaust gases pass from the cylinder through a particular pipe, known as the *exhaust manifold*, and thence to the back of the car. As there remains considerable pressure in these gases when allowed to escape freely, they make much noise and considerable smoke, so that all cars are required by law to carry and use a *muffler*. The exhaust gases pass through this and thence out into the atmosphere. This whole group of parts is called the *exhaust system*.

Ignition System. The *explosion* comes in an intermediate stage. It is produced by means of an *electric spark*, made within the cylinders by means of a *spark plug*. The electric current, which is the original source of this spark, may be produced by a rotary current producer, known as a *magneto*, or it may be taken from a *battery*. In either case, the current must be brought up to a proper strength, and the various sparks must be produced at the exact time they are needed. All this calls for auxiliary apparatus. Moreover, the current producer, if it be a magneto, must be driven from some rotating shaft, and there must be a suitable place provided on the engine to attach it in such a way as to provide for quick and easy removal. All this, as a complete unit, is called the ignition system. A complete treatment of this subject will be found under "Electric Equipment for Gasoline Cars".

Cooling System. A great amount of heat is created by the following explosion and subsequent expanding and exhausting of the gas. Some idea of this may be gained from the two following state-

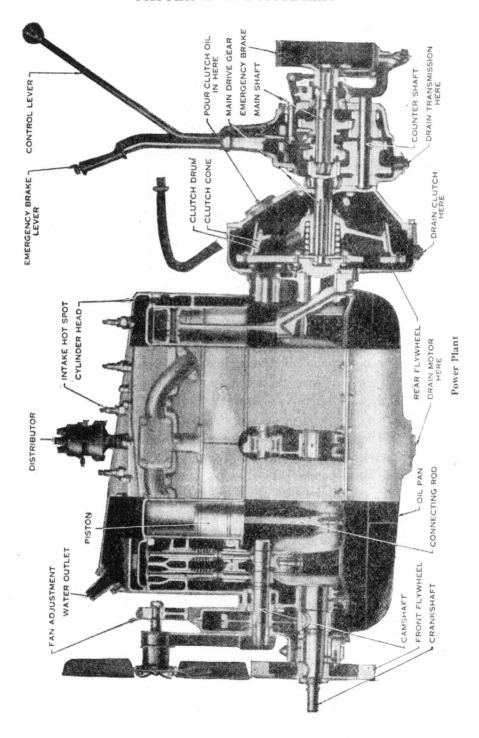

CONTROL LEVER

EMERGENCY BRAKE LEVER

POUR CLUTCH OIL IN HERE

MAIN DRIVE GEAR

EMERGENCY BRAKE

MAIN SHAFT

COUNTER SHAFT

DRAIN TRANSMISSION HERE

CLUTCH DRUM

CLUTCH CONE

DRAIN CLUTCH HERE

INTAKE HOT SPOT

CYLINDER HEAD

REAR FLYWHEEL

DRAIN MOTOR HERE

DISTRIBUTOR

OIL PAN

CONNECTING ROD

PISTON

FAN ADJUSTMENT

WATER OUTLET

CAMSHAFT

FRONT FLYWHEEL

CRANKSHAFT

Power Plant

15

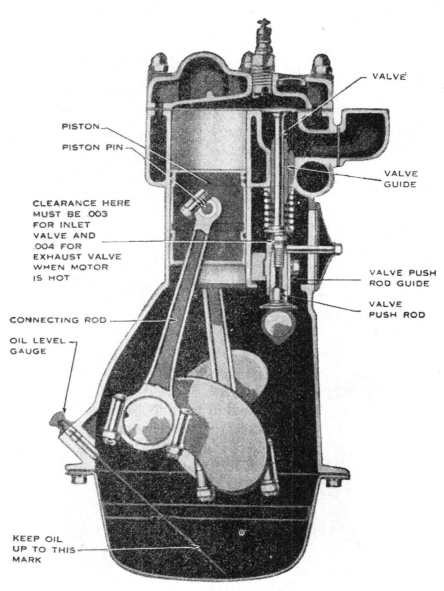

PISTON

PISTON PIN

VALVE

VALVE GUIDE

CLEARANCE HERE MUST BE .003 FOR INLET VALVE AND .004 FOR EXHAUST VALVE WHEN MOTOR IS HOT

VALVE PUSH ROD GUIDE

VALVE PUSH ROD

CONNECTING ROD

OIL LEVEL GAUGE

KEEP OIL UP TO THIS MARK

Cross-Section of Engine
Rickenbacker Motor Company

ments: The explosion temperature often runs up as high as 3000° F., and the exhaust temperature frequently is as high as 1500° F. In order to take away this heat, which communicates itself to the walls and to parts of the engine wherever it comes in contact with them, and, by conduction, to other parts with which it does not contact, the parts which are exposed to the greatest heat are surrounded by hollow passages, called *jackets*, through which water is forced, or allowed to flow. This might be called a collector of the heat, for it is then conducted to the *radiator*, a device for cooling the water. It is there cooled off and then used again. In order to circulate the water, a removable *pump*, driven from some rotating shaft, is used. All this, with the necessary piping to connect the various parts, is called the *cooling system*.

On some cars, notably the Franklin, and on motorcycles, there is another type of engine with an *air-cooled* system. This type will be taken up later.

Lubrication System. To make the various parts rotate within one another, *bearings*, or parts specially designed to facilitate easy and efficient rotation, must be used. In and on all such bearings a form of *lubricant* is necessary, also between all sliding parts. In order to have a copious supply of oil at certain points, various forms of *lubricators* or *oil pumps* are needed to circulate it; pipes must be provided to carry it; a *sight feed*, or visible indication that the system is working, must be placed in sight of the driver (usually on the dashboard); an *oil tank* for carrying the supply must be provided; and a location found for the lubricator or pump, as well as means for driving, removing, adjusting, and cleaning it. All this comes under the head of the lubrication system. This system covers, in addition, isolated points requiring lubrication and the different ways used to supply them.

Starting System. In order to start the engine, a *starting handle* is provided on all older cars, with possibly a *primer* working on the carburetor, and other parts. On modern cars, this work of starting is done by electricity, which requires a *starting motor*, a *battery*, a *switch* for connecting the two, wiring, buttons, and other parts. All this combined is called the *starting system*. For a complete treatment of Starting and Lighting Systems see the section on "Electrical Equipment."

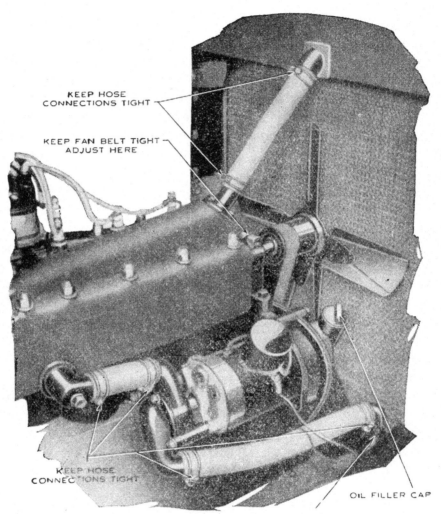

KEEP HOSE
CONNECTIONS TIGHT

KEEP FAN BELT TIGHT
ADJUST HERE

KEEP HOSE
CONNECTIONS TIGHT

OIL FILLER CAP

IN COLD WEATHER WHEN ANTI-FREEZE IS NOT USED DRAIN ALL
WATER FROM COOLING SYSTEM EVERY NIGHT AT THIS POINT

Cooling System
Rickenbacker Motor Company

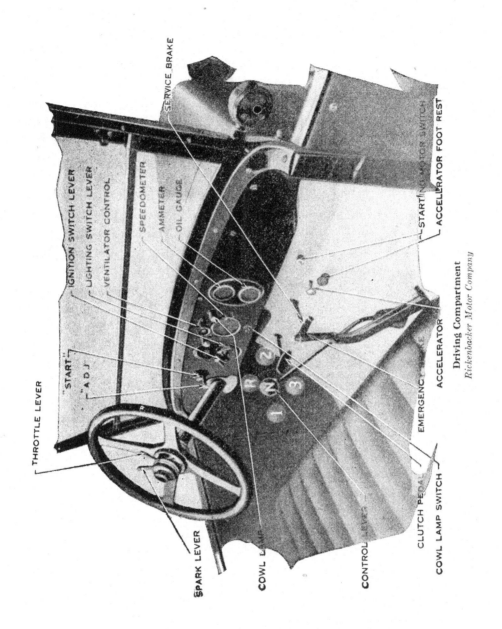

THROTTLE LEVER

"START"

"ADJ"

IGNITION SWITCH LEVER

LIGHTING SWITCH LEVER

VENTILATOR CONTROL

SPEEDOMETER

AMMETER

OIL GAUGE

SERVICE BRAKE

STARTING MOTOR SWITCH

ACCELERATOR FOOT REST

SPARK LEVER

COWL LAMP

CONTROL LEVER

EMERGENCY BRAKE

ACCELERATOR

CLUTCH PEDAL

COWL LAMP SWITCH

Driving Compartment
Rickenbacker Motor Company

19

Lighting System. Nearly all modern motor cars have an *electric lighting system.* This includes an *electric-current generator;* a *battery* to retain the electric current until needed; suitable governing devices to control the generation and flow of current; *lamps* to use the current; *wiring* to connect them with the source; *switches* to turn the current on and off; and other parts.

Flywheel. At one end of the engine shaft is the flywheel. This is a large, wide-faced member of metal, comparatively heavy, the function of which is to store energy (by means of rotation) as the engine produces it and to give it back to the engine at other parts of the cycle when energy is needed, and none is being produced. In short, it is a storehouse of energy, absorbing the same from the engine and giving back the excess when it is needed. In general, this effect is greatest when the mass of metal is farthest from the center, consequently flywheels are made of as large a diameter as is possible, considering the frame members. Note this in the illustration, Fig. 1.

Clutch Group. .The *clutch* is generally located inside the rim of the flywheel. This is a device, by means of which a positive connection can be made with the engine or a disconnection from it effected at the driver's will. When such disconnection is made with the engine running, it will continue to run idly, and the car will come to a standstill. Conversely, when the positive connection is made, the motor will drive the clutch and such parts beyond it as are connected-up at the time. This arrangement is necessary because of a peculiarity in the gas or gasoline engine which cannot start with a load, but must be started and allowed to get up speed before any load is thrown upon it. The function of the clutch, then, is to disconnect the balance of the driving system from the engine, so that it may attain the necessary speed to carry a load. When this has been done, the proper gear is engaged, the clutch is thrown in, and the engine picks up its load.

Like other groups, this must have a means of connecting and disconnecting, a proper place, proper fastenings, means for adjustment and removal, means for lubrication, and easy access to its parts. All this, collectively, is called the clutch group.

Transmission Group. As has just been pointed out, the gasoline engine cannot start with a load; it must get up speed first. When the load is first applied it must be light. This necessitates certain *gearing,* so that, when starting, the power of the engine may be multiplied

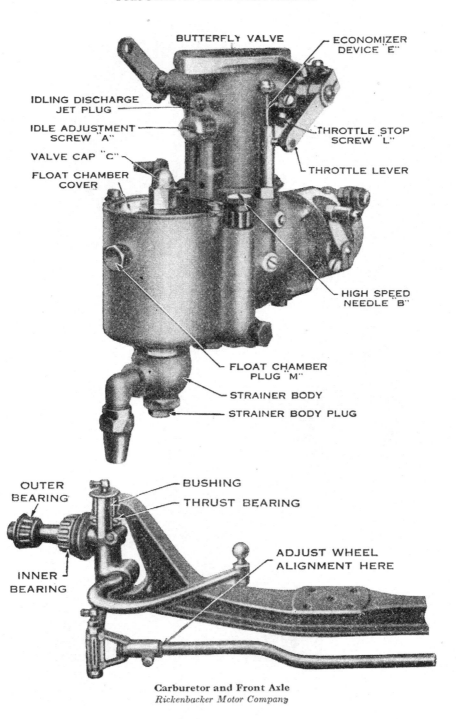

BUTTERFLY VALVE

ECONOMIZER DEVICE "E"

IDLING DISCHARGE JET PLUG

IDLE ADJUSTMENT SCREW "A"

THROTTLE STOP SCREW "L"

VALVE CAP "C"

THROTTLE LEVER

FLOAT CHAMBER COVER

HIGH SPEED NEEDLE "B"

FLOAT CHAMBER PLUG "M"

STRAINER BODY

STRAINER BODY PLUG

OUTER BEARING

BUSHING

THRUST BEARING

ADJUST WHEEL ALIGNMENT HERE

INNER BEARING

Carburetor and Front Axle
Rickenbacker Motor Company

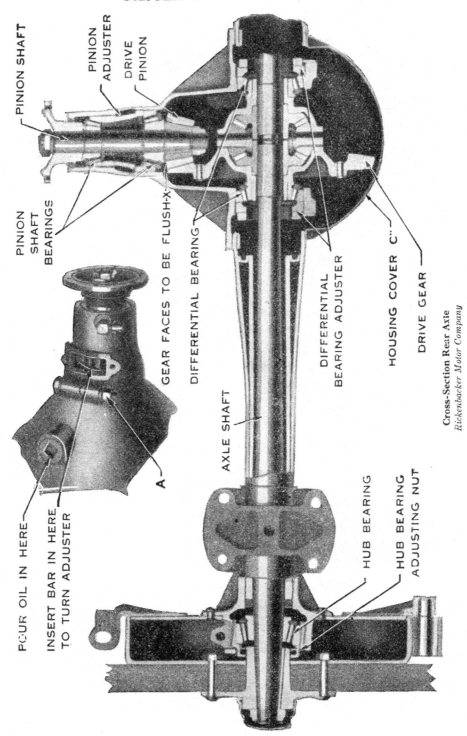

Cross-Section Rear Axle
Rickenbacker Motor Company

PINION SHAFT

PINION ADJUSTER

DRIVE PINION

PINION SHAFT BEARINGS

GEAR FACES TO BE FLUSH-x

DIFFERENTIAL BEARING

DIFFERENTIAL BEARING ADJUSTER

HOUSING COVER "C"

DRIVE GEAR

AXLE SHAFT

HUB BEARING

HUB BEARING ADJUSTING NUT

POUR OIL IN HERE

INSERT BAR IN HERE TO TURN ADJUSTER

A

many times before reaching the wheels and applied to the propulsion of the car. Furthermore, it has been found convenient to have a series of such reductions or multiplications. These correspond to the various speeds of the car, for, obviously, if the power is multiplied by means of gearing, it is reduced in speed in the same ratio. This whole group of gearing is the *transmission* or *gearset*, and the various reductions are the *low, intermediate,* and *high speed* in a *three-speed gearbox;* and *low, second, third,* and *high* in a *four-speed gearbox.* A gearbox is always spoken of by its number of forward speeds, but there is in all of them, in addition to the forward speeds, a *reverse speed* for backing the car.

In the usual form, these gears are moved or shifted into and out of mesh with one another, according to the driver's needs. For this purpose, *shifting gears* must be provided within the *gearbox*, that is, the arrangement must be such that the proper gears can be moved back and forth, with a *shifting lever* outside for the driver's use, and proper and accurate connections between the two. The gears must be mounted on *shafts*, these in turn on *bearings*, the bearings must be supported in the *gear-case*, and this must be supported on the frame. In addition, there must be suitable provision in the *gear-case cover* for inspection, adjustments, and repairs; all the moving parts must be lubricated; all parts must be protected from the dust, dirt, and moisture of the road, etc. All this comprises the *transmission* or *gearing group*, which properly ranks second to the engine group in importance.

Final Drive Group. *Driving Shaft.* The connection from the transmission to the rear axle in pleasure cars is usually by shaft, called the *driving shaft*. On the majority of motor trucks, however, it is by means of the worm drive, which will not be discussed here. This shaft is sometimes inclosed in a hollow *torque tube*, with suitable connection at the front end to a frame cross-member, and at the rear to the *axle housing*. Its construction is generally such that it contains a *bearing* for the driving shaft at both front and rear ends. In addition, the majority of final drives contain at least one *universal joint*, and many of them contain two. As its name indicates, this will work universally, that is at any angle, its particular function in the driving shaft of an automobile being to transmit power from a horizontal shaft—that of the engine clutch and transmission—to an inclined one—the driving shaft—with as little loss as is possible. The drive shaft is often called "propeller" shaft.

Rear Axle and Differential. The driving shaft drives the rear axle through some form of gear, either *bevel, worm,* or other variety, and is usually a two-part shaft. The reason for cutting the rear axle is that each wheel must be driven separately in rounding a curve, for one travels a greater distance than the other. This seemingly complicated act is produced by a simple set of gearing called the *differential,* which is located within the driven gear in the rear axle. Each half of this is fixed to one part of the *axle shaft.* All these gears and shafts must have bearings, lubrication, means for adjustment, etc. On the outer ends of the axle shafts are mounted the *rear wheels,* which carry some form of tires to make riding more easy. The *brakes* are generally in a hollow drum attached to the wheels. All this goes to make up the driving system.

Steering Group. The front wheels perform a different function. They are hung on the *steering pivots,* so that they can be turned to the right or the left as desired. In order to have the wheels work together, a rod, called the *cross-connecting rod,* joins them, while the motion is imparted to them by means of another rod, called the *steering link,* which joins the *steering lever* or *arm* with the right-hand, or left-hand *steering pivot.* The last-named lever projects downward for this purpose from the *steering-gear case* and is moved forward and backward by the rotation of the *steering wheel* in the driver's hands.

The transformation of the rotation or turning motion of the hand wheel into a longitudinal movement is accomplished within the steering-gear case by means of a worm and gear, a worm and partial gear, or by a pair of bevel gears. All these parts need more or less adjustment, lubrication, fastening means, etc., the complete group being designated as the steering group.

In addition, the steering wheel and post carry the *spark* and *throttle levers,* with the rods, etc., for connecting them to the igniting apparatus (magneto, timer, etc.) and the carburetor, respectively. The purpose of the spark lever is to allow the driver to vary the power and speed of his engine by an earlier or later spark, according to his driving needs. Similarly, the throttle lever is for the purpose of opening or closing the throttle in the intake manifold of the carburetion system and regulates the amount of gas entering the engine, thereby increasing or decreasing its power output, or speed. Actually, these are parts of the ignition and carburetion systems, respectively, but they are usually classified with the steering group, because they are located on the steering wheel and post.

Frame Group. Little need be said about the frame. The *side members* are generally supported by the *springs* at the front and rear ends. The springs are connected to the axles and support the car. The *front cross-member* usually supports the radiator and sometimes the front end of the engine, too. The *rear cross-member* usually supports the gasoline tank when a rear tank is used. The other cross-members may support the engine, transmission, shifting levers, and other parts, according to their location. In general, the number and character of frame cross-members is slowly changing; the modern tendency is toward their elimination. By narrowing the frame at the front, the engine can be supported directly on the side members. With the units grouped, the same is true of the other important units.

Formerly, practically all motors and transmissions were supported on a *sub-frame*, but it has been found that the same results can be obtained when this extra weight is eliminated. A sub-frame is shown on page 4.

When the shifting levers are placed on the outside, they are fastened to the frame, as is the steering gear; all step, fender, and body parts, the *under-pan*, or *splash-pan*, for protecting the mechanism from road dirt; and usually the headlights. The frame is constructed with this idea in view, six bolts generally being used. The muffler is usually hung from a rear-frame member. When electric lighting and starting are used, the battery is very often hung in a cradle, supported by the frame, while the *hood* or *bonnet* is supported equally by the side members of the frame (usually covered with wood), and by a rod running from radiator to dash.

On page 4 it will be noted that the engine group and the clutch group are together, forming one unit. The transmission is mounted on the front end of the drive shaft, thus forming another unit. When the motor and the transmission are so located, they form a two-unit power plant. The single-unit power plant, in which the transmission and the motor are in one unit, is the most used construction at the present day. A few manufacturers still mount the transmission on the rear axle.

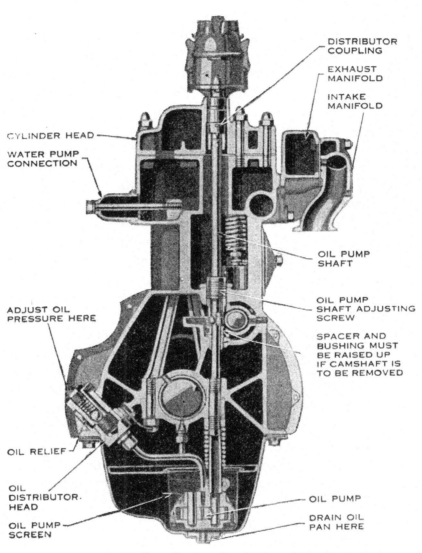

DISTRIBUTOR
COUPLING

EXHAUST
MANIFOLD

INTAKE
MANIFOLD

CYLINDER HEAD

WATER PUMP
CONNECTION

OIL PUMP
SHAFT

OIL PUMP
SHAFT ADJUSTING
SCREW

ADJUST OIL
PRESSURE HERE

SPACER AND
BUSHING MUST
BE RAISED UP
IF CAMSHAFT IS
TO BE REMOVED

OIL RELIEF

OIL
DISTRIBUTOR
HEAD

OIL PUMP

DRAIN OIL
PAN HERE

OIL PUMP
SCREEN

Cross-Section of an Engine
Rickenbacker Motor Company

CUTAWAY VIEW OF PACKARD SINGLE-EIGHT ENGINE

EXPLOSION ENGINES

ELEMENTARY PRINCIPLES

General Description. The term *explosion motor* as herein used refers primarily to gasoline engines such as are used on aerial crafts, automobiles, motorcycles, motorboats, and small stationary installations. There is nothing mysterious about this form of engine, it being similar in most respects to the ordinary steam engine, except that the force which develops the power is not derived from the expansion of steam but from the explosion of a gaseous charge consisting of a mixture of oil, vapor, and air.

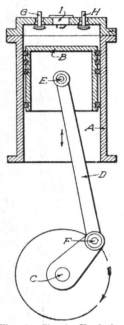

Fig. 1. Simple Explosion Motor

The simplest type of motor, Fig. 1, consists of a cylinder *A* in which there is a hollow piston *B* (free to slide up and down), a crankshaft *C*, and a rod *D*, connecting the piston through the piston pin *E* to the crank on the shaft. As the piston moves up and down in the cylinder this reciprocating motion is converted by the operation of the connecting rod on the crank *F* into a rotary motion, as shown by the arrow near *C*. The whole action may be compared to that of a boy on a bicycle, *D* representing the boy's leg and *F* the pedal. At the head of the cylinder are shown two valves, *G* and *H*, and a spark plug *I*, whose functions are to admit the charge, explode it, and permit it to escape, by which operations and their repetition the reciprocating motion of the piston is set up and maintained. The successive explosions of the charges produce considerable heat and, therefore, in actual practice the cylinder *A* is usually surrounded by a jacket. Water is circulated around in the space between this jacket and the cylinder, thus cooling the cylinder. Another cooling method is by air, in which case the outer wall of the cylinder is constructed as shown in Figs. 2 and 3. In order, there-

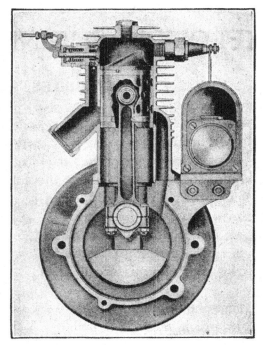

Fig. 2. Single-Cylinder Motorcycle Motor
*Courtesy of Excelsior Motor Manufacturing and
Supply Company, Chicago, Illinois*

Fig. 3. Excelsior Twin Motor

fore, to secure the above action, the following mechanical devices must be provided: (1) A cylinder containing a freely moving piston, capable of being lubricated effectively; (2) a combustion chamber in whose walls are valves for the admission and exhaust of the gas, and valve seats so arranged that the joints will remain gas-tight when desired; (3) an outside, dependable means of ignition, with sparking points inside the combustion chamber; (4) a source of fuel supply, which, in the ordinary engine, must convert liquid into a vapor; and (5) a cylinder construction which will carry off the surplus heat or allow of its being carried off.

Historical. The first workers in this field were perhaps Huyghens, Hautefeuille, and Papin, who experimented with motors, using gunpowder as a fuel, in the latter part of the seventeenth century. A patent was obtained in England by John Barber, in the closing years of the eighteenth century, on a turbine using a mixture of gas or vapor and air for the fuel. A few years later Robert Street, another Englishman, built an oil engine in which the vapor was ignited by a flame at the end of the first half of the outward stroke.

From 1800 to 1854 several French and English patents were granted for internal combustion engines, most of the engines being double acting, that is, one explosion acting on one side and the next explosion acting on the other side of the piston, and some using electrical ignition. In 1858, Degrand made a big advance by compressing the mixture in the cylinder instead of in separate pumps.

First Practical Engine. The first commercially practical engine was developed about 1860 by Lenoir, who marketed in Paris a 1-horsepower, double-acting gas engine closely resembling a horizontal steam engine. This used what is now called jump-spark ignition and was made in sizes up to 12 horsepower. It gave considerable trouble in many cases, but the principal reason for its failure was the excessive amount of gas required—60 to 100 cubic feet of illuminating gas per brake-horsepower hour*—which was more than three times the consumption of a modern gas engine and prevented competition with steam.

Otto Engine. The gas engine industry as we know it today was really started in 1861, when a young German merchant, N. A. Otto,

---

*Brake horsepower (b. h. p.) is the power delivered from the shaft of the engine. When delivered for one hour it is called a b.hp.-hour.

developed an experimental engine in which admission, compression, ignition, and exhaust were accomplished in the one working cylinder. Otto failed to realize fully the great promise held out by his engine and temporarily abandoned its development.

De Rochas' Theory. In the year 1862 it was pointed out by a French engineer, Beau de Rochas, that in order to get high economy in a gas engine certain conditions of operation were necessary, the most important being that the explosive mixture shall be compressed to a high pressure before ignition. In order to accomplish this, he proposed that the cycle of operations should occupy four strokes or two complete revolutions of the engine and that the operation should be as follows:

(1) Suction or admission of the mixture throughout the complete forward stroke.

(2) Compression of the mixture during the whole of the return stroke, so that it finally occupies only the clearance space between the piston and cylinder head.

(3) Ignition of the charge at the end of the second stroke and expansion of the exploded mixture throughout the whole of the next forward stroke.

(4) Exhaust beginning at the end of the forward stroke and continuing throughout the whole of the last return stroke.

De Rochas had developed a brilliant theory but never put it into practical use. The pamphlet containing this idea remained practically unknown until about 1876, when it was discovered and published in the course of a patent-lawsuit against Otto and his associates, who were using this cycle in their engine, Otto having returned to the development of his engine in 1863. Although the original idea was perhaps Beau de Rochas', the credit really belongs to Otto, who made practical use of what would otherwise have been an unknown theory. In recognition of this fact the four-stroke cycle which Otto adopted in his engine and which is used in the majority of our modern motors is generally known as the Otto cycle.

CYCLE OF EXPLOSION ENGINE

The cycle of the explosion engine, therefore, consists of four distinct steps: (1) *admission* of the charge of explosive fuel; (2) *compression* of this charge; (3) *ignition* and *explosion* of this charge; and (4) *exhaust* or expulsion of the burned charge. If this complete process requires four strokes of the piston rod in any one cylinder, the motor is designated as a four-cycle motor, although it would be more exact to call it a four-stroke cycle. If the complete process is accomplished in two strokes of the piston, the motor is designated as a two-cycle motor.

Four=Stroke Cycle. One complete operation of a single-cylinder Otto or four-cycle explosion motor is shown in Figs. 4, 5, 6, and 7. Fig. 4 shows the end of the first or suction stroke of the cycle. At the beginning of this stroke when about $\frac{1}{16}$ inch past the dead center, the inlet valve A is opened by an eccentric rod whose movement is controlled by the eccentric on a secondary shaft driven through gears at half the speed of the motor. This allows the vapor supplied by the carburetor, which is an instrument for converting the liquid fuel

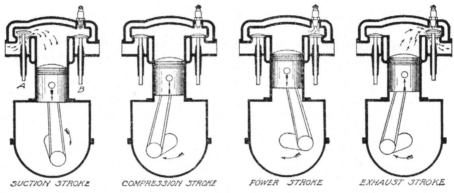

SUCTION STROKE   COMPRESSION STROKE   POWER STROKE   EXHAUST STROKE

Figs. 4, 5, 6, and 7. Diagrams Showing One Complete Cycle of a One-Cylinder Explosion Motor

into a vapor or gas, Fig. 8, to be drawn into the cylinder by the suction produced by the downward-moving piston. During this stroke the exhaust valve B has remained closed.

The conditions shortly after the beginning of the second or compression stroke are shown in Fig. 5, both valves being closed. The piston, traveling as indicated by the arrows, compresses the charge to a pressure of about 60 pounds, when it is ignited at or before the end of the stroke by a spark taking place in the spark plug as shown in Fig. 6. Its arrangement is shown in detail, Fig. 9, the spark passing between the points A and B. The force of the explosion drives the piston downward as shown in Fig. 6, which represents the power stroke. During these last two strokes, namely, the compression and working strokes, both valves if correctly timed should be completely closed.

Fig. 7 illustrates the conditions existing after the piston has begun the fourth or exhaust stroke. The exhaust valve *B* has been opened slightly before the end of the third stroke, and during this fourth stroke the gases are expelled from the cylinder through the

Fig. 8. Typical Modern Carburetor with
Water Jacket
Courtesy of Rayfield Carburetor Company, Chicago

open valve as shown. At the end of this stroke, piston and valves are again brought to the proper positions for the beginning of the suction stroke, illustrated in Fig. 4.

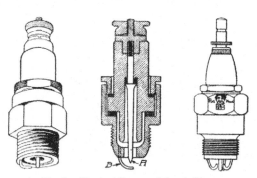

Fig. 9. Typical Forms of Spark Plug

The two strokes, suction and compression, as shown in Figs. 4 and 5, are completed in one crankshaft revolution. This may be termed the first revolution. The two strokes, power and exhaust, Figs. 6 and 7, are also completed in one crankshaft revolution, and this may be termed the second revolution. Therefore it takes two revolutions of the crankshaft to complete the cycle in a four-stroke cycle engine. Speaking in terms of crankshaft movement, these two revolutions are referred to as so many degrees of crank-shaft travel. A circle consists of 360 degrees and this circle, Fig. 10, is divided into four divisions of 90 degrees each. If the crank is at the point marked *A*, it will be at the zero point. If the crank is moved one-quarter of the distance around the circle, it will have moved or traveled 90 degrees, and if the rotation is continued back to the zero point, it will have moved or traveled 360 degrees. It will be seen that to complete the two revolutions necessary for the four piston strokes, the crankshaft must travel through twice this dis-

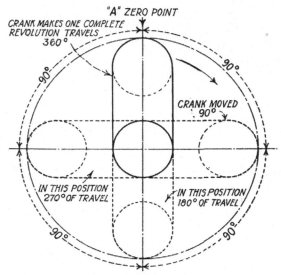

Fig. 10. Crankshaft Travel

tance, or 720 degrees. The mechanic must understand this per-fectly for it is the basis of the operation of the automobile engine. The complete cycle is shown in Fig. 11. We also have a two-stroke cycle engine that completes the cycle in two strokes of the piston.

Two=Stroke Cycle. An increased frequency of the expansion or motive stroke can be obtained by a slight modification of the Otto cycle which results in the cycle being completed in two strokes and is consequently called the two-cycle method. Single-acting motors using the two-cycle method give an impulse every revolution, and consequently not only give a more uniform speed of rotation to the crankshaft, but also develop 60 to 80 per cent more power than

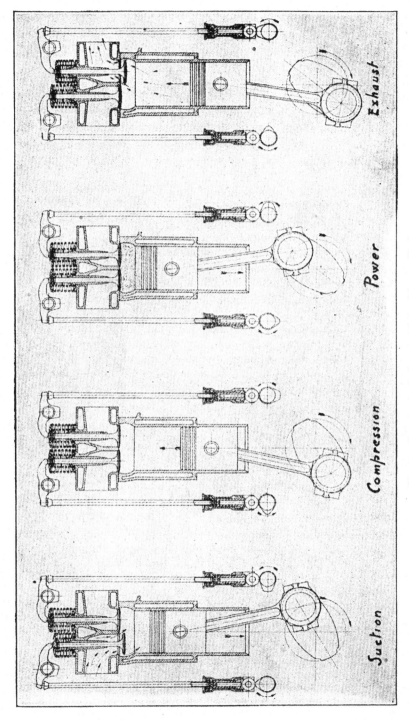

Fig. 11. Four Stroke Cycle as Applied to Marmon Engine
Courtesy of Marmon Company

four-cycle or Otto cycle motors of the same size. Moreover, they are generally of greater simplicity, having fewer valves than the four-cycle motors. An example is shown in Figs. 12 and 13 of a two-cycle motor of small size and of the two-port type; Fig. 12 is a vertical section showing the piston at the bottom of its stroke, and Fig. 13 is a vertical section in a plane at right angles to the previous section plane and showing the piston at the top of its stroke. As the trunk

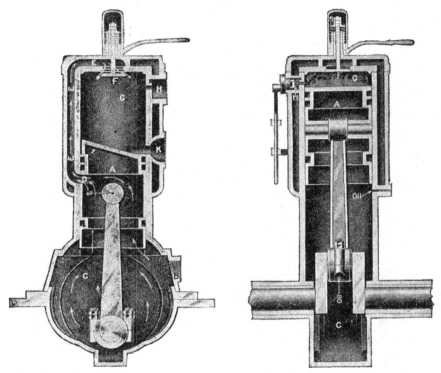

Fig. 12. Vertical Section of Two-Cycle
Smalley Motor

Fig. 13. Vertical Section at Right
Angles to View in Fig. 8

piston A makes its upward stroke, it creates a partial vacuum below it in the closed crank chamber C and draws in the explosive charge through B. On the downward stroke, the charge below the piston is compressed to about 10 pounds pressure in the crank chamber C, the admission through B being controlled by an automatic valve (not shown) which closes when the pressure in C exceeds the atmospheric pressure. When the piston reaches the lower end of its stroke, it uncovers exhaust port K and at the same time brings admission port D in the piston opposite the by-pass opening E, and permits the compressed charge to enter the cylinder G through the automatic admission-valve F as soon as the pressure in the cylinder falls below that of the compressed charge. The return of the piston shuts off the admission through E, and the exhaust through K, and compresses the charge into the clearance space. The charge is then exploded, Fig. 13, and the piston makes its down or motive stroke. Near the end of the down stroke, after the opening of the exhaust port K, the admission of the charge at the top of the cylinder sweeps the burned gases out, the complete escape being facilitated by the oblique form, Fig. 12, of the top of the piston. The motor is so designed that the piston on its return stroke covers the exhaust port K just in time to prevent the escape of any of the entering charge. The processes described above and below the piston are simultaneous, the up-stroke being accompanied by the admission below the piston and compression above it, while the down-stroke has expansion above the piston and a slight compression below it. In large engines the charge is compressed by a separate pump, and not in the crank case.

We find in comparing the crankshaft movement, or travel, in the two-stroke engine that the cycle is finished in 360 degrees of crankshaft travel as against the 720 degrees in the four-stroke engine. In the four-stroke engine only one power stroke is given in every four strokes, and in the two-stroke engine every down-stroke is a power stroke.

By referring to Fig. 14 it will be found that the cranks are laid out in degrees in regard to their relation with each other. The division of the circle in degrees is used here. A crankshaft layout for a four-cylinder engine is shown at D and the cranks are set at 180 degrees. It will be noticed that cranks 1 and 4 are directly opposite cranks 2 and 3 and therefore are on opposite sides of the circle, or 180 degrees apart. At E the cranks are set at 120 degrees and are so arranged that they are one-third of the total circle distance apart. The diagram shows a six-cylinder shaft and cranks 1 and 6 move together, 2 and 5 together, and 3 and 4. A four-cylinder engine shaft can be used in an eight-cylinder engine and a six-cylinder shaft can be used in a twelve-cylinder engine. There is a definite distance that the crankshaft travels between explosions and consequently there are a certain number of power strokes given for every revolution of the crankshaft.

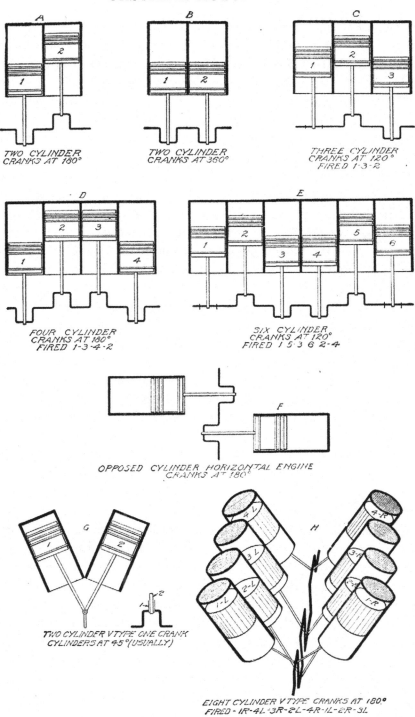

TWO CYLINDER
CRANKS AT 180°

TWO CYLINDER
CRANKS AT 360°

THREE CYLINDER
CRANKS AT 120°
FIRED 1-3-2

FOUR CYLINDER
CRANKS AT 180°
FIRED 1-3-4-2

SIX CYLINDER
CRANKS AT 120°
FIRED 1-5-3-6-2-4

OPPOSED CYLINDER HORIZONTAL ENGINE
CRANKS AT 180°

TWO CYLINDER V TYPE ONE CRANK
CYLINDERS AT 45°(USUALLY)

EIGHT CYLINDER V TYPE CRANKS AT 180°
FIRED - 1R-4L-3R-2L-4R-1L-2R-3L

Fig. 14. Crank and Firing Arrangements for Multicylinder Four-Cycle Motors

GASOLINE AUTOMOBILES

With the cranks set at 360°, Fig. 14*B*, we get a power stroke at each revolution. This arrangement, however, requires careful balancing to counteract the vibration which results from all parts moving in the same direction at the same time. The order of action in the two cases is given as follows:

180°		360°	
FIRST CYLINDER	SECOND CYLINDER	FIRST CYLINDER	SECOND CYLINDER
Suction	Exhaust	Suction	Firing
Compression	Suction	Compression	Exhaust
Firing	Compression	Firing	Suction
Exhaust	Firing	Exhaust	Compression

If the amateur finds the above difficult to follow, it may be simplified as follows: Duplicate the actions below those given, that is, repeat the action in two revolutions. Then mark off at the left the revolutions, indicating the first pair of actions for one, the second for two, etc. This applies right across the table. Then one notes that the firing in the first cylinder comes on the second revolution and the first stroke, while that in the second cylinder comes on the same revolution but the second stroke. This gives two firing impulses on one revolution, followed by another with none, then two more firing, etc. In the cylinders set at 360°, it will be noted that the second cylinder fires on the first stroke of the first revolution, while the first follows, firing on the first stroke of the second revolution, then the second on the first of the third, and the first on the first stroke of the fourth, etc., thus distributing the firing evenly.

Four-Cylinder Motor. In the four-cylinder motor of the four-cycle type, we have two power strokes for each revolution of the crankshaft or flywheel. In order to secure smooth working, these power strokes should occur exactly one-half revolution apart. From Fig. 14*D* it will be seen that the four-cylinder crankshaft has two pairs of cranks just about one-half revolution apart. Pistons *1* and *4* move up, while pistons *2* and *3* move down, or *vice versa*.

Suppose, for instance, that piston *1* has just been forced down on the power stroke. Then pistons *2* and *3* will be up and *one* of these should be ready to receive the force of the explosion and should have, therefore, just compressed an explosive charge in its cylinder ready to be ignited. For the sake of illustration let us choose piston *3* to make the next power stroke. Piston *3* now moves down and pistons *1* and *4* move up. Since it is evidently impossible to have piston *1* contain an explosive charge without giving it one more up and down motion, piston *4* must make the next power stroke.

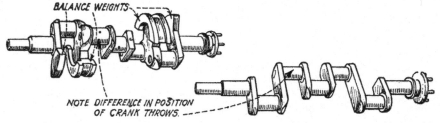

Fig. 15.   View of Crankshaft
Courtesy of Cadillac Motor Company

This piston, therefore, moves down as a result of the explosion in cylinder *4*, and it is now necessary for piston *2* to make the next power stroke.   Thus the order of firing is 1-3-4-2.

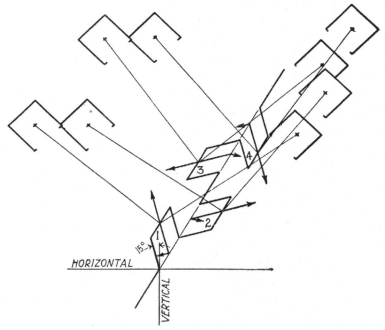

Fig. 16.   Balance of New 8-Cylinder Crankshaft
Courtesy of Cadillac Motor Company

The most recent addition to the perfect operation of the automobile engine is a crankshaft of a different design, as used in the Cadillac.   The ordinary four-throw crankshaft, as used in the old Cadillac engine, caused a certain amount of vibration due to uneven balance. A different arrangement of the crankshaft throws is used in the new shaft, Figs. 15 and 16. The explosions still occur at the same intervals as formerly but the new design reduces the vibrations at all speeds. The object of the designer in the past was to keep the shaft as short as possible to avoid distortion. That is one reason for the V-type engine. The Packard Company have made a straight 8-cylinder engine but the design of the shaft does away with any chance of whip or distortion. Fig. 17 shows the shaft used in this

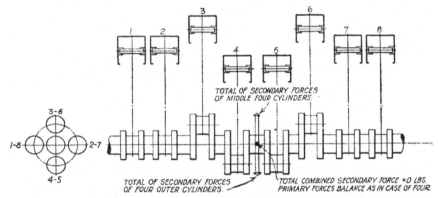

Fig. 17. View of Packard Shaft
Courtesy of Packard Motor Company

type engine. The firing order of an engine depends upon the position of the throws of the crankshaft, therefore these two engines have a somewhat different firing order as compared to the standard 8-cylinder engine. The firing order for the Cadillac is 1L—4R—4L —2L—3R—3L—2R—1R. The order in the Packard is 1—3—2—5 —8—6—7—4.

Theory of Crank Effort. *One-Cylinder Motor.* In a single-cylinder motor, four strokes of the piston are required to complete its cycle—the suction stroke, compression stroke, power stroke, and exhaust stroke. Note that only one of these strokes, the third, makes power. Roughly speaking, power is not produced throughout even the entire part of this stroke, but only through about four-fifths of it. Hence, in a single-cylinder motor with a 5-inch stroke, the piston travel for one complete cycle will be 20 inches. In only about 4 inches of this distance is power produced. (See Fig. 18.)

Hence four-fifths of the total piston travel is a non-producer of power.

Two-Cylinder Motor. In the two-cylinder motor we have two power strokes in two revolutions, as follows:

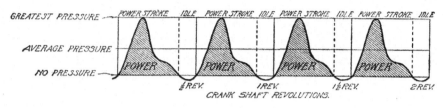

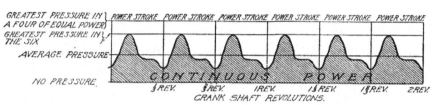

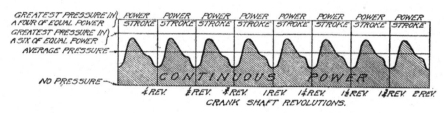

Fig. 18. Curves Showing Duration of Power in Four-, Six-, and Eight-Cylinder Motors

FIRST STROKE	INCHES OF POWER
Cylinder *1* Suction	0
Cylinder *2* Power	4
SECOND STROKE	
Cylinder *1* Compression	0
Cylinder *2* Exhaust	0
THIRD STROKE	
Cylinder *1* Power	4
Cylinder *2* Suction	0
FOURTH STROKE	
Cylinder *1* Exhaust	0
Cylinder *2* Compression	0
	—
Total inches of piston travel representing power...	8
Total inches of piston travel...................	20

Hence, the motor furnishes power during only 40 per cent of the cycle.

Four-Cylinder Motor. With the four-cylinder motor we have one power stroke during each half revolution of the crankshaft. This gives us power during 16 inches of piston travel or power during 80 per cent of the entire cycle.

Six-Cylinder Motor. In the six-cylinder motor, (Figs. 19 and 20) the cylinders being the same size as those considered previously, and the stroke the same—we have 4 inches of power produced by each cylinder, making a total of 24 inches of power with a total

Fig. 20. Electrical Side of Six-Cylinder Engine
Courtesy of Marmon Motor Car Company

piston travel of 20 inches. On the basis of the percentage values given in the two- and four-cylinder types this would mean an application of power during 120 per cent of the cycle. As this is impossible and as the six cylinders are evenly spaced, the power in the cylinders must overlap each other. This results in continuous power. Diagrams showing the relation between the application of power in the four-cylinder, six-cylinder, and eight-cylinder motor are shown in Fig. 18.

Eight-Cylinder Motor. In the eight-cylinder motor—the cylinders being of the same size as those considered previously, and the stroke the same—we have 4 inches of power produced by each cylinder, making a total of 32 inches of power with a total piston travel of 20 inches. On the basis of the percentage values given for the other types, this would mean the application of power over more time in the cycle than is possible, so, as in the case of the six-cylinder motor, there is an overlap. In this instance, however, the overlap is three times as great as in the six-cylinder, consequently the delivery of power is that much more even and continuous.

Twelve-Cylinder Motor. In the twelve-cylinder motor, with the same size cylinders as before, we have the same 4 inches of

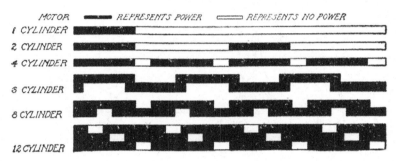

Fig. 21. Power Distribution Chart in Various Motors

power in each cylinder, or 48 inches total, with a total piston travel of 20 inches, showing again a large amount of overlap. Here the overlap is seven times as great as in the six-cylinder form, consequently the output of power should be that much more even.

The diagram, Fig. 21, gives a clear idea of this distribution of power in the various motors discussed. The six-cylinder motor has a small overlap, while the eight-cylinder has a wide overlap. The twelve-cylinder motor has a power overlap of two cylinders continuously, while the power impulses from three cylinders overlap part of the time, thus giving greater flexibility.

Effect of Dead Centers. In both the two- and four-cylinder motors, the cranks being set 180 degrees apart, each piston is always one complete stroke ahead of the succeeding one. When the cranks of the motor are in direct line with the connecting rod, Fig. 22 (*a*), the entire motor is on dead center. Fig. 22 (*b*) shows the same condition with offset cylinders.

In the six-cylinder motor, the cranks are set at 120 degrees, Fig. 22 (*c*), and therefore we have no condition when the entire motor is on dead center. It is impossible to have more than two of the cranks on dead center at once. Hence, there is never a time in the six-cylinder cycle when the motor does not produce power.

In the eight-cylinder V-type motor, Fig. 23, the cranks are set 180 degrees apart, as in the four-cylinder, but the cylinders are set at 90 degrees, 45 on each side of a vertical, as shown in Fig. 22 (d). The connection of the side by side cylinders of each pair of fours

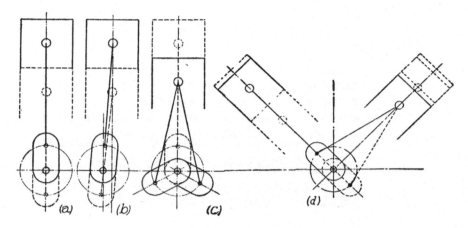

Fig. 22. Diagram of the "Dead Center" Problem

to a common crank pin—the two number one cylinders, for instance, working on the first pin, the number twos on the second, etc.— eliminates all dead centers. This is one advantage of the V-type over the straight-line type, for the latter has a dead-center cylinder.

In the twelve-cylinder V-type motor, Fig. 24, the cranks are set at 120 degrees as in the six, but the cylinders are set at 60 degrees, 30 on each side of the vertical, the only difference from that in Fig. 22 (d) being in the angle. The crank-pin attachment in the twelve is similar to that in the eight, the first two cylinders working on the first crank pin, the second two on the second pin, and so on. Obviously the form of the crank and the setting of the cylinders at an angle eliminate all dead centers.

By comparison, the respective cylinder forms show these relative overlaps, the piston travel of 20 inches being the same for all: 6-cylinder—24 inches; 8-cylinder—32 inches; 12-cylinder—48 inches. The dead center consideration is entirely eliminated in the twelve-cylinder engine.

A mechanic may have to fit some kind of an ignition device to an engine and it is practical to have a set rule in finding the number of power strokes given per crankshaft revolution for engines of different number cylinders. The sparks for firing the gas in the cylinders must come in a definite order and at certain intervals

Fig. 23. Front View of Eight-Cylinder V-Type Motor
Courtesy of Cadillac Motor Car Company, Detroit, Michigan

of crankshaft position. The ignition device must revolve at a certain speed according to the number of sparks required, since a definite number of power strokes is given for every crankshaft revolution. To find the number of power strokes—this will also give the number of sparks required—divide the number of cylinders by two. Suppose we have a twelve-cylinder engine and want to find the number of power strokes for one crankshaft revolution. Dividing 12 by 2, gives 6, which is the number of sparks required to fire the gas charges in the cylinders for one revolution.

Repair Man's Interest in Multiple Cylinders. Every repair man should be well posted on eights and twelves for two reasons. In the first place, the average owner knows very little about them. He thinks the repair man knows all about every kind of motor and so goes to him for information at the first sign of trouble. In the second place, the repair man should be able to handle and repair

Fig. 24. View of Packard Twelve-Cylinder V-Type Motor Mounted in Chassis

these forms of motor, for the fact that they have more parts and are more complicated makes them more likely to need skilled attention. Moreover the average owner, knowing of this greater complexity of construction, will be averse to turning his eight or twelve over to any but the best repair men—skilled mechanics with a thorough working knowledge of the principles of the new motors. Any intelligent repair man with a thorough knowledge of the principles around which these new motor forms are built and with an equally thorough and intimate knowledge of how fours and sixes are constructed, adjusted, and repaired, need have no fear to tackle any kind of engine new or old.

GASOLINE AUTOMOBILES

Horsepower. The unit of power used in the automobile is horsepower and is equal to raising 33,000 pounds one foot in one minute. The calculation is made in two or three different ways. The brake horsepower is power actually delivered at the crankshaft and is obtained by test under working conditions. The indicated horsepower, which is obtained by a test indicator, shows the working pressure inside the cylinders.

There is one formula everybody should know who has an automobile or is in any way connected with the business and that is the method for calculating the taxable horsepower for license application.

$$\text{Horsepower} = \frac{(\text{Bore of cylinder})^2 \times \text{number of cylinders}}{2.5}$$

This is termed the S.A.E. formula.

AVIATION ENGINES

Aviation vs. Automobile Engines. One of the great results of the War has been to produce some very large and high-powered engines for use in airplanes, seaplanes, and dirigibles and to call popular attention to them. This fact was perhaps most strikingly presented to the aeronautic show in Madison Square Garden in the spring of 1919, when there was exhibited no less than six different eight-cylinder, one nine-cylinder rotary, five different twelve-cylinder, two sixteen-cylinder, and one eighteen-cylinder engines, developing up to 800 horsepower.

At present great interest is being taken in the development and calculation of freight transportation in all steel planes, using an 800 hp. engine as the power unit. It is also excellent practice to use two or more 400 hp. engines for a single plane. This allows the use of smaller propellers, resulting in greater efficiencies.

The production of airplane engines by the thousands for war use and the wide publicity given to the details of these have produced much popular interest in the special airplane engine. This, it should be understood, is not by any means an automobile motor adapted to other work. The most important of the essential points of difference is the fact that the airplane engine requires first of all light weight, not just low weight, but the minimum weight possible consistent with regularity of operation. This requirement has been the cause of much additional machining to remove useless weight and has forced the use of various light materials or of heavy materials in a new way. Both of these practices have had the effect of making the cost of air engines tremendously high, approximating $10,000 per engine; whereas, a very good automobile engine can be produced for one-tenth of this sum, and a fair engine for a low-priced car, such as a Ford, a Maxwell, and the like, for one-hundredth of it.

Another point of difference relates to the service demanded of the motor. An automobile engine starts at low speeds and then probably runs first fast then slow, its speed constantly varying; in fact, it has been estimated that no average touring-car motor is run at its maximum speed in excess of 18 per cent of its useful life. The airplane engine, on the other hand, operates at high speed from the start all the time it is in use and then is shut off entirely; that is, it operates at high or highest possible speed for 90 to perhaps 97 or 98 per cent of its useful life.

There is also an important difference in the matter of regularity of operation. If an automobile engine does not work well or needs adjustment, the car can be stopped and the driver can get out and fix it; in an airplane, on the contrary, not only can this not be done, but such irregular operation or lack of adjustment may mean the death of pilot or passengers or all.

An automobile engine works always upon the level, with the exception of climbing or descending hills—and then the angle is comparatively slight. The airplane engine must work as well upside down as right side up; must work at all intermediate angles from zero to 90 degrees, and must work inclined sideways at any or all angles.

The automobile engine works practically always at the one altitude above sea level and consequently at the one air pressure and under the one set of air conditions. The aerial engine works at all altitudes and may pass from a level of a few hundred feet to an altitude of 15,000 to 20,000 feet within twenty minutes. The differences in air pressure and conditions at these radically different levels, succeeding one another with rapidity, have a tremendous influence upon the engine as well as upon the machine and the driver.

GASOLINE AUTOMOBILES

All these points have been emphasized because they indicate how and why the automobile and the airplane engine not only are at present but always must be radically different in design, construction, and use. In outward appearance and in number and functions of parts and units used the two may be alike, but there the resemblance ceases.

Moreover, aside from differences in details of design and construction, the search for maximum power and speed, combined with minimum weight and minimum space occupied, or, more correctly, minimum head resistance, has brought out many types of motor not used for any other purpose. Thus, the rotary form of engine was used on only one automobile, which was built in very small quantities and given up many years ago. It is widely used in airplane work, its use is steadily increasing, and there are dozens of different designs. Similarly, the radial form of engine with stationary air-cooled cylinders has never been tried for motor cars, but finds wide and increasing use in airplanes. These two forms also involve the use of an odd number of cylinders. Except for the one car already mentioned (which had a five-cylinder motor) and another of about the same general description and fate (which had a three-cylinder vertical compound engine), all automobiles of recent years have had an even number of cylinders, such as two, four, six, eight, and, most recently, twelve. For airplane use the three-, five-, seven-, and nine-cylinder forms are common; doubles of these are also used, giving ten, fourteen, and eighteen cylinders.

The air-cooled motor is coming into more prominence as its construction is better understood and its efficiency is much higher than that of the water-cooled motor. The Franklin and Holmes are both air-cooled motors, the Holmes being a comparatively new car in this field. For aeroplane work, the air-cooled motor is fast losing its prestige. American makers are using the water-cooled motor and almost all altitude and speed records are now held by planes equipped with water-cooled motors.

The crying demand for speed and more speed and the equally great outcry for enormous carrying capacity have produced some airplane engines of tremendous size, and have brought about their use in multiples. The practical limit of horsepower output per cylinder in airplane engines has been found to be between 45 and

50. The matter of securing greater power has now settled down to a question of how many cylinders can be used advantageously and with very high powers, such as 2,000 horsepower, and how many engines can be used and where they should be located.

We have already mentioned that altitude has a tremendous effect on the operation of an engine. The air becomes less dense the higher the altitude, and this causes the mixture in the carburetor to become richer and also reduces the compression volume—thereby reducing the power. This is one reason why an automobile seems to have less power in mountainous country. Water boils at a lower temperature in high altitudes, but this should not be taken as an indication of serious overheating.

FRANKLIN AIR-COOLING SYSTEM FOR CYLINDERS

53

CYLINDERS

Method of Classifying Cylinder Forms.   Cylinders are generally named according to two things: first, the method in which they are cast or produced; and second, the shape of the combustion chamber, or arrangement of the valves.   Thus, according to the first method, they are divided into those which are cast separately, that is, each cylinder by itself; cast in pairs, or each two cylinders cast together; cast in threes, a modern modification fitted to the six-cylinder engine;

Fig. 1.   Typical T-Head Cylinder Units with Other Cylinder Parts
Courtesy of Locomobile Company of America, Bridgeport, Connecticut

and cast together, or *en bloc*, that is, all of the cylinders cast as a single unit.

According to the second method of naming, cylinders are of the **L**-head type, in which the combustion chamber has the shape of an inverted capital letter **L**, formed by the placing of all valves on one side; of the **T**-head type, with the combustion chamber shaped like a capital **T**, because the valves are equally distributed; of the **I**-type, or valve-in-the-head type, so called because the combustion chamber is left perfectly straight and round by placing the valves in the head; and modifications of these.

Usually in speaking of the cylinders, both names are used as one, as, for instance, those of Figs. 2, 3, and 4, all of which happen to be alike, would be spoken of as **L**-head blocks, Figs. 1 and 2 as **T**-head pairs, etc.

Methods of Casting Cylinders. *Cast Separately.* The early and still common practice in the building of multi-cylinder gasoline motors is the casting of cylinders separately. This policy makes it easier to secure sound castings, simpler to machine and finish them, and less

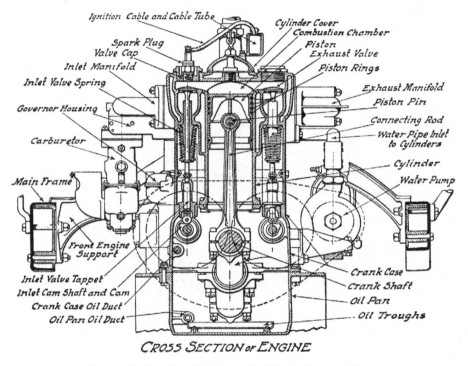

CROSS SECTION of ENGINE

Fig. 2. Section through Locomobile Cylinder Shown in Fig. 1

troublesome to disassemble parts of the motor without disturbing the rest.

In a number of cases, where extremely light weight was desired, this method was followed, but the cylinders were machined all over and a sheet-copper water jacket was applied in assembling. The separate cylinder has been most successful in aeroplane work and also for motor cars, but when the Cadillac changed its form this construction lost its principal American adherent. In addition to this construction, there have been a number of motors built with an applied water jacket of sheet metal of the built-on form. These have shown splendid cooling abilities, but, under the twisting and racking of automobile frames, particularly in later years, with the use of more flexible frames, they have shown too much tendency toward leakage to become popular.

Cast in Pairs. Just as soon as two-cylinder and four-cylinder engines were produced, the cast-in-pairs form of cylinder appeared and is almost as widely used today as then. While the modern tendency toward smaller bores, compactness, and light weight has greatly increased the number of cylinders cast *en bloc*, the paired

Fig. 3. Studebaker Six-Cylinder Motor, Showing Block Castings of the Six Cylinders

form, including the cast-in-threes modification for six-cylinder engines, holds its own.

Cast Together. The great advantage of having the several cylinders of one motor cast together—*en bloc*, as the French term it— is that the alignment and spacing of the different cylinders is thus rendered absolute and permanent, regardless of any differences in adjustment that may otherwise occur in assembling.

This construction has been applied to a large proportion of the small and of the medium-sized fours, a fair proportion of the larger fours, and to a considerable number of sixes, Fig. 3.

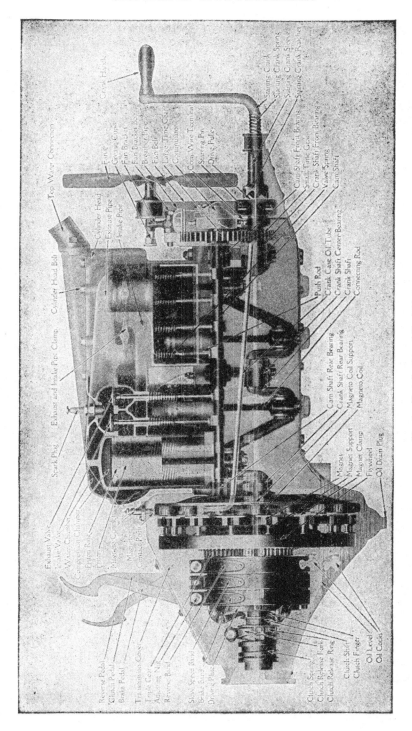

Fig. 4. Part Section of Ford Motor
In this engine cylinders are cast together

Another advantage is, that the water connections, exhaust and intake manifolds, etc., are rendered simpler both in their form and the number of their points of attachment.

In some advanced motor designs, the passages for the incoming mixture and for the exhaust gases, and in one case even the carburetor itself, are all incorporated in the main casting.

Fig. 5.   Section Through Continental 7R Cylinder Showing the L-Head Valve Construction

Another example of simple construction is that illustrated in Fig. 4, which depicts one of the latest Ford motors, in which the cylinders and the upper half of the crankcase are all cast in one piece. The lower half of the crankcase and the gearbox are similarly constituted of another simple pressed steel unit, while a second casting is used for the heads of the cylinders and for the water connection.

Cylinders Classified as to Fuel Chamber or Valves. *L-Head Forms.* In the **L**-head form, the valves are all located on one side, and usually because of this, all the accessories are on the same side. This makes a lop-sided engine, with carburetor, inlet pipe or manifold, magneto and wiring, exhaust manifold, and sometimes electric generator and other parts all grouped on one side, with little or nothing on the other. While a disadvantage in four- and six-cylinder motors, this is somewhat of an advantage in eight- and twelve-cylinder forms, for all the parts and auxiliaries can be grouped in the V between the cylinders, leaving the outside clear. On the other hand, where this grouping has been found undesirable for four- and six-cylinder motors, it has been possible to overcome it in part by taking the magneto and carburetor over on the other, or plain side, of the cylinders, leading a conduit back for the wires in the one case, and a long inlet manifold in the other. An L-head cylinder is shown in Fig. 5.

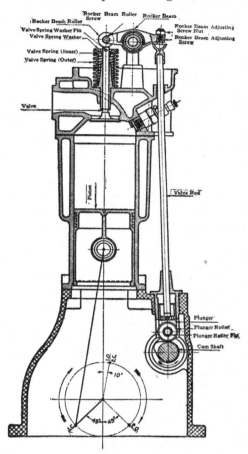

Fig. 6. Section through Dorris 1920 I-Head Cylinder as Used with Valve-in-Head Motors

T-Head Forms. A desire for more symmetry and a better arrangement has brought about the **T**-head form, which has the inlet valves, carburetor, and inlet manifold on one side, and the exhaust valves and manifold on the other. This separation gives more space on both sides, and allows the distribution of the other engine accessories so that each has more accessibility. This is important, for some parts, like the magneto, do

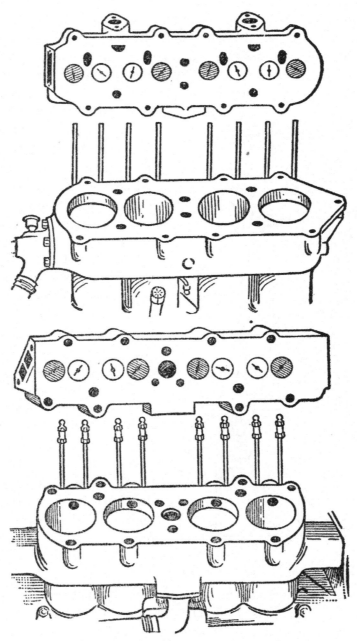

Fig. 7.   Cylinder and Cylinder-Head Assembly of the 1920 Chevrolet
Showing the Valve in the Head Construction

not withstand the heat well, and consequently should be far away from the heat of the exhaust manifold. See Figs. 1 and 2.

I-Head Forms. The valve-in-the-head, or overhead valve, motor requires an I-head cylinder, because, with this location of the valves, there is no necessity for the valve pockets of the other forms. Consequently the cylinder can be straight and plain, while the head, which is separate, is fastened on instead of being cast integrally. It may have either the L- or T-form, according to the location of the valves and the inlet and exhaust manifolds. Fig. 6 shows an I-head in which the manifolds are located on the opposite side. Note that in this form the cylinder head is removable, the valves being set directly in the head, as shown in the view of the Chevrolet motor, Fig. 7.

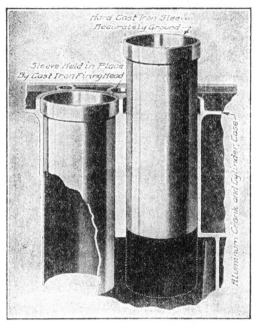

Fig. 8. Detail of Marmon Cylinders Showing Cast-Iron Sleeves Inserted in Aluminum Casting

The forms are not so clearly separated as they were formerly, for the inclusion of cylinder heads in one case, and their exclusion in another; the integral casting of manifolds, water passages, etc.; the casting of crankcase upper halves and also of gear covers, flywheel enclosures, transmission cases and other parts, all of which are quite common; no longer leave the cylinder casting as a single simple clear-cut unit.

An I-head motor with a removable head is also shown in Fig. 7. In removing the valves on this motor, the rocker arms and shaft should first be removed by taking out the shaft bearing bolts. Care should be taken in marking the rockers, as they will operate best in their original position.

The cylinder head is then removed and the valve keys taken out of the valve stems. This valve construction predominates when the motor is of this type. Better valve cooling is secured by having the valve in the cylinder proper instead of in a removable cage. The inserted sleeve, shown in Fig. 8, has been discarded in recent years but there are still some cars in service with this installation. The trouble with this design is that the sleeves are difficult to remove in repair work or for replacement when worn. The new sleeves are also hard to install and must have perfectly tight joints to prevent water leaks. The aluminum outer-casing would expand

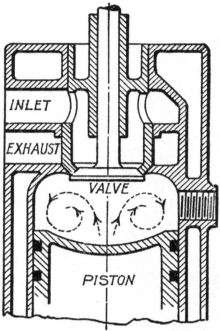

INLET

EXHAUST

VALVE

PISTON

Fig. 9.   Turbulence Combustion Chambers

and cause a leak unless the machine work on the outside of the sleeve was very accurate in allowing the correct amount of clearance for expansion.

Combustion Chamber Design. Considerable attention is being paid by the engineer to the design of the combustion chamber in the present-type engine. To obtain the best possible efficiency out of the engine, the fuel must burn thoroughly and quickly and the combustion chamber is designed to this end. The object is to make the fuel swirl around the chamber and then compress it in a compact mass around the spark-plug points. This swirling movement is called turbulence. The rate at which the fuel will burn is directly dependent on the rate of turbulence. There are two effective ways of causing turbulence: (1) a great velocity of incoming gas on the suction stroke; (2) causing the charge to flow on the compression stroke. If the first method is used, there should be no sharp corners in the combustion chamber which would tend to stop the turbulence. The desired effect is best obtained by designing the chamber so that the up-stroke of the piston will cause a rapid movement of the charge. Fig. 9 shows a spherical-shaped chamber similar to that used in the Knight-sleeve engine. As the piston rises it will cause the fuel to swirl in a circular motion. Fig. 10 shows a design that will cause the gas to be greatly agitated and compressed into a very dense mass around the spark plug points and it is in the

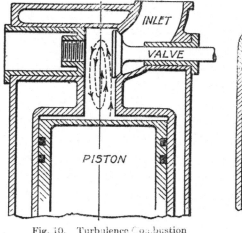

Fig. 10. Turbulence Combustion
Chambers

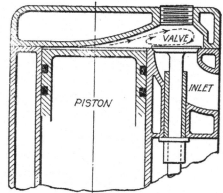

Fig. 11. Turbulence Combustion
Chambers

best possible shape for ignition. In this design there is a great amount of space occupied with the intake header and the overhead part of the engine. A better design in which the overhead part is done away with is shown in Fig. 11. The gas would obtain a great amount of velocity in this design and, of course, it would be greatest at the end of the stroke. The gas is highly compressed when ignition takes place.

Spark Plug Position. The position of the spark plug is important. It should be placed where it can be kept as cool as possible and where no dead exhaust gases can accumulate. In cylinders where a turbulence is obtained and where the exhaust and intake ports are open to each other, the plug position should be out of the path of the oil thrown up by the piston and away from the wet incoming gases which are found at the time of starting. The plugs should also be as close to the center of the gases as possible.

Water Jackets. The water jackets around the cylinders should be of ample capacity in order to give uniform cooling and eliminate steam pockets. The water should enter at the bottom and be free to flow to the top. Its temperature is increased as it comes in contact with the hotter parts of the cylinder. It is a distinct advantage to have ample cooling around the valves and spark plugs. This prevents the valve from warping and the spark-plug electrodes from getting red hot, causing pre-ignition.

Cylinder Troubles. If the cylinder casting is not heat-treated correctly, it will warp in service. Heat treatment relieves the internal strains in the casting and some manufacturers season the casting by leaving them out in the weather. This method is considered by many to be the best treatment because it is a natural one. The only cure for warping is to refinish the bore of the cylinder. In the rush of production, a bad cylinder block will often pass inspection. An engine that pumps oil in the early part of its service may show signs of warping if the cylinder bore is measured closely.

Scored Cylinders. This is caused by several things, and in most cases can only be cured by regrinding or reboring. If the score is light, it can often be lapped out but, in any case, new pistons must be fitted.

A cylinder that is scored or worn will cause the engine to run unevenly and also cause a loss of compression. A hissing noise in the crankcase is an indication of this trouble. In testing, place a piece of rubber hose on the breather pipe or at the point where the oil is poured into the crankcase. Place the other end to the ear and the hissing noise can be heard distinctly. To find the cylinder which is actually faulty the engine must be disassembled for inspection and measurement.

CYLINDER REPAIRS

Worn Cylinders. Where a cylinder of an automobile engine has become worn slightly out of shape or where the rings do not bear equally on the surface of the cylinder wall, the defect may be remedied entirely or to a great extent, depending on the magnitude of the defect, by lapping the cylinder wall. This measure will not cure the cylinder which has become scored but applies only to one which has been worn a very few thousandths of an inch out of round.

Lapping by Hand. The job can be done satisfactorily only by using an old piston of the same bore as the cylinder which is being worked upon. If one does not have a drill press, the hand operation,

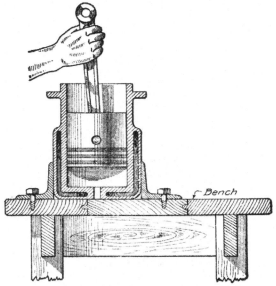

Fig. 12.   Cleating Casting to Bench

which will give a very satisfactory job, should be done as follows: Support the cylinder in its inverted position on the work bench. Inasmuch as practically all motors of present-day construction are of the block cast type, this heavy casting should be well supported in an upright position in order that the lapping may be done conveniently.

Cleating Down the Casting. Probably the best and easiest way to support the casting is by cleating it to the bench, as shown in Fig. 12. If the motor is a four- or six-cylinder block-cast type, use three sets of cleats on each side. These consist of a block of wood laid against the side of the cylinder block and clamped in place by wood pieces mitered off at a 45-degree angle, the mitered edge of one end nailed to the block and the mitered edge of the other end nailed to the work bench. This cleating will support the block substantially.

Proper Fit for Piston. Before proceeding with the work, one must determine that the old piston which is to be used is a proper fit in the cylinder to be lapped. It must be such a tight fit as to require considerable pressure to move it up and down. On the other hand, a loose fit will mean uneven grinding and a great deal more work to obtain the proper lapped surface.

The piston should have a connecting rod fitted into it, or better still, a rod of such a length that it will protrude about 18 inches above the top of the piston. If one contemplates an extensive

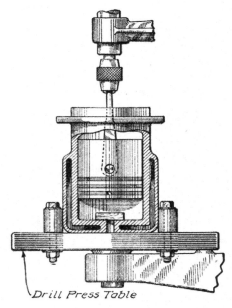

Drill Press Table

Fig. 13. Cylinder Mounted on Drill Press
Bed for Lapping Job

business in cylinder lapping by the hand method, it would be well to fit up a number of standard size pistons with rods such as just described. The connecting rod itself, however, will serve the purpose if the jobs are so few that they do not merit the special tools.

Emery Paste. With the cylinders blocked up on the work bench and a suitable piston at hand, one is ready for the lapping operation. There are several pastes on the market made up of fine emery and an oil body which are excellent for lapping work. However, one can make the necessary material himself with very fine emery dust, ordinary motor oil, and a bit of graphite worked into the paste.

This compound should be made up to the consistency of library paste and applied thoroughly to the walls of the cylinder to be lapped and to the surface of the piston to be used for the lapping.

When applying the paste, watch the surface upon which it is being applied with great care, especially if the paste has been made up previously and allowed to stand around the shop for some time. It is very easy for metal chips and filings to be dropped into the paste, and if these get into the cylinders when the lapping operation is under way, they are liable to scratch, or score, the surface.

Grinding Process. Lower the piston into the cylinder and proceed with the lapping. In performing this, lower and raise the piston, at the same time maintaining a circular motion, thus turning the piston around so that all surfaces of the piston will be brought to bear upon all parts of the cylinder.

This operation should be continued for a period of from 15 to 30 minutes, depending upon the condition of the cylinder interior. It will not remove scratches and scores and will not iron out a warped or egg-shaped cylinder, but it will dress down the small humps and impart a very smooth glass-like finish to the cylinder walls.

Lapping by Drill Press. If the repair shop is equipped with a fair size drill press, lapping can be performed quickly on this machine. It is especially easy when one has to deal with separate cast cylinders inasmuch as these can be clamped into the drill-press bed without need of special supports, Fig. 13. However, if the job is a block-cylinder casting, one must provide some means of support outside of the drill-press bed and inasmuch as it is a matter of blocking from the floor, it is for the ingenuity of the repair man to devise the best method.

Piston Rod. In drill-press lapping of cylinders it is, of course, necessary that a rod be used to take the place of the connecting rod, this rod to fasten to the wrist pin at one end and be so shaped as to lock into the chuck of the drill press at the other end.

It is well to cut a block of wood which when dropped into the inverted cylinder will come up to the line which marks the top of the piston stroke. To lap the cylinder, the old piston is coated with the lapping paste as previously described and let down into the cylinder. The drill press must be turned at its lowest possible speed. When the lapping is going on, the drill-press arm should be let up and down so that the position of the piston is constantly changing within the cylinder. Of course lapping by this method can be accomplished in about half the time required by the hand method.

Cleaning after Grinding. At the completion of hand or machine lapping, the cylinder interior should be thoroughly washed out with gasoline and the surface polished with a soft cloth. It is imperative that all emery be removed from the cylinder as it would undoubtedly injure the bearings or some other part of the motor, after the motor has been assembled and run.

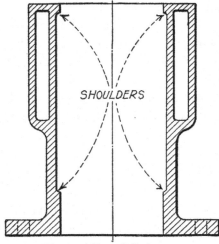

Fig. 14.   Worn Cylinder

Fitting Piston Ring to the Cylinder. When the fitting of piston rings is entailed in the repair of an engine, accurate and close measurements must be taken to see if the cylinder bore is parallel and round. A good job of fitting piston rings cannot be done unless the cylinder bore is perfect in every way. One of the conditions often overlooked by the mechanic is a shoulder, worn in the bore, at the point in the bottom of the cylinder where the bottom ring travels. This is found particularly in the engine whose piston has only three piston rings. Fig. 14 shows the condition mentioned. If the ring is fitted to pass through the small part of the bore it will expand in the large part and leave a large gap at the ring ends, allowing the compression to pass by, which will defeat the object in the fitting of new rings. The top of the cylinder bore should also be examined for a shoulder, and if there is one, it should be removed because the ring at the top of the piston would strike against it and cause a knocking noise. The top ring of the piston is usually made to overrun the cylinder bore about a half-width of the piston ring. In this case no shoulder would be left at the top of the cylinder bore.

Checking Up Cylinder Bore. Before any work is done upon the cylinder bore, such as turning, grinding, etc., it should be checked up very carefully, Fig. 15. An expert workman, accustomed to the tool, would use an inside micrometer, but when this tool is lacking,

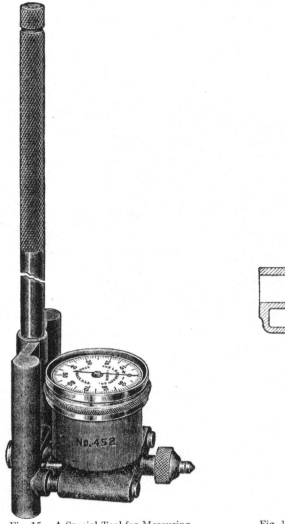

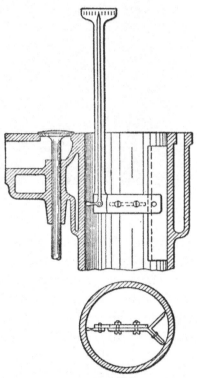

Fig. 15. A Special Tool for Measuring
Cylinder Bores
Courtesy of Starrett Tool Company

Fig. 16. Construction of Simple Rig for
Measuring Worn Cylinder Bores

as well as the experience necessary to use it, a fairly simple tool which can be used by almost anyone may be constructed as follows: As shown in Fig. 16, a short angle iron forms one side of the bore-measuring part; its length is sufficient to keep the entire tool perfectly vertical when the cylinder is vertical, and thus gives an accurate right-angle measurement of the bore. A central arm is fastened to this and the framework adjustably bolted to it. This includes the indicating dial at the top. At the lower corner is the indicating member, which is simply an L-shaped piece with a very short base and a very long stem; this is pivoted at the center of

Fig. 17. Grinding Engine Cylinders
View Shows Exhaust for Dust, Jig for Holding Cylinders, and Eccentric Wheel Spindle
Courtesy of Heald Machine Company, Worcester, Massachusetts

the bend. It is held against the side of the cylinder by means of a light spring. After adjusting the tool to the approximate cylinder bore, it is inserted, and a reading is taken; the tool is then moved, and another reading taken. The length of the arm is so great that any movement of the small arm is magnified about 15 times. In this way a difference of $\frac{1}{1000}$ in the bore shows as $\frac{15}{1000}$ on the dial, or $\frac{1}{64}$. In a shop where most of the work is on one motor, the micrometer could be improved by eliminating the adjustable feature and making the frame and angle face a solid piece.

Grinding Out Cylinder Bore. As the usual amount of metal which would be removed from a worn cylinder would not exceed a few thousandths of an inch, grinding should be the process used. Other processes, except possibly lapping or hand grinding, are too inaccurate. For this reason, a typical grinding set-up is shown in

Fig. 18.   Boring Tool
Courtesy of Universal Tool Company

Fig. 17. This shows the cylinder bolted against a large angle plate, attached to the grinding machine table. The angle plate is drilled out to take the bolts which hold the cylinder casting to the crankcase. When bolted up for work, the air hose is connected up through the cylinder head to blow out the dust or particles ground off. Not more than three or four thousandths of an inch should be taken off at one time; if more must be removed, a second operation over the surfaces is necessary.

If the cylinder is worn badly enough to warrant re-boring, which calls for new pistons and rings, it should be borne in mind that a standard set of oversizes has been adopted by the Society of Automotive Engineers, and that all manufacturers are working to them, by stocking pistons and rings according to these dimensions:

Oversize Standard	Inches Large
For 1st Oversize	10 thousandths (.010″)
For 2d Oversize	20 thousandths (.020″)
For 3d Oversize	30 thousandths (.030″)
For 4th Oversize	40 thousandths (.040″)

In shops where expensive regrinding and reboring equipment cannot be purchased, cheaper ones can usually be obtained. This equipment will usually be in the shape of an attachment which will do very accurate work, especially if there is not a great amount of metal to be removed to put the bore in shape for new pistons and rings. Fig. 18 illustrates an attachment of this kind. The better grades of machines are provided with a micrometer adjustment, which allows an accurate setting of the cutting tools. The tool is bolted to the top of the cylinder and a fine thread on the rod regulates the amount the cutters move through the bore. In the tool shown, there is a split ring ahead of the cutters which guides the tool and one behind the tool which holds the tool true after the cutters have removed the metal. Fig. 19 shows the tool being adjusted with the aid of a micrometer. Too much metal should not be removed at one cut, because lighter cuts will give smoother surfaces. It is claimed that a cylinder can be refinished with this tool in a much shorter time and more accurately than by lapping.

Cause of Scored Cylinders. (1). Lack of lubrication; which may be caused by the failure of the oil pump to operate, loss of oil by leakage, or inattention. This lack of lubrication causes friction between the piston and cylinder. With the expansion of the piston and its tendency to stick to the cylinder walls, the metal starts to wipe over the surface and scoring occurs. Often the piston will stick fast and to help break the two apart a little kerosene and oil should be poured into the cylinder and the engine allowed to cool.

(2). Lack of water in the cooling system, or through obstruction, causing failure of the water to flow in the system. The excessive

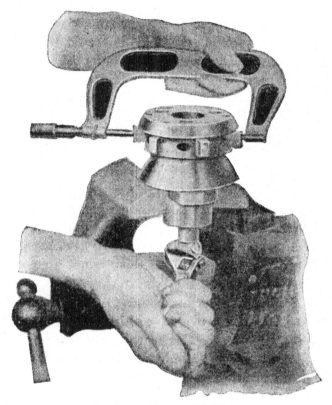

Fig. 19. Setting Cutters with Micrometer
Courtesy of Universal Tool Company

heat generated causes the above result. The obstruction will often be found to be inside the rubber-hose connections. After the hose has been in service some time it will swell inside and make the obstruction. The pump impeller may become loose on its shaft and water will not be forced through the system. The hose-connections should be closely examined in the thermo-syphon system when there is overheating.

(3). New pistons that are fitted too tight are apt to score unless great care is taken when the engine is started for the first time. An engine that has been reground and new pistons fitted should not be run faster than 15 miles an hour for the first 500 miles.

(4). Piston pin working loose in the piston and projecting beyond the piston wall, rubbing against the cylinder. This will wear a deep groove in the cylinder bore in a very short time. In repairing it is necessary to fill the score with a special metal called silver solder or have the cylinder welded. This will necessitate the bore being reground and new pistons fitted.

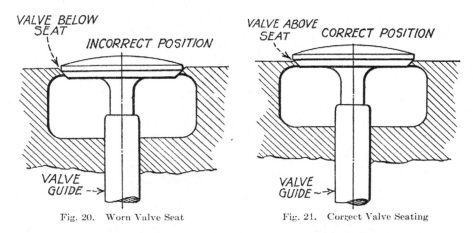

Fig. 20. Worn Valve Seat   Fig. 21. Correct Valve Seating

Reconditioning of Valve Seats. A common repair is the reconditioning of the valve seat. The constant pounding and grinding of the valve will bring it below the top of the seat as shown in Fig. 20. Its correct position is shown in Fig. 21.

The top of the valve seat should be recessed to correct this condition, and a simple tool for this work is shown in Fig. 22. Care should be taken to see that the pilot fits the valve guide snugly, so that the tool will cut true. The seat will also need refacing and a tool for this purpose is shown in Fig. 23. Care should be taken in selecting a tool of the right angle. An even pressure that is not too heavy should be used on these tools to prevent them from chattering and leaving a rough surface.

Replacement of Valve Guides. The valve guide is the part that the valve slides in, and this becomes worn after a period of service and needs renewing. An illusive knock in the engine can often be traced to this trouble. The worn guide will not allow the valve to

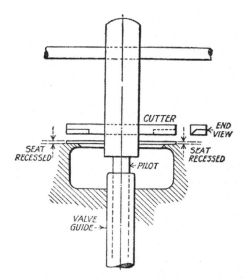

Fig. 22. Recessing Tool

Fig. 23. Valve-Seat Refacing Tool

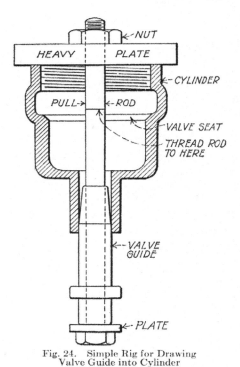

Fig. 24. Simple Rig for Drawing Valve Guide into Cylinder

seat directly. The valve will touch one side of the seat and then drop over to the other side and cause the clicking or knocking noise, which is very hard to locate. If the intake-valve guide is worn, it will cause an air leak and the excessive air drawn into the cylinder will cause missing at low speed and hard starting. An over-size valve can often be fitted to the guide after it has been enlarged a trifle with a reamer. Where a replacement is to be made the guide should be pressed or driven out and the new guide fitted. Where a press is not handy, a tool can be made. A piece of steel should be reduced until it will go into the guide up to a shoulder on the piece and a hammer used to drive the guide out. This method should not be used when fitting the guide. It should be drawn in, when a press is not used. Fig. 24 shows a tool in use—when drawing in the guide.

Removing Carbon. *Scraping.* The two standard methods of removing carbon are by scraping and by burning with oxygen. If the carbon is to be removed by the scraping process, the cylinder head is first taken off and the carbon then removed with

Fig. 25. Oxygen Regulator for Carbon Burning

a putty knife or carbon scraper. While this is a satisfactory method, it requires considerable time. This operation can be done with but little expense if the cylinder head is easily removed.

Oxygen Process. In removing carbon by the oxygen process, a spark is first applied to a mixture of carbon and oxygen and then combustion takes place. The carbon will continue to burn until it is completely exhausted or until the supply of oxygen is cut off.

Setting the Motor. The motor should be turned by the crank until piston *1* is on upper dead center, ready to fire. When the piston is in this position, both valves are closed and the carbon on top of the piston is nearer the oxygen supply. The spark plugs are then removed and a little oxygen allowed to escape from the torch into the combustion chamber through the spark-plug hole. This is done so that there will be sufficient oxygen to support combustion when a match is dropped through the spark-plug hole before the oxygen torch is inserted. After the regulator, Fig. 25, has been adjusted to a pressure of about 15 pounds, the torch nozzle is inserted through the spark-plug opening, which causes the carbon to burn very rapidly. It is important always to have at hand a reliable fire extinguisher as some sparks or hot carbon may drop in the oil pan and cause a fire. It is unnecessary to turn off the gasoline supply to the carburetor or to remove the carburetor, as the closing of the inlet valves prevents any chance of a fire in this instrument. Fig. 26 shows an operator removing carbon by this method.

Sequence of Burning. After the carbon is removed from cylinder *1*, the crank should be turned until the piston of the next cylinder in firing order is at upper dead center. If the motor is a six-cylinder type, the crank may be turned one complete revolution and the carbon then removed from cylinder *6*. It will then be necessary to find the firing position of cylinder *2* and, after burning, the crank should be turned one complete revolution; then cylinder *5* will be in its firing position and ready for the burning process. After the carbon has been removed from this cylinder, it is necessary to find the firing position of cylinder *3*, and after the carbon is burned, the crank should be turned one revolution and then cylinder *4* will be in position for carbon burning.

Fig. 26. Burning Carbon with Oxygen

If the motor is a four-cylinder type, the same method may be used; first finding the firing position of cylinder *1* and cleaning it and then removing the carbon from cylinder *4*, after the motor has been turned a complete revolution. The firing position in cylinder *2* is then found, and after one complete turn of the crank, cylinder *3* will be in position for carbon burning.

Finding Firing Position. There are several methods of finding the firing position. If the motor is equipped with battery ignition, the best and quickest method is to turn on the ignition switch, having the spark lever fully advanced and holding No. *1* spark-plug wire near the cylinder. The crank should be turned until the piston is brought to the top of the stroke, and then the carbon should be removed. The firing position of the other cylinders is found by the same method. In any four-cylinder motor, cylinder *1* is ready to fire when exhaust valve *4* has just closed. In the case of any six-cylinder motor, cylinder *1* is just ready to fire when exhaust valve *6* just closes and other cylinders at every 120° of crankshaft travel after cylinder No. 1 has fired.

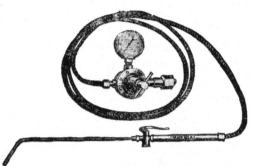

Fig. 27.   Imperial Oxygen Burning Outfit. (Without Oxygen Tank)

Precautions. In burning carbon one should guard against using a too high pressure on the oxygen nozzle as this is likely to cause sufficient heat to melt the nozzle, thereby making it necessary to stop the operation and refit a new nozzle. It is also important to see that the valves are seated, as they are likely to warp if not in this position. The oxygen regulator hose and torch, Fig. 27, can be purchased from welding equipment supply houses or from the manufacturers.

Removing Carbon by Scraping Tools. When the carbon cannot be burned with oxygen, the repair man must go back to hand scrapers. In any case, these are the most simple and fully as effective as any provided the extra time needed to use them and do a good job is available. When the offending member has been brought out so it can be handled, the removal of the carbon can be accomplished in a few minutes. A flat piston head can be scraped off with any knife or chisel, but a special scraper made from an old file, flattened out at the end and ground down so as to present one sharp edge is better. Every garage man should accumulate from five to a dozen shapes and sizes of scrapers for various work, including a flexible one with which to reach into corners. The carbon is brittle and comes off readily. After its removal the surface should be cleaned with air and gasoline to make it smooth, in order to delay the formation of a second coat. This is true of carbon in other places, but usually it is impossible to smooth the surface, in which case the process must stop when the part is scraped clean.

PORTABLE CYLINDER GRINDER
Courtesy of Gisholt Machine Company

PISTONS

Piston Construction. The pistons of automobile motors have long been made of cast iron, with the piston pin held in bosses on the piston walls. For all ordinary service this construction, well carried out, serves every purpose, but with the development of very high-speed motors, with piston speeds twice and three times as high as past practice has sanctioned, there is a growing tendency to substitute steel for cast iron in this important reciprocating element.

Particularly in aviation motors this has been the case; the pistons of one well-known revolving motor, for example, are machined to the thinnest possible sections, out of a high-grade alloy steel. In

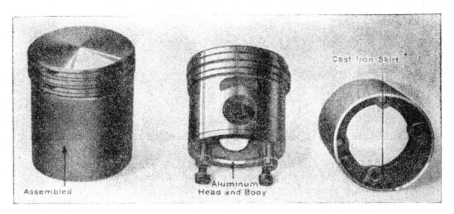

Fig. 1. Marmon Two-Piece Piston as Used on the 1920 Car

this motor, the connecting rods are hinged to the head of the piston instead of to the walls, which can be made much thinner than otherwise would be possible. This practice has been followed to a slight extent by some automobile manufacturers. There are now a few stock cars of established quality provided with pressed-steel pistons.

In cars, too, the movement toward smaller bores and higher efficiency has brought about the use of much lighter pistons; this is done by making them thinner and shorter. The latest development has been the use, not only of aluminum pistons and die-forged aluminum alloy connecting rods, but also of aluminum cylinders having cast-iron sleeves driven in to form the actual cylinder surfaces.

Marmon Two-Piece Piston. The body of this piston, Fig. 1, is of aluminum, and the cast-iron sleeve is bolted on to this body.

The aluminum part is die cast and carries three rings and the piston pin as well as the four studs which hold the skirt of the piston. The skirt is a light cast-iron cylinder whose only connection with the head portion is at the flange, where they are bolted together. This construction allows the aluminum head to expand or contract without affecting the cast-iron skirt and thereby combines the aluminum and cast-iron pistons.

Modern Tendencies. The modern tendency is to cut down the weight. This has been done by lightening the piston all over and by taking out rings. With fewer rings, it is necessary that each should be more efficient, consequently there has been much experimenting

Fig. 2. Old and New Types of Pistons
Former Heavy Piston at Left; Present Lighter Type at Right
Courtesy of Locomobile Company of America, Bridgeport, Connecticut

done with new forms. The lightening of piston weight has not materially changed the old open-end trunk form, although the use of aluminum has modified its straight shape somewhat in the hour-glass and similar forms. Attempts to utilize so-called free pistons, in which the upper part is flexibly connected to the lower, and the use of combinations of pressed steel and other metals have done much to modify the general form.

Fig. 2 shows how a certain piston was lightened by taking out two rings at the top, one rib inside, and generally using thinner metal. The old form is shown at the left, the new at the right. Fig. 3 shows a piston cast in aluminum alloy. Note how this is cast to have less metal at the piston boss and also to be strong without extra ribs.

The use of lightweight pistons has cut down the reciprocating weight, which tends to lessen the vibration and increase the speed and power to be obtained from the engine. A certain amount of metal must be allowed at the top of the piston so as to withstand the pressure exerted on the piston at the time of the explosion, and also as a means of conducting some of the heat of the combustion away. The latter is necessary to prevent too great expansion, causing the piston to stick, which, in turn, will score the cylinder.

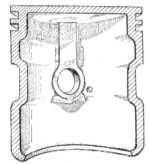

Piston Pin Position. The position of the piston pin is important. The piston should be evenly balanced above and below the piston pin. Therefore there should be the same amount of metal in weight above and below the pin, which tends toward the elimination of piston slap. In fitting new pistons, it is

Fig. 3. Typical Piston Cast in Aluminum Alloy for Minimum Weight

essential to relieve the piston at the point where the pin passes through the piston. This part of the piston is called the piston pin boss and is a great deal thicker than the other parts of the piston.

Fig. 4. Relieved Piston by Grooving

Fig. 5. Relieved Piston by Recessing

For that reason, there will be more expansion at this point. If the piston is not relieved, the expansion will cause slight scoring and pitting of the metal. The method used for this is either to machine a groove, Fig. 4, around the piston the same width at least as the diameter of the piston pin hole, or to recess a portion of the piston just around the hole, Fig. 5.

Piston Clearance. The different parts of the piston are as follows: the piston ring groove—the part in which the piston ring is placed; the ring land—the part between the groove; the skirt—the part below the lower piston ring groove, see Fig. 6. The repair man should be careful to check the clearance when installing new pistons. Clearance is the difference in size between the piston diameter and cylinder diameter. The piston should be much smaller at the ring lands than at the skirt, because there is greater heat at the top therefore greater expansion. A good rule for cast-iron piston clearance is here given. Two thousandths (.002) inch should be allowed

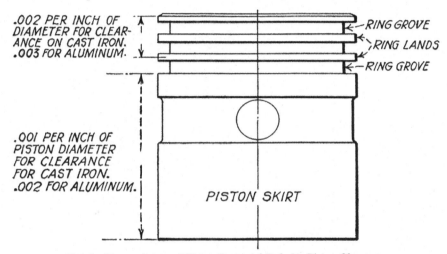

Fig. 6. Nomenclature of Piston Parts and Rule for Piston Clearance

at the ring lands for each inch of piston diameter, and one thousandth (.001) at the skirt. Aluminum expands more than cast iron, therefore aluminum pistons must have more clearance. For this type of piston the rule is three thousandths (.003) inch at the ring lands and two thousandths (.002) at the skirt for each inch of piston diameter, Fig. 6. This rule is not hard and fast but is a safe one to follow. Oversized pistons have been spoken of in a previous part and the standard sizes given. The piston should be measured with a micrometer to see if it is perfectly round before fitting it to the cylinder.

There are two ways of testing the clearance of a piston: one by the use of the outside and inside micrometers; the other, by the use of a thickness gauge. To use the micrometer it is necessary to find the size of the piston and then the size of the cylinder, Figs. 7 and 8. Subtracting the size of the piston from the size of cylinder will give the clearance. The piston must be measured at the top and at the skirt to get the exact measurements. The feeler, or thickness gauge, is used as shown in Fig. 9. The piston is slipped

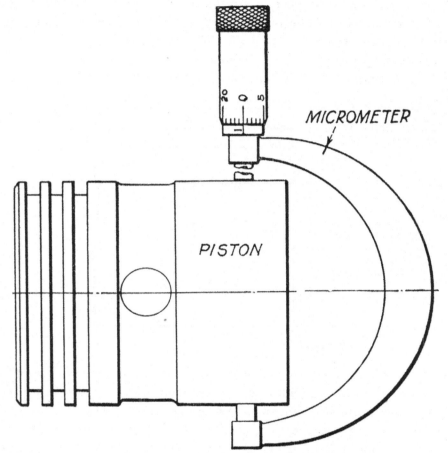

Fig. 7. Measuring Piston with Micrometer

into the cylinder and a leaf of the gauge is put between the piston and the cylinder walls. When the piston slides into the bore snugly with a certain thickness leaf in position, the clearance will be the thickness of the leaf. The leaf should be tried in several different positions and the piston in different positions. If the correct amount of clearance is not allowed, there is a great risk of scored cylinders; if too much is allowed, it will cause piston slap. The speed of the engine has something to do with the amount of clearance allowed. If the engine is to operate part of the time at medium speeds, the clearance should be less than that allowed in an engine that is to run at full load at all times, as in a racing engine.

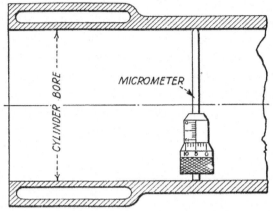

Fig. 8.   Measuring Cylinder with Inside Micrometer

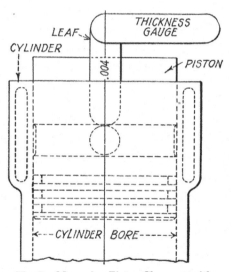

Fig. 9.   Measuring Piston Clearance with
Thickness Gauge

Piston Rings. Good compression is the basis of perfect operation and economy in an engine. Good compression depends upon the wearing quality and the fit of the piston ring to the piston and cylinder. If the piston rings are soft and wear quickly or are fitted incorrectly, there will not only be a loss of compression and power, but there will be a leakage of gasoline past the rings into the crankcase. This causes the rapid thinning out of the oil and the quicker and greater wear on the bearings and all moving parts.

Miscellaneous Adjustments of Rings. There are several things to be looked for to determine whether the piston rings are functioning as they should. If gas has been working its way past the rings or if the rings have not been fitting the cylinder walls properly, points where the gas passed will be evidenced by burned, browned, or roughened portions of the polished surface of the piston and rings. Points where this discoloration is noted will more often be at the thin end of an eccentric ring, the discoloration being apparent about $\frac{1}{2}$ to $\frac{3}{4}$ inch each side of the slot. Possibly the rings were not true when put in.

It is well to bear in mind that before replacing pistons in the cylinders one should make sure that the slots in the piston rings are spaced equidistant on the piston. If pins are used to keep the rings from turning, one should be careful to make sure that these pins fit into their holes in the rings and that they are not under the rings at any point. Putting pistons in cylinders really requires the use of two pair of hands.

Fitting New Rings. Fitting new rings will not prove of advantage unless the cylinders are in good condition. Before making a new ring installation, make sure that the cylinders are not out of round, warped, or scored. If found to be so, they should be reground and oversize pistons and piston rings installed. Piston rings must have a uniform wall pressure of sufficient strength to maintain a bearing against the cylinder walls during every revolution of the engine. Piston rings that will assume the shape of the worn or warped cylinder do not have the necessary wall pressure and will collapse under the force of expansion.

Where oversized rings are to be fitted to an engine care should be taken in their selection. If the ring is too large, it will necessitate more work in the fitting. A greater amount of metal will have to be filed off of the end in this case also, which will destroy the roundness or concentricity of the ring and it will not fit the cylinder bore. If the ring used is composed of two or three parts, extreme care should be taken when it is fitted to the top groove. Some pistons are so made that the top ring overtravels the cylinder bore. Where such a ring is used, one of the parts might expand over the bore when the piston is at the top and cause serious damage. The writer has seen a piston fitted with this type of ring which had the top of the piston pulled completely off. A safe plan is to use only one-piece rings in the top-ring groove of any piston.

There is a correct and an incorrect way of placing a ring in the ring groove. If the repair man will examine a piston ring closely, he will notice that at least one side of the ring has a better finish

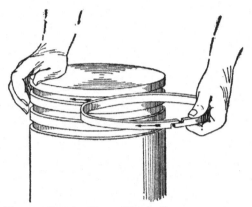

Fig. 10. Starting Piston Ring in Groove
to Test the Fit

than the other. This side has been ground to a smooth surface for a special reason. Both sides are finished in better class rings. The ground side of the ring should always be placed toward the bottom side of the ring groove, because a perfect seal is needed at this point on the compression stroke of the piston, as the ring is pressed against this side on the up-stroke. If it is necessary to reduce the thickness of the ring to make it fit the groove, it should always be done on the unground side. If both sides are ground, only one side should be reduced and the ground side that is untouched should be placed downward in the groove.

Fitting Ring in Groove. In fitting rings, the piston should be immersed in gasoline and sprayed thoroughly to remove the least particle of dirt from the grooves and guides. Much time may be saved by trying the rings in the various grooves to see which ring most nearly fits a given groove.

Fig. 10 shows how the ring should be started in the groove, and the arrows show the direction in which the ring should be moved.

The entire circumference of the ring should be rolled around the groove. Of course, if the ring will not fit into the groove, try another groove. The reason the back end of the ring is fitted first instead of the inner is because the latter fitting would require that the ring be put in its usual position around the piston. Slipping the rings over the piston head is not easy in itself and would be difficult were the rings not of the proper size.

Testing and Correcting Length of Ring. The ring should next be inserted into the cylinder to determine whether the ends are the proper distance apart. The distance between the ring ends, when

Fig. 11. Filing Piston Ring to Give
Proper Spacing

the ring is in the cylinder, varies with the different designs. An electric lamp dropped into the cylinder, while the ring is in, will show immediately whether the ends of the ring are touching. If they do touch, they should be filed slightly, as shown in Fig. 11. The ring should be placed in a vise with one end protruding about an inch. A little of the ring is left sticking out so that it will not sway when filing is being done. The file—a very fine mill file—is placed between the ends as the sketch shows, with the left hand pressing the long end of the ring lightly against the file. The operation should continue for a short time only, about twelve strokes of the file being sufficient. The ring should be put back in the cylinder and the distance between the ends measured with a thickness gauge, or as it is called by factory men, a feeler. Fifteen-thousandths inch is a good distance to allow if the factory measurements cannot be obtained.

Lapping In the Ring. The next step is to make the ring fit its groove properly. Lapping is the term applied to the operation of grinding the ring down so that it fits. A level steel surface is used, upon which is sprinkled enough very fine emery dust to cover it. Enough water is added to make a pasty mass. The ring is then placed on the steel plate and a block of wood about 6 by 6 inches placed on top of the ring; by exerting a slight pressure on the block and applying a rotary motion, the ring is moved about over the emery.

If the ring will not stay under the wood block, cut a little notch in the block to hold the ring still. After grinding for a few strokes

Fig. 12. Putting Piston Ring on Piston End

on one side, the ring should be tried in the groove, and the process repeated until the proper thickness is obtained.

The entire operation should not last longer than one or two minutes. After lapping, the ring should be immersed in clean gasoline and fitted to the groove which it most nearly fitted before. If every part of the circumference of the ring fits every part of the groove, then the lapping is complete and the ring may be tagged to designate its location. The figures 1-1 on a tag usually represents the first cylinder ring No. 1, this ring being the one nearest the top of the piston. If one part of the ring fits and another does not, the place that is too tight will show up when the ring is dipped in gasoline and then rubbed with a cloth. The high spot will be more shiny than the rest. Lay the ring perfectly flat and with a fine file take a little off from both sides of the ring. Only a little should be taken off at a time, and the ring should be tried after each filing.

Replacing the Rings. When all the rings have been filed in this way, the next step is to place them in their respective grooves, making them occupy their proper position when in use. In Fig. 12 is shown a method for doing this. First place the bottom ring in position.

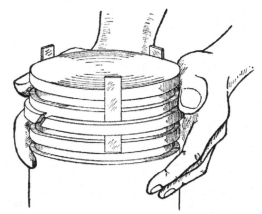

Fig. 13. Using Metal Strips in Properly Placing
Piston Rings

For this operation, three pieces of saw blade with the teeth ground off are used. Hold one blade against the piston with the left hand and with the right hand bring one end of the ring in contact with the blade. Get the blade about $\frac{1}{2}$ inch from the end of the ring, so that the blade can be held in place by pressure against the ring. Then slip the ring over the piston top. There is a space on either side of the blade through which the other blades may be inserted. Push the blades around until they appear as shown in Fig. 13. By sliding the ring on the three blades, it may be placed easily in its groove. With the lapped ring in its groove, the ring must fit so that it may be turned around easily. No up and down play must exist.

To have a perfectly smooth running engine all reciprocating parts should be evenly balanced in weight. The parts are usually balanced at the factory, but this is not always attended to in replacements. The parts should not vary more than $\frac{1}{4}$ ounce in weight. The repair man is often asked to speed up the revolutions of an engine, and an excellent way of doing this is to lighten the pistons by drilling.

In order to get out any amount of metal worth the trouble, it will be necessary to drill from 12 to 20 or more holes of from $\frac{1}{2}$-inch up to 1-inch diameter, depending upon the size of the piston as to bore and length. In a six-cylinder motor, this amounts to almost 100 holes (even more in some cases), and as these must be drilled with considerable similarity in the pistons, it is well worth while to construct a fixture to aid or speed up this work.

One idea of the way such a lightened piston should look when finished is given in Fig. 14, which shows the steel pistons used in the

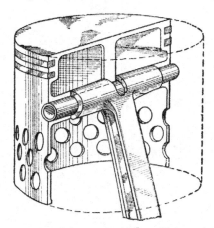

Fig. 14. Appearance of Piston Lightened for Racing Purposes

Sunbeam racers. These are made this way to give the maximum of lightness with strength. Although made from steel, this is done simply to get very light side walls, and the general appearance of the skirt with its many drilled holes is just what the repair man should try to get when he starts to cut down the weight of standard pistons for racing or speed purposes.

Clamp for Pistons. The first requisite is a clamp, Fig. 15, to keep the piston from turning, so that it will not break the drill. A good way to begin is to construct a base with a pair of uprights having deep 90-degree **V's** in them; this is made so that it can be bolted to the drill-press table. The **V's** should be lined with leather or fabric. Discarded clutch or brake linings answer this purpose very well. To one of the uprights is pivoted a long handle, having a lined **V** which matches with that of the upright below it, and gives a good grip on the piston.

Drilling Holes. When drilling to save weight, the holes are put in close together and in regular form, the idea being to take out as much weight of metal as is safe. In doing this, it is well to work out a scheme of drilling in advance, to make a heavy brown paper template, and fasten to each piston in turn.

Piston Repairs. If an engine is to be efficient, new piston rings will often have to be fitted. The piston-ring grooves do not wear evenly, as shown in Fig. 16. It will be seen that the groove-wears

Fig. 15. A Home-Made Wooden Stand to
Facilitate Drilling Out Pistons

taper, that is, are smaller at the rear. A good job of fitting rings to a piston in this condition can not be done until these grooves are made square and true in every way. Put the piston in a lathe, and using a square tool, machine the groove until the sides are parallel. There are a few hand tools on the market that do very satisfactory work. A tool for this purpose is shown in Figs. 17 and 18. This is a ring-shaped tool with rollers that fit the groove and guide the cutter. The cutter is set and the tool rotated around the piston, squaring the groove. It will then be necessary to fit oversize piston rings to the groove. It is very important that the piston rings fit the groove, for if there is side play between the groove and the ring, the gas or compression will leak around behind the ring and the engine will lose power. If this condition exists, the ring will move from the top to the bottom side of the groove or vice-versa, every time the piston changes its direction of movement. This not only causes wear on both the ring and the groove, but it also causes a knock in the engine. Sometimes it is found necessary to fit over-size piston pins to the piston. A reamer is the correct tool to use for this purpose. The tool should not cut too much metal at one time for it may leave a rough surface. The tool should be placed in a vice, Fig. 19, and the piston placed over it and rotated around the reamer. This is repeated until the hole is the required size. The piston pin should be inserted into the hole occasionally to be

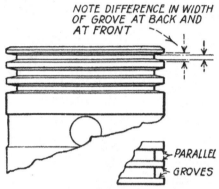

Fig. 16. Worn Piston Ring Grooves

certain that the hole is not becoming too large. When the piston pin can be driven into the piston with light hammer blows it is considered to be a good fit. Some makers—the Marmon Company, for instance—fit the pin so that it is necessary to expand the piston by immersing it in hot water before the pin can be put into place. The pin should not be fitted to a tight-driving fit because it is apt to distort the piston and often cause the latter to split. At the same time it should fit so that it will not loosen in service and cause wear on the pin and in the piston-pin hole.

Piston Pins. Piston, or wrist pins, as they are variously called, are usually very simple. In general, when the pin is a light drive fit or any easy fit in the piston, it is made from a high quality of carbon steel tubing of considerable thickness, ground on the outside to size, and drilled for the locking pin (when one is used). It is then hardened and finish ground. In some instances it is simply a tight fit, with a ring fitted around the outside of the piston at its center,

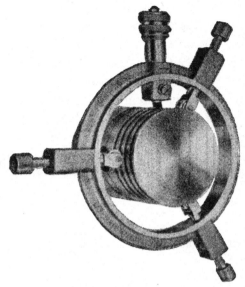

Fig. 17.   Tool for Squaring-Up Piston Ring
Grooves
Courtesy of The Dyer Company

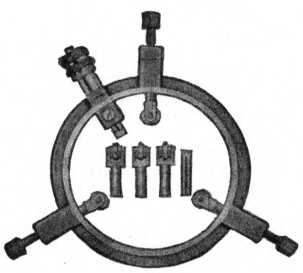

Fig. 18.   Tool Parts
Courtesy of The Dyer Company

to form a lock. In other forms it is clamped in the connecting rod and turns in bushings in the two piston bosses. The general method, however, is the use of a hollow pin, the variation coming in the method of locking. Thus there is the use of two locking pins which project into holes; of two set screws which bear against grooves for

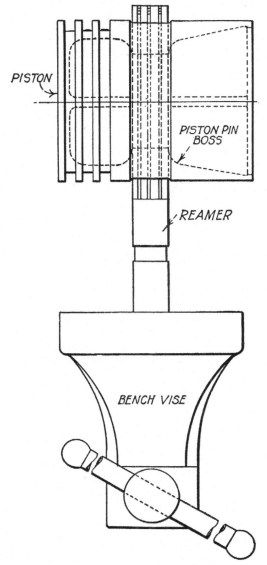

PISTON

PISTON PIN BOSS

REAMER

BENCH VISE

Fig. 19. Reaming Piston

this purpose; expansion plugs screwed into the split ends; spring plungers in holes in the piston; and of complex built-up pin sections with tapers bearing upon each other so as to be self-locking. The really important point is to have the pin so locked in place that it can never work out and score the cylinder walls, and yet be easy to disassemble. Piston pins are made hollow to reduce the reciprocating weight and thereby give more power and speed to the engine. Being hollow, they also form an oil way for the lubrication of the piston pin bearings.

Piston Pin Knock. To find this noise a test can be made as follows. Short out or disconnect the spark plug while the engine is running at idling speed. This will cause the engine to misfire. If the wrist pin is loose, the knock will be more pronounced when the engine is thus treated than when the engine is firing correctly.

Mandrel for Turning Pins. Because of its being hollow in many cases, the wrist pin is difficult to handle when any work must be done upon it. For this purpose, a mandrel is needed. The

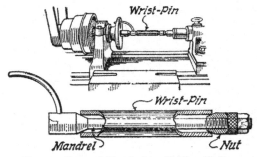

Fig. 20. Tapered Mandrel for Holding Hollow
Piston Pin for Lathe Work

method of constructing and using this is shown in Fig. 20. This consists of a shaft with a taper at one end and thread at the other, for a tapered nut. The wrist pin is slipped on the outer end, the taper nut put in place against it, and the backing nut put on behind that. These are screwed up until the two tapers hold the pin firmly, after which it may be placed in the lathe and worked upon.

Removal and Replacement of Pistons. Speaking of pistons, there are several things that the beginner should learn about their removal and replacement. While it is not a difficult matter to pull a piston out of a cylinder, when both have been previously lubricated and all proper precautions taken to loosen connecting parts, there are a few important things to remember.

The piston should be drawn out as nearly parallel to the axis of the cylinder as is possible, accompanied by a twisting motion not unlike taking out a screw, in case it sticks a little. If the piston sticks badly, pour in a little kerosene and work the piston in and out so as to distribute the kerosene between the two surfaces.

To get at the spaces the rings must be removed, and as they are of cast iron and very brittle, this is a delicate task. Two methods of accomplishing this are illustrated in Fig. 21. If the owner has a pair of ring-expanding pliers, the rings can easily be expanded enough to lift them over the edge, as shown in (a). As very few owners possess this useful tool, however, a more common

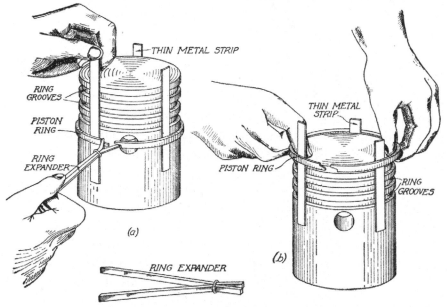

Fig. 21. Method of Removing Piston Rings

way is shown in (b). Secure a number of thin, flat steels about $\frac{1}{2}$-inch wide and $\frac{1}{16}$-inch thick—corset steels, flat springs, or hack-saw blades may be used, although the latter require more care on account of the teeth along one edge. The length of these steels should be such as to reach from about an inch below the last ring, to the top. Lift out one side of the ring with a small pointed tool and slip one of the steels between the ring and the piston, then move around about one-third of the way and insert another, taking care to hold the first in place; repeat the operation with a third steel.

When these are in place, the steels will hold the ring out from the piston far enough to be slid over the "lands" between the grooves and along the steels to the top.

Always begin at the top and work down when removing rings, and just the opposite, from the bottom up, when replacing them. After one is mastered, the removal of the others is a simple matter

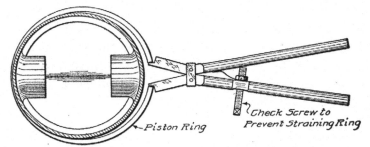

Fig. 22. Tool for Moving Piston Rings Which Prevents Breakage

of repetition. The grooves can now be scraped free of the offending carbon, a process which is but an inversion of the previous method. After this it will be necessary to replace the rings.

A modification of the simple home-made ring spreader is shown in Fig. 22. This is made with a stop, which prevents opening the

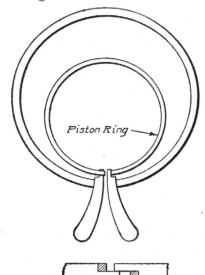

Fig. 23. Simple Piston Ring Remover

pliers beyond a predetermined distance and thus prevents breaking a ring by continued pressing on a stiff or stuck one until it gives suddenly and is then spread beyond the resisting ability of the iron. It is applicable to all forms of rings, except those with diagonal slots. In addition to the construction shown, it is desirable to fit a spring which will draw the handles together when not in use. This closes the jaws and keeps them closed, ready for immediate use.

An even better and more simple form, but without the safety feature of that just mentioned, consists of a large diameter steel spring, shaped not unlike a very big piston ring, which has a pair of handles fitted to the ends. This is shown in Fig. 23, which indicates how the nubs on the two handles are shaped so as to take hold of stepped joint rings. By making these nubs differently, any form of ring can be handled. A device of this sort saves the repair man lots of time.

Loosening Seized Pistons. When the pistons and rings freeze into the cylinder, or seize because of a lack of lubricant, there is nothing quite as good nor quite as quick acting as kerosene. The cylinder head should be opened as quickly as possible, and the kerosene poured in liberally on top of the pistons. This should be done in each cylinder. Kerosene is thin and will work down between

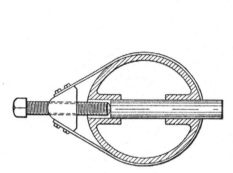

Fig. 24. Simple Piston-Pin Pulling Outfit

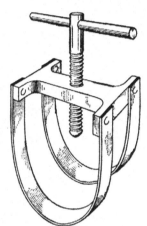

Fig. 25. Piston Ring Puller Which Allows for Exit of Pin

cylinder wall and piston rings, gradually cutting away the two where they have frozen together. If kerosene is not available, take the thinnest lubricant at hand; heat it so that it will be still thinner and more penetrating, then pour it in. At times, olive oil can be combined with kerosene to advantage.

Freeing Wrist Pins and Bushings. When the piston pin or wrist pin is inserted directly in the piston, it is usually a tight fit, so tight, sometimes, that the repair man experiences difficulty in getting it out. To overcome this difficulty, a piston pin puller is needed. One of these, shown in Fig. 24, is made from a piece of steel, a steel strap, and a large cap screw. This piece of steel is drilled and tapped for the cap screw, and for the bolts to hold the steel strap. Then the latter is fastened so as to be about $\frac{1}{4}$-inch larger in diameter than the piston, or still larger if a long cap screw is available. When a pin is to be removed, the strap is put around the piston and the cap screw screwed in until it bears against the end of the pin. This can be done by hand. Then a wrench is applied, and as the screw is forced in, the pin is forced out on the opposite side. Be careful to see that the far side of the steel band is below the piston pin hole, so the pin will be able to come out without touching it.

This can be simplified by having an endless steel band with a nut on the inside of it to form a backing for the cap screw to work against, or, the steel band can be welded to the nut.

A form which removes the above difficulty is that shown in Fig. 25. This is made so that it holds around the piston at two

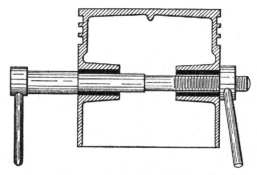

Fig. 26. Piston Pin Bushing with Shouldered Mandrel

points, above and below the piston pin, leaving room for the pin to come out. While more elaborate than the first one described, it is still very simple. For hollow piston pins, a different form of tip on the screw is needed, as the point, or tip, must press against the outer circular ring instead of against the center. This can be obviated, however, by laying a special round piece of metal over the end of the hollow pin before starting to apply pressure to force it out.

Bushing Removers. When the piston pin is fixed in the connecting rod and rotates in bushings in the piston bosses, it is sometimes necessary to remove these bushings. A somewhat similar device will do this work, except that a shoulder or stop is needed to come up home against the side of the bushing, while the screw or threaded end must be small enough to pass through the hole in the bushing and long enough to come out on the other side so a nut can be applied. One of these is shown in Fig. 26. The disadvantage of this type is that the nut shown on the right, which is operated to force the bushing out, must rest against the surface of the piston while being turned around. If a small U-bar be made to rest against the piston side, with a central drilled hole through which the threaded end passes, the nut will bear against the outside surface, so that even if the nut should scratch, no harm will be done to the piston. These pullers are used as substitutes for an arbor press, but this is desirable, as the use of the press is likely to distort the more or less delicate piston. With aluminum and the lighter weight cast-iron pistons, this is a thing which it is desirable to avoid.

Some motors have the wrist pin locked in place by means of an expanding nut with a sunken square hole for turning. To start these, a wrench with a square projection or tit to fit this is needed.

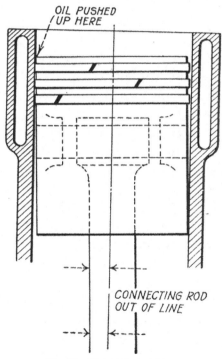

Fig. 27. Piston Out-of-Line

Such a wrench is used on certain lathe chucks, so one can always be borrowed in a machine shop or tool room.

Oil Pumping. One of the greatest troubles experienced in the automobile engine is oil pumping. The indication of oil pumping is the continual fouling of the spark plugs, a great amount of blue smoke coming from the exhaust, and the quick formation of carbon, especially if wet and sticky.

Some of the causes of this trouble are relative to piston condition. There is only one permanent cure and that is to install new pistons and piston rings.

(1). *A cocked piston in the cylinder, Fig. 27, which pushes the oil up into the combustion by the edge of the piston.* The cure is to check the alignment of the connecting rod and straighten it so that the piston will have equal space all around it.

(2). *Rings that do not fit the piston ring grooves or cylinder walls.* Check the cylinder condition and fit new rings if satisfactory.

(3). *Loose pistons.* Fit new pistons throughout if cylinder conditions are right. If not, then the cylinder block must be reground.

(4). *Leaky valves.* Regrind.

(5). *Loose main bearing in force-feed lubrication.* This allows the oil to seep out at the ends of the bearings and down the webs of the shaft to be thrown up into the cylinders, consequently supplying more oil than the rings can handle and flooding the engine. The play in the bearings must be taken up.

Some excellent temporary cures are given in the following paragraphs.

Curing Excessive Lubrication. *Holes in Pistons.* When it comes to drilling holes to provide an outlet for the excess oil in the cylinders and to reduce smoking, small holes, $\frac{1}{8}$-inch for example, are sufficient. They may be drilled in on any spiral plan by simply beginning near the bottom and working up close to the piston-pin bosses along a spiral track. The advantage of the spiral arrangement is that no hole is above another; the dripping from each hole is therefore distinct, and the quantity which runs down is greater.

Grooving Pistons. Another method of curing the excessive lubrication to which the older cars—particularly those with splash

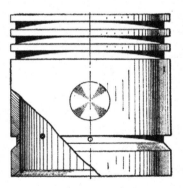

Fig. 28. Method of Grooving and Drilling Piston to Overcome Excessive Lubrication and Smoking

lubrication—are subject, is to turn a deep groove in the bottom of the piston, about like a piston-ring groove but with a lower edge beveled off. When this is done, as shown in Fig. 28, a series of small holes—made with a No. 30 drill —are put in at the angle of the bevel; six or eight holes, equally distributed around the circumference, are probably enough. The sharp upper edge acts as a wiper and removes the oil from the cylinder walls into the groove, whence it passes through the holes to the piston interior and there drops back into the crankcase. No ring is placed in the slot as it would prevent the free passage of the oil. This device stops the smoking immediately.

Loose Pistons. Many times the pistons will wear just enough so that they are loose in the cylinder all the way around. This causes leakage of gas, piston slap, and other similar troubles. If the owner of the car does not care to buy new pistons, or if the car is an "orphan", or if, for other reasons, pistons cannot be obtained, the clever repair man can remedy the trouble at small expense. The process consists in heating and expanding the old pistons. The heating is done in charcoal and must be done very carefully and slowly. After the pistons become red hot the fire is allowed to go out slowly, so that the piston is cooled in its charcoal bed. Sometimes as much as $\frac{4}{1000}$ of an inch can be gained in this way. When the pistons are so far gone that they cannot be handled in this way, they must be replaced with new ones.

Piston Slap. A piston slap is caused by the movement of the piston from one side of the cylinder to the other by the action of the connecting rod.

This noise can be detected in the following manner. Remove the spark plug and pour into the cylinder a small quantity of heavy oil and then crank the engine so that this oil will be spread over the cylinder walls. Start the engine and if the knock has gone or is diminished, the heavy oil has cushioned the piston. Of course as the heavy oil gradually thins out under the heat the knock will increase in volume.

Mounting Pistons on Lathes. It is difficult to handle a piston in the lathe, or machine the outside in any manner, as a chuck does

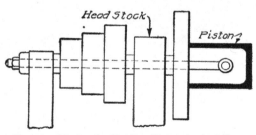

Fig. 29. Rigging for Holding Piston Against Face Plate of Lathe

not get enough of a hold on it, and is likely to mark the surface. When work on it is necessary, the piston can be handled effectively by using a small rod with an eye at one end. This is made to fit the piston pin in the case of an old piston. The rod is run through the hollow spindle and bolted at the outer end. The tightening of the nut pulls the piston up against the face plate as Fig. 29 shows. This same method can be used when making a new piston. In the latter case, it is held in the chuck to finish the outside and inside, then the wrist-pin hole is drilled, bored, and reamed, and the wrist pin fitted. Finally, the finishing cut, or grinding of the outside, is completed.

Replacing Pistons in Cylinders. When cylinders or pistons have been removed to be worked on, replacing these is a difficult job.

Fig. 30. Method of Re-Assembling Piston Mechanism

There are two ways of doing this: either by a special form of ring closer or by hand, using a string. The ring closer is a shaped device which is clamped around the ring and squeezed together with pliers, using one hand, while with the other hand the ring is guided into the groove. The second and more usual method is illustrated in Fig. 30, and requires two men, unless the cylinder is of such a shape that it can be clamped in a vise. As the picture brings out, one man holds the cylinder while the other forces the piston carrying the rings into place. The piston is shoved in until the expanded top ring pre-vents further movement, when a heavy cord is placed around the spring, and the ends are crossed, thus closing up the ring and allow-ing the piston to slide in as far as the next ring. The operation is repeated successively for the other rings. This is a very simple method but it requires patience.

When a block cylinder is to be replaced, this job is not so easy, for all the pistons, four or six as the case may be, must be lined up, and two of them entered at one time. This requires either special apparatus to help hold them or the services of several men. Most

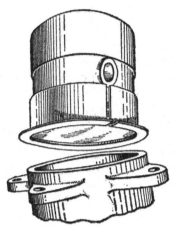

Fig. 31. Simple Rig to Assist
Pistons Entering Cylinder
Casting

cylinders have a small bevelled edge at the bottom to facilitate this, but it is best to make a rig for a motor which is handled in sufficient numbers to warrant this. A handy form, and one easily made, is that shown in Fig. 31. This consists of a sheet-iron band of a depth equal to the total depth of the rings in the upper part of the cylinder and is flanged over at the top to give it extra stiffness and prevent its entering the cylinder. It is made a little bit small for the size of the pistons over which it is to be used, so it will have to be sprung into place. When this is done, it will have a tight hold on the rings, compressing them so they will enter the cylinder. In applying it, care should be used to put it on squarely, and similarly in pushing it down by forcing the piston upward into the cylinder. It should not be moved off of a ring until that ring has been entered in the cylinder enough so it is held therein. That is, the spring clamp should not be moved down below a ring until that ring is engaged and held within the cylinder. Its use is restricted to one size of motor, which is no hardship in a big shop where one make of car is handled exclusively. The small shop handling a variety of work would find half a dozen different sizes useful and economical. Moreover, the cost of this device is very small.

A modification of the above device consists of a similar small-sized band of sheet metal, made very wide but without the upper flange. It is made, however, with a pair of right-angle lips where the two sides meet; these are drilled for a clamping bolt. This bolt has a wing nut with clamping rings to compress the lips of the band.

Another modification of this is a loop or strap of narrow sheet metal having an additional loop to go over the two ends. These ends are made with a right-angle bend close to the piston-curve portion, and the compression of the rings is effected by pressing the sides of the clamp tightly against them, then sliding the small loop along the ends to hold this tightness.

SECTION OF NASH CAR, SHOWING ENGINE AND TRANSMISSION DETAILS AND REAR SPRING SUSPENSION

Courtesy of The Nash Motors Company, Kenosha, Wisconsin

VALVES AND THEIR MECHANISM

PART I

Importance of Valves. Probably the most important thing about a four-cycle gasoline engine is the valve, or, more correctly, are the valves, for the usual number is two per cylinder. The opening and closing of these control the functions of the engine; for if the valve does not open and allow a charge of gas to enter, how can the piston compress, and the ignition system fire a charge? Similarly, if the exhaust valve is not opened and the burned gases allowed to escape, they will mingle with and dilute the fresh, incoming charge, possibly to the extent of making the latter into a non-combustible gas. This is purposely stated in this way because both methods mentioned have been utilized for governing the engine speed, although not to any great extent in automobile work.

Summary of Valve Features. In the valves and valve mechanisms of modern gasoline engines there have been and are impending more interesting changes than seem in prospect in any other portion of the mechanism of the modern automobile. Particularly is this the case with reference to the present tendency to discard the poppet valve with its many objectionable features. Even where there is no tendency toward the use of a sleeve-valve or slide-valve form of motor, much experimenting has been done with increasing the number and changing the position of the valves.

Poppet Valves. Though the very first internal-combustion engines ever made were operated with slide valves, the poppet valve was introduced very early in the history of this art and has reigned supreme in practically all types of gas and gasoline engines.

The chief advantage of the poppet valve is its capacity for continuous operation at excessively high temperatures, but since the cooling of engines has progressed to the status of high reliability, this advantage is of less importance than formerly. And the disadvantages of poppet valves—the small openings that they afford, the noisy and hammering action they involve, their tendency to leak and in other ways give out, and the necessity for frequently regrinding them—are objections so serious that it is no wonder the prospect of their elimination is so widely welcomed.

About the only recent improvement that has been made in poppet valves is in the quality of material used in them. Many valves now used have cast-iron and nickel heads, which offer a maximum resistance to warping from the heat to which they are subjected. These are fitted with carbon-steel stems, which are superior in their wearing qualities. More use has been made recently of tungsten as a material for valves. Steel containing this is even harder than nickel steel, and experiments have shown that it does not warp as much. In practice, the objection found to cast-iron heads was that the fastenings to the carbon-steel stem were not sufficiently strong to withstand the constant pulling and pushing to which a valve was subjected. As a result they separated, causing trouble.

In the operation of poppet valves, the cams become an important factor. These are the parts which, in revolving, raise the valves so that they open at the proper time. In addition, the cams are so shaped as to hold the valves open for just the right length of time and allow them to close, through the medium of the valve-spring pressure, at the proper point in the cycle. The importance of this can be seen if we consider that opening the slightest fraction of a second too late will reduce the amount of the charge very much and thus lessen the power developed by the motor.

Enclosures. The use of casings to enclose the valve stems, springs, and push rods, so as to keep these elements from exposure to dirt, and at the same time silence, in a large degree, the noise they make, is also becoming usual.

Many excellent examples of this may be seen in modern motors. The whole side of the motor where the valve mechanism is located is covered with a long removable plate, keeping in noise and lubricant and keeping out dirt. Usually, however, on a six-cylinder motor the valve enclosure is made in two parts, one half enclosing the mechanism of the valves in the first three cylinders, the other half, those in the last three. This is, of course, the preferred construction on those six-cylinder engines which have the cylinders cast in threes, instead of in a block, as the one referred to. On some motors where this construction has not found favor, the designers have followed the plan of enclosing the individual valve mechanisms. While more expensive, this method is equally as efficient. On the other hand, it adds to the parts, and the whole modern tendency has been to reduce the number of parts.

Sleeve Valves. This type of valve, while not at all new, has only within the past few years come into considerable prominence, chiefly as a result of the truly remarkable performances of the Knight motor, which is equipped with the most advanced examples of this type of valve.

Contrary to past opinion, it has been conclusively demonstrated that sleeve valves do not, to any perceptible degree, increase the tendency of a motor to overheat, nor do they wear at any very measurable rate. They afford, moreover, in the best constructions, a much higher thermal and mechanical efficiency than it is possible to secure from the average poppet-valve motor, this improvement being due to the better-shaped combustion chamber that can be used and the greater areas of valve opening, which facilitate the ingress and egress of the charges.

Another advantage in favor of the sleeve valve is that its timing is permanent and unchangeable and does not alter materially with wear. Not the least of the merits of the sleeve valve is found in the fact that it lends itself to positive operation by eccentric mechanisms, which are in every way greatly superior to the non-positive cam mechanisms universally used to actuate poppet valves.

Sliding Valves. Sliding valves of other than the sleeve type, embracing a considerable variety of piston valves and valves similar to those employed in steam engines, have not found as much favor with designers of automobile engines as have other types herein referred to.

One exception is the successful use of a "split-ring" valve sliding up and down in the cylinder head just above the piston, which has found successful application in a few motors recently built by the Renault Company, France.

Rotating Valves. A number of engines with rotating valves have been built from time to time, but none of these seem to have survived the test of time, for not one which was in evidence two years ago is made now. However, they are under development and it is hoped that an improved engine of this type will be successfully completed.

The flat-seat valves and the valves with a seat having a 45- or a 30-degree angle are of the poppet type. The flat type is not used to any great extent because the carbon particles are apt to lodge on the seat and cause trouble. The edges of the valve must be made very thick, or else they will get red hot, causing preignition. This would not only add to their weight but also would cause more wear on all parts of the valve mechanism.

Valves at an Angle to the Cylinder Bore. Some engines have the valves so placed that their stems are not parallel to the bore of the cylinder. There are two distinct advantages in this arrangement. (1) It allows a little larger valve-port area, which gives a larger explosive charge to the cylinders, and therefore a higher power output. In overhead camshaft positions, it allows the shaft to be placed between the valves. (2) It eliminates the side thrust of the cam against the push rod and the wear on the push rod and the guide is reduced. (3) It eliminates certain parts, as the rocker arms. An example of this type of installation is shown in Fig. 1.

Typical Valve Actions. Figs. 2 and 3 illustrate the complete valve action very well. In Fig. 2, the cam works against a roller in the bottom of the push rod. This works upward in the push-rod guide and has a dirt excluding arrangement at the top. The top of the push rod bears against the bottom of the valve stem with an adjustable hardened screw, forming the contact. The valve is held down on its seat in the cylinder by means of a strong spring which the upward movement of the push rod opposes. The valve is guided in and has its bearing in the valve guide, which is made long to give large bearing surface. As the Locomobile motor is of the T-head type, the exhaust and inlet valves are on opposite sides of the cylinders and are operated by separate camshafts. The valve mechanism is completely enclosed.

Fig. 3 shows the valve action used on Haynes cars. The difference is in the elimination of the roller at the bottom of the push rod which forms the point of contact with the cam. In this form, a flat hardened surface makes the push rod more simple and reduces the number of parts. It has been said against this form that the cam scrapes across the push-rod face and thus wears it, but in actual use it has been found that the push rod rotates and in this

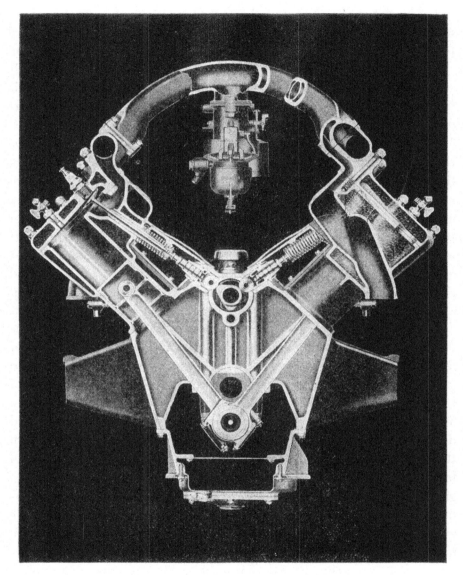

Fig. 1.   Sectional View of the LaFayette Eight-Cylinder Motor Showing the Valves Set at an Angle to the Cylinders

way the wear is distributed over the whole flat face, which in this construction can be made much larger than can the face of the roller. The push rods are of the "mushroom" type and are made of nickel steel. The push-rod adjustments are completely enclosed but may be readily reached without disturbing any other unit.

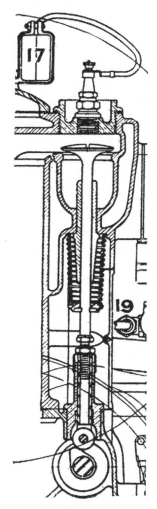

Fig. 2. Complete Valve
Motion with Roller Push-Rod
*Courtesy of Locomobile Company
of America, Bridgeport,
Connecticut*

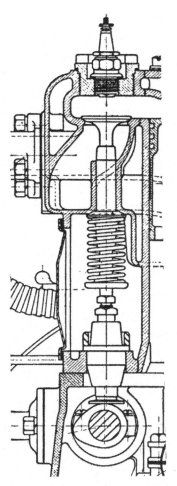

Fig. 3. Complete Valve Motion
with Mushroom Push-Rod
*Courtesy of Haynes Automobile
Company, Kokomo, Indiana*

They may be removed and replaced without removing the valve springs or valves.

Neither of these systems is in decided favor, designers being about equally divided between them.

The construction and operation of the cam mechanism is the same whether used in connection with an exhaust or an inlet valve, as the same line of reasoning and the same method of procedure, in both cases, would lead to the same results.

It has many times been tried and still more often urged that the straight surface of the side of the cam is not conducive to the best results, because of the fact that when the first straight portion of the cam surface strikes the cam roller it does so with so much force that it tends to wear the latter in that direction. As for the receding face, it has been urged that the ordinary closing of the valve is too slow and that the straight surface can be altered so as to allow of speeding up the downward movement of the valve. This idea works out into a curve. The back of the surface is hollowed out so that as soon as the cam roller passes the center it drops vertically, owing to the tension of the spring. This method has been tried, but without success.

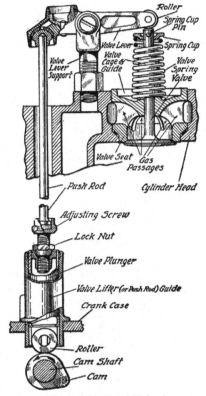

Fig. 4. Typical Overhead-Valve Layout, Showing Complete Mechanism

Other Parts of Valve System. Fig. 4 shows an overhead-valve system in which the camshaft is in the usual place in the crankcase; long push rods are used with rocker arms, or levers, at the top. This is mentioned because many, in fact, the majority of motors with overhead valves have an overhead camshaft like the Wills Sainte Claire.

The rotation of the camshaft brings the cam around so that it lifts the roller and valve lifter. The valve lifter has the adjusting screw and its lock nut at the top. The top of the roller bears against the bottom of the push rod, and the upper end of the push rod operates the valve rocker lever, which is held in the support. At the other end of the valve-rocker lever a roller presses against the top end of the valve stem and pushes it down from off the valve seat against the pressure of the spring, the upper end of which is held by the cup and cup pin and the lower end rests upon the upper surface of the valve cage. The latter is made so that its central upward extension also forms the valve guide. The valve cage is screwed down into the cylinder head with packing to make a gas-tight joint. It carries the valve seat and is cored out for the gas passages through which the gas enters (or leaves).

When the valve in pockets is substituted for the long push rod, in either the L-head or in the T-head cylinder, the construction is about the same as if the upper right-hand valve group were lifted bodily, turned upside down, and placed so that the upper end of the valve stem, upon which the roller rests, comes into contact with the adjusting screw. In that case, the valve lifter would be called the push rod, and the valve cage would become a part of the cylinder with an integral or, in some cases, a removable valve guide.

There is a small amount of play between the push rod and the valve stem which is called clearance. The overhead valve must always be given more play than other types, because the expansion is a great deal more in this type than in the ordinary installation. The valve stem gets hotter and expands more, consequently, the adjustment should be made when the engine is warm so that the valve is sure to close properly. Where the ordinary valve clearance is about .004 inch, the overhead valve has an average clearance of .008 inch to .010 inch.

What Good Modern Practice Shows. A more modern way, which is fast becoming universal, is to use straight sides for the cams and take advantage of rapid closing in another way, the benefits of which more than offset the benefits of the old way and have no corresponding disadvantages. In the ordinary automobile engine running at 1000 revolutions per minute, the gases are traveling into the cylinder at the rate of 5000 to 6000 feet per minute, and traveling out at from 7000 to 10,000 feet per minute. At this tremendous speed, the gas inertia is very high, and experiments go to show that the gases by means of this inertia will continue to force their way into the cylinder even against the return motion of the piston. So it is now common practice to hold the inlet valve open about 30 degrees on the upstroke of the piston, which results in a much larger piston charge. The same practice is carried out with the exhaust, but as the pressure is higher, as large an angle is not necessary. These actions take place on the back—flat side—of the cam surface and have given to the high-speed automobile engine a larger charge and a more complete scavenging effect, resulting in more power and speed from the same size of cylinder.

As proof of this statement, the power curve of an engine of but 3½-inch diameter of cylinder is shown in Fig. 5. This size of six-cylinder engine would be rated by any formula at about 29 horsepower at the maximum speed, and a commercially obtainable

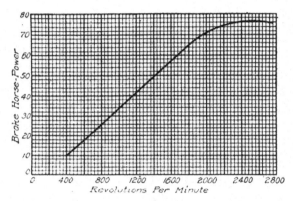

Fig. 5. Power Curve of an American Engine with
Superior Cams and Balancing

type in this size would doubtless be guaranteed to deliver between 20 and 25 horsepower. This engine, which is not built for racing purposes, displays a power curve which continuously rises; a speed at which it would turn downward has not been obtainable in the tests. This curve shows also that the maximum power obtained was over 80, which is nearly three times the power of the ordinary engine of this same size. This result is ascribable to superior valves and superior attention to the valve angles as governed by the cams.

Number of Valves per Cylinder. *Three Valves per Cylinder.* When it was stated that but two valves per cylinder were ordinarily used, with one cam for each, the majority case was spoken of. The most important advocate of air cooling in this country and the

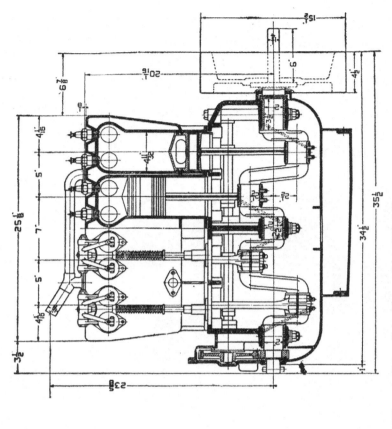

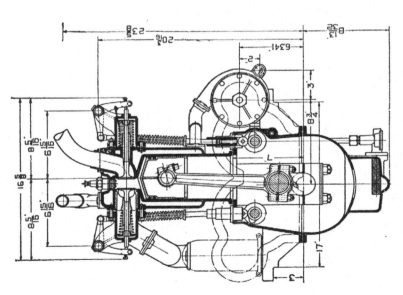

Fig. 6.   Sections through Wisconsin Sixteen-Valve Motor—Side and End Views

Courtesy of Wisconsin Motor Company, Milwaukee, Wisconsin

117

world, the H. H. Franklin Manufacturing Company, used three valves, and consequently three cams, per cylinder. These three were the ordinary inlet; the usual exhaust; and the additional auxiliary exhaust. By re-designing later, this complication was avoided and the third valve eliminated.

The Wisconsin Motor Company has developed another motor with four valves per cylinder and, after a notable racing success, has placed it upon the market. Any maker desiring to do so may

Fig. 7. Exhaust Side of the Stutz Sixteen-Valve Motor

purchase this and incorporate it in his chassis. This emphasizes the distance which the sixteen-valve four-cylinder motor has progressed in a short time. A section through this motor, both side elevation and end view, showing all the details of the construction, is shown in Fig. 6. The exhaust manifold of the Stutz motor is shown in Fig. 7.

Four Valves per Cylinder. The very latest practice in the way of multiple valves is the use of four valves per cylinder—two inlets and two exhausts. There are a number of reasons why this construction is a good one. The area through which the gases enter and leave the cylinders is made greater, thus giving the same or greater supply of gas more quickly and a better scavenging effect.

GASOLINE AUTOMOBILES

The volumetric efficiency of the cylinder is greatly increased in this way, giving more power and speed from the same size of cylinders—so much more as to give a four-cylinder engine with sixteen valves as great a flexibility as that of a six-cylinder with but twelve valves. Another big advantage claimed for the smaller lighter valves of this construction is that very much lighter valve springs can be used. This advantage was discovered by using sixteen valves on a four-cylinder racing engine where the compression and other pressures were enormous. The valve springs for the ordinary eight-valve engine had to be very stiff and, consequently, gave much cam trouble. The stiff springs dug out the sides of the cams very rapidly and also failed rapidly themselves.

Valve Timing. This increase of speed without material alteration in the engine is what every repair man aims to get when he goes over the timing of the motor. Valve timing has been called an art, but it is not; it is only the application of common sense and the known valve diagram to the motor in an attempt to get the best all-around results. These, as might be expected, are a compromise, and that repair man does the best timing, who realizes this and, instead of attempting the impossible, simply produces the most desirable all-around compromise.

General Rule. Although the manufacturers usually have a valve timing which is suitable for their particular product, the following is a general rule which can be used when timing engines. *Rotate the crankshaft until the piston in number one cylinder comes to the top of its stroke. With the camshaft gear out of mesh, move the shaft in its proper direction of rotation until the exhaust valve has just closed, and then mesh the gears.* If the work has been done correctly, the intake valve should start to open as soon as the piston starts to move down on the suction stroke. The exact point of closing can be found by inserting a thin piece of paper between the tappet and the valve stem and lightly pulling on it. When the valve closes, the paper will be free and can be pulled out. The timing gears are coarse enough so that an error will show when the work is checked. To check the timing, insert a piece of paper between the tappet and the valve stem. Rotate the crankshaft, lightly pull on the paper, and when the paper is free, the piston should be at the top of the stroke.

GASOLINE AUTOMOBILES

In finding the top dead center, insert a stiff wire in the cylinder and mark the point at which the piston ceases to rise. Move the piston and mark the point where it starts to move down. The midway between the two marks is the top dead center.

Where the actual valve timing is not known, the average setting —which can be used for the trial setting—is as follows: intake valve opens between top dead center and 10 degrees past top dead center, and closes 45 to 50 degrees after bottom dead center; exhaust valves open from 45 to 40 degrees before bottom dead center and close 10 to 18 degrees after top dead center. The exhaust valve is opened

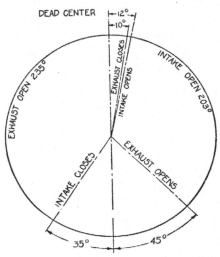

Fig. 8. Overland Four Valve Timing

at this point because all of the useful expansion of the gas is gone. This insures a clean exhaust and prevents over-heating and back pressure on the piston.

Flywheel Markings. Nearly all motors now have the timing marked upon the rim or face of the flywheel, so that it is unnecessary to bother with the crankshaft and pistons. This has been found by experience to be the best and handiest way, for the flywheel is generally accessible without removing many other parts. The same is true with the valves. This is not the case with pistons and crankshaft; moreover, with these it is difficult to determine the exact upper and lower dead centers, and still more difficult to work to angles.

GASOLINE AUTOMOBILES

To use these settings marked on the flywheel, a stationary pointer on the upper surface of the crankcase hangs over the flywheel surface as closely as possible and indicates the reading. The flywheel is turned by hand or by means of the crank at the front of the engine until a mark or the desired mark is brought up to the pointer. Thus the cylinders are marked from front to back always, that nearest the radiator being 1, the next 2, then 3, and the last, in the case of a four-cylinder motor, 4. In a six-cylinder motor the method is the same with the addition of two cylinders, the one nearest the dash being, of course, 6. The flywheel sometimes has the positions marked on its surface, as well as the valve operations. Fig. 8 shows the valve-timing diagram of the Overland Four. Notice in this that none of the valve operations begin or end on a dead center point so that even if the centers are marked on the flywheel (as they are in this case) this is of little benefit except as will be pointed out. The marks on the flywheel are as follows, this showing also what they indicate. In referring to these it will be remembered that on a four-cylinder crankshaft the first and fourth crankpins are up (or down) together, while the second and third are down (or up) together:

1-4 UP   Means that pistons in cylinders 1 and 4 are in their uppermost position, or at upper dead center.

2-3 UP   Means that pistons in cylinders 2 and 3 are in their uppermost position, or at upper dead center.

1-4 I-O   Means that inlet valve cylinder 1 or 4 (not both) opens.

1-4 I-C   Means inlet valve of cylinder 1 or 4 closes.

1-4 E-O   Means exhaust valve of cylinder 1 or 4 opens.

1-4 E-C   Means exhaust valve of cylinder 1 or 4 closes.

2-3 I-O   Means inlet of cylinder 2 or 3 opens.

2-3 I-C   Means inlet of cylinder 2 or 3 closes.

2-3 E-O   Means exhaust of cylinder 2 or 3 opens.

2-3 E-C   Means exhaust of cylinder 2 or 3 closes.

The firing order of the cylinders is 1- 3- 4- 2. To apply this knowledge, open the pet cocks so the motor will turn over easily; selecting cylinder 1 to start with, turn the flywheel until the mark 1-4 UP comes to the pointer at the top. Now continue turning to the left (at the rear end) about an inch more when the mark 1-4 I-O will be seen. Bring this slowly up to the pointer, when the inlet valve should just begin to move. This can be noted by feeling the stem, or by placing a wire upon the top of the valve and noting when it begins to be pushed upward by the valve movement. If this should happen in cylinder 4 instead of 1, turn the flywheel one complete revolution, bringing the same point to the top. If this is entirely correct, the flywheel can be turned in the same direction about 5 or 6 inches more than half a turn, when the mark 1-4 I-C will appear. Turn slowly until it reaches the pointer, when the valve in cylinder 1 should be completely closed. This can be determined again by feeling of the valve stem which should come down to its lowest position, or by the wire on the top of the valve. At this point the valve-tappet clearance comes in. When the valve tappet has reached its lowest point, and the valve has been allowed to seat, the tappet should go down slightly farther than the valve, leaving a very small space between the two. This is the clearance and it varies in normal engines from .002 inch to .012 inch. In the motor which is being described it is .012 inch. The closest approximation to this is an ordinary visiting card, which is about .012 inch thick; when a motor is handled which has less, very much less, this can be approximated by means of cigarette papers which are very close to .003 inch thick. These are used in the absence of precise metal thickness gages, or feelers, as they are called.

Valve-Stem Clearance. This clearance is necessary to compensate for the expansion of the valve stem when it becomes highly heated during the operation of the engine; the tappet or push rod does not become heated, consequently it does not expand. Practically all motors are made with an adjustment here in the form of a screw with a hexagon head which is hardened where it strikes the valve stem or it is recessed out for a piece of hard fiber to deaden the noise, Fig. 2, and the fiber is locked in the desired position by means of a lock nut. If the clearance is less than the required amount or greater so that the motor is very noisy, the lock nut is loosened, and the screw gradually turned upward until it just begins to grip the visiting card. This should be done very carefully, for if the clearance is made too small, the valve will not seat fully when the motor is hot and the valve has expanded; on the other hand, if the clearance is made too large, the push rod will come up against the valve end each time with a bang, and eight of these repeated a thousand times a minute make a great deal of disagreeable and useless noise. In the modern motor, the cams are made an integral part of the cam shaft. If the driving gear for the camshaft is in its right place, and the camshaft bearings are all in good shape, this push rod adjustment is the only valve adjustment possible. If the timing is not correct, that is, if none of the valve operations correspond with the marks on the flywheel and the maker's instructions, then the cam gear has been misplaced.

It is not possible to set a definite amount for valve clearance in engines where the best possible performance is required, as racing and aeroplane engines. An equal amount of mixture must be obtained in all cylinders, therefore, all valves must be open at the same piston position. If this can be obtained by giving one valve more or less clearance than another, it should be done. Each valve should be tested individually, the position found, and the clearance given. The opening and closing positions of the valves are equally important. There is a difference in the amount of wear or in the shape of cams on the same shaft, and this should be taken into account when setting valve clearances on the engines mentioned.

The best position for setting the valve clearance is with the piston at the top of the compression stroke. Watch the intake valve when it opens and closes, and bring the piston to the top of that stroke. In this position the push rod or tappet is resting on the dead side of the cam.

Exhaust-Valve Setting. The same procedure is followed through for the exhaust valve of the same cylinder, continuing past the 1-4 UP mark to the mark 1-4 E-O. At this point the exhaust valve of cylinder 1 should just begin to open. Then continue around to the 1-4 E-C point where the exhaust valve of cylinder 1 is just completing its downward, or closing, movement. If there should be any need for adjustment here, as described previously, this should be made before proceeding to the other cylinders. It should be stated that many makers give the exhaust-valve stems slightly greater clearance than the inlets, on the assumption that they work with hotter gases, are subjected to more heat, and should therefore expand more. The make being described has the same clearance for both valves; .004-inch clearance on the intake and .005 to .006-inch on the exhaust are recommended.

Relation of Settings in Each Cylinder. Now, having checked up
and adjusted both valves for cylinder 1, follow through the same
process for cylinder 4, and, after that, for cylinder 2, then 3. The
diagram, Fig. 8, shows but the cycle in each cylinder, while the
description above simply listed the markings to be found on the
flywheel, so the additional diagram, Fig. 9, is given to show the

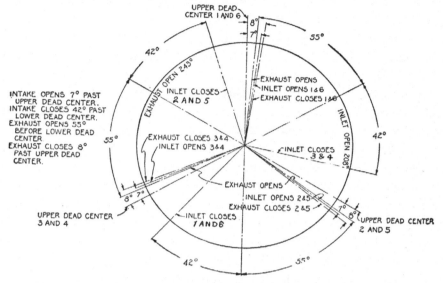

Fig. 9. Valve Timing Diagram for Hudson Super-Six Motor, Showing All Cylinders

relation of these marks to one another. This diagram refers to a
different motor, a Hudson Super-Six model, and the timing is indicated on the face, but the repair man will understand that this is
done simply for convenience, and that these marks are actually
found on the rim. So, too, the lines drawn down to the center are
simply shown for convenience in indicating the angles and do not
appear on the flywheel. In this a different timing will be noted, in
that the inlet opens later and closes earlier, while the exhaust opens
earlier and closes earlier.

System Applies to All Types of Motors. There is now, and
always has been, a wide divergence among designers on the subject
of valve timing, so that the repair man must look for a different
setting with each different make, and often a different setting with
each different model of the same make. All that can be used for all
cars is the general method. The general method, however, is appli-

cable whether the valves are all on one side (L-head cylinders), half on each side (T-head cylinders), all in the head or half on one side and the other half in the head, in short, regardless of the valve position. Similarly with regard to numbers, the method holds good regardless of the number of valves per cylinder. Moreover, it applies regardless of the number and arrangement of the cylinders, as it is just as good for eights and twelves as for the four described. On V-type motors there is a close relation between the opposing cylinders, right-hand No. 1 and left-hand No. 1, and this must be taken into

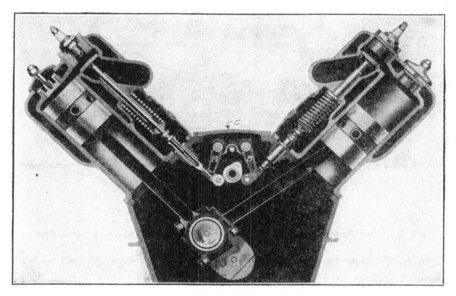

Fig. 10. Section through Cadillac Eight, Showing Camshaft and Valve Mechanism
Courtesy of Cadillac Motor Car Company, Detroit, Michigan

account. In some motors there is a cam for each valve, in which case no trouble would ensue; but in others there are but eight cams for the sixteen valves (of an eight-cylinder motor). This type of shaft will influence the timing diagram, and in setting, the repair man will have to concern himself with the same cam for two different valves—one in a cylinder of the right-hand group and one in a cylinder of the left-hand group.

This statement will be more plain perhaps if reference is made to Fig. 10, which shows a section through the Cadillac-Eight and indicates how the one cam operates two valves through the hinged rocker arms *A* on the left-hand cylinder and *B* on the right for the right-hand cylinder. By comparison, see also Fig. 11, which shows the plate *C* in Fig. 10 removed and turned upside down, with the camshaft and rockers complete. Not all eights and twelves are like this, nor do all have a single camshaft set in the middle of the V; on the contrary, one well-known twelve-cylinder motor, the National, has the valves on the outside of the two groups of cylinders, and thus has two camshafts. In such a case, the timing method just described would be followed through for all the cylinders on one block, then the same system would be followed through on the other side of the engine, one cylinder after another, on that block.

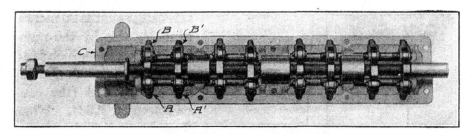

Fig. 11. Cadillac Camshaft, Cam Followers, and Covers Removed from Motor

How to Divide Flywheel Circumference for Valve Timing. In most engines the top dead center is marked, but the position of valve operation is not always shown on the flywheel rim. Valve operations—as discussed—take place so many degrees before r after top or bottom dead center. This means that a line which indicates the top dead center must be so many degrees past or before the center when a certain valve operation takes place. It is not always convenient to make a protractor for measuring the distance in degrees, but the distance can be laid out in inches on the circumference or surface of the flywheel. A circle consists of 360 degrees—so a degree will equal a certain distance in inches or parts of an inch on the circumference of the flywheel. The amount depends on the size of the flywheel. To find the number of inches per degree of flywheel circumference, multiply the diameter by the number of degrees, and divide by 114. The formula can be written thus: $\dfrac{\text{diameter} \times \text{degrees}}{114} = $ inches per degree. The *diameter* refers to

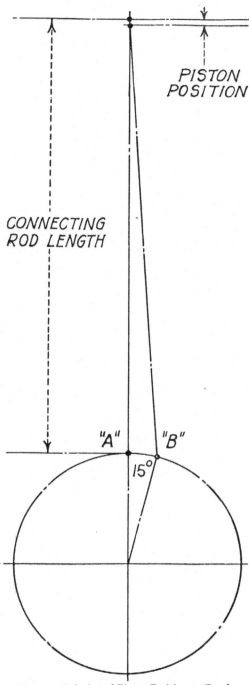

PISTON
POSITION

CONNECTING
ROD LENGTH

"A"   "B"

15°

Fig. 12.   Relation of Piston Position to Crank
Position

the diameter of the fly-
wheel; *degrees* equal the
number of degrees the line
must move; and *114* is a
constant.

To illustrate: suppose
an intake valve must open
15 degrees after the center
line has passed the dead
center point and there is no
marking. Find the diam-
eter of the flywheel, and in
this case, say it is 20 inches.
Multiply this by the num-
ber of degrees—which is 15
—and we have 300. Divid-
ing 300 by 114 (the con-
stant) equal 2.631. When
the center line is moved
this distance beyond the
center point, the valve
should be open. To mark
this distance on the fly-
wheel, take a flexible rule
and lay it on the circumference of the flywheel. Measure back from the center
line, or against the flywheel
rotation, 2.631 inches, which
is $2\frac{41}{64}$. When this new
line or mark comes in line
with the center line of the
cylinders, the crankshaft is
in the correct position for
the valve to open. The
center line and flywheel
markings are not always
easy to obtain or read, and

if the engine is not dismantled it is a difficult matter to get the flywheel diameter and mark it. Let us suppose that a new set of timing gears or chain must be installed and that the valve position is not marked. Therefore, we must find the piston position for the valve operations. Find the length of the stroke, and draw a circle which has a diameter equal to the stroke, as shown in Fig. 12. Mark a point at the top of the circle, which represents the center of the crankshaft throw, as at A, and from this point draw a perpendicular line equal to the length of the connecting rod. Since the crankshaft revolves in a circle, the basis of the calculation is 360 degrees. Suppose the intake valve must open 15 degrees past upper dead center, and the engine has a stroke of 6 inches, with a connecting rod 12 inches long. Proceed as shown in Fig. 12. Draw the circle and the perpendicular and mark the point B, which is the 15-degree mark on the circumference. This can be laid off with a protractor, but if one is not to be had, the previous formula can be used to find the distance. From this point on the circumference, measure the length of the connecting rod—12 inches—to a point on the perpendicular line. The distance from the top of the line to the second point will be the distance that the piston must be down from the top when the valve opens. The length of the connecting rod is obtained by measuring the distance between the piston pin hole center and the center of the connecting rod big-end bearing.

Valve Troubles and Cures. Good compression depends upon good valve performance, both with regard to movement and seating. Exhaust valves give the most trouble in the automobile engine, because they are subjected to the hot exhaust gases. The results of this are as follows:

(1). *The seats become pitted;* carbon settles on them, and the constantly rapid pounding of the valve causes little holes to form, which means a loss of compression. The remedy is to grind in the valves.

(2). *Hot gases pass down through the valve guide, forming a carbon deposit on the stem.* This makes a sluggish valve action and a sluggish engine, which will not pick up speed quickly. Take out the valves, polish the stems, and clean the guides thoroughly with emery cloth. This trouble can be prevented by squirting some kerosene on the stems occasionally.

(3). *Valves holding open:* caused by not enough tappet clearance. This will cause the valve face and seat to burn and warp, missing at low speed, and uneven running. Burning of valve seat is also caused by a very rich mixture and late exhaust-valve opening. Take the valves out, grind them in, reset the tappets, readjust the carburetor, and check the valve timing.

(4). *Troubles with Inlet Valve.* The inlet valve is often the seat of trouble, and missing here is generally caused by a weak or broken spring, a bent stem, or a carbonized valve. If the valve spring has lost its temper and broken down, the tension will be insufficient to properly hold the valve on its seat, and the gas will partially escape and cause missing. The insertion of an iron washer or two will increase the tension of the defective spring and serve as a temporary road repair. A broken spring may be similarly repaired by placing a washer between the broken ends. A bent valve stem should be taken out and carefully straightened by laying it upon a billet of wood with another block interposed between it and the hammer. Only a very little force is needed, and the stem should be repeatedly tried until it slides freely in its guide.

Intake valves do not become carbonized very quickly because they are closed when the explosion takes place, and they are not subject to the heat of the gases. They do not need grinding as often as the exhaust valves. A weak valve spring will allow the valve to bounce on its seat with a consequent loss of compression and power. The valve spring should be removed and tested and a new one installed where needed. An intake valve with not enough clearance will also become burnt, because the valve will hold open and the hot gases will strike the face seat and stems, causing the stems to become sticky. The valves must be taken out, stems cleaned, valves ground in, and a proper clearance given.

VALVES AND THEIR MECHANISM

PART II

REPAIRING VALVES

Curing a Noisy Tappet. When the clearance between the end of the tappet and the end of the valve (usually from .003 to .008 inch) is too great, a metallic click results. Often this noise from the tappet is mistaken for a motor knock; but the skilled repair man has little trouble in finding and remedying it. Ordinary thin wrapping paper is well known to be about .005 inch; with this

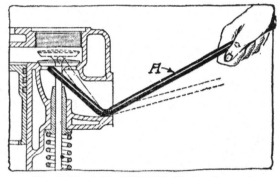

Fig. 13. Bent Tool Which Facilitates Removal
of Stuck Valves

alone, or in combination with cigarette papers, .003 inch thick, he can obtain .005, .008, .010, and .011 inch, practically all the variation he is likely to need.

Removing Valve. Getting the valve out frequently gives much trouble; the valve is often found frozen to its seat or to the stem gummed in its guide. A tool to meet this difficulty is a plain bar or round iron about $\frac{1}{4}$ inch in diameter, Fig. 13, with one end, for a distance of perhaps 2 or $2\frac{1}{2}$ inches, bent up at an angle of about 120 degrees. To use the tool, insert the short bent end in the exhaust or the inlet opening, according to which valve is stuck, until the end touches the under side of the valve head, then lower the outer end until the bottom of the bent part or point at which the bend occurs rests against solid metal. The outer end can now be pressed down, and, with the inner end acting as a lever, the valve can be pressed off its seat and out very quickly.

To make this clearer, the rod, Fig. 13, is indicated at *A*, while the dotted line shows how it is pressed down and the valve forced out. The garage man can elaborate upon the tool when making it for himself by using square stock; it has the inner end forked so as to bear on each side of the valve. The form pointed out above is the simplest, cheapest, and easiest to make.

Removing Valve Spring. Taking out the valve spring is frequently difficult for various reasons; perhaps the springs are very stiff, or they

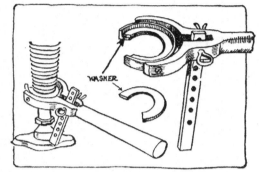

Fig. 14.   Easily Made Tool for Removing Valve Spring

may have rusted to the valve cups at the bottom, or the design may not allow room enough to work, etc. At any rate the removal is difficult, and a tool which will help in this and which is simple and cheap, is in demand. Many motor cylinders are cast with a slight projection, or shelf, opposite the valve-spring positions, so that one only needs a tool that will encircle the lower end of the valve spring and rest upon this ledge and give an outer leverage.

Types of Valve Removers. In working on cylinders that do not have this cast projection, a tool like that shown in Fig. 14 is useful. It consists of a yoke for encircling the lower end of valve spring and cup, with a long outer

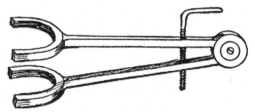

Fig. 15.   Type of Valve-Spring Tool Which Leaves the Hands Free

arm for prying, and a slot into which a drilled bar is set. This bar is placed in various positions according to the kind of motor which is being worked on; when removing a valve-spring key, the lower end of the bar rests upon the crankcase upper surface, or upon the push-rod upper surface if that is extended. After slipping the grooved yoke under the spring cup, a simple pressure on the outer end raises the valve so the key can be withdrawn. Then the removal of the tool allows the valve spring to drop down, and the valve is free.

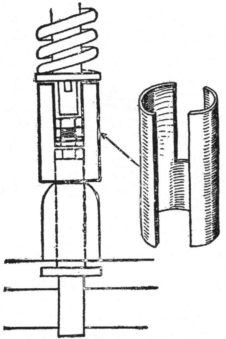

The valve spring may be removed in two other ways by the use of the two tools shown in Figs. 15 and 16. In the former, the idea is to compress the spring only, no other part being touched. This tool, once set, will continue to hold the spring compressed, leaving the hands free—a decided advantage over the tool shown in Fig. 14. This device consists, as the illustration shows, of a pair of arms with forked inner ends and with outer ends joined by a pin. A bent-handled screw draws the ends together or separates them, according to which way it is turned.

Fig. 16. Substitute for a Valve Spring Remover Which Pushes Spring away as Motor is Turned

The simplest tool of all is the one shown in Fig. 16. It is a formed piece of stiff sheet metal which is set into place when the valve is open, and when the valve is closed by turning the motor, the sheet-metal piece holds the spring up in its compressed position.

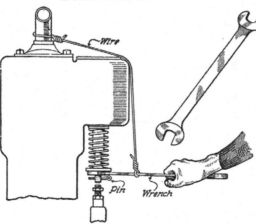

Fig. 17. Method of Compressing Valve Spring without Special Tool

Courtesy of "Motor World"

There are almost as many different valve and valve-spring removers as there are different cars or different motors. However, the simple makeshift shown in Fig. 17 is worthy of mention. Lacking a form of valve- or spring-removing tool, this repair man simply supported a plain double-ended wrench by means of a wire attached to the water pipe on top of the motor; adjusting the length of it so that the end of the wrench would just slip under the valve key, he was able to remove the pin, which freed the spring and thus the valve. Practically the same thing was evolved by another repair man who took a wrench of this type and drilled a hole through the center of the handle which was first twisted through a right angle. Then he bent a piece of stout wire into the form of a hook, one end through the wrench, the other over some projection on the engine. With the hook removed, the wrench was not radically different from any other and could be used as freely; with the hook in, he had a simple valve-spring removing tool.

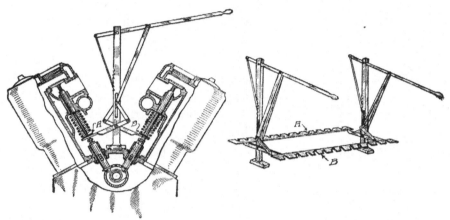

Fig. 18.   Method of Compressing All Twenty-Four Packard Valve Springs at Once
Courtesy of "Motor World"

Twelve-Cylinder Valve Remover.   One of the objections raised to the twelve-cylinder motor is the trouble of removing and grinding all the valves. The Philadelphia Branch of the Packard Company has overcome this disadvantage by constructing the special tool shown in Fig. 18. This lifts the whole 24 valves at once. It consists of the central stand, which rests on the flat top of the crankcase, having a long arm and connected levers at the bottom to work the spring compressors. These, as will be seen at *A* and *B*, are really the special feature of the outfit, as they are specially constructed to fit around the valves in sets of 12 each. A ratchet holds the device locked, so that after it is applied and fitted to all the valves, they can be forced up and locked; then the matter of valve removal, regrinding, and replacement can be handled for the whole 24. At its conclusion, the rigging can be unlocked and all 24 valves freed at once.

Holding Valve Springs Compressed. Many times there is a need for holding the spring in its compressed form, as, for instance, when the valve is removed with the positive certainty that it will be replaced within four or five minutes. In such a case a clamp which will hold it in compression is very useful, for it saves both time and work. These may be made to the form shown in Fig. 19 in a few minutes' time, for they consist simply of a pair of sheet-metal strips with the ends bent over to form a very wide U-shape. A pair of these is made for each separate make of valve spring, because of the

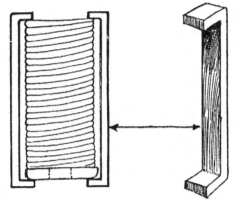

varying lengths, but they are so easily and quickly made that this is no disadvantage.

In many shops, after getting in the habit of making these clamps, the workmen take this way of replacing the spring in preference to all others. After removal of the valve, the spring may be compressed in a vise and a pair of the clamps put on. Then when the valve is ready to go back in, the spring is as easy

Fig. 19. Spring Clamp, Which Is Easily Made and Saves Much Work and Trouble

to handle as any other part. This is especially true when replacing the spring retainer and its lock.

Stretching and Tempering Valve Springs. Many times when valve springs become weakened, they can be stretched to their former length, so that their original strength is restored. This can be done by removing them and stretching each individual coil, taking care to do it as evenly as possible. When well stretched, it is advisable to leave the coils that way for several days. This method will not, of course, restore the strength permanently; it is at best a makeshift, for in the course of a few thousand miles the springs will be as bad as before.

Sometimes weakened valve springs may be renewed by retempering, on the theory that the original temper was not good or they would not have broken down in use. The tempering is done by heating to a blood-red color and quenching in whale oil. If this is not successful, new springs are advised.

Adjusting Tension of Valves. Unless all the valves on a motor agree, it will run irregularly, that is, all the exhausts must be of the same tension, and all the inlets must agree among themselves, though not necessarily with the exhausts. Many times irregular running of this kind, called galloping, is more difficult to trace and remove than missing or some other form of more serious trouble, and it is fully as annoying to the owner as missing would be.

To be certain of finding this trouble, the repair man should have a means of testing the strength of springs; a simple device for this purpose is shown in Fig. 20. As will be seen, this consists of sheet-metal strips and connecting rods of light stock, with a hook at the top for a spring balance and a connection at the bottom to a pivoted hand lever for compressing the spring. By means of the center rod at R and the thumb screw at the bottom, the exact pressure required to compress the spring to a certain size may be determined. Suppose the spring should compress from 4 inches to

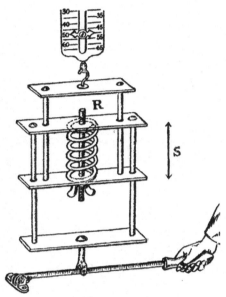

Fig. 20. Simple Rigging for Testing Valve-Spring Pressure and Strength

$3\frac{1}{2}$ inches under 50 pounds. By compressing it in the center portion of the device, so that the distance between the two adjacent strips of metal indicated by S is just $3\frac{1}{2}$ inches, the spring balance should show just 50 pounds. If it shows any less, the spring is too weak and should be discarded; if it shows any more, it is stronger than normal —which is desirable if all the other springs on the same engine are also stronger.

If only a quick comparison of four springs is desired, the device can be made without the bottom lever, as the setting of S at a definite figure—say to a template of exact length—would call for a certain reading of the scale of the spring balance.

Cutting Valve=Key Slots. Cutting valve-key slots in valve stems is another mean job which the repair man frequently meets. He runs across this in repairing old cars for which he has to make new valves; and at other times for other repairs. The best plan is to make a simple jig which will hold, guide, and measure all these things at once, as all are important. Such a jig is shown in Fig. 21. It consists of a piece of round or other bar stock, in which a central longitudinal hole is drilled to fit the valve stem, one end being threaded for a set screw. Near the other end of the jig, three holes, of such a diameter as to correspond with the width of key slot desired, are drilled in from the side. These are so placed that the length from the top of the upper hole to the bottom of the lower gives the length of key seat desired. Opposite the three drilled holes and at right angles to them, another hole is drilled and tapped for a set screw.

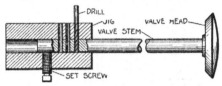

Fig. 21. Cheap Jig for Slotting Valve Stems

To use the device, slip the valve in place and set the bottom screw of the jig so as to bring the three drilled holes at the correct height for the location of the key seat. Then the three holes are drilled, and the valve is moved upward so that the space between the holes is opposite a guide hole, and two more holes are drilled to take out the metal between. The five holes will give a fairly clean slot, which needs a little cleaning out with a file before using.

Grinding the Valves. The new driver must learn when to grind his valves, that is, how often, and he must also learn to do the work properly. There is no hard and fast rule which can be given aside from grinding when it is necessary. A careful driver may get four to five thousand miles out of his valves with one grinding, while another may get only one or two thousand miles with the selfsame car and engine. There are many factors which enter into the life of a valve seat, and, in the frequency of grinding, all of these have to be taken into account. Some of these are: imperfect cooling of the seats; too strong springs, which cause hammering and thus wear out the seats prematurely; over-lubricating, which causes spitting and sooting, both of which reduce the active life of the valve seat.

Another cause for frequent grinding is contributory negligence on the part of the driver. He does not examine them as often as he should, and the result is failure to discover something in the way of soot or dust caught in between the valve and seat, which is being gradually pressed into the seat.

Regrinding Process. Before grinding in the valves, care should be taken to see that the guides are well cleaned, and that the valve stem slides freely in them. A quicker and better job of grinding

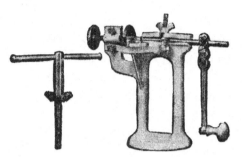

Fig. 22. Valve Refacing Tool
Courtesy of Whitney Manufacturing Company, Lewiston, Maine

Fig. 23. Electric Valve Regrinder
Courtesy of Whitney Manufacturing Company, Lewiston, Maine

can be done if the valve is refaced; a valve face will become grooved when ground two or three times. Unless the groove is taken out first, there is danger of an imperfect seat. A tool, Fig. 22, which is similar to a small lathe, will do very well to reface the valve. The ideal method to reface valves· is to grind the pits out first. Fig. 23 shows such a tool in use. It is a time saver, since it is an electrically driven motor and leaves a smooth finish on the valve before grinding.

When either the valve head or seat has become worn or pitted, it must be reground as follows: Secure a small amount of flour of emery, the finer the better, and mix this into a thin paste using cylinder oil, or graphite, or both. Loosen the valve, disconnect all attachments, remove the valve cap above, and free the valve in a vertical direction. Now lift it out, place a daub of the emery paste on the seat, and replace the valve. With a large screwdriver

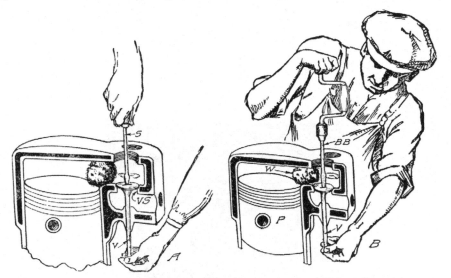

Fig. 24. Two Methods of Grinding-In Valves: (A) by Hand, Using a Screwdriver; (B) with Brace, Screwdriver and Bit

press the valve firmly in place, at the same time rotating it about one-fourth of a turn to the right and then the same amount to the left.

This is shown in Fig. 24A, in which S is the screwdriver, V the valve, and VS the valve seat. Note how the right hand presses down on the screwdriver and turns it at the same time. A light spring can be placed under the valve so that it will automatically raise off the seat when pressure is released. After moving back and forth about eight or ten times, let the valve rise off its seat and turn it through a quarter-turn, and press it back into place. Then repeat the grinding until the whole circle has been covered several times. Then remove the valve and clean both moving member and seat with gasoline. Mark the seat on the valve with a slight touch of Prussian blue, replace the valve, and twirl it around several times so as to distribute the color. Remove the valve without touching the seat portion on it or in the cylinder, and examine both. If the grinding process has been complete and accurate, the color will have been distributed in a continuous band of equal width all around the surface. On the first attempt at this rather delicate piece of work, it is well to call in an expert repair man to examine and pass upon the job.

In Fig. 24B the same process is shown, but a brace, screwdriver, and bit are used in place of the slower screwdriver. This method would hardly be advocated for an amateur attempting his first job of valve grinding, but as soon as some proficiency has been attained, it is the best, quickest, and most thorough method.

Noisy Valves. Sometimes the valves get very noisy and bother the driver a great deal in this way, that is, the wear in the valve-operating system becomes so considerable as to make a noise every time a valve is opened or closed. With the engine running at slow speeds, each one of these is heard as a separate small noise and not much is thought of it, but when the motor is speeded up, the noises all increase and become continuous and very noticeable. This may be remedied by taking up the valve tappets which usually are made adjustable for this purpose, until there is but a few thousandths of an inch between the valve tappet and the lower end of the valve stem. A good way to measure this is to adjust until one thickness of tissue paper will just pass between the two; then there is approximately 0.003 inch between them.

The clearance between the ends of the valve stems varies a great deal in different motors. This depends mainly upon the cam clearance, the length of the valve stems and the cooling of the stems. A variable thickness gauge may be had from any supply house.

There is often one noisy valve which stands out above the rest after the proper valve clearances have been given. This can often be traced to the adjustment screw at the top of the push rod. A hole will be worn in the head of the adjustment screw, due to the pounding of the push rod against the valve stem. The gauge seems to be tight between the stem and the push rod, but there is more clearance than is necessary because of this hole. The screw should be taken out and the head of the screw dressed down on a fine emery wheel. The head should be ground square and flat.

Push Rods and Guides. As can be seen from Fig. 5, Part I, the push rod and its guide, or lifter and guide, become important. The shape of the cam is such that it deals the roller and lower end of the push rod, or lifter which holds it, a fairly heavy blow sideways each time it comes against it. If the roller and rod are not a perfect fit, something will yield each time, and the roller will wear oval in a short time. The movement and noise will increase rapidly and soon become very objectionable. The only remedy is replacement. These guides are held in place in one of two ways; either individually by means of a pair of bolts or in pairs by means of a yoke and a single central bolt and nut of large diameter. The Locomobile is an example of the former method and the Haynes, the latter method. In Fig. 25, the arrow points to the nut midway between the two push rods, which holds down the yoke that rests upon shoulders on the push rods and holds them in place. From a repair man's point of view, the latter construction is better, for the push rods can be removed and replaced much more easily and quickly.

Noisy push rods may be caused by the roller and roller pins becoming worn or the roller sticking and wearing flat in one place by the action of the cam. In the case of the mushroom type, a hole will be worn in the mushroom causing considerable play and noise when the cam comes up against it. Worn push-rod guides will also cause trouble and noise and all parts concerned should be replaced. When fitting new guides and push rods, the rod should slide freely in the guide and the clamp, that holds the guide in position, should not pinch the guide and cause the rod to stick. If the rod sticks, it will cause a knock to develop quickly and the camshaft to bend, necessitating the installation of a new camshaft.

Valve Cage Repairs. When the valves are in overhead cages, it is highly important that they fit tightly in the cylinder head; they must be ground in as carefully and as tightly as the valves are ground into their seats. Where a shop handles a good many motors of the overhead-valve type, it is desirable to make a rig to do the grinding easily. One of these rigs is shown in Fig. 26. It consists of a shaft and handle with lock nuts for the valve cages used on Buick cars. On these cars, it is in two parts; the cage proper, and the locking member which screws into the cylinder. Obviously the cage is the one to be ground in. The rig shown slides in the central opening, that is, fits in the valve guide, and has a lock nut top and bottom to fasten it tightly. When fitted into place firmly, the right-angle bend in the rig gives a handle by means of which the cage can be

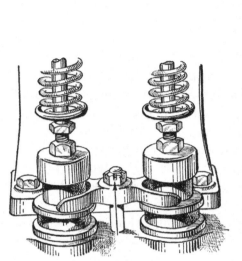

Fig. 25. Method of Holding Two Push Rods
with Yoke and Single Central Nut

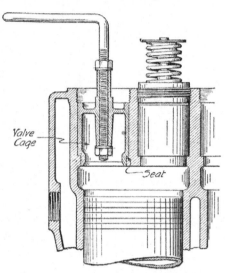

Valve Cage

Seat

Fig. 26. Simple Fixture for Grinding-In
Overhead Valve Cages
Courtesy of "Motor World"

lifted in and out and, what is more important, rotated on its seat. When the cage is prepared, the seat is given a little oil and emery or oil and powdered glass or prepared valve grinding composition, the cage is set in place and ground in the same as a valve, that is, with one-third to one-half rotations in one position, then lift, move around, and repeat in the new position, continuing this until the whole surface of the cage in the cylinder has been covered twice. This should result in a good seat.

When the valves in an overhead motor need grinding, the valve and cage are taken out completely and held in an inverted position in a vise or other clamp, and the valve ground in to the seat in the cage in the regular way. It is said this can be done very rapidly and well by chucking the valve stem, as it projects from the cage, in a lathe rotating at a very slow speed, and operating the cage by hand, that is, slide the cage back, apply grinding compound, then move the cage up to the rotating valve and hold it with the hand while the valve is turning with the lathe. In holding it thus, the pressure endwise should be very light.

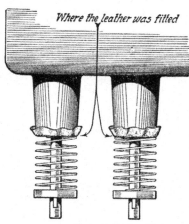

Fig. 27. Method of Curing Valve-Guide Leak Quickly and Cheaply

Valve Guides. The valve stem must be a tight fit in the guide, otherwise air will leak through into the combustion chamber and dilute the mixture, or the compression will leak out, or both. Any valve leak will affect the running of the motor, so it should be stopped at once. Two methods of temporarily remedying small leaks are shown in Figs. 27 and 28. A simple leather washer with a small hole through the center, which fits tightly over the valve stem, is pressed up around the outside of the guides, as shown in Fig. 27. This simple repair was very effective, and the leather washers lasted an astonishingly long time. The other method, Fig. 28, shows practically the same result arrived at differently. In this case, old spark-plug shells, with considerable recesses in the center part, were turned down so as to fit around the bottom of the guides. These recesses were packed with felt or other available packing, care being taken to pack the recesses tightly. Then the whole thing was held up in place by a lighter spring put inside the main valve spring. By adding a few drops of oil to the packing now and then to keep it soft, it lasts almost indefinitely.

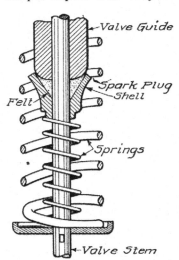

Fig. 28. Remedy for Leaky Valve-Stem Guide, Using Old Spark Plug and Felt

The valve-guide hole in the cylinder is generally made as long as possible, both to give a straight and true hold on the valve stem and thus maintain its straightness in spite of the heat, and to give a long wearing surface. This length and the need for accuracy throughout makes the valve-guide hole an awkward surface to repair. When worn beyond any hope of simple repair, it is best to ream it out and press in a bronze bushing so that the valves can still be used. An excellent tool for this purpose, developed for Dodge motors but which is usable for almost any motor, is shown in Fig. 29. This consists of a high threaded bushing which is clamped to two diagonal cylinder studs. The thread inside the bushing is very fine. A long tube, with the lower end bored out to take a standard reamer, is screwed into it. The top is squared and a handle is made to fit it.

When the handle is turned, the tube is gradually screwed down into the cylinder, carrying the reamer slowly but truly down through the valve guide. This rigging is simple, easily made, and gives accurate results. When the valve-guide hole is reamed, the bushing can be turned up and pressed in with any form of shop press.

Valve Caps. The plug which fits into the top opening in the cylinder through which the valve is put in place and removed is called the valve cap. Sometimes it has external hexagonal sides so it can be easily removed, but

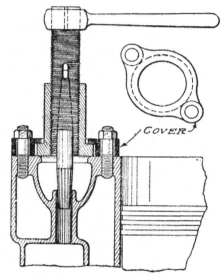

Fig. 29.   Rigging for Reaming Out Valve-
Stem Guide Holes
Courtesy of "Motor World"

more often it has an internal hexagon, or internal ribs. The latter form can be removed most easily by constructing a special tool, consisting of a cylindrical member, with a bottom diameter slightly larger than the opening in the valve cap, with four (or more) teeth, or projections, set into the bottom of this to match the ribs inside the cap. A central hole is drilled for a bolt with spark-plug threads at the bottom. To use the member, remove the spark plug, set the device in place, slip the central bolt in and screw it down into the plug to hold the whole thing in place, then apply a wrench to its upper square surface and remove the valve, cap and all.

It can be laid aside just as removed, and when the work is concluded, the whole thing can be screwed back in, the central screw loosened, and the rig should then be removed from the cap.

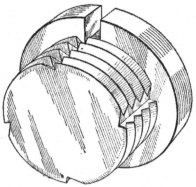

Fig. 30. Reamer for Clearing Out Threads of Valve Cap
Courtesy of "Motor World"

Sometimes the threads in the cylinder into which the valve cap screws become dirty, slightly cut up, or marred so that the cap does not screw in or out readily. By taking an old valve cap of the same motor and same threads and fluting these in a milling machine, as indicated in Fig. 30, a neat tap can be made which will clean out the threads in a jiffy. It is simple, effective and cheap.

DETAILS OF SLIDING= SLEEVE VALVES

A method of avoiding cams, and with them all cam troubles, is the use of a sliding sleeve in place of a valve, slots in the sleeve corresponding to the usual valve openings both as to area and timing. The sleeves may be operated by means of eccentrics by various lever motions, or by a direct drive operated by means of a gear mounted on a separate shaft.

Gear control. A good example of the application of a worm and gear for this purpose to a French two-cycle engine is shown in

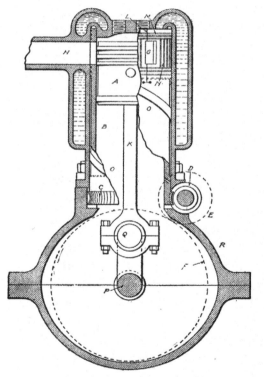

Fig. 31. Section through Ledru (French) Camless Engine. The Rotary Gear-Driven Sleeve Displaces All Cams

Fig. 31, although there is nothing in its construction which would prevent its use on the more usual four-cycle engine.

In this figure, P is the usual crankshaft, Q the large end of the connecting rod K, while A is the piston and R the crankcase, no one of these differing from those in other engines. On the crankshaft there is a large gear F, which drives a smaller gear E, located on a longitudinal shaft above and outside of the crankcase. On this shaft is located a worm gear D, which meshes with a worm C formed integral with the sleeve surrounding the piston A. Aside from this worm gear, the sleeve is perfectly cylindrical, being open at both ends. It is placed outside of the piston, between that and the cylinder walls. At its upper end, it has a number of ports, or slots, cut through it, which are correctly located vertically to register, or coincide, with the port openings in the cylinder wall when the sleeve is rotated. One of these is seen at $H;$ the exhaust, while 90 degrees around from it, and hence invisible in this figure, is a similar port for the inlet. As the crankshaft rotates, the side shaft carrying the worm is constrained to turn also. This turns the worm which rotates the worm wheel on the sleeve. In this way, the openings in the sleeve are brought around to the proper openings in the cylinder, and the combustion chamber is supplied with fresh gas, the burned gases being carried away at the correct time in the cycle of operations.

With a motor of this sort, the greatest question is that of lubrication. The manner in which it is effected in this case is by means of the large wide spiral grooves shown at OO and the smaller circular grooves at the upper end M. Another method which renders this problem more easy of solution is by the machining of the sleeve; during this operation much metal is cut away along the sides so that the sleeve does not bear against the cylinder walls along its whole length but only for a short length at the top and a still shorter length at the bottom.

Knight Sleeve Valves. In the last few years, tremendous progress has been made here and abroad with the Knight motor, named after its Chicago inventor. In many important factories this valve has displaced the poppet valve. In a regular four-cylinder four-cycle engine, the valves consist of a pair of concentric sleeves, the openings in the two sleeves performing the requisite functions of valves in the proper order. These sleeves, as Fig. 32 shows, are actuated from a regular camshaft—running at half the crankshaft speed and driven by a silent chain—by means of a series of eccentrics and connecting rods. In the figure, A is the inner and longer sleeve and carries the groove or projection C at its lower end. The collar actuating the sleeve is fixed around and into it. This collar is

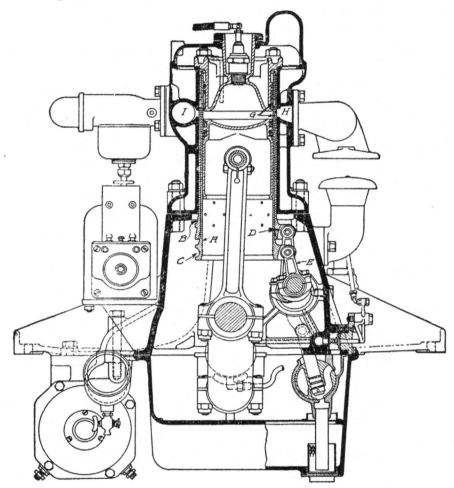

Fig. 32. Willys-Knight Engine in Which Eccentrics and Sliding Sleeves Replace Cams and Valves

attached to the eccentric rod E, which is driven by the eccentric shaft shown. The collar D performs a similar function for the outer sleeve B.

At the upper ends of both sleeves, slots G are cut through. These slots are so sized and located as to be brought into correct

GASOLINE AUTOMOBILES

TABLE I

Royal Automobile Club's Committee Report on Knight Engine

Motor horsepower—R. A. C.	38.4		22.85
Bore and stroke	124 by 130		96 by 130
Minimum horsepower allowed	50.8		35.3
Speed on bench test	1200 r.p.m.		1400 r.p.m.
Car weight on track	3805 lb.		3332.5 lb.
Car weight on road	4085 lb.		3612.5 lb.
Duration of bench test	134 hours 15 min.		132 hours 58 min.
Penalized stops	None		None
Non-penalized stops	Five—116 min.		Two—17 min.
Light load periods	19 min.		41 min.
Average horsepower	54.3		38.83
Final bench test	5 hours 15 min.		5 hours 2 min.
Penalized stops	None		None
Light load periods	15 min.		1 min.
Average horsepower	57.25		38.96
Mileage on track	1930.5		1914.1
Mileage on road	229		229
Total time on track	45 hours 32 min.		45 hours 42 min.
Average track speed	42.4 m. p. h.		41.8 m. p. h.
Fuel per brake horsepower per hour	First bench test	.679 pt. .613 lb.	.739 pt. .668 lb.
	Final bench test	.599 pt. .541 lb.	.749 pt. .677 lb.
Car miles per gallon	On track	20.57	22.44
	On road	19.48	19.48
Ton miles per gallon	On track	34.94	33.37
	On road	35.97	31.19

relation to one another and to the cylinder ports and the exhaust at *H* and inlet at *I*, in the course of the stroke.

It might be thought that the sliding sleeves would eat up more power in internal friction than would be gained, but a very severe and especially thorough test of an engine of this type, made by the Royal Automobile Club of England, an unbiased body, proved that for its size the power output was greater than that of many engines of the regulation type. Moreover, the amount of lubricating oil was small.

The results of the test are shown in Table I. After the test was concluded, both the sleeves, Fig. 33, were found to show still the original marks of the lathe tool. This proved conclusively that the principle of this type was right, for the tests were equivalent to an ordinary season's running.

The slots which serve as valve ports are at *G*, Fig. 33. The longer sleeve *A* is the inner one. At the bases of the sleeves are the collars and pins *D* by which the connecting rods are attached.

The surfaces of the valves are grooved at *J* to produce proper distribution of oil.

The Knight type of motor has been adopted by a number of well-known firms in America, such as the Stearns, Willys, F. R. P., Brewster, and Moline Companies. These engines are noted for their silent running and for their efficiency. The Moline-Knight motor was subjected to a severe continuous-run test of 337 hours, under the auspices of the A. C. A. authorities, in January, 1914. During this time the motor developed an average of 38.3 brake horse-

Fig. 33.   Sleeves Which Replaced Valves on Knight Engine, after
137-Hour Bench Test and 2200 Miles on the Road

power. During the 337th hour the throttle was opened, the motor developed a higher speed and a brake horsepower of 53. After the test, the motor parts showed no particular evidence of wear. The test gives abundant evidence of the endurance and reliability of the sleeve-valve type of motor and of the sterling qualities of the product of the American automobile manufacturers.

In addition to the four-cylinder forms just mentioned, the Knight type of motor is also made as a six, and, more recently, as a V-type eight. In these forms, the basic principle of sliding sleeves and their method of operation and timing is not changed.

Originally, the Knight motor was installed only in the highest-class cars. The firms in Europe which took it up ranked among the very first—notably the Daimler, Panhard, Minerva, etc.—but in this country it has made little progress among the better cars. It is now assuming the rank of a low- and medium-priced motor, being available for about $1000, and as an eight, for approximately $2000.

Timing the Willys=Knight. While the connection between the Knight motor sleeves and eccentric rods, and between the rods and the eccentric shaft, is more or less permanent, there is the possibility of the shaft being bent or twisted during running or dismounting. The repair man should know how the motor is timed, in order to cor-

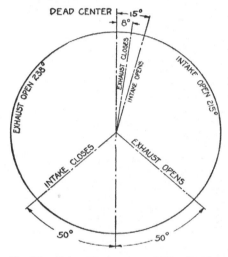

Fig. 34. Valve Timing 1920 Willys-Knight

rect any faults. As will be noted in the timing diagram shown in Fig. 34, this is not radically different from the poppet-valve type. The inlet opens at 15 degrees past the upper center and closes 50 degrees past the lower center, a total opening of 215 degrees. The exhaust opens 50 degrees before the lower center and closes 8 degrees past the upper center, a total opening of 238 degrees.

The various positions are clearly shown in Fig. 35, and make the action of the motor much more clear than the simple timing diagram. The figures, reading from the left, are as follows: *1* shows the inlet just beginning to open; the inner sleeve is coming up, and the outer sleeve is going down, so the port opening is increasing in area with unusual rapidity. At *2* the inlet is fully open; the inner sleeve is coming up, but the outer has reached the bottom of its travel; the two ports are fully open and register exactly with one another and with the opening in the cylinder. At *3* the inlet has just closed, the inner sleeve is still coming up, while the outer sleeve has come up a considerable distance. A slightly further upward movement of both inner and outer sleeves shows the motor in *4*, the top of the compression stroke, with all ports closed. This is the point of explosion. In *5* the exhaust

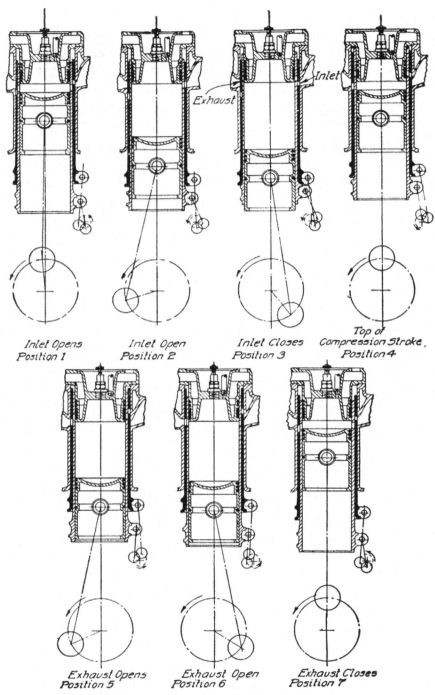

Fig. 35.   Various Stages in Cycle of Knight Sliding-Sleeve Motor

is beginning to open, the inner sleeve has reached the top of its movement and started down, while the outer is almost at the top. At *6* the exhaust port is fully open, the slots register exactly with each other and with the cylinder outlet, both sleeves are traveling down, the outer having reached and passed its highest point. At *7* the exhaust has just closed, the inner sleeve has reached its bottom position and is about to start up, while the outer sleeve is close to the bottom. The cycle of inlet, compression, explosion, and exhaust has now been completed and is about to start over. Note that position *7* is almost exactly like position *1*, but a slight additional movement of the sleeves is needed to produce the latter.

The eccentric rods are very similar to connecting rods, as will be noted by referring back to Fig. 33. Here *E* is the eccentric rod operating the inner sleeve *C*, while *D* is the eccentric rod which operates the outer sleeve *B*. As will be seen, these have an upper end exactly like a piston, or wrist pin, except that no bushing is provided. At the lower end, it will be noted that the fastening and arrangement is just like the big end of a connecting rod. It should be cared for, adjusted, and tightened in just the same way to get the best results.

Method of Timing the Sleeve Valve Engine. To check the timing of the sleeves in the Knight engine, it is necessary to remove the exhaust manifold so that the operation of the sleeves may be observed. Take the spark plug out and drop a small electric light into the cylinder. Turn the crankshaft over by hand and watch the light. When a small ray of light is barely seen between the upper edge of the port in the outer sleeve and the lower edge of the exhaust port in the cylinder block, the exhaust port closes. If the marks on the flywheel "EC" should be in line with the line on the cylinder block, the timing is correct.

There are few troubles with sleeve valves, but the one that is most important has to do with the junk ring. These rings will wear like other machinery and cause a clicking noise. If this noise is noticed, the ring should be renewed as soon as possible. The clicking is caused by the ring being loose in the ring groove.

DETAILS OF ROTATING VALVES

Successful Operation Requires Two Valves. In addition to rotating and reciprocating sleeves and reciprocating valves, the rotating valve has been tried, in common with any number of other devices intended to supplant the ordinary poppet valve. This arrangement on a multi-cylinder motor consists of a single valve for all the cylinders, which extends along the top or side of the

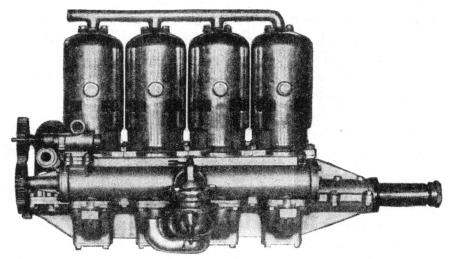

Fig. 36. Roberts Two-Cycle Motor with Rotating Crankcase Valve
Courtesy of E. W. Roberts, Sandusky, Ohio

cylinder head and is driven by shaft, chain, or otherwise, at one end. Naturally, this necessitates having the ports cut very accurately in the exterior of the valve, or rather the sleeve—as it usually assumes

Fig. 37. Rotating Inlet Valve of Roberts Two-Cycle Motor

the form of a hollow shell—for not alone does it act as inlet and exhaust manifold but also as the timing device. This multiplicity of functions seems to have been its undoing, for the latest types using valves of this form have no longer one shell as at first but a pair, one for the exhaust valves and one for the inlet valves. In the latter shape these have been more successful, but not sufficiently so to bring them into competition with the poppet and Knight sleeve-valve forms.

Roberts Rotary Valve. A motor—a two-cycle motor, by the way—which has been very successful in motor-boat and aeroplane work, although it is not used for motor cars, is the Roberts, shown in Fig. 36, with the valve in Fig. 37. This valve is for the inlet ports only and is located inside the crankcase, while the cylinders exhaust freely into the open air, the exhaust issuing directly from the cylinders.

CAMSHAFTS

Half=Time Shafts. For the actuation of the valve mechanism of any four-cycle motor, it is necessary to have a shaft (or in the case of rotary valves, to run the valve itself as a shaft) turning at one-half the speed of the crankshaft through a two-to-one gear ratio.

Ordinarily the half-time shaft is the camshaft, but in motors of the Knight type it is, of course, an eccentric shaft. Camshafts, particularly, call for good workmanship and high-grade materials, as well as sound design, since the constant pounding of the valve stems or push rods on the cams is a prolific source of trouble if anything but the soundest of sound construction be employed.

In laying out or designing a set of cams for a gasoline engine, such as is used on an automobile, it is first necessary to decide upon the exact cycle upon which to operate the engine. By this is meant the exact length of time, as referred to the stroke, in which the valve action will take place. Upon this subject designers all over the world differ, and no wonder, as this cycle can but be judged by results, for it is impossible to watch it as it operates. Deductions differ, therefore, as to what happens and, consequently, as to the effect of various angles of beginning and ending the valve actions. A camshaft changes rotary motion to reciprocating motion.

Cam Function. Granting the necessity for proper means to regulate the inflow and outgo of the charge and consequent products of combustion, as exemplified by the valves, the next most important part is the one which controls the movement of the valve, and is, therefore, essential to the success of the latter. This is what is known as a cam and in the usual case amounts to an extension of, or projection from, the so-called camshaft. Inasmuch as the valve functions only come into play upon every other stroke of the crankshaft, this camshaft is gear-driven from the crankshaft so as to rotate at half the speed of the latter. This is very simply effected by having the cam gear twice as large as the crankshaft gear. As the same valve is never used for both the inlet and the exhaust, so the cams are seldom made to do more than the one thing, namely, operate one set of the valves. From this has grown the custom of referring to them according to the function of the valve which they operate—inlet cam, exhaust cam, etc.

The speed at which the valve opens and closes is governed by the shape of the cam outline as well as by the size and shape of the

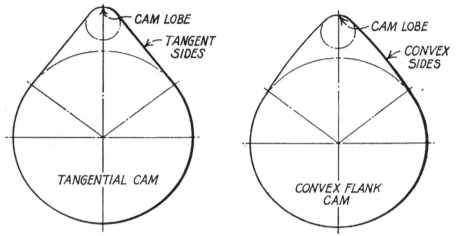

Fig. 1. Tangential Cam   Fig. 2. Convex-Flank Cam

cam follower. To get the largest amount of gas into the cylinder it is often necessary to have the valve open and close quickly and, at the same time, have it remain open as long as possible. On the other hand, the valve gear must operate as quietly as possible, and therefore the drop and lift must be gradual. There are three types of cams and cam followers. The tangential cam, Fig. 1, and the convex-flanked cam, Fig. 2, both of which can be used with a mushroom-type follower, and the cam with the concave flank, called the constant-acceleration cam, Fig. 3. The tangential cam requires a stiff valve spring, which causes extra wear and strain on all valve parts. This type has been in use the longest and gives excellent results. The mushroom-type cam and

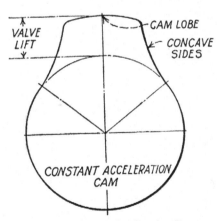

Fig. 3. Constant-Acceleration Cam

follower does not need as strong a spring as the tangential cam. It opens the valve very quickly, giving a larger volume of gas for compression. Unless the cam is especially designed and machined, the cam strikes the mushroom a very sharp blow when it strikes the follower. This is very true when the clearance between the valve stem and push rod is large. The constant-acceleration cam

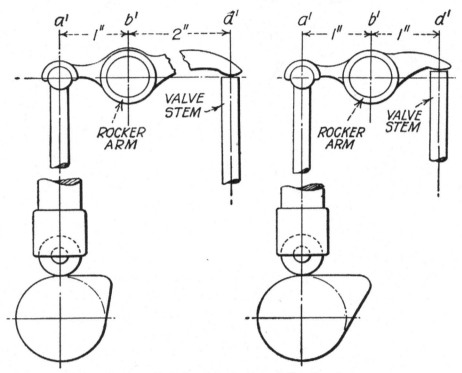

Fig. 4. Relation of Rocker Arm to Cam Travel

does not need as strong a spring as the tangential cam. It raises the valve less suddenly than the mushroom cam and decreases the speed gradually. It is, therefore, a compromise between the other two.

If the constant-acceleration cam is used, the exhaust-valve cam can be picked easily, because the lobe or top of the cam is broader than the intake cam. The reason for this is because the exhaust is open longer than the intake valve. If there is trouble in the valve system, it can be readily noticed whether it is the exhaust or intake cam that is causing the trouble. For example, a camshaft has been removed for inspection. One cam shows more wear than another, and by knowing the two shapes, no time is lost in inspecting the wrong valve parts to find the trouble, and in most engines, the exhaust cam with a large lobe is used. The lift of the valve is the distance that the valve is lifted or raised off its seat, and this is governed by the height of the cam lobe, Fig. 3. Where overhead valves are used and the camshaft is in the crankcase, heavier valve mechanism and stronger springs are needed, because of the inertia of the parts. One way to reduce the spring tension is to increase the travel of the cam by the use of a longer valve-rocker arm, Fig. 4. The distance between a' and b' in ratio to b' and d', Fig. 4, doubles the travel of the follower and, therefore, it only has to travel half as far. This reduces the speed at which the cam must travel as well as the amount of acceleration or lift of the cam.

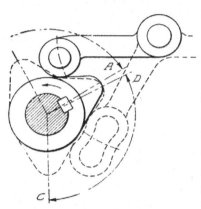

Fig. 5. Cam Mechanism of Peugeot Single-Cylinder Engine

The things to be aimed at in the design of cams and valve mechanisms are greater volume and the least possible strain on all valve parts. Of course, silent operation is a desirable feature, but the best possible performance of the engine should come first. Therefore the rapid opening and closing of the valves with lightness of parts is to be commended. The use of more than two valves per cylinder tends toward the use of lighter valve parts and weaker valve springs, and, therefore, less reciprocating weight and wear on cams and camshaft and shaft bearings.

A cam follower which differs from the usual direct-lift push rod may or may not affect the shape of the cam. Usually it does not, so that the shape does not have to be taken into account. Ordinarily these followers are used to prevent side thrust on the push-rod guide, the follower itself taking all the thrust and being so designed as to be readily removable or adjustable to take care of this. In cases where this does not obtain, the object usually sought is the removal of noise. The two objects may be combined, as shown in Fig. 5, which represents an enlarged view of the cam mechanism of the famous one-cylinder French car, Peugeot. The action is that of one cam operating both the exhaust and the inlet valves through the medium of a pair of levers upon which the cam works alternately.

A cam follower of somewhat different form will be noted in the Cadillac eight-cylinder motor, shown in Fig. 6.

Relation of Valve Opening to Crankshaft Travel. The valve opening bears a definite relation to the crankshaft and piston travel, since for good operation the valves must remain open as long as

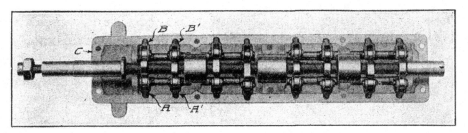

Fig. 6. Cadillac Camshaft, Cam Followers and Covers Removed from Motor

possible. It is often necessary to vary the length of time that the valve is open or to make some change in the valve timing, and to find the length of time that the valve is open before making any change. The crankshaft makes two revolutions to complete the cycle in a four-stroke cycle engine, and the intake valve is open a certain number of degrees the first revolution, and the exhaust valve is open a certain number of degrees the second revolution. Therefore, each valve is open for a certain number of degrees in 360 degrees of crankshaft travel. Fig. 7 shows a valve timing in which the intake valve opens at 10 degrees after top dead center and closes at 45 degrees after bottom dead center. It will be noticed that the valve is open one-half a revolution less 10 degrees, or 170, plus 45 degrees, which is the amount that the valve is open after the bottom dead center point is past, which makes a total of 215 degrees of crankshaft travel.

The rule for the intake valve is as follows: *Deduct the amount that the intake is closed after top dead center from 180 and add to that result the amount that the valve remains open after bottom dead center.*

The rule for the exhaust valve is as follows: *Add to 180 the number of degrees that the valve is open before bottom dead center plus the amount the valve is open after top dead center.*

For instance, in Fig. 7, the exhaust is open 50 degrees before bottom dead center and remains open 10 degrees after top dead center. Therefore, the valve is open 180 plus 50 plus 10, or a total of 240 degrees of crankshaft travel. If the timing of the valve is made earlier in opening, the closing will also be earlier, or vice versa, and the piston will not be as far down on its stroke or will be farther down, according to whether the timing is advanced or made later. This has a distinct bearing on the amount of gas drawn into the cylinder. The cam is so arranged that there will be a slight vacuum in the cylinder when the intake valve opens, because this causes a quicker intake of gases and the quick valve opening aids this condi-

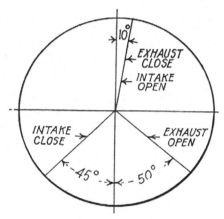

Fig. 7. Valve Timing Diagram

tion. The opening should not be delayed too much or the suction will be greatly decreased and the power output lessened. A change in timing can be made with little trouble if the above rules are remembered.

Difficulties in Making Cams. There was a time when the production of an accurate camshaft was a big job in any machine shop, well-equipped or otherwise, and represented the expenditure of much money in jigs, tools, and fixtures. Now, however, the machine-tool builder has come to the rescue of the automobile manufacturer, and special tools have made the work easy. So it was with the production of the shaft with integral cams; this used to be a big undertaking, but today special machinery has made it an easy matter. The illustrations, Figs. 8 and 9, show some of the product of a cam milling machine. This is now the favored way of putting cut engines, for the integral cams and shaft have the advantage of much lower first cost and, with proper hardening, will last fully as long as those made by mounting the separate cams directly on the shaft.

Grinding Increases Accuracy. An even later improvement in the way of a machine for producing cams on an integral shaft is the grinding machine which has been developed for this purpose. This works to what is called a master camshaft, that is, a larger size of shaft which has been very accurately finished. This master shaft is placed in the grinding machine, the construction of which is such that the grinding wheel follows the contour of the very accu-

Fig. 8. Cams Integral with Shaft—Milling Machine Job

Fig. 9. Another Camshaft with Integral Cams

rate master shaft and produces a duplicate of it, only reduced in size, a reducing motion being used between master shaft and grinder-wheel shaft.

The result of this arrangement is a machine which is almost human in its action, for it moves outward for the high points on the cams and inward for the low spots on the shaft. Moreover, it has the further advantage that all shafts turned out are absolutely alike and thus accurately interchangeable. It allows also of another arrangement of the work, the drop forging of the shafts within a few thousandths of an inch in size, the surface of skin is easily ground off in one operation, then the hardening is done, and the final grinding to size is quickly accomplished. In this way, the shafts may be produced more cheaply than was formerly the case and have, in addition, greater accuracy, superior interchangeability, and quicker production.

The same process is applicable to, and is used for, other parts of the modern motor car; thus crankshafts are ground, pump and magneto shafts are finished by grinding, and many other applications of this process are utilized. The process can be extended indefinitely, the only drawback being that a master shaft is very expensive.

Old Way Required More Accurate Inspection. With the old method of making the cams and shaft separate, the amount of inspection work was very great and represented a large total expense in the cost of the car. Thus, it was necessary to prove up every cam separately as well as every shaft, and later the cams and shaft assembled. One of the forms of gages used for inspecting cams is shown in Fig. 10. It is in two pieces, dovetailed together. This

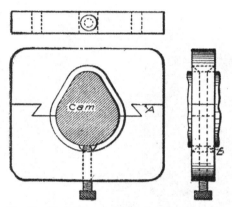

Fig. 10. Useful Form of Gage for Separate Cams

allows of the testing of many shapes of cam with but one base piece and a number of upper, or profile, pieces equal to the number of different cams to be tested. To test, the cam is slipped into the opening, and if small, the set screw forces it up into the formed part of the gage, showing its deficiencies; while if large, it will not enter the form.

Camshaft Drives. There are two methods of driving camshafts —gear drive and chain drive. Gear drive has been very popular in the past, but, owing to the noise and the hum caused by the gears, they are being replaced rapidly by chain drives. The use of gears determines the position of the camshaft, because the camshaft must run at half the speed of the crankshaft. Therefore the gears must be of a certain size to obtain this ratio and this is often the cause of a less compact engine. When valves are placed on both sides of the engine, it needs three gears, which means increased noise and wear. The crankshaft and camshaft gears are meshed directly together, where there is a single camshaft, which eliminates a little of the noise. An idler gear is used to drive the magneto gear, and when the gears become worn they rattle and hum badly. There is no adjustment for the meshing of the gears, and it is often necessary to install new ones. Two or three different sets of gears are often tried before a quiet set is obtained. Manufacturers of gears have tried many things to cut down the noise, using many materials, as compressed fiber, and others, with some satisfactory result. If lubrication should fall short, they are likely to tear and cause con-

Fig. 11.   Automatic Chain Adjuster
Courtesy of Link Belt Company

siderable damage. Some of the material has been found to swell, causing tight meshing, with the rapid failure of the gears. Most of these types of gears are run between two steel gears and this has been found to be the best arrangement.

The chain drive holds many advantages: They can be adjusted when worn; are easily replaced; are silent in operation; and, with their use, the camshaft can be placed anywhere the designer desires. The ratio of two to one is maintained, that is, the camshaft gear has twice as many teeth as the crankshaft gear, but the gears can be smaller and this tends greatly toward a more compact engine. In past years the chains were not adjustable and when the chains needed tightening it was necessary to remove the chain and take out a link and replace it. The next improvement was a hand adjustment, as used in the Cadillac and Packard, in which an eccentric bushing was used to take up the slack in the chain. When a chain becomes loose, it will often jump a tooth and the valve and ignition timing are altered. The timing chains should be kept as tight as possible to prevent this trouble.

In the present-day cars there is an automatic adjustment in the form of a spring and an eccentric bushing, Fig. 11. As the chain

Fig. 12. Front View of Eight-Cylinder V-Type Motor
Courtesy of Cadillac Motor Car Company, Detroit, Michigan

wears, the spring moves the eccentric bushing and takes up the slack in the chain. This gear does not do any driving but simply acts as an idler gear and adjuster. Fig. 12 shows the Cadillac hand adjustment and Fig. 13 shows the automatic adjustment in use. The chain drive absorbs the many small shocks of the explosions and the inertia of the rapidly moving parts, such as the piston and connecting rods, which causes the noise in the gear-driven type of timing gear. The use of chain drives brought out vibrations in the crankshaft which were never suspected by the engineer and, consequently, helped to develop the smooth operation in the present-day automobile. It is therefore becoming very popular.

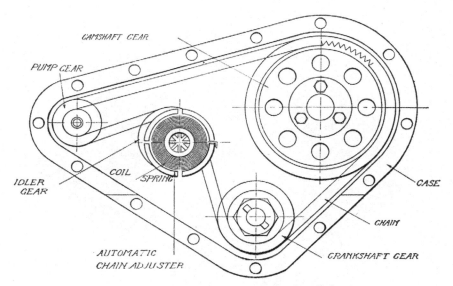

Fig. 13.   Automatic Chain Adjuster Installed
Courtesy of Motor Life

Twisted Camshafts. With the present form of camshaft having the cams forged integral, troubles and irregularities between one cylinder and another, which the repair man finds difficult to trace or run down, sometimes develop in the running of the engine. A fairly light camshaft will sometimes become twisted, usually right at a cam where the stress is. When trouble of this kind is indicated, the camshaft should be removed and tested. A good way to do this is to place the shaft in the milling machine with the index head set so that one revolution of the shaft can be divided into four equal parts. Place a thin disc in the arbor, then mount the shaft and bring it up to the disc. Choose one of the cams and set the disc to the exact center of the point of it. Then, by turning the shaft a quarter-turn each time, the other cams can be tested with their relation to this one. Sometimes a difference of $\frac{1}{8}$ inch will be found in this way. The lay-out for this is seen in Fig. 14.

Sometimes it is not convenient to take the camshaft out to make a test for a twisted camshaft and the following method can be used to make a test with the camshaft in position: Give all the valves the same amount of clearance, rotate the crankshaft, and notice if the valves all open at the same point relative to piston position. If they do, the shaft is in good condition; if they do not, the shaft is bent and the valve that shows the change will indicate the position of the twist or bend. The shaft will have to be removed to straighten.

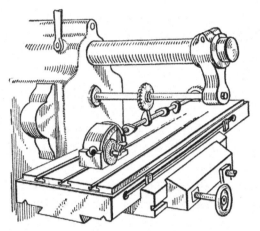

Fig. 14. Checking up Camshaft in Milling Machine

A bent or twisted shaft will cause a very noisy timing gear, where either gears or chains are used, and a very uneven running engine. Of course, in the latter case, it must be determined that all other conditions are correct which might cause the engine to run unevenly.

Worn Cams on the Shaft. Worn cams on the shaft will cause noise and erratic valve action. The constantly changing valve clearance adjustment is an indication of worn cams. If the valve clearance is set at one point and the shaft is rotated, and brought back to its original position, there should be no change in the valve clearance; but if the cam is worn, there will be a decided difference. It is the best plan to install a new camshaft when this trouble occurs. Close inspection will often show a hollow worn in the part of the cam where the lift starts to take place, and this will cause a slapping noise, especially in the mushroom type of cam follower when the cam hits the tappet.

Worn Bearings. Worn bearings will cause noisy timing gears and sometimes cause the chain to jump a tooth or two, which will alter the timing of the engine. The only satisfactory repair is to replace the bearings with new ones. In some bearings there is a set screw that can be tightened to take up the wear. Where the split-type of bearing is used, the bearings can be tightened by filling the faces and covering the outside of the bearings with solder, and when it is pressed back into place, the bearing will be tight on the shaft and in its housing.

End Play or Movement of the Camshaft. This trouble will cause a knock in the engine and often cause the cam to wear more on one side than on another, which in turn causes uneven wear on the push rods or tappets and their guides. Where spiral-type timing gears are used, this trouble can be located by rocking the crankshaft. The action of the gears will cause the gear and shaft to move backward and forward, and the knock will be distinctly heard. Where chains are used, removal of the gear case, and pulling and pushing on the shaft is the only way to locate the trouble. The front-end camshaft bearing usually has a flange on it to take the thrust of the shaft. The insertion of a metal or fiber ring between the gear and the thrust face of the bearing will cure the end play of the shaft.

Worn Camshaft Gears. Worn camshaft gears will cause a very noisy or rattling timing gear. The only cure is to replace the gears. There should be at least .005 inch play between the different gear teeth. The gears should be carefully and truly bolted on the camshaft flange so that they do not weave or run in an eccentric manner. The crankshaft gear should be on the shaft truly and not cocked on the key. The timing gear should never be touched with a file to reduce the size of the teeth if they do not mesh properly, because it will throw them out of alignment.

Camshaft Rocker Arms. Where rocker arms are used in conjunction with the camshaft, as in the Cadillac, a great deal of noise can be caused by worn rocker-arm bushings and bearings. It is best in this case to replace any worn parts rather than repair them. The rollers and pins will wear, tending toward noise and incorrect valve clearance adjustments.

Cleaning Camshaft Gears. On the majority of engines the camshaft and other gears, or the silent chain which replaces them, are lubricated automatically by the running of the engine as they are by-passed in on the engine lubricating system. This is an excellent feature, but it leads to neglect. These gears or sprockets are sure to wear, and the metal worn off remains in the case. Moreover, dust and the impurities of the oil are bound to get in. The foreign matter has a cutting action on gears, chains, or bearings, so the gear case should be cleaned out frequently. This is done best by thoroughly flushing out the case and the gears, or sprockets and chains, as the case may be, with kerosene. After using the kerosene, use gasoline along with the kerosene to clear away any remaining dirt or oil. After applying the gasoline, wait long enough for it to evaporate before replacing the parts.

CONNECTING RODS

The purpose of the connecting rod is to transmit the power developed by the combustion of the gases in the combustion chamber to the crankshaft, and with the aid of the crankshaft to change the reciprocal motion of the piston to rotary motion, which is necessary to drive the automobile. The connecting rod has to withstand two strains which are set up by two conditions of its operation. A compressive strain is set up by the weight and inertia of the reciprocating parts, and the other strain is the centrifugal force of the revolving crankshaft transmitted through the rod. Therefore, the design of the connecting rod is an important feature in its manufacture. The explosive pressure is also a compressive pressure which amounts to more than the pressure set up by the reciprocating parts.

The length of the rod is also important. It has been found that the shorter the rod, the greater the side thrust on the cylinder walls, owing to the greater angularity of the rod. A long connecting rod will reduce the wear in cylinder and piston. A shorter connecting rod is lighter, and as weight is an important factor in the present-day cars, it appears to be the correct installation. The length of the connecting rod is in proportion to the radius of the crank throw, which should be about $3\frac{1}{2}$ times the radius.

There is a bearing at the top and the bottom of the rod. In some cases the bearing at the bottom is cast in the rod itself, while in others the bearing is a separate unit. The latter is the best arrangement, for it is possible to renew the bearing with little trouble when necessary.

Design Characteristics. *H-Section Form.* Established practice in connecting-rod design is almost all in favor of the common H=section rod, usually with two bolts to attach the cap. In some cases four bolts are used, since with four bolts a flaw or crack in one is less likely to cause damage than is the case when only two are used. The old scheme of hinging the cap at one side is now practically obsolete, having been discarded because it made accurate adjustment of the bearing surfaces almost impossible.

GASOLINE AUTOMOBILES

Tendency to Lighten Rods. The modern tendency toward lightening the weight has extended to the connecting rods, since a portion of the rod is considered as reciprocating. This lightening has been accomplished by external machining. Thus, in the typical connecting rod of forged alloy steel, Fig. 1, the form at the left is that formerly used, while that at the right is its present shape. Note

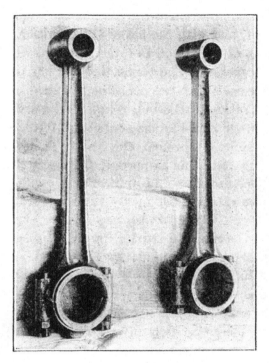

Fig. 1.   Old and New Connecting Rods Showing How They Can Be Lightened
Courtesy of the Locomobile Company of America, Bridgeport, Connecticut

how the rounding sides of the **H**=part, necessary in forging, have been machined off; how the fillets at big end and piston end have been machined down; how the upper end has also had its central rounding part machined off; and the whole, file finished. Another excellent feature of the work done to lighten the rods in this way is that they can be brought to an absolute standard of weight, so that every rod weighs exactly the same as every other. This was not possible previously, as the variation of the exterior surfaces, due to differences in forging, made considerable difference in weight. In both, the bushings are in place.

Tubular Rods. Tubular rods, in place of the H=section, are giving good service in several of the long-stroke foreign motors, and it is difficult to see why this form is not superior to that in common use. The question of cost, however, is a consideration, since it is necessary to bore the hole through the inside of the rod, whereas a forged rod of H=section requires no machining except at the end.

The wonderful progress in welding, however, has made it possible to construct a tubular connecting rod at a very low expense, and, owing to its many advantages, this is finding much favor for small motors. The two ends are machined and a section of tubing welded to them.

One advantage of the tubular rod, in addition to its superiority for withstanding the compression load to which a rod is chiefly

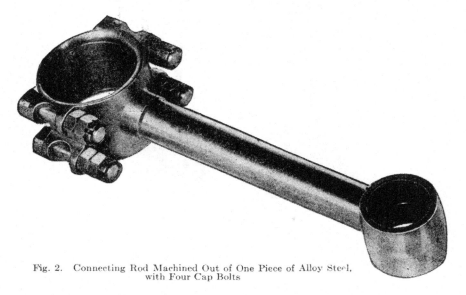

Fig. 2. Connecting Rod Machined Out of One Piece of Alloy Steel, with Four Cap Bolts

subject, is that it can be used as a pipe to convey oil from the big end to the piston-pin bearing.

Fig. 2 is an example of a very light-weight, high-quality, aviation-motor connecting rod, machined out of a solid bar of alloy steel, and provided with four bolts in the cap.

Connecting=Rod Bearings. *Usual Types.* Connecting rods have two different forms of bearings. This is due to the difference in their service. At the upper or piston end, the bearing is usually a high-grade bronze tubing, machined all over and pressed in place.

When in place, it generally has a central oil hole drilled through rod and bushing, and then a couple of oil grooves are scraped in by hand to start from this hole and distribute the oil outward in both directions on its inner surface.

At the lower or, as it is usually called, big end, the connecting rod must have a better bearing. This end is bolted around the crankshaft pin and must sustain high rubbing speed, as well as the load of explosions. Bolting it on, and the need for removing it occasionally, call for a form which is split horizontally. Generally, this bearing is of high-grade bronze with a softer, or babbitt, central lining which can be replaced easily and quickly. The harder bronze back will sustain the stresses of bolting up tight and stand up under the constant pounding, while the softer and renewable center takes all ordinary wear. These bearings are fitted with great care. They are reamed by hand after machining, and then hand scraped to a precise fit. They are pinned in place, drilled for oil, and grooved to distribute it.

Eight- and Twelve-Cylinder V Types. The eight- and twelve-cylinder V-type motors have altered the design of connecting-rod bearings somewhat, in that there are two connecting-rod big ends working upon one crank pin, that is, an eight-cylinder V-engine uses a four-cylinder form of crankshaft with two connecting rods on each pin. This modifies what was good connecting-rod bearing practice, one of two different forms being utilized. When the rods are placed side by side with individual bearings, the pins are made very large and as long as possible, in order to give adequate bearing surface. The other form is the forked rod in which one rod works within a slot in the other. In this type, a split bearing of the usual form is placed in the forked or long rod, and the outer surface of the central part of this prepared as a pin surface for the other or central rod. The requisite area of the smaller rod bearing is made up by its larger diameter. This is well shown in Fig. 3, the rods and bearing are assembled, and the separate big-end bearing is at the right. In another type of V-motor connecting-rod bearing, the larger bearing is slotted for the central rod and its bearing, the slot being made large enough to permit a rotation, which never exceeds a quarter of a turn. This arrangement is more complicated to install and repair than the form shown in Fig. 3.

Aluminum Connecting Rods. A number of manufacturers are now developing aluminum connecting rods as this metal is very light and will combine very readily with other metals, thus forming an alloy of great strength. The lighter the reciprocating weight, such as the piston and connecting rod, the greater will be the efficiency, power, and speed of the motor. It is for this reason that

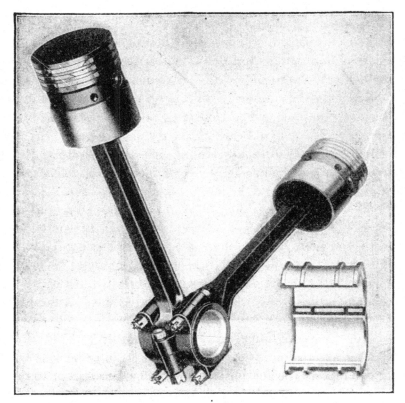

Fig. 3. Connecting Rods for V-Type Engine, Showing Method of Forking One Rod
Courtesy of Cadillac Motor Car Company, Detroit, Michigan

the engineers desire to develop a much lighter rod. While it is true that the entire rod does not act as reciprocating weight, in general practice, the upper half of the rod is considered reciprocating while the lower half is rotating weight.

The Triple Lite connecting rod, Fig. 4—an alloy with aluminum as its base—is constructed with a section somewhat different from the ordinary drop forged connecting rod. A comparison with Fig. 3 shows that the *H* section in the Triple Lite connecting rod has its flange between the bearing pins while the flange in the drop forged steel rod is at the side of the bearing pins. The Triple Lite is also used as a bearing, making it unnecessary to equip these rods with a babbitt bearing face. This rod weighs but 14 ounces.

Rebabbiting Bearings. Sometimes through failure of lubrication or lack of oil, a bearing will melt or burn out. It then becomes

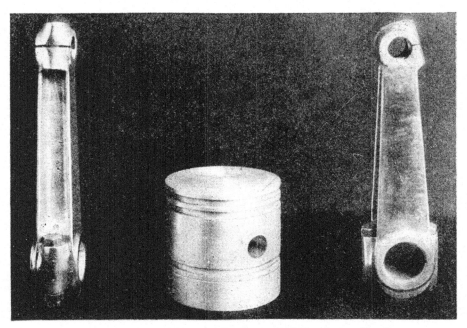

Fig. 4. Triple Lite Piston and Connecting Rod Manufactured by the Laurels Motor Company, Anderson, Indiana

necessary to replace the bearing shells with new bearings or to refill or rebabbit them in cases where the new parts cannot be obtained or where the bearing is a part of the rod. Special jigs or fixtures can be purchased but they are not always at hand. Therefore it is a good thing to know how to do the work with other tools that can be made on short notice.

The majority of connecting-rod and crankshaft bearings are bronze shells or backs, lined or faced with babbit as a wearing metal. The bronze provides the stiffness and long life, the babbitt, the softer wearing face which is easily and cheaply replaced. In this replacement, a form or jig to simulate the crankpin and approximate its size must be used for a center. A form made of wood is shown in Fig. 5. This is simply a round member of hard wood, turned up slightly smaller than the actual crankpin at the upper end, while the lower end is left large to form an under surface for the metal. Next, the upper part is split or rather has a cut taken across it, equal in thickness to the shim to be used when the bearing is assembled in place. Then, when the babbitt is poured in, a metal member is set across the rod to form the shim, which is shown in the sketch at the right in the figure.

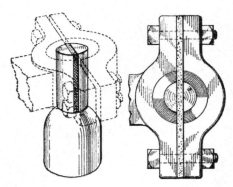

Fig. 5. Wooden Core for Babbitting Connecting-Rod Bearings

This method has the advantage over that of using the pin when pouring the metal in position, because it gives a little surplus to machine off, and thus makes the surface more accurate before it is scraped. If broaching to harden the surface of the metal is resorted to, it gives a little metal to broach down. Moreover, by making it so simple and easy to handle, the work of babbitting is made easy. This cannot be said of trying to babbitt in place. The core need not necessarily be of wood; it can be of metal or of anything else desired. But the wood has the advantage of being easily worked, or of being cheap and quickly obtained.

It is not good practice to use the main shaft for the purpose of casting the bearings, because the hot metal is apt to spring the shaft. A better plan is to use a wood jig such as shown in Fig. 6.

It is unfortunate but true that a new jig will probably have to be made for every different size of job, but the jig is easily turned in a lathe in one set-up of the chuck. The solid flange A should be about 1 inch thick and should have a diameter 1 inch or so greater than the outer diameter of the bearing. The shaft C should be turned to a size $\frac{1}{64}$ inch smaller than the size of the bearing surface, and should be about $\frac{1}{8}$ inch longer than the length of the bearing itself. Then on the shaft side of the flange A a groove B should be turned, having a depth of $\frac{1}{4}$ inch and a diameter equal to the diameter of the hole through the connecting rod when the babbitt metal is removed.

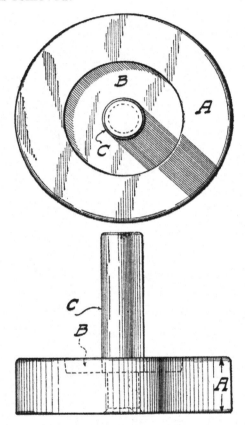

Fig. 6. Jig for Rebabbitting Bearings

Pouring the Babbitt. The jig is now ready for use. Fill the groove B with plastic fire clay even with the surface of the flange and place the bearing container over the shaft of the jig, as shown in Fig. 7. The bearing container should be adjusted over the shaft of the jig so that the space on all sides is exactly the same, determining this with a tapered steel gage, Fig. 8. Drop the gage into one side and note the mark on the taper where it comes to rest when touching the jig shaft and the bearing container. Then move the gage about and determine whether the other side is too close or too far away. Continue this operation until the space to be filled is the same on all sides. It is important that the machined surface of the bearing container rests perfectly flat on the block.

With everything properly located, lay a rim of fire clay about $\frac{1}{4}$ inch thick around the top of the bearing container, as shown in

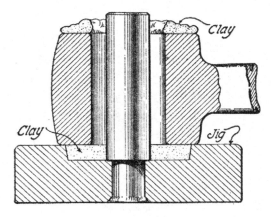

Fig. 7. Jig and Bearing Container
Ready for Pouring

Fig. 7, so that the space between can be filled with bearing metal above the edge of the container to take care of contraction.

Everything is now ready for the pouring of the bearing metal, which has been melted in a ladle. Before starting to pour, make

Fig. 8. Tapered Steel Gage

sure that all impurities which have risen to the top are skimmed off. These impurities, if allowed to pass into the bearing, might cause trouble later. Pour the metal from the ladle into the hole quickly and with a circular movement about the rim of the hole. It is important that it be poured in quickly, because babbitt cools very rapidly. However, this does not imply that the metal should be splashed in recklessly with the probability of throwing out the setting of the jig.

Finishing the Bearing. Allow the metal to cool for a period of 30 minutes and then remove the jig by pulling it out of the hole with a screwing motion. If care has been taken in placing the clay, the babbitt bearing will be held firmly in the bearing container. If the bearing is too tight for the crankshaft, it may be scraped to a proper fit as described in the next section.

When babbitt bronzes are to be relined, it is also necessary that there be a core to fit within the bronze, this core to be the size of the piece upon which the bearing operates.

Of course it is necessary, after the pouring has been done, to chip off the excess babbitt on the upper and lower surfaces of the bearing, smoothing down these edges after the bigger portion has been chiseled off by the use of a coarse file. The final polishing may be done with a fine file.

Fitting parts by means of a grinding compound has heretofore been limited to hard metals such as iron and steel. Ordinary grinding compound cannot be used on soft metals as the compound is embedded in the metal and has a bad effect upon the wearing qualities. One of the latest developments in the method of bearing fitting is a compound for use on soft metals only, which can be used in fitting a soft metal bearing such as connecting-rod bearings, main bearings, wristpins, bronze worm gears, bronze bushings, etc. This compound is composed of two distinct crystals—large or grinding crystals and small or neutralizing crystals. The large crystals continue to cut the soft metal until they are ground down to the size of the small crystals. These crystals are then broken up, thereby neutralizing the cutting crystals and leaving a compound harmless to metal and readily dissolved by oil.

A small amount of compound is made into thick paste by mixing with oil. If the bearing is new, a scraper is used until the bearing "bottoms." The paste is then applied to the bearing, after which it is bolted together rather snugly. Then the rod is turned a few times and the cap taken up. Two or three applications of this compound should give a good fitting.

Connecting=Rod Bearing Fitting. The fitting of connecting-rod bearings is a very important part of the manufacture and repair of the automobile. Bearings that are not correctly fitted will wear out quickly, causing noise and vibration. This applies to both the upper or piston-pin bearing as well as to the lower or crank-pin bearing, sometimes called the "big end."

Whether it is the fitting of a new set of bearings or the refitting of old ones, the principles are the same and just as much care is necessary. It is important that the bearing fits the connecting rod and cap tightly and that it has a perfect bearing in its housing. If the bearing can move in its housing, the bearing and the housing will both suffer wear and cause a noise in the engine which is hard to find and cure. When screws are used to hold the bearing in place, the screws should fit the hole snugly and hold the bearing tightly in place. In fitting new bearings to cap and connecting rod, cover the rod or cap with lampblack as a marking medium and

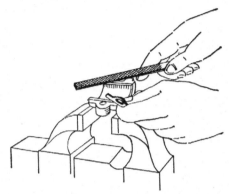

Fig. 9. Filing Crankpin Bearing Cap

then place the bearing in position. If the black marking is equally distributed over the back, the bearing has a good bearing in the housing. If not, the high spots, shown by the black marks, must be filed off and the bearing tried again. This process should be repeated until the bearing has a good bearing.

The bearing should not be below the faces of the cap and the rod for that will allow it to move in its housing. If this condition does exist, the rod and cap should be filed until the bearing is level or stands a little above the faces of the cap. The edges of the bearing will come against each other, when the rod and cap are bolted together, and hold the bearing firmly in place. If shims are used, the edges of the bearing will be tight against them.

If the faces of the rod or cap have to be filed, Fig. 9, it is essential that they be filed true and square with each other, or there will not be a perfect bearing obtained, for the bearing will only be touching in one place, whereas it should touch all around the shaft. The conditions are shown in Figs. 10 and 11. In Fig. 10, the outside of the bearing holder has been filed too much so that when the faces are pulled together with the connecting-rod bolts, the bearing will pinch the shaft at the points *a* and *b* while the opposite sides of the bearing will not touch at all. This bearing will soon wear loose and the rod will knock in a very short time. In Fig. 11, the inside of the holder has been filed too much with the result that the top and bottom of the bearing touch while the sides do not. This condition will cause the same trouble as in the first

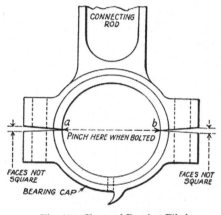

Fig. 10.   Faces of Bearing Filed
Unevenly

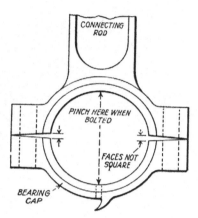

Fig. 11.   Faces of Bearing Filed
Unevenly

case. Care should be taken in the case of a rod that uses a solid shim between the connecting rod and its cap when the shim is filed.

The safest way to reduce the rod and cap is to place a piece of emery cloth on a flat surface, invert the cap, press it firmly down on the cloth, and move it in a circular manner. In this way the parts will be reduced squarely and truly. The file should be used when a lot of metal is to be removed. A face plate should be used to test the work and keep the faces true. After the part has been filed a little, it should be inverted and moved around on the face plate on which is spread a thin layer of marking. The spots, where the file has touched, will be shown by the marking. These high spots can then be filed off, thus keeping the faces true and square with the bearing.

After the bearing has been fitted to the connecting rod, it will be found that the edges of the bearing have been pinched. It

Fig. 12. Jigs for Connecting-Rod Reaming

will be necessary to cut away the corners to allow the bearing to touch the crankshaft journal or crank pin.

The next important step and one on which the satisfactory fitting of the bearing depends is to see that the crankshaft journal or pin is round and parallel. If close measurements are taken of a shaft that has been in service some time, it will be found that the journal has worn oval, and in cases where an off-set connecting rod is used, the journal will also taper. It will readily be seen that satisfactory work of bearing fitting cannot be done to a shaft in this condition because the bearing would only touch the large part of the shaft. The shaft should be put into a lathe and the journal ground or lapped down until the latter is true in every respect. The tools and method for lapping are given under main bearing fitting. In the absence of a lathe or lapping tool, a good job can be done in the following manner. A micrometer should be used to find the large parts of the shaft and a fine file used to reduce these places to a uniform size. The work should be tested often to see that the size is becoming uniform. A fine piece of emery cloth on which some oil has been poured should be used to bring the shaft to a smooth finish and a high polish. It requires patience and care to do this work, but the end justifies the time and care spent on it.

There are two methods of fitting connecting rods: (1) by alignment reamers; and (2) by scraping. The reamer process is quicker and absolutely accurate because, with the tools used, it insures the piston-pin bearing being true with the big-end bearing. This is not always true in hand fitting and the rod has to be aligned after the work of bearing fitting is finished.

Alignment Reamers. Fig. 12 shows an excellent tool for alignment reaming. The piston-pin bearing is held in correct position by two taper bushings and an adjustable stop holds the big end in position while it is being reamed. A study of the jigs shows that the bearings are certain to be in perfect alignment after the job is completed in this way. The reamer not only cuts a true hole but also burnishes the bearing, giving a smooth and accurate finish. A perfectly round bearing surface is obtained and there is no need to scrape the bearing later. Some mechanics like to "spot in" the bearing after reaming, and this is an excellent method. It does not make any difference if there is a slight amount of play in the bearing after fitting because the oil film will take care of the play. If the bearing is given .001 inch play when fitted, it will give better service, because oil has a chance to work into the bearing before the metal starts to overheat and flow. If the bearing is fit very tight, the metal will wear away very fast and a loose bearing will be the result. Some manufacturers use the broaching method on their connecting-rod big-end bearings. A broach is a tool having a series of cutting edges on the same bar and of various sizes which begin quite small and finish with a cutting edge of the required size. The tool is pushed or pulled through the bearing and cuts the metal as it passes through. It performs three operations at one time—cutting and forcing the metal into a hard mass and burnishing the babbitt, leaving a smooth accurate sized bearing.

Fig. 13. Crank Shaft in Vertical Position for Adjusting Bearings

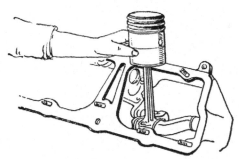

Fig. 14. Testing for Play in Connecting-Rod Bearing

It is a good plan to ream the piston-pin bearing before using a jig or fixture to ream the big end. It gives a better locating point for the bushings and the less accurate hand work is done first. If the big end is reamed first, there is a chance of the pin bearing being reamed out of line with the big-end bearing.

Hand Scraping. The process of hand scraping a bearing is a long and tedious job. It requires a lot of practice for a man to quickly and accurately fit a bearing in this way.

Holding Crankshaft. A means of holding the shaft upright on the bench must be devised. Usually on the end of the shaft there is a flange with a number of holes drilled through. Place the flange end of the shaft on the bench, as shown in Fig. 13 or Fig. 14, and mark on the bench with chalk the places under the holes. Drill holes through the bench where the chalk marks appear, and bolt the shaft to the bench, using as many bolts as you have holes. The bolts should be long enough to run through the bench and have 1 inch left over.

Cleaning Parts. Immerse the connecting-rod parts in gasoline, and then rub them dry. The connecting rods, like the cylinders, are numbered from the front to the back of the motor and, in working with them, never put a rod in any but its proper position; that is, rod No. 1 should always be fitted to wrist No. 1. The connecting rods are now ready for an initial fitting.

If it is noticed that the rod does not fit snugly when the initial fitting is given, then the shims should be filed. These are the thin

Fig. 15.   Shims Mounted for Filing

pieces of metal which rest between the two halves of the connecting-rod bearing and regulate the tightness of the bearing. A filing block of wood should be made as shown in Fig. 15. The block should be gouged on its surface in two places so that the resulting shapes resemble those of the shims. They need not fit perfectly, but the indentations must be of the same depth but not too deep to prevent filing the surface of the shim. The shims, when placed in these grooves, are ready for filing. Both shims should be filed at the same time. The block should be placed in the bench vise or in a metal vise. Then a fine mill file should be run over the surface of the shims by holding the file as previously instructed. Do not file much, the object of filing being to bring the two halves of the bearing halves closer together so as to touch the shaft. It will be seen from this that considerable accuracy is necessary in filing shims. The shims should be perfectly level.

GASOLINE AUTOMOBILES

Putting Prussian Blue on the Crankshaft. The crankpins on the crankshaft having been cleaned and polished with emery, the pin corresponding to the rod to be fitted is covered with a thin layer of prussian blue. Let us say that rod No. 1 is to be fitted. A little prussian blue mixed with oil to the consistency of cream is rubbed on the pin with the finger. Rod No. 1 is then placed in position and tightened. Care should be taken that the nuts are

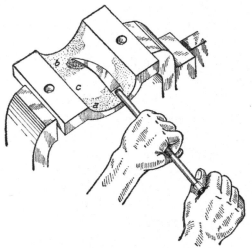

Fig. 16.   Inside of Bearing Showing Spots Which Need Scraping

tightened properly as many repair men make the mistake of assuming that the nuts may be drawn up in any order whatever. This is wrong. First tighten one nut a little, then the opposite one a little, and then a third—if there are more than two—and the opposite one the same amount. Go back over the nuts in the order that they were first drawn up. This should be continued until all the nuts are tight and the bolts drawn up as much as possible without splitting them. As these bolts are very easily stretched, care should be taken that they are not tightened excessively.

Marking Bearing. When all the bolts have been drawn up, turn the rod around in one direction for awhile, then run it back and forth for a few minutes, and then all the way around again. The entire operation of cutting-in the bearing, as it is called, should last about 2 minutes. Then take off the connecting rod. The connecting-rod bearing will be covered with little black spots, caused by the lampblack being embedded in the soft metal of the bearing.

Scraping Process. With the shims filed, place them in position and give the bearing another fitting. Remember the filing was done to bring the bearing together. When it is properly closed, the rod should fit tight enough to require some effort to push it around. Taking for granted that the bearing has been given a fitting and that it has been found to contain a number of blue spots, these must be scraped off, as shown in Fig. 16. For this operation a bearing scraper, Fig. 17, is used. This may be procured at any supply store. The scraper is held as shown in Fig. 16. However, one who is accustomed to scraping may be able to handle the instrument better in another position. One very important point must be borne in mind and that is that the word scraping does not mean—as it usually does—scratching; scratching is detrimental to the bearing. By

Fig. 17.   Type of Bearing Scraper

scraping is meant cutting from the surface of the bearing a very thin shaving of metal and at the same time leaving the surface of the bearing smooth.

The real object of scraping is to get the bearing to touch the crankshaft at every point. A bearing may be said to be a good one if every $\frac{1}{32}$ inch of the surface touches the crankshaft. It will be supposed that the bearing needs scraping. It does not show little blue spots every $\frac{1}{32}$ inch. Instead there are groups of spots, at each end as at a and b, Fig. 16, while in the center portion c there are no spots, which means that at this point the bearing is not touching the shaft at all. The object of the scraping is to make the center portion as well as the two ends touch.

The little blue spots are scraped off one at a time or nearly so, using short clean strokes with the scraper and taking care not to roughen the surface of the bearing. The scraper should be moved sideways and at the same time a little forward. One hand is necessary to manipulate the scraper and the other to guide the tool.

After all the blue spots have been removed, the bearing is thoroughly cleaned with a cloth. The wrist of the crankshaft is again blued with blueing and the rod given another fitting. If at this fitting the rod is loose, due to the bearing having been scraped too much, the shims should be filed a little. After the rod has been turned on the crankshaft for about 2 minutes, it should be removed and the bearing again examined.

Little blue spots will again be seen, but this time they will be more evenly distributed if the bearing was properly scraped before. If the entire surface of the bearing contains blue spots about $\frac{1}{32}$ inch apart, then the bearing is in good condition. But this holds true only if the rod holds snugly on the shaft. If the blue spots are again grouped as shown at a, b, and c, then the individual spot scraping is repeated until the rod gives a snug fit and at the same time has the

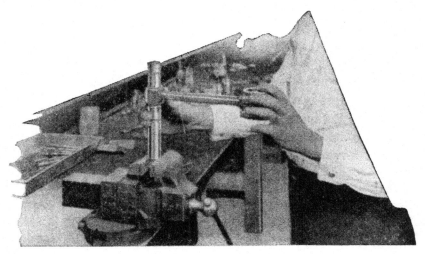

Fig. 18. Reaming Piston-Pin Bearing

bearing touching uniformly. It is often necessary to fit a new bearing to a shaft that is still in the crankcase. A great deal of time can be saved if a mandrel or shaft is machined to the same size as the journal to which the bearing is to be fitted, and the bearing fitted to nearly a finish fit on it and then to the journal itself.

Correct Fit of Bearing. A bearing may be said to have a correct fit when the marking shows an even fitting bearing and when the rod will make two revolutions when given a sharp push. When it stops, it should remain in position. Of course, there must be oil in the bearing when making this test. Another test can be made with the piston attached to the rod. The rod should be tightened in position and then given a slight push. If the fitting is right, the rod should fall slowly down by the weight of the piston.

Fitting the Piston Pin to the Small End. The fitting of the piston pin in the rod is usually done by hand. Fig. 18 shows how this is done. The pressure on the rod should be equal at both ends when forcing the rod over the reamer. Too large a cut should not be taken at one time because it will cause the reamer to vibrate and will leave a rough surface behind. The pin should be fitted so that it can be driven through the bearing with light hammer blows. If the pin is a little tight, some mechanics will tap around the end of the connecting rod. This is poor practice because it stretches the metal and often loosens the bushings in the rod, causing wear on both and in time a knock. This can only be repaired by fitting an oversize bushing to the rod.

The following is a good test for the fit of a piston pin. Assemble the pin in the rod and hold the pin. If the rod drops by the weight of the big end, it is a good fit.

Bearing Scrapers from Old Files. Old files, when properly worked into shape and tempered, make excellent bearing scrapers. One great advantage in favor of the use of a homemade scraper

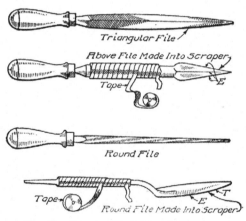

Fig. 19. Scrapers Made from Old Files

is that it is possible to make a scraper that will be more adaptable to the hands of the workman than the standard type.

In Fig. 19 is shown some of the types of scrapers best made from old files. The way to go about making a scraper is to select an old file resembling the type of scraper desired. Heat the file to a light-red heat and forge with a hammer, or bend in a vise as required.

When this is done, allow the file to cool slowly in the ashes at the side of the forge. When cool, it will be much softer than in its original state and most probably will be soft enough to be filed readily into the exact shape desired. If too hard to file conveniently, an emery wheel may be brought into service to shape the tool.

When the proper shape has been obtained, the next operation is to temper the tool. This is done by heating it again to a light

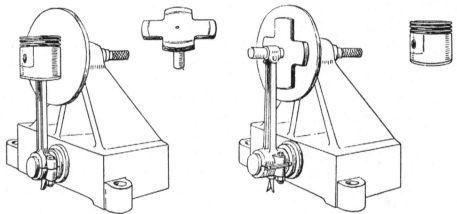

Fig. 20.   Fixture for Checking Piston and Connecting-Rod Alignment

red, then immersing the scraper portion in cold water and moving it about for a few seconds until it has entirely lost its red color. It should now be withdrawn and its bright surfaces quickly sandpapered so that the changes of color can be noticed. When a light yellow or straw color appears, the whole tool should be immersed in water, moved about therein for a few minutes, and then left there until cold.

The last step in the manufacture of the homemade scraper is to grind the surfaces of the tool so as to get smooth sharp-cutting edges. The sharp-edge scraper will of course have its three cutting edges formed by hollow-grinding the surfaces so that about $\frac{1}{16}$ inch of the original flat surface remains on either side of the edge. These surfaces remain flat and afterward are smoothed up on an oil stone.

Piston Pin and Piston Alignment. After the big-end bearing and piston pin have been fitted, it is very important that the pin is in perfect line with the bearing and the piston, so that the latter will be true in the cylinder. Oil pumping is often caused by a piston being out of line or a bent connecting rod. A connecting rod can be out of line by a twist or a bend in the rod. There are several methods of testing the rod: (1) by using a fixture as shown in Fig. 20, in which the rod is bolted to a mandrel with the piston against a true face. The amount of light passing between the

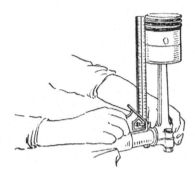

Fig. 21. Checking Connecting-Rod Alignment by Shaft and Square

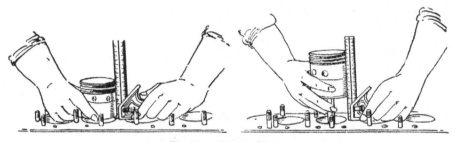

Fig. 22. Aligning Pistons

piston and the face of the fixture will indicate the distance the rod is out of line. In Fig. 21, the rod is bolted to a true shaft and a square is used. The blade of the square is placed close to the piston and the amount of light passing between the blade and the piston will be the indication. It can be tested also after the rod is bolted to the crankshaft and in the crankcase. This method is shown in Fig. 22. The square is placed on the crankcase face to which the cylinders are bolted. This face being true with the bore of the cylinder will give a true indication when the blade of the square is placed against the piston. If the rod is slightly bent, it may be sprung sufficiently to bring it true by the use of a wrench or by twisting the bar.

A bent connecting rod will not only cause oil pumping but will also cause undue pressure upon the cylinder and piston walls, with quick and uneven wear which can only be cured by regrinding or reboring. It will also cause piston slap and loss of compression and power.

Straightening Bent Rod. The need for a straight and true rod is apparent, but it is surprising how many rods are not straight, particularly in old motors. Many erratic and bad-sounding motors have all their trouble caused by a bent rod. A connecting rod can be bent either of two ways, and one gives as much trouble as the other. If bent in the plane of rotation, the rod will simply be shortened, the piston will not go as high as it should, and it will go down a little lower than normal. Moreover, the bend will press it with unusual force on the cylinder wall on one side and cause it to wear more than the other. The combination will soon result in trouble. When bent in a longitudinal direction, that is, fore and aft, the upper end of the rod will run against one side of the piston or perhaps only knock against it on each stroke. At any rate, this, too, will give trouble.

Testing Straightness. The first thing to do when a connecting rod is suspected is to take it out and test it. One way of doing this

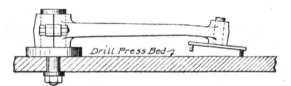

Fig. 23.   Method of Testing Connecting Rods
with two Mandrels

is to attach the lower end to a mandrel, which can be bolted into a drill-press table, Fig. 23. Before doing this, the small end is also fitted with a mandrel, the lower part of which is of considerable length and has two short vertical pegs. When the big end is bolted down, if both the small pegs on the other end touch, it proves at least that the two holes (big end and small end) are parallel. If one of these pegs is off the table as shown, it proves that the two holes are not parallel. In the latter case, the rod would need to be straightened, as nothing but the bending of the rod would throw the holes out of parallel when they were bored correctly.

Another method, which is very similar, consists in forcing two mandrels of equal length into the two holes, until each is centered in the rod. Then, if the rod be placed on supports on the surface plate, or other similar true surface, so that one mandrel is horizontal, the surface gage will show at once if the other end is also horizontal, and thus, if the rod is straight and true. It will also show how much it is twisted, if out of true. If the mandrels are made long enough, ordinary calipers can be substituted for the surface gage with equally accurate results.

A method almost the same as that just described is utilized in the testing fixture shown in Fig. 24. The advantage of such a

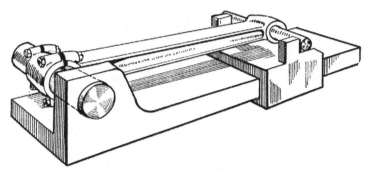

Fig. 24. Complete Connecting-Rod Testing Fixture

fixture is that it always works the same, while the use of surface gages and calipers varies from one workman to another, and even with the same man, from day to day, according to his moods and feelings. As the sketch shows, there is a mandrel for each end of the rod, that for the big end being pivoted in the fixture. When the rod is forced into this, and the other mandrel put in place in the piston end, if rotated down to a flat position (as shown), the small end mandrel should touch both of the fixture stops. If badly twisted, it will not be able to go down on one side.

Straightening Jigs. When it has been proved that the rod is not straight, it is necessary to have a device for applying pressure in order to straighten it. The simplest way is an ordinary straightening press consisting of a pair of ways with V=blocks upon which the work is supported and a lever or screw to apply the pressure in the middle. The work is supported on the V=blocks, the distance apart varying with the amount it is to be bent—far apart for a big bend, close together for a small one. For as short a member as a connecting rod, however, this is not sufficiently accurate, and besides, the form of the rod does not suit it to good results by this method.

A simple fixture for bending a rod, Fig. 25, consists of a pair of hooks for holding it and a central screw for applying power. The

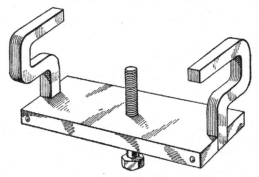

Fig. 25. Connecting-Rod Straightener Constructed from Three-Quarter-Inch Bar Stock

rod is slid into place inside the hooks and the screw turned until the rod is straightened. Then to prevent its springing back when the pressure is released, it is peened on the side opposite the screw. The advantage of this method is that it throws all stresses upon

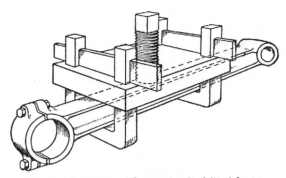

Fig. 26. Box Type of Connecting-Rod Straightener

the rod itself and none on the bearing surfaces. The hooks are forged from high-carbon steel of $\frac{3}{4}$-inch square section. The screw should be not less than $\frac{5}{8}$ inch to $\frac{3}{4}$ inch in diameter and fine threaded.

Another fixture is on the box order, Fig. 26. This has a pair of end clips which hold the rod tight by means of wedges which are driven into place. When this has been done, the rod is straightened by means of the central screw. As will be noted, the principal difference between the two forms, Figs. 25 and 26, is in the holding method. There are other forms, as well as forms of mandrels for lapping in big-end bearings, which are so constructed as to give a check on straightness and to allow of remedying the situation if the rod is not straight. Some of these will be described.

Offsetting. Many motors have been constructed with offset connecting rods, that is, the perpendicular center line of the wrist-pin, located in the piston where the pressure is applied, is not upon the center line of the bottom end. This resultant wear on the bearings is exaggerated in Fig. 27, which indicates also how this situation causes wear on the upper left end and lower right end of both bearings. The sketch also shows how this unequal wear is greater on the crank end, which is offset, than upon the piston end. The cause of this wear is simple, the pressure is unbalanced on the left side, so a downward push on that side is taken up by extra wear there, and on an upward push, as on the compression stroke when the flywheel is driving the pistons, the extra resistance of the left side causes unusual upward pressure on the right side. So the ends continue to wear, until a rocking motion of the pins results, and this causes a noise. New bearings help temporarily, but a stiffer connecting rod will often remedy it more or less permanently. This rocking motion also causes uneven wear on piston and cylinder walls.

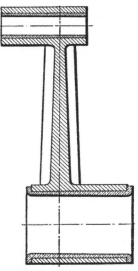

Fig. 27. Offset Connecting Rod Showing How Bearings Wear

Connecting=Rod Bearing Knock. A great deal of time can be saved in bearing adjustment if the loose connecting-rod bearing can be identified easily. This can be done with the aid of a sounding rod. Take a piece of round stock and place one end on the crankcase of the engine. Place the thumb over the other end of the rod and place the knuckle of the thumb in the ear. Move the rod about from place to place on the crankcase and as the rod comes nearer to the loose connecting rod the noise will sound louder at the ear.

To find out if the connecting-rod bearings are loose proceed as follows. Drive the car up a hill so that the engine is pulling hard and if the knock is slight or heavy and it has a muffled sound, either once or twice during a revolution, it indicates a loose connecting-rod bearing.

Kinks in Adjusting Bearings. Usually crankshaft and connecting-rod bearing adjustment is a difficult job. This is particularly true when the engine is not removed from the chassis. The

Fig. 28. Homemade Creeper

connecting-rod bolts are tight and hard to reach, and the operator, who is lying on his back, has all dislodged dirt or oil dropping in his face. Work like this calls for an easy means of getting under the engine and out again. For this, a form of creeper is necessary. There are many forms made and sold, but a simple one which any repair man can construct for himself is shown in Fig. 28. This consists of a wood frame with casters at the four corners and longitudinal slats for the floor. By making the ends concave, the surface is made concave. With a pillow or other head rest, it is more comfortable to use.

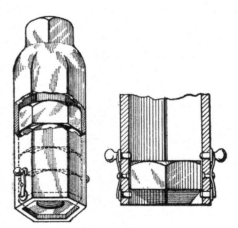

Fig. 29. Spring Clips on Socket Wrench for Use in Inaccessible Places

Another way in which this work may be facilitated is to make a special socket wrench for connecting-rod nuts and to make it deep enough to hold four nuts, one over the other. Then with a spring-stop arrangement, Fig. 29, the nuts from two rods can be taken off without stopping; or if lock nuts are used, the nuts and lock nuts may be removed from one rod. This is accomplished by means of four spring-operated pins. When the first nut is removed, it sticks in the end of the tool, but pushing this into the second one moves the first nut on up inside the socket. In replacement, when the upper pins are pulled, a nut drops down and is held by the lower pins enough to start it on the bolt end. When tightened, the socket can be pulled off, and the next nut dropped down and fixed in place by hand. The four pins have hardened ends, and the springs are old clock springs to which the upper pair of pins are brazed. The lower pins can be free. This form of socket wrench can be used with equal advantage in many other inaccessible places. Its single drawback is that it can only be of one size; and a set of them have to be constructed to take care of all needs.

In the ordinary bearing adjustment, the nuts are taken off, the connecting-rod cap removed, and the shims taken out, Fig. 30; say,

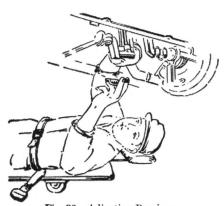

Fig. 30. Adjusting Bearings

a shim of .001-inch thickness for very small wear, .002 inch for considerable wear, and .003 inch for severe wear. If more than this has been worn off the bearings, they need re-scraping, as this is about the maximum that can be taken out without scraping. Usually, when the bearings have been taken up in this way, the caps are put back on pretty tight, a little bit tighter than they were previously. Then they are flooded with oil and run in this condition. The combination of excess oil and tight caps soon gives the entire bearing surface a fine polish which will last for many miles.

Special Sleeve Replaces Shims. In one motor (Reo), the shim is replaced by an ingenious arrangement of a threaded sleeve around the bearing bolts, Fig. 31, in which the sleeves are marked *A* and the bolts *B*. It will be noted that the sleeves rest against the upper part of the bearing and have a head against which the bolts rest, so that the latter can be tightened only as far as the sleeves allow. With this construction, when it is desired to tighten a bearing, the socket wrench is slid on so as to hold the heads of both bolt and sleeve, and then turned to unscrew both. Then the socket is drawn off the sleeve head, in the position shown at the left, and the bolt screwed back to pinch the bearing together and lock it. As will be

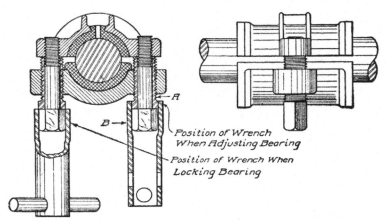

Fig. 31.   Connecting Rod and Main Bearings Constructed Without Shims
Courtesy of Reo Motor Car Company, Lansing, Michigan

noted, the two halves of the bearing metal are separated a considerable distance so that this arrangement is good for many thousand miles. Two years' running will usually exhaust the possibilities of the original bearing and its shims, which calls for re-babbitting, re-scraping, new shims, or for an entirely new bearing. This form of construction could be used anywhere that the bearings are likely to need frequent readjustment.

Mandrel for Lapping. In order to give the connecting-rod bearings the best possible surface, a mandrel should be used to lap them in. This is the equivalent of running in. The rod, with bearings in place, is put on the mandrel, and the bolts tightened a little; then it is worked back and forth, until the flattening down of the surface will allow more tightening of the bolts. This is continued until, with a mandrel the exact size of the crankpins, the bolts can be pulled up dead tight. Then the rod is removed; it is finished.

Such a mandrel, Fig. 32, is usually a piece of steel turned up on one end to the exact size of the crankpin, with a flat spot machined in the other end to allow holding in the vise. By making it perfectly

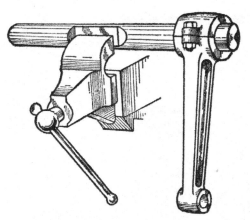

Fig. 32. Standard Mandrel Method of Lapping
Big-End Bearings of Connecting Rods

straight, a try square against the mandrel will show the correctness of the rod. On the other hand, if the outer end be made with a very slight taper, it is easier to work the rod on and off and easier to inspect the inside surface without unbolting.

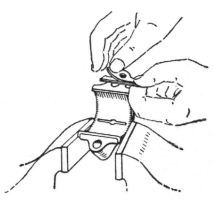

Fig. 33. Peeling Laminated Skin

Drilling Thin Shims. When thin brass shims are used, and the shape is formed by the workman, it is difficult to get a good true hole because of the extreme thinness of the metal. By collecting a number of these together and clamping them between two blocks of wood, a straight true hole can be bored through wood and brass with an ordinary bit and brace. The use of laminated shims avoids all this, as they come in the required thickness and are drilled to size. With these, adjustment is simply a matter of peeling off one of the laminations, as shown in Fig. 33.

PACKARD EIGHT-CYLINDER-IN-LINE MARINE MOTOR

CRANKSHAFTS

The crankshaft might be termed the backbone of the engine because it stands all the strain and stress of the power developed. The purpose of the crankshaft is to change the reciprocating movement of the piston and connecting rod into rotary motion and is the first part through which the power developed above the piston is transmitted in the automobile.

The engineer who is designing automobiles today is directing his effort toward the development of a smoother and more flexible running engine, and the design of the crankshaft has a great deal to do in regard to it. Perfect balance of the crankshaft is absolutely necessary where vibration is to be eliminated and smooth operation

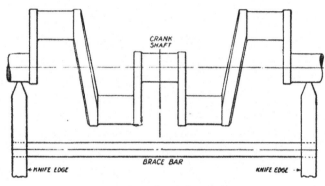

Fig. 1. Static Crankshaft Balance

obtained. Every piece of revolving machinery has its critical speed at which a vibration is set up in the revolving mass. This critical speed vibration will start other parts vibrating which are close to it.

So in the automobile, the crankshaft has its critical speed vibration. Where close attention is not paid to the balance of the crankshaft, it will be found that at this critical speed the whole car will vibrate. Sometimes the shaft is so designed that the vibrating speed is not within the speed range of the engine and consequently no vibration is felt.

Crankshaft Balance. There are three distinct types of balance that the engineer has to take into consideration when he designs the crankshaft for an engine, especially in the high-speed class—static, dynamic, and deflecting.

Static Balance. Static balance is the state of balance when the shaft is at rest. When the crankshaft is made so that it will stay in any position in which it may be placed, without moving, it is said to be in perfect balance. After the crankshaft has been machined, the first test for balance is the static test, Fig. 1. A pair of knife edges are made perfectly level in every way and the shaft is placed on these edges. If the shaft is in balance, it will not move or revolve. If it moves, the side that is heaviest must be made lighter until the balance is obtained. The heaviest side will, of course, be the side that drops to the bottom. The throws of the crankshaft should balance each other.

Dynamic Balance. The dynamic balance requires a special machine for the test, Fig. 2. The test is made while the shaft is revolving at different speeds and special indicators show exactly where and how much the shaft is out of balance. The parts that are out of balance are dressed down until there is no vibration. With the testing machine, Fig. 2, the static and dynamic test can be made at the same time. The shaft to be tested is placed in the machine and rotated above its critical speed. The drive is released and an indicator reading is set on a calculating rule which shows how much the shaft is actually out of balance. A weight is placed according to the reading of the rule to offset the "out of balance" factor and the shaft tried again. An indicator shows exactly where metal should be removed to balance up the shaft.

Deflecting Balance. Deflecting or bending balance is the ability of the shaft to withstand the continual twisting and distortion caused by the strain of taking the drive. It is dependent upon good dynamic balance. It does not matter if the shaft shows good dynamic balance at low speeds, there will be bending or deflection of the shaft if the dynamic balance is poor at high speeds. The strength of the shaft will govern this and therefore the design and calculations of the stress that the shaft will stand in operation are important.

In a shaft where counterbalance weights are used and they are removed for any reason, the shaft should be tried for both static and dynamic balance before being put back into service. Where balance weights are installed on a crankshaft with the idea of cut-

Fig. 2. Dynamic Crankshaft Balance Machine
Courtesy of Gisholt Machine Company

ting down the vibration, it will often be found that the trouble is worse instead of better and therefore the balance of the shaft should be tested before putting into service.

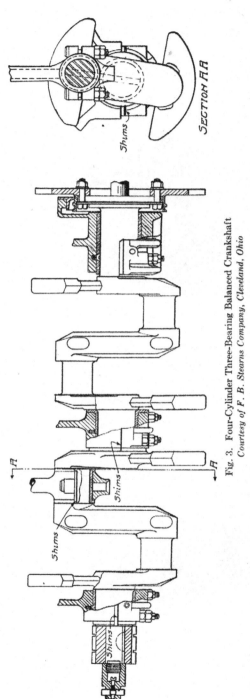

Fig. 3. Four-Cylinder Three-Bearing Balanced Crankshaft
Courtesy of F. B. Stearns Company, Cleveland, Ohio

Material. The crankshaft in all but heavy slow-running motors should be made of the finest alloy steel obtainable, for it carries the practical equivalent of thousands upon thousands of heavy blows.

Variation of Design. The greatest variations in automobile crankshaft design, aside from those permitted or made necessary by differences in the quality of material, are due to the conditions involved in the different combinations of cylinders that can be utilized. Thus the number of crank throws, as well as their position, varies with the type of motor.

As the repair man knows crankshafts today, they are of two kinds. The first is the four-cylinder form, in which each pair is in a single plane. This type of shaft has four pins, one for each connecting-rod big-end bearing. It may have either three bearings, as shown in Fig. 3, or five bearings. The second type, which the repair man is likely to meet, is the six-cylinder shaft, which will have six pins for connecting rods; these are grouped in pairs, and each pair in a different plane, the angle between them being 120 degrees. This type of shaft may have either four or seven bearings. In the four-bearing form, there is a bearing at each end, and another between each pair of cylinders, as shown in Fig. 4, with pistons and connecting rods attached. In the seven-bearing form, there is a bearing on each side of each connecting rod. These are the modern types, but older shafts may be encountered occasionally, in the way of four-cylinder shafts with two bearings, one at each end only; also with four bearings, the latter having the usual center bearing eliminated. The modern tendency is toward simplification, compactness, and lowered first cost; and the shafts with the fewer number of bearings are on the increase.

Crankshafts may be found which are drilled out for lubricant passages. In such cases, the repair man must look for attachments

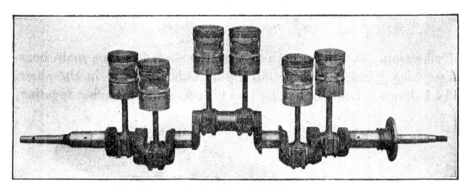

Fig. 4. Six-Cylinder Four-Bearing Crankshaft with Pistons and Connecting Rods Assembled
Courtesy of Nordyke & Marmon Company, Indianapolis, Indiana

which feed the oil into the hollow interior. Also, he may meet a ball-bearing form of shaft which has been built up to allow the bearings to be assembled. Such a shaft should be handled with extreme care.

Eight-cylinder engines generally use a four-cylinder form of shaft, with two connecting rods on each of the four pins. This is explained previously under connecting rods. Similarly, twelve-cylinder motors have a typical six-cylinder crankshaft, with two rods on each of the six pins.

An excellent example of one of the latest crankshafts that are not counterbalanced is shown in Fig. 5. This is the crankshaft used on the Packard "Straight-Eight" cylinder engine. The difficulty in an engine of this type was in keeping down the vibration, owing to the whip and distortion found in a long crankshaft, and to keep the bearing surface adequate with the least possible weight and absence

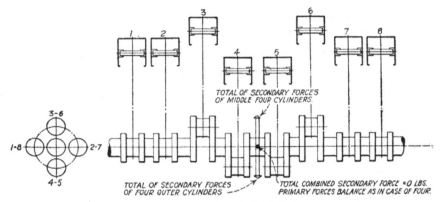

Fig. 5.　Non-Balanced Crankshaft

of vibration.　It will be noticed that the shaft has nine main bearings which do away with practically all twist or whip in the shaft. The balance is kept by having two pistons always moving together,

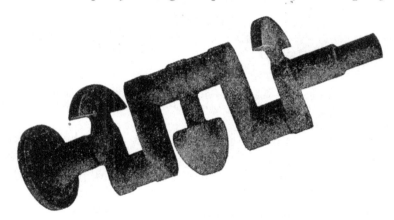

Fig. 6.　Typical Drop-Forged-Balanced Crankshaft
Courtesy of Park Drop Forge Company, Cleveland, Ohio

the two pistons moving up being balanced by two pistons moving down, and in this way a perfect balance is maintained.

Balanced Crankshafts.　While not an assembled shaft in the sense just referred to, the balanced form is meeting with great favor, and is being widely adopted.　This will be met by the repair man in two forms. One is like Fig. 3, except that the weights are machined to fit on the crank cheeks and bolted there. The repair man should not remove these unless it is absolutely necessary, as they vary in size and weight. They are fitted in place with extreme care and fastened extremely well. The other type—the kind being introduced into the latest models—has its counterweights forged as a part of the crankshaft, Fig. 6. In this type, the weights are adjusted to make the proper balance when the shaft is being machined.

A departure in crankshaft design is found in the Cadillac crankshaft which is now of the counterbalance type, Fig. 7. Here again

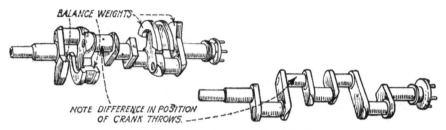

Fig. 7. Counterbalanced Crankshaft

the designer has tried to prevent all possible vibration and it will be seen that the shaft is different in regard to the position of the crank throws, so that the weight of the moving pistons is balanced. A comparison between the old shaft and the new will show the difference in the positions of the crank throws. The firing interval has not been altered but the firing order has. This new design of shaft gives perfect balance and therefore there is no vibration found in this eight-cylinder V-type engine.

Flywheels and Flywheel Attachment. Although the flywheel is a separate part of the automobile, it is very closely allied to the crankshaft. The purpose of the flywheel is to keep up the momentum of the revolving shaft and to carry the shaft over the points where no power is being developed by the engine. In engines that do not have a continuous flow of power, as in the 4-cylinder engine, the flywheel must be heavier than in an engine that has a continuous flow, as in a 6-cylinder or one of higher power. In high-speed engines, a lighter flywheel is being used which is consistent with the multiple-cylinder engine. The flywheel should not be too light or the power developed will not be up to the standard required, and it should not be too heavy, or the engine will be very slow in picking up speed and in acceleration.

The position of the flywheel has a great deal to do with the balance of the engine. In the Rickenbacker, the weight of the flywheel is divided between the front and the rear of the crankshaft. It is claimed that this arrangement cuts down the whip of the shaft and, if the timing gears are located at the end of the engine where the flywheel is placed, it prevents a great deal of wear on the gears. This arrangement was used by the Mercedes Company in Germany, years ago, and was very successful. Of course in the chain-driven gear it would make very little difference.

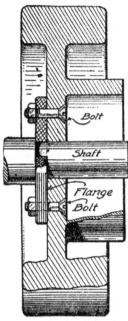

Fig. 8. Cross-Section of Flywheel Showing Flange Attachment

The flywheel must be tested for static and dynamic balance just as was the crankshaft, and practically the same methods are used. If there is a heavy side to the wheel, it may be made lighter by drilling holes in that side. The light side may be made heavier by drilling holes and filling them with lead to balance the wheel.

The usual method of attaching the flywheel to the crankshaft is by bolting the wheel to a flange that is a part of the crankshaft itself, Fig. 8. Sometimes the bolts take the drive as well as hold the flywheel in place, while in other cases, there are circular pieces of metal, called dowels, which take the drive. They are inserted between the flywheel and the flange in small recesses. In the latter case, the only function of the bolts is to hold the flywheel in place.

If the flywheel is removed from the crankshaft, it should be put back in exactly the same position. Some manufacturers make provision for this by either inserting dowel pins, drilling a hole off center or out of position, or by marking the flywheel and the crankshaft flange so that the marks line up when the two parts are in correct relation to each other. It is necessary that the flywheel be put back correctly for balance and for timing purposes. It will often be found that there are some marks on the rim of the flywheel which are used in the timing of the spark or the valves, and if the flywheel is not put back correctly it will throw out the timing marks in relation to the position of the crankshaft. When replacing a flywheel, care should be taken to see that it is securely bolted in position or else it will cause a knock.

Knock Caused by Loose Flywheel. A test for this trouble can be made by running the engine, then turning the switch off for a few revolutions, and then turning the switch on while the engine is still revolving. If there is a distinct knock when the switch is turned on, it is a good indication of a loose flywheel.

Bearing in Flywheel. A bearing will be found in the end of the crankshaft which supports the end of the clutch in the flywheel. This bearing may be a ball bearing or a bronze oilless bearing. When the flywheel is taken off, this bearing is often removed with it. The bearing should be tested for wear, because it will cause a knock if it is in poor condition. It should be thoroughly lubricated before putting back as there is no provision made for its lubrication.

Shapes of Flywheels. Flywheels do not vary in shape very much. A cross-section of a flywheel is shown in Fig. 8. It is made of a heavy outer rim with a central web or spoke. The outer rim is reduced in thickness when a lighter wheel is used.

In some flywheels, the clutch housing is a part of the flywheel, and in others, the clutch drum, as it is called, is bolted to the wheel. When cone clutches are used, the cone is machined in the flywheel. The starting gear, which is located on the outside circumference, is sometimes shrunk on the flywheel or the teeth are cut into the cir-cumference of the flywheel itself.

Portable Engine Stands. Unless the repair man has the proper tools to work with he cannot do real first-class work. One of the essential tools that should be in every automobile service station is the engine stand. A mechanic cannot scrape or fit the bearings to the crankshaft of an engine unless the case is held firm and can be moved in any position without disturbing the crankcase position in the stand. If the engine is removed from the chassis, the first thing needed is a suitable engine stand, Fig. 9. The frame is made of tubing, which gives a maximum of strength in a minimum of space. The stand can be moved around readily and it can be clamped so as to hold it steady in any position.

This form of engine stand holds the motor in its natural, or upright position. But it is not always desirable to have the engine in

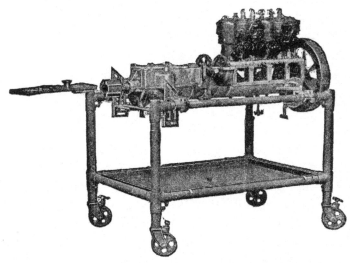

Fig. 9. Handy Form of Engine Stand Constructed from Piping
Courtesy of Shewaller Manufacturing Company, Springfield, Ohio

that position; in fact, when working on crankshaft bearings and other parts on the under side, it is necessary to have it inverted. There also is work which makes an intermediate position desirable. For this purpose, an engine stand is needed which can be turned to

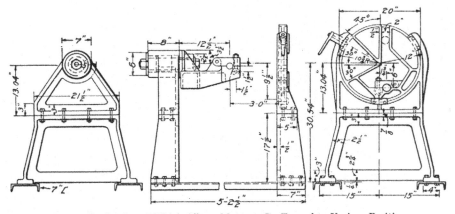

Fig. 10. Engine Stand Which Allows Motor to Be Turned to Various Positions

any desired angle and fastened there. Such a stand is shown in Fig. 10. It is made by the International Motor Company, Plainfield,

New Jersey, for its own use. It would hardly pay to make one of these, as the ends are castings which require a pattern, but if a couple of garages wanting, say two each, would go in together, it would pay to have patterns made for the four. After making castings for their own frames, the garage owners could later make them for sale if they wanted to go into the business. The sketch explains the construction, but this explanation might be added: the central part, projecting from the left-hand member is attached to the rear crank-case arms, and when the engine is turned, this turns with it. The

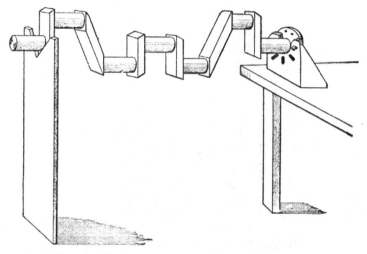

Fig. 11. Set-Up for Supporting Crankshafts out of Motor

central rotating member on the upper part of the right-hand unit is made to take the starting crankshaft, and the clamp at the upper left is to lock it in the desired position. Eight holes are provided, but a person making one could have as many as he wished, since they are drilled. As will be noted, there are six pieces, but the two bases are made from the same pattern, so five patterns are all that would be needed.

Holding the Crankshaft. When the shaft has been removed from the engine and work is to be done upon it, it is an awkward thing to handle. It is just delicate enough so that it cannot be handled carelessly, yet its size and weight make it difficult to move around. Thus, in lapping the shaft pins, in fitting connecting-rod bearings, or doing other work upon it, a support which is simple, easily moved around, yet adequate, is needed. Ordinarily a shaft is clamped in a vise, but this is not always satisfactory when working on an end bearing. The method shown in Fig. 11 has many advantages. This consists of a special bench fixture and a notched board. The latter should be at least 1-inch stock, that is, it should be $\frac{7}{8}$-inch when dressed on both sides. The former is simply a metal angle with a series of radial slots to take the flywheel bolts, with a

Fig. 12. Dogs for Use in Turning Four-Cylinder Crankshafts

central hole for the shaft to rest in. The metal above the hole is well cut away to facilitate putting the shaft in and taking it out.

Handling Shaft in Machines. When the crankshaft is to be machined, no matter what the form of lathe, grinder, or other machine, the fact that the pins are eccentric necessitates a special dog or jig for holding it. If an ordinary flange is bolted on the end, the main pins can be turned, smoothed down, or ground, but the crankpins cannot. What these latter need is a form of flange or plate with two exact centers on either side of the central one at distances exactly equal to the crank throw. One is shown in Fig. 12, which is attached to a four-cylinder shaft all ready for the machine and above it is another shaft without machining flanges. The bolts which attach the flanges to the shaft can be seen beyond

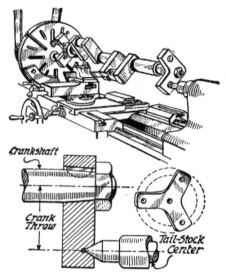

Fig. 13. Fixture and Lathe Jig for Turning Six-Cylinder Crankshafts

the right-hand flange and at the far end. The rack in the background, on which these shafts are placed, is of interest also, forming, as it does, a simple and efficient means of holding the shafts, yet it is convertible for holding other parts or units. It is simply a stout form of horse, rather high, and with three legs instead of the usual two. The braces are all put on the inside to leave the surface clear, while the supporting pins differ only in length. In this case they have been made long enough and strong enough to hold two or three shafts at once. In this way, the one horse can hold some 48 shafts at once.

Handling Three-Throw Shafts. The rigging just described is for four-cylinder shafts only, as these have the throws all in one plane, so that, although three different centers are required, they lie in one straight line, and the flange can be very simple for this reason. With a six-cylinder shaft, on the other hand, this is not the case; and a much larger flange is needed, for the three pin centers are spread out fan-like around the main bearing center. A form is shown in Fig. 13, which can be used for a shaft of this general type, although the one shown in the lathe provides for two pins only, not for three. For a six-cylinder engine of ordinary crankshaft construction, this would have to be like the triangular sketch at the lower right, if it is carried out on the same plan; or with the same

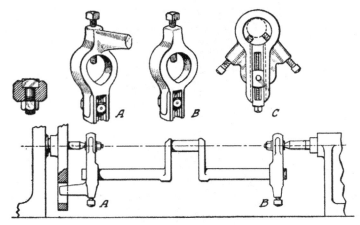

Fig. 14. Dogs with Adjustable Centers for Handling Crankshafts

bearing and pin centers, and a round outline as shown by the dotted line, if there was no necessity for saving metal.

Adjustable Crankshaft Flanges. In the small shop the general run of work varies so much that the principal difficulty lies in having flanges, dogs, or fixtures for handling the variety of crankshafts that come in. Diameters vary so much that a wide range of central holes is needed, because throws are all different. This gives a different center to center distance; then, too, there are still one- and two-throw, and other old forms of shafts in use, which come in occasionally for repairs. For these reasons, it is not wise for the small shop to go too far into special crankshaft fixtures; it should stick to simple dogs, with adjustable center distances, like the three shown in Fig. 14. While the shaft indicated is a single-cylinder form, dogs of this type can be used on other forms. This constitutes their biggest advantage. The variation in the three is self-explanatory to any machinist.

Bearings cannot be fitted correctly to a shaft unless the shaft is perfectly round and parallel. That is why a shaft should always be tested before any attempt is made to fit a bearing to it. Not only should the crankshaft bearings be tested for wear but the shaft should be tested for bend or twist. In testing, the shaft should be put in a lathe and revolved. Place a surface gage pointer close to the shaft. If the shaft is bent, the pointer will touch the shaft on one side but not on the other. A dial indicator will show by the

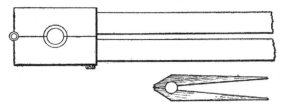

Fig. 15. Lapping Fixture of Simple Construction
for Crankshaft Pins

fluctuation of the needle how much the shaft is out of line. A bent or twisted crankshaft will not allow a good fitting bearing to be tight in one position and loose in another. It will also cause a knock in the engine.

Crankshaft Lapping. The pins of a crankshaft need lapping the same as other pins where a grinding machine is not available. There are two ways of doing this: by hand, which is slower but more simple so far as apparatus is concerned; and by machine, which requires special fittings for this purpose. In the sketch, Fig. 15, a form of hand lapper is shown. This consists of a pair of hinged members, with a central hole large enough to take various sizes of bushings such as would be required on different shafts. A long handle is provided; also a bolt to hold the two halves together when the bushing has been inserted. The babbitt bushing must be split and have end flanges to hold the halves in place sideways. The handle gives leverage for working the tool, which is made effective by the application of fine emery and oil on the pins to be lapped. In the same way, the pins are polished by means of a pair of long wooden clamps, Fig. 15, and made in somewhat the same way. There is a hinge at the back; and the abrasive used is fine emery cloth, which is flooded with oil.

The throws on the crankshaft can be lapped in the lathe by putting it between centers for the main bearings and by using a special flange for the other pins. A method which can be used is shown in Fig. 16. This consists of a special fixture, made from a

Fig. 16. Lathe Set-Up for Lapping Crankshaft Pins

large casting with a base to fasten to the face plate; a long extension arm, having a split end for attaching and detaching, to encircle the throw to be lapped. When this is used, the shaft is supported in V-blocks, somewhat flexibly it is true, but sufficiently.

Crankshaft Bearings. The bearings of the crankshaft in the crankcase do not differ materially from the connecting-rod bearings previously described. They may be a little longer, but the type is the same. They are pinned or otherwise fastened in the crankcase so as not to rotate, while the connecting-rod bearings are fastened in the connecting rods so as to rotate with them. A few shafts will be met which have ball or roller bearings, but the great majority have the split bronze-backed, babbitt-faced bearing described for connecting rods.

Crankshaft Bearing Shims. Practically all split or two-piece bearings for either crankshafts or connecting rods are assembled in place with shims. These are very thin flat pieces of metal set between the two halves of the bearing when it is assembled new to spread it apart. The shaft bearings are scraped to an exact fit on the pins with these shims or expanders in place. Then when wear occurs in the bearing, so that its inside diameter is enlarged, the bolts may be taken out, a shim or shims of the required thickness removed, and the bolts put back and tightened. This removal reduces the diameter of the inside of the bearing. To facilitate this action, the shims are generally put in so as to allow taking out a number of thousandths of an inch, there being two shims of $\frac{1}{1000}$, two or more of $\frac{2}{1000}$, possibly one of $\frac{5}{1000}$, and a thicker one, or more of the very thin ones. These shims enable the taking-up of wear amounting to $\frac{1}{1000}$ of an inch, when one of the thinnest shims is removed; $\frac{2}{1000}$ by removing one of that thickness; $\frac{3}{1000}$ by removing a $\frac{1}{1000}$ and a $\frac{2}{1000}$; $\frac{4}{1000}$ by taking two 2's, etc.

Of course, a crankshaft bearing or a connecting-rod bearing will not wear entirely round, but the work of adjusting either bearing is reduced to a minimum by the use of shims. When the wear is very bad, the bearings should be re-fitted and the shims left out.

An entirely new form is the laminated shim. The total thickness required is built up of very thin laminations, either one or two thousandths of an inch thick, so that in adjusting a bearing as many laminations are peeled off as are necessary to take up the wear, then the original shim, slightly lessened in thickness, is replaced.

In Fig. 3, the end view shows both connecting-rod and crankshaft bearing shims in place, and indicates how they perform their function of holding the halves of the bearing apart when the bearing is being fitted.

BEARING TROUBLES AND REMEDIES

Bearings. Bearings of the two-piece, or split, type give the auto repair man fully as much trouble as anything, in fact, the crankshaft bearings should not be tackled until considerable repair experience has been had. In general, wear on the bearings is due to one of two causes: either to a soft metal which has caused vertical wear on the inside or outside of the lower half of the bushing, or to a vibrating shaft which has worn an oval hole somewhere in the length of the shaft, as at the inner or outer end.

In the former case, the height of the worn half must be reduced. This is usually done by taking as much metal from the upper face as is necessary. When this has been done—either by filing or by rubbing across emery cloth wet with oil—the two halves of the bushing will approach so close together that the hole will be smaller than the

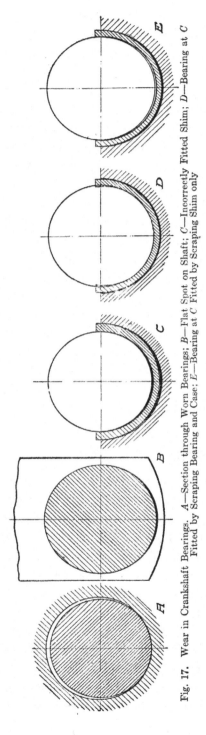

Fig. 17. Wear in Crankshaft Bearings. A—Section through Worn Bearings; B—Flat Spot on Shaft; C—Incorrectly Fitted Shim; D—Bearing at C Fitted by Scraping Bearing and Case; E—Bearing at C Fitted by Scraping Shim only

shaft. This will necessitate scraping out, or reboring, according to the amount which has been taken off. In the case of very small amounts, this wear can be taken up by removing shims, as mentioned above.

When the second form of wear is found, that is, when the bushing is worn oval by a wobbling shaft end, the only remedy is to bring the bearing halves together as before and rebore. It may be that this operation robs the bearing plates of so much metal that they will not fit the holes in the case; or possibly the wear may have communicated itself to the case, so that the hole there is out of true. If this be slight, refilling the cases with babbitt metal or building-up may be resorted to, but if the wear is considerable, a new set of bearings is the only remedy. In building up the bearing, strips of soft metal are placed in the worn spots, after cutting or filing them to fit as closely as possible, and the bearing driven down upon them as firmly as possible. In this way, it is often possible to build up a worn crankcase to answer for many thousand more miles running.

Bearing Wear. It is important to know how and why bearings wear. Normally, between the crankshaft bearing and the pin, there is a space of perhaps .002 inch divided into .001 inch all around, and this space is occupied by a film of lubricant. So long as this is the case, if the metal remains hard and does not give under the constant pounding, and the film of lubricant stays unbroken, it remains a perfect bearing. But the film does get broken or reduced, and the softer metal does give, so we have a condition shown at *A*, Fig. 17. Instead of a cylindrical pin centered in a cylindrical hole, one or the other is worn oval. This is usually the bearing, for the weight of the shaft, coupled with the pressure on it, keeps it at the bottom of the hole. The tendency is to increase this eccentricity. In this condition, the pin is running against the bearing metal at only one very limited surface, so all the pressure and all the wear are concentrated there. If the bearing is hard, or if a hard spot develops, the pin is likely to wear flat on the bottom side, as shown at *B*. When the bearing is fitted to the case, great care and accuracy are required, or an incorrect fitting, shown at *C*, is the result. Here the shim does not entirely fill the opening for it, and the bearing metal rests on the case at one point; on the shim at another; and does not touch either at a third. This is remedied by scraping both bearing and case, as shown at *D*, or the shim alone, as seen at *E*. In the former it will be noted how the full shim has raised the bearing so that its points project into the pin, where scraping will be needed. In the latter case scraping the bottom of the bearing will be necessary, as using a fully fitted shim has raised the center more than the sides.

Crankshaft Pounding. When the dull throbbing noise is found to come from within the crankcase, possibly between two of the bearings, this indicates a crankshaft or a connecting-rod pound. That is to say, either the rod is loose on the shaft or the shaft is loose in one of its bearings. Whenever the force of an explosion comes on the piston and drives it down, this looseness is taken up quickly, and a pounding noise is made. The loose rod may become disconnected and thrash around and, in so doing, wreck the crankcase; if the pound comes from the shaft, the bearing may continue to loosen and finally that part of the shaft become entirely free to thrash around. These troubles can be overcome by tightening the bearing caps.

Main Bearing Knock. If the engine had a distinct knock during each revolution, with a muffled sound similar to that of a block of wood striking the ground, it indicates main bearing trouble.

Holder for Bearing Caps. When a number of bearing caps have to be scraped, or filed down, it is worth while to make a holder for them. A plain form is shown in Fig. 18. This consists of a semi-circular piece of metal which fits into the hollow part of the bearing, with each end pivoted on two L=shaped members. The members are held tightly in the vise, and the tighter they are gripped the tighter the bearing cap is held. This jig holds the cap with the desired firmness, yet it leaves the whole upper surface free and clear so the workman can work at it readily and do a neat quick job of

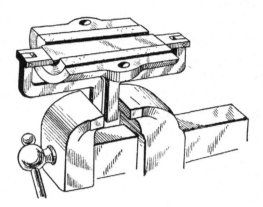

Fig. 18. Holding Fixture for Crankshaft
Bearing Caps

filing. The same layout is suitable for connecting-rod caps, except where they have an oil scoop or other central projection which interferes.

Handy Wrench. The form of the crankshaft-bearing cap and also of the connecting-rod bearing cap are such that no space is wasted. Very often the nut is so close to the cap that it is difficult to turn, unless the cap is taken out of the motor where the wrench can be applied at right angles. The use of the socket form of wrench, however, does not make it necessary to take the cap out of the motor. Aside from the socket wrench it is hard to get any other form of wrench to use on these nuts that is not so small and thin that it has no particular strength. In Fig. 19, a form is shown which has all the strength of the very stiffest forms, and yet it can be applied to these inaccessible nuts with ease. Moreover, its construction is such that it can be applied and used readily. It consists, as the sketch shows, of a solid socket wrench, as distinguished from the form made of tubing, and has part of one side of the socket cut away. This makes its quick application to the nuts easy, although it also limits the amount of turn possible. Generally the case nuts are different in size from the connecting-rod nuts; so it is advisable to make the wrench double ended with a size at one end for the rods, and one at the other end for the case.

Fitting Crankshaft Main Bearings. When the crankshaft is correct in every respect, the shaft should be placed in position and the caps bolted down tight for the initial fitting. Two things of importance should be noticed. (1) In engines where timing gears are

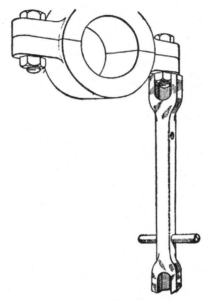

Fig. 19. Semi-Socket Wrench for Crankshaft Bearing Nuts

used, the meshing of the gears should be examined to see if there is enough play to allow for scraping or refitting of the bearings. The engine should be upside down so that the weight of the shaft will force it against the top half of the bearing. In this position, the amount of play between the gears can be easily seen. If there is not enough play, a shim must be placed back of the bearing, that is, between the case and the back of the bearing. (2) There should be no end play in the shaft. By end play is meant the movement of the shaft, from front to rear, or vice versa. If this condition exists in an engine, it will cause a knock.

The bearings should fit their holders tightly. If the bearings do not fit or are not held tightly in position, there will be a knock in the engine. The same method as that used for connecting rods may be used for fitting the main bearings to the case and cap.

Fitting Shims to the Bearing. There should be at least .005 inch play between the timing gears. This is immaterial when chains are used in the timing gear, but the fitting of the shim is just as important. The reason for the insertion of a shim between the bearing and holder is to give more material for refitting or scraping.

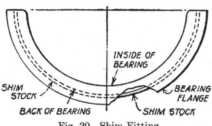

Fig. 20. Shim Fitting

The thickness of the shim would be governed by the amount of play in the bearings found on the initial fitting and the amount of play in the timing gears. The material used for shims should be governed by the amount of play in the timing gears. It should be sheet steel or sheet brass and can be purchased in different thicknesses from .002 inch to .015 inch, and from $1\frac{1}{2}$ inches to 3 inches wide. Paper should not be used to make shims for this work, for it compresses, especially when oil soaked; and it also holds the heat, which helps to break down the oil film.

After the desired thickness of shim stock has been found, the shim should be cut so that it covers the whole back of the bearing, as shown in Fig. 20. When the bearing is put into place this will draw in the edges of the bearing and insure the fitting of the bearing edges against the crankshaft. If the bearing does not fit all the way around the shaft, it will be found that there is an oil leak. This trouble often happens in the rear main bearing of an engine. It will also cause flooding of the engine with oil because it allows the oil to seep out of the ends of the bearing and to be thrown up into the cylinders by the webs of the shaft. This is especially noticeable in force feed lubricated shafts. The placing of this shim will raise the babbitt above the face of the holder and will necessitate the babbitt being filed down. A slight amount of the bearing may be allowed to stand above so that when the cap is bolted down it will force the bearing firmly into place. After the shim is fitted, the oil hole should be perfectly free from obstruction.

Taking Up Crankshaft End Play. On the crankshaft center or rear main bearing will be found flanges that rub against the flanges on the babbitt bearing and these in time wear so that it allows the shaft to have a lateral movement. There are two ways of curing this, either by the installation of a new bearing or by building up the flanges on the babbitt bearings. The method of building up the flanges is to drill $\frac{3}{16}$ inch holes as close together as possible in the flange. Make a thread in the holes and screw brass wire pegs into the threaded holes, Fig. 21. Dress the brass pegs until the bearing will go between the

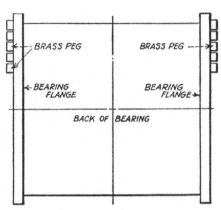

Fig. 21. Method of Taking Up End Play

webs of the crankshaft without any end play being evident. After the shims and end play have been corrected, the bearings should be fitted. Sometimes it is necessary to file the bearing caps to take up the play, just as in the case of the connecting rod. The same care should be taken in regard to the faces of the bearing cap. The faces should be true and square with each other.

Fitting Bearing by Alignment Reamer. The best, quickest, and cheapest way of fitting main bearings is to use an alignment reamer. This is the only way that a perfectly aligned bearing can be obtained. Figs. 22 and 23 show an alignment reamer in use, while Fig. 24 shows the different parts of the tool and reamer. The method of using the reamer is as follows: The caps, with the desired amount of shims between them, and the crankcase are bolted into place just as they would be if the shaft was in place. The diameter of the shaft should be obtained and the micrometer adjustment on the reamer set to the size of the shaft plus a certain amount for an oil film. The reamer bar should be passed through the bearings, and the threaded bushings, Fig. 25, should be put into position, Fig. 23. The reamer, Fig. 26, may then be fastened to the bar and the first bearing reamed. Remove the threaded bushing from the next bearing and insert in the reamed bearing which will support the bar while the next bearing is being reamed. This process is repeated for all the bearings. The type of reamer shown has an adjustment by which more metal can be taken off one side of the bearing than the other and is especially

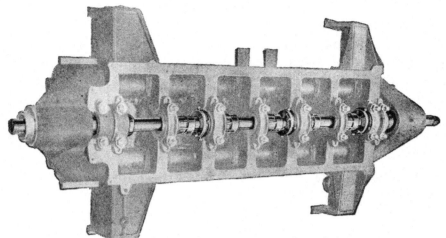

Fig. 22. Alignment Reaming of Seven-Bearing Crankshaft
Courtesy of Taft-Pierce Company

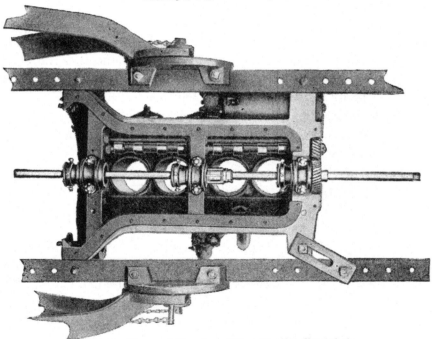

Fig. 23. Alignment Reaming of Three-Bearing Crankshaft
Courtesy of Taft-Pierce Company

useful where the meshing of timing gears must be taken into consideration.

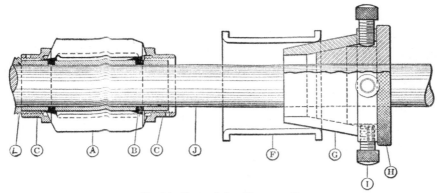

Fig. 24. Parts of the Alignment Reamer

A Reamer Cutter	F Bearing	I Adjusting Screw
B Adjustment Wedges	G Threaded Sleeve	J Reamer Bar
C Locking Nut	H Adjustable Bushing	L Thread Adjustment

Courtesy of Taft-Pierce Company

Fig. 25. Threaded Bushings
Courtesy of Taft-Pierce Company

This same method can be used when a new set of babbitt bearings have to be fitted. In the fitting of new bearings it is necessary to make new shims to go between the faces of the bearing. Obtain the diameter of the crankshaft and deduct the inside diameter of the bearing. Deduct the amount to be reamed out and the answer will be the thickness of the shims. For example:

Diameter of the crankshaft 2.875
Diameter of bearings............................. 2.800
                                                        .075

Amount to be reamed out .... .040
Proper thickness of the shim .... .035

The thickness of the shim that is placed behind the bearing shell, that is, between the bearing and the case, should be the same for each bearing.

Fitting the Bearing by Hand. Fitting main bearings by hand is complicated, tedious, and difficult unless a certain method is decided

Fig. 26. Reamer Head   Fig. 27. Marking Bearings
Courtesy of Taft-Pierce Company

upon and carried throughout the process. The best plan is to fit the shaft to the rear and front bearings. Use them as a guide to fit the rest of the bearings. After the bearings have been shimed, the shaft should be covered with the marking medium, put into the bearings, and revolved, Fig. 27. The marking shows the points at which the shaft touches the bearings. The marks should be cut away from both the front and rear bearings at the same time and this process repeated until the shaft touches both bearings at all points. This is called "bedding in" the bearing. The other bearings should not be in place while this is being done. After the front and rear bearings have been bedded in, the center main bearing may then be put into the holder and the shaft bedded into it, without touching the bearings already fitted. When the marks show all over the center bearing, the other bearings may be put in place and fitted the usual way.

After the shaft has been bedded into the top half of the bearings, that is the part that is in the crankcase, the caps should be placed into position and bolted down. The front and rear caps should be fitted first and for preference the rear should be the first to be scraped in. The same method is used for scraping as used in the case of the connecting rod. The shaft should be covered with a thin layer of the marking and the spots cut away from the bearing surface which are shown when the shaft is revolved in the bearings and which indicate the high spots. After the front and rear caps have been fitted,

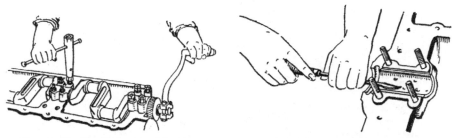

Fig. 28.   Testing Tightness of Bearings   Fig. 29.   Scraping Bearings

the center one should be fitted next, and the other caps in any order that may suit. The reason that it should be done in this way is in order that the bearings that are the most important may act as a guide for the alignment of the rest. After the caps have been fitted, they should be tightened down evenly and the shaft rotated, Fig. 28, for a number of times. The caps should be removed and the shaft taken out of the case and the high spots lightly cut away, Fig. 29, in both the case-half of the bearing and in the cap. This process is called "spotting in".

In fitting main bearings there should be about .001 inch play all around the bearing for an oil film, especially where force feed lubrication is used. It is not good practice to tighten up a bearing so that the automobile must be towed to get the engine to break away and start. The oil film between the surfaces of the bearing will give lubrication immediately and prevent any wear or heating of the metal bearing; whereas, if the bearing is made very tight, a certain amount of metal must be removed before the oil can get i between the surfaces and lubricate the bearing. To test the bearing clearance of play proceed as follows: Cut a piece of thin stock about $\frac{1}{4}$ inch wide and a little shorter than the length of the bearing, and .002 inch thick. Lay it in the bottom of the bearing and bolt the cap into position. If the shaft can be rotated with this strip in position, the bearing is not tight enough. It has been found that a newly fitted bearing has a tendency to stick even when oil is on the bearing. If a little powdered graphite is mixed with the oil, that is, put on

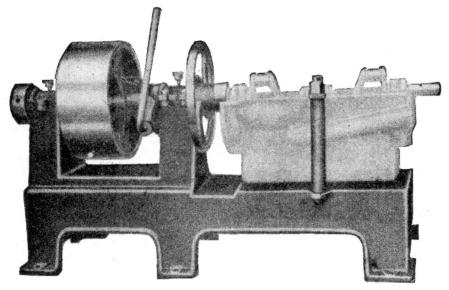

Fig. 30. "Burning In" Machine

the bearing at the time of assembling the bearing and shaft after overhauling it, it will give a better lubrication and reduce the tendency to stick. There is a compound sold which is excellent for this purpose. It is composed of oil mixed with finely ground graphite which does not leave any sediment in the oil. A little of this compound put in the oil makes an excellent lubricant and prevents bearing seizure which sometimes takes place in a newly fitted bearing.

"Burning In" Bearings. The process of fitting a bearing by the "burning in" method is not to be recommended where a well fitted and resilient bearing is desired. The heat generated in the bearing during the process often destroys the virtue in the babbitt metal and causes it to granulate and crystallize; and, moreover, if the crankshaft is not in perfect alignment with the burning machine, the bearings will not have a good bearing with all the bearings in line. The very fact that a bearing is pulled up tightly in order to wear in the bearing quickly, throws a twisting strain on the crankshaft that is not good for the shaft. As this method is used a great deal, a description of it is given. The shaft is fitted to the bearings in the usual way but no attention is paid to spotting in. The shaft is attached to the "burning in" machine, Fig. 30. The bearings are not flooded with oil while the shaft is being revolved under power, either by a belt or directly coupled to an electric motor. The babbitt metal is caused to flow and form itself to the shaft and the bearing is thus formed. The shaft should be in perfect alignment with the "burning in" machine because there is sometimes a little difference in the height of the cylinder block, and this will throw the shaft out sufficiently to cause a poor bearing to be made. The centers of the two shafts should be exactly level and parallel, and the block should not tilt or the shaft will be bent when the block is bolted on.

After any kind of work has been done on the bearings of an engine, all oil ways and channels should be cleaned so that no chips or grit remain to block the passage of the oil or score the bearings. Compressed air is excellent for this purpose. Be certain that all grooves in the babbitt bearing are deep enough to carry the oil properly. Be sure that all cotter pins are in the places allowed for them before assembling, and that all nuts are tight and properly locked in place on all bearing studs and bolts. If in tightening, any of the nuts show signs of striping, put in new bolts, studs, and nuts.

PACKARD SIX-CYLINDER MARINE MOTOR

CRANKCASES

Function of Crankcase. The lower part of the motor car, truck, or tractor engine is generally enclosed for the purpose of assisting the circulation of the lubricant, and for keeping the dirt and dust out. This enclosure is called the crankcase, and covers the crankshaft, the connecting rods, the bearings for both, and the lubricating system and lubricant reservoir. In general, the crankcase forms the support for the entire engine, as arms extend from it for this purpose. It also supports the cylinders upon its upper face or faces, and the crankshaft bearings upon inner integrally cast bosses. This is worded in this way, for formerly many marine engine cylinders, and even today, all high-powered marine engine cylinders are set upon posts and the sides between the cylinders and crankshaft left entirely open.

The crankcase also has suitable housing in its interior for camshaft bearings and for flanges or brackets for the attachment of accessories such as the starting and lighting equipment on the outside of the case. In general, the length and size of the crankcase depends upon the length of the crankshaft, the piston stroke, and the connecting rod.

Crankcase Construction. In designing the case, the engineer must take into consideration the many stresses and strains that the case is subjected to in service. Not only does the case have to stand the twisting or weaving of the frame but it also must withstand pressure when the explosion takes place in the cylinder, which is a pulling strain on the bolts and studs that hold the cylinders in place on the case. The flanges to which the cylinders are bolted should be of ample thickness. The thread in the case should not be depended upon to hold the cylinder. A lock nut should be used to give additional strength to the case and stud.

Most crankcases are split longitudinally along the center line of the crankshaft. The upper half supports the cylinder and crankshaft and the weight of the engine on the chassis frame, and also has proper provision for the support of the various accessories upon it. The lower half, in such cases, is formed as a simple enclosing pan, with oil reservoir in the bottom. When the lubricant is circulated by pump, this is generally attached to the lower half of the crankcase, either inside or outside.

A section through a modern crankcase is shown in Fig. 1, which illustrates a twelve-cylinder motor. Note the inclined upper surfaces of the upper half to which the cylinders are bolted and the stiffening rib at the center line where the two halves meet. Note also how the lower half is simply an enclosure, carrying only the oil strainer (shown) and the oil pump (not shown). It has cooling fins cast on its lower surface to keep the temperature of the oil down. The shelf, which is cast on the upper half to close the space between

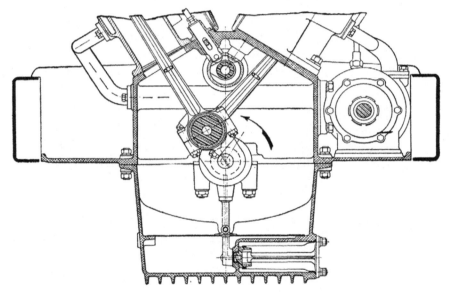

Fig. 1. Section through Crankcase of Box Type for Twelve-Cylinder
V-Type Packard Motor

the sides of the crankcase and the chassis frame, serves the double purpose of a protecting pan to keep out road dirt and water and of a supporting shelf for accessories. Fig. 2 shows the same engine from the front.

Crankcases are made mostly in two forms: the box type, which has more or less straight sides, with a flat top and bottom; and the barrel type, which is round or a modified round with a flat bottom and top. The one shown is of the box type; the barrel type is generally not split along the center line, but it has removable end plates which allow the insertion of the crankshaft and a very simple bottom plate which carries the oil supply. The one-piece type is supposed to give greater rigidity, but this is at the expense of accessibility.

Modern Tendencies in Design. There are two modern tendencies shaping toward a modification of, or the entire elimination of,

Fig. 2. Assembled Motor Shown in Section in Fig. **1**
Courtesy of Packard Motor Car Company, Detroit, Michigan

the lower half of the crankcase as it is now known. One is the minimizing of its functions, so it can be made of pressed steel, when it becomes a cover only, and the oiling system is made so that the supply is carried elsewhere. The other is the casting of parts of the crankcase integrally with the cylinders. This has been done successfully with the Marmon, the Ford, and with others, in which the cylinder block and the upper half of the crankcase are cast as one. If this casting is considered as a cylinder unit, there is no upper half of crankcase. By extending this practice a little further, the lower half may be combined with the cylinder block and upper half, so that the crankcase as we know it now would cease to exist.

All these combinations save weight and reduce cost. They also reduce the number of parts and make the car as a whole more simple. In some cases they go hand in hand with large production, as the pressed steel lower half of the crankcase calls for a big expenditure for dies. On the other hand, they make the repair man's work greater. As, for instance, when the cylinders are combined with the crankcase, it is an all day's job to take out a piston and replace it. When the cylinders are separate, cast in pairs, or bolted on, a piston can be taken out and replaced in a couple of hours.

While lightness is a big asset, the matter of strength is also important and should not be sacrificed too much for the former. The crankshaft must have adequate support through its bearings or the shaft will be influenced greatly by the twist and distortion of the frame and case. If the support is not adequate, the bearing can easily get out of alignment, which causes difficulty in correctly fitting main bearings to the case or shaft. The places in which the bearings are placed should be well ribbed to give the strength and support required. At the point where the rib is attached to the bearing holder and case, there should be a fillet of metal which will help prevent breakage at those points.

Crankcase Materials. It is important that the repair man should know the materials of which both upper and lower halves of the crankcase and the gear cover are composed, for these may need repairing. In general, crankcases are of aluminum alloy, the exact composition varying. When this is the material, the gear cover is of aluminum alloy also. A few crankcases are made of cast iron, on very low priced cars. Others have the pressed-steel oil pan, previously mentioned. A few high-grade cars have bronze crankcases which are made of either government bronze or vanadium bronze.

Crankcase Arms and Engine Supports. The engine is generally supported by crankcase arms extended from the sides or ends of the upper half of the crankcase and cast integrally. However, this is not always the case. In many unit power plants, the rear pair of supporting arms may be fixed to the flywheel housing or to the transmission case. This may be done to allow the engine freedom of slight rotation and relieving it of twisting due to road inequalities;

it may be done because of lack of confidence in the strength of the crankcase material as an engine support; it may be done to facilitate foundry work on the crankcase, and thus reduce its cost. Separate supporting members bolted or hinged in place may be used. These are heavy steel forgings, stout bronze castings, or heavy gage steel tubing. In taking out an engine, the repair man should find out about this, as it may simplify or complicate the removal.

Three-Point Suspension. There is a great deal of distortion given to the automobile frame which, in turn, is passed to the engine through its supporting arms or attachments. If there is no way of allowing for this distortion, there would be a great strain thrown on the engine and its shafts. It would cause the bearings to suddenly pinch or clamp the shaft tight. This would give a twisting tendency and also throw a heavier driving strain on the shaft.

The most popular method used to allow for these twisting strains is the "three-point suspension" in which the rear engine supports are attached rigidly to the frame and the front support is allowed to move in a bracket or swivel. In this way the frame can move on the front pivot without throwing any strain on the shaft or case. A variation of the above method is found in the latest Maxwell installation in which the rear supports are of the swivel type and the front support is on a spring. It is claimed in this type of installation that the vibration natural to a four-cylinder engine is not felt at all.

Breather Pipes. The reciprocating movements of the piston in the cylinder tend to create a compression in the crankcase. If there is no opening to relieve this compression, the oil will be forced out of the crankcase through the attachments and the crankcase joints. The leakage of gas past the piston is another cause of increased pressure and it must be allowed to escape. There are several methods for allowing the air to escape, but the following two are important: (1) holes in the valve covers, and (2) the installation of a breather that is incorporated with the filler through which the oil is poured into the crankcase. The breather should be placed so that the oil that is splashed by the connecting rods is not carried out with the air.

Gear Cases or Gear Covers. At the front end of the great majority of engines, the gears which determine the working of the engine and its accessories are placed. These may include the crankshaft driving gear and any or all of the following driven gears: camshaft gear, magneto gear, water-pump gear, lighting-generator gear, oil-pump gear, and sometimes fan gear and air-pump gear. These may be driven directly by gear contact or by means of silent chains. In either case the gears are enclosed by a case or cover, variously called the gear case, gear cover, or cam-gear cover. This housing is generally simple in shape and is bolted in place with as few bolts as possible in the lower half of the crankcase in order to facilitate its removal for crankshaft or other bearing inspection or for repair.

TROUBLES AND REMEDIES

General Nature of Troubles. The most general crankcase trouble, aside from bearing trouble, is breakage. The usual bearing troubles require in their handling much special apparatus, such as stands, jigs, fixtures, and tools, which can be developed by the ingenious repair man. Worn main bearings cause a knock. If this comes from any one bearing, it can usually be traced quickly. The use of the stethoscope is recommended for any crankcase or gear-cover noises or troubles. A squeak from any part of the crankcase usually means a lack of oil or the rubbing of parts which should not rub.

The bolts that hold the engine to the frame should be kept tight at all times or they will allow the engine to move and perhaps result in a broken engine support. A knock that occurs in an engine can sometimes be traced to loose engine bolts, allowing the engine to move up and down on the bolt or support. If the front bracket is loose, it will often give a knock that is like a main bearing knock. A squeak in an engine can also be traced to the engine support rubbing against the bracket. This noise would be noticed most when driving over bumpy roads.

Mending Breaks. If the case is of aluminum, it should be watched carefully for breaks or cracks. If a crack develops, it should be drilled, plugged, and welded, as cylinder water jackets. This will prevent the crack from spreading. Any fairly large break means either undue stress or a weakness in the metal. The latter can be remedied by patching, by building up in the welding operation, or by the use of a new part. The repair man who is in doubt about his ability to repair a break or crack should always consult a welding expert, for welding can be done, and is being done daily, which would astonish those unfamiliar with the scope of the process. Moreover, it is relatively inexpensive. Quite often, a weld which would not cost more than $4 or $5, can be made the same day even by a fairly busy shop; otherwise it would mean a new case at a cost of perhaps 10 or 12 times as much, two weeks' delay or longer for delivery of the order, and the additional time and delay of detaching all the old accessories and fittings from the old case and re-attaching them to the new case.

Cleaning Aluminum. Aluminum can be cleaned externally by means of a weak sulphuric-acid solution, say not more than 10 per

Fig. 3.   Method of Boring Crankcase Bearings with Special Boring Bar
Courtesy of Pierce-Arrow Motor Car Company, Buffalo, New York

cent sulphuric acid. This should be well scrubbed into the surface with a stiff brush, then washed off with water. Care should be taken to wash well enough and long enough to remove all the acid. Moreover, it should be kept from clothes or from any wood parts, as it is strong enough to attack fabrics and wood.

Machining Crankcases. Generally speaking, the repair man will not be called upon to do any machining on crankcases beyond something like chipping or filing, or in the case of a break, patching or welding. But in case such a job should come along, it is important to know how to handle it, for there is no more important crankcase job than the machining of the main bearings. The necessity here is to keep them in perfect alignment, and this necessitates machining all of them at once with a long boring bar, as shown in Fig. 3. The method of support upon the flat upper, or cylinder, face will be noted, also the holding down blocks bolted to the table of the machine, after being bolted to the cylinder studs. The provision for lubricant on each one of the boring cutters will be seen in the small copper pipes above and at the back. As the average shop does not have a boring tool of this kind, this work will have to be approximated. It could be done by hand, using the now well-known Martell aligning reamer, to ream the bearings out and put in new and larger bushings. This also has a series of cutters, much like the boring bar shown, and is actuated by hand. So the principal requisite would be a large flat surface on which to work. Possibly this will be found at the drill-press platen, the planer table, or the working table of whatever large machine tool the shop possesses. Unless the case is held firmly throughout, it is likely to give or spring, and this will spoil the whole job, no matter how good it may be otherwise.

In all crankcase repairs, the repair man should remember that the case is really the foundation of the engine, and if it is not firm of itself and firmly supported, the action of the engine cannot be positive nor continuous. Consequently the case should be handled with unusual care. Gear-cover troubles are few and far between, consisting mostly of breaks or trouble inside the cover with gears or driving chains. Usually, too, gear-cover lubrication is automatic, that is, one end of the crankshaft and crankcase-bearing lubrication system is continued forward to the gear cover, so that it gets all the surplus oil. In this way lubrication is cared for automatically, but the repair man should take no chances on this with cars under his care. He should remove the gear cover occasionally for inspection. Gear noises, too, emanate from the timing gears and are often due to a lack of lubricant there, or, to not enough thick lubricant to deaden the sound. Sometimes the construction of a gear causes a ringing noise, according to the form of construction used. Often whirring noises from the gear case are caused by burred teeth. The repair man can remove the burr with a file. Sometimes a chip of metal will get in between two gears and be pressed into the softer of the two; from that time on, it will cause noise continuously, and will also cut the other gear.

GASOLINE AUTOMOBILES

LUBRICATION

The purpose of lubrication is to prevent friction between two surfaces that slide or roll over each other, and a film of oil should be kept between these two surfaces. The oil used as a lubricating medium in the automobile engine should be one whose film is not easily broken down under heat generated in the bearing and it should not be greatly affected by cold weather.

Crankcase Dilution. The fuels that are in use today contain a great deal of heavy distillate which does not burn when combustion takes place in the cylinder. These distillates flow past the piston and piston rings into the crankcase and dilute the oil until it becomes so thin that there is hardly any oil film between the bearing surfaces. This is termed "crankcase dilution" and is one of the chief causes why the oil should be changed in the crankcase of an automobile engine at least every 500 miles.

A certain amount of grit is bound to get into the crankcase, mix with the oil, and circulate. It will cause wear on the crankshaft as well as on the bearings and cylinder walls. The act of combustion generates moisture and a certain amount of this also passes down into the crankcase and a certain amount of condensation occurs. This moisture mixes with the oil and forms an emulsion which destroys the lubricating property of the oil and therefore the bearings and other parts are not lubricated properly. A thick slimy sludge, caused by the mixture of grit dust and carbon particles will form on the inside walls of the crankcase. This sludge is a great detriment to the lubricating system and the case should be washed out thoroughly.

The inside of the crankcase will be cleaner the more often the oil is changed, and the life of the engine will be longer, its operation smoother, and the visits to the repair shop less frequent. The oil should be changed when the engine is warm, after the car has finished a long run. The oil will flow freely and run out of the case easily and at the same time wash out any grit or foreign substance that may be in the crankcase. Oil that is recommended by the manufacturer of the car should be used when possible.

If the oil becomes thin in a very short time, the adjustment of the carburetor should be looked over and corrected. In vacuum-feed systems the valve mechanisms may go wrong and allow gasoline to be drawn into the intake manifold in its raw state and pass down into the case, causing the oil to thin out very rapidly. Where a great deal of emulsion is found, water leaks should be looked for. These are usually found at the header gasket between the cylinder top and the removable cylinder head.

There are two or three manufacturers of automobiles who are installing, as standard equipment, some device which purifies the

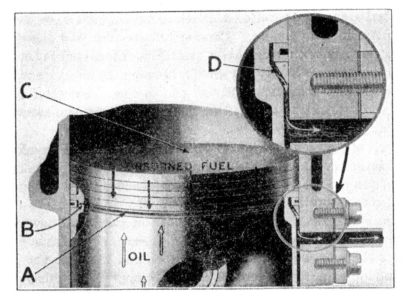

Fig. 3-a. Skinner Oil Rectifier
Courtesy of Skinner Automotive Device Company, Inc., Detroit

oil while it is in circulation. One method is to draw the gasoline from around the pistons by a vacuum, and the other is to pass it through a specially made filter.

The oil and gasoline mixture, which is drawn from around the pistons, is made to pass over or near a heated surface, which vaporizes the gasoline, which is again introduced into the intake system. The oil is allowed to cool and is then passed back into the crankcase. Fig. 3-a shows a piston with a groove behind the lower piston rings from which the oil and gasoline is drawn. The groove is marked *B* and *A* is the hole in the piston ring through which the oil and gasoline is drawn. This installation saves gasoline and also insures a good oil film for the engine bearings, because it prevents crankcase dilution.

The filter method takes out the grit particles from the oil by passing the oil over some cotton-like material which removes the foreign matter in the oil. The filter material can be renewed and will last at least one year before it needs replacing.

Interior and Exterior Demands. The engine of a motor car requires two distinct kinds of lubrication. The interior parts, which are subjected to the greatest heat, rotate or slide at the highest rate of speed, and generally do the greatest amount of work, must have what amounts to a continuous stream of good lubricant. With the exterior parts, which do not rotate so fast, do less work, are not subjected to much heating, and will be kept cool by the atmosphere, there is no need for this continuous stream, nor for such a quantity or high quality of lubricant.

The exterior and interior systems must be considered separately. With reference to the internal oiling, there are two general systems in use: the pressure and the splash. A third system which is now coming rapidly into use is a combination of the two, called the splash-pressure system.

Splash Lubrication. The feeding of oil to bearing surfaces by the simple expedient of enclosing a quantity of it in a reservoir in which the working parts are also contained is a successful and widely used scheme in automobile motor construction.

In the splash lubrication system the lower ends of the connecting rods "splash" up the oil which is in the bottom of the crankcase in the form of a huge puddle. Since this method, formerly almost universal, has been criticised as wasteful of oil as well as productive of much needless smoke, it has been modified by the majority of makers so that the scoops on the ends of the connecting rods dip into small narrow troughs provided for this purpose. Another objection to this system is that at high speeds too little oil is thrown around the interior of the cylinders and crankcase, since the initial rotation of the rods has churned or beaten the entire supply into a mist, while at low speeds too much is thrown around for the work the engine is doing.

The latter objection has been overcome in the newer engines by making the troughs into which the connecting-rod scoops dip movable and attached to the throttle lever, so that when the latter is opened wide to develop maximum power, the troughs are brought up higher, allowing the scoops to dip down deeper and thus supply a greater amount of lubricant.

Splash=Pressure Feeding. One of the best and most successful types of lubrication systems is that in which the oil is fed under pressure to the different bearings.

In the splash-pressure system, the oil to all the crankshaft and connecting-rod bearings, to the timing gears, and to the upper portion of the cylinder walls is supplied through the medium of a

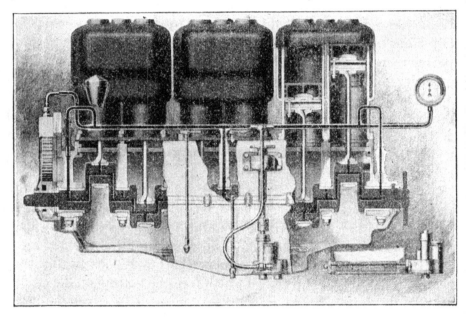

Fig. 4. Pressure-Feed Lubrication System on Pierce-Arrow Cars
Courtesy of Pierce-Arrow Motor Car Company, Buffalo, New York

gear-oil pump driven usually by worm gearing from the camshaft. The other bearings within the engine are lubricated by oil spray thrown from the crankshaft. Such a system is shown in Fig. 4.

Overland. The same units are necessary in all splash-pressure systems, but they can be and are used in widely different ways. It is of interest to the repair man to know the details of a number of these methods so as to be able to repair and adjust the mechanisms more readily, also to more quickly point out their troubles. One of the most simple systems in use is that of the Overland, Fig. 5. In this, the oil pump at the bottom of the oil sump A is driven from the camshaft rear end. After passing through the strainer B, the oil continues through an outside pipe to the sight feed C on the dash. This simply indicates that the system is working continuously. From here it passes back through the pipe D to the inner distributing pipe E; this serves to keep the troughs FF filled. At the middle part of the downward stroke, the scoop on the bottom of each connecting

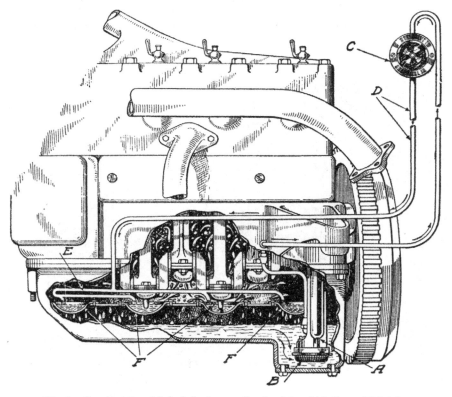

Fig. 5.   Constant Level Splash System on Overland, in which Pump Maintains
Oil Supply at Predetermined Level

rod dips into its own oil reservoir and splashes up a fine spray of oil. At high speeds, the four rods fill the whole interior of the crankcase and the lower parts of the four cylinders with a mist of oil. This is sufficient to lubricate everything thoroughly. In a system of this kind the strainer is of great importance and must be kept clean. Similarly, the oil sump should be drained very frequently—at least every 500 miles.

Studebaker. The Studebaker system is very similar, except that the oil pump is outside of the crankcase and set higher up. It is of the simple gear type and is not liable to derangement. The system is equipped with an oil-level indicator on the side of the case, which shows the quantity within the case.

Force=Pressure Feeding. The drilled crankshaft, as shown in Fig. 4, is a necessity in all pressure systems—as it also is in all combination splash-pressure systems. This can be seen and perhaps

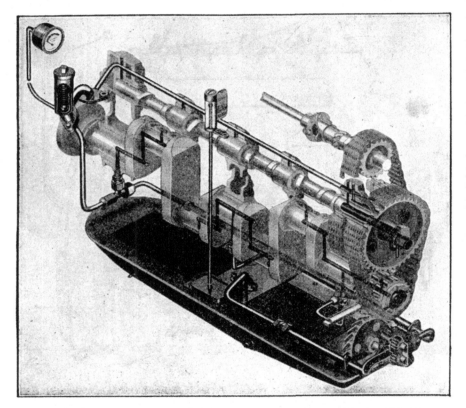

Fig. 6. Lubrication System of Cadillac Eight, Showing Pump and Path of Oil, Also Auxiliary Circuit for Crankshaft

the whole system explained more clearly by referring to Fig. 6. In this the single pump working direct is used. The oil is forced to flow through the three bearing leads to the interior of the crankshaft, whence it follows in to the pins upon which the connecting rods work. These rods are drilled, and the oil is thrown out by centrifugal force, passing up through the rods to the piston, thence onto the cylinder walls. In addition, the latter are sure to receive sufficient lubricant, for the rotating shaft and rods throw off a good deal in the form of a mist which settles upon the cylinder walls.

Generally pockets are provided inside the motor to catch the mist and force it to flow to the camshaft and other bearings besides

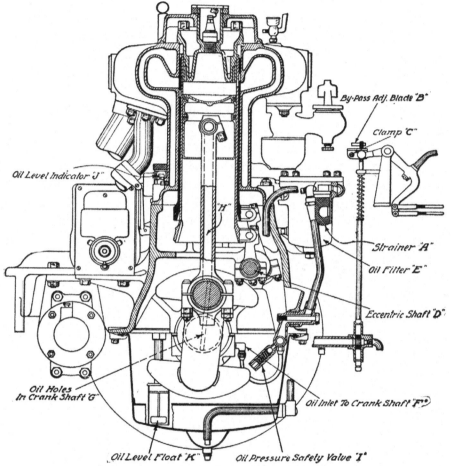

Fig. 7. Pressure Lubrication System Used on Stearns-Knight Motors
Courtesy of F. B. Stearns Company, Cleveland, Ohio

the crankshaft, but in this case it will be noted that the camshaft bearings have individual supplies through the medium of a camshaft oiling pipe.

An objection to lubricating systems of this type is that in case there are several leads to different bearings one of them may become

obstructed without anything to indicate this condition or to overcome it until the bearing involved becomes overheated and ruined.
If one lead becomes obstructed, the oil can still continue to feed out
through the others, thus relieving the pressure in apparently the
normal manner and failing to reveal a serious derangement.

Stearns. The Stearns-Knight system is shown in Fig. 7.
The oil is circulated by a pump (not visible in this sketch) at the
front end of the eccentric shaft D. After passing through a screen
and the pump, it is forced through a strainer A in the filter E, thence
through pipes to the pump-shaft bearings, eccentric-shaft chains,
and main crankshaft bearings. It reaches the crankshaft bearings
through the oil inlet F, the drilled holes in the crankshaft being indicated at G. From these holes, it reaches the hollow center of the
connecting rods H, and thus to the piston pins and piston outer walls.
At the bottom of each connecting rod there are three small radial
holes through which sufficient oil escapes to lubricate the inner and
outer sleeves which take the place of the valves. A gage on the dashboard, or cowl-board, indicates the oil pressure and should read from
1 to 5 pounds with the throttle closed and the motor idling, and from
40 to 60 pounds when the throttle is wide open and the motor running
normally or at high speed.

The variation on this pressure is controlled entirely by the
by-pass in the main oil lead, which is connected directly to the
throttle-control mechanism. This by-pass consists of a body with
an oil port and a piston with a series of holes. When the throttle is
closed, and the motor idling, these holes and port register, so oil
passes through freely, relieving the pressure on the bearings. When
the motor is speeded up and more oil is needed, the piston is turned
by the throttle connection so that the holes and ports no longer
register and the oil cannot escape as freely and must be forced through
to the bearings. This by-pass is adjustable by means of the small
blade B, Fig. 7, which is rotated from the center to right or left and
locked by the clamp bolt C. The safety valve I within the crankcase
is set at the factory for the maximum pressure to be used in the
system. If this is approximated, this valve is forced open and the
oil escapes back into the crankcase, thus lowering the pressure.
The oil-level indicator J is operated through the float K in the oil
well and indicates the quantity. In cleaning and replacing filter

screen *A*, be sure the holes register. The system used on the Stearns-Knight eight-cylinder V-type motor is essentially the same, with a few differences of location due to the form of engine.

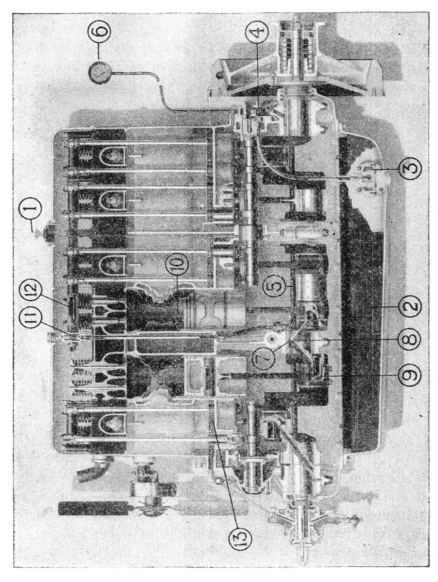

Fig. 8. Pressure System with Many Individual Features on Marmon Engine
Courtesy of Nordyke & Marmon Company, Indianapolis, Indiana

On high-speed and multi-cylinder motors (which are almost invariably high-speed forms), the lubrication assumes an importance not hitherto attached to it. This is responsible for the pressures used and for the wide spread use of mechanically driven positive pumps.

Formerly, pressures of from a few ounces to 4 or 5 pounds were considered sufficient. Now, pressures as high as 60 and 70 pounds are not unusual. These tremendous pressures, however, have necessitated a system much more carefully constructed, assembled, and used than was the case previously.

Marmon. The Marmon system is not radically different from that just described, but there are a number of small individual points worthy of mention. The filling is not through the usual crank-

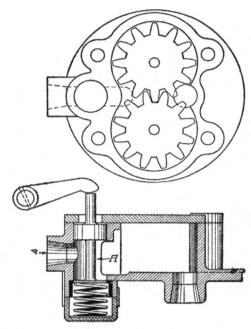

Fig. 9. Detail of Throttle-Connected Plunger
in Marmon Oil Pump

case breather pipe, but through an opening in the top of the cylinder head *1*, Fig. 8. From this opening the oil flows around the valve push rods down into the bottom of the oil pan *2*. After screening at *3*, it passes through the throttle-controlled regulator to the oil pump *4* on the rear end of the camshaft. The main feed pipe is marked *5*, the pressure gage *6*, lead to crankshaft bearings *7*, hollow in crankshaft *8*, connecting-rod bearing *9*, cylinder walls *10*, ball check valve *11*, which governs pressure in main feed pipe and excess oil through hollow rocker-arm shaft *12*, connecting to oil container *13* above valve tappets.

In Fig. 9, a detail of the regulator is shown. Oil enters the pump body from the left through the opening B. The passage from B to the gears is controlled by the opening in the plunger A, which is operated by the movement of the throttle lever through the small tappet seen on top. When the throttle lever is depressed, the plunger moves down, and its upper, or piston, portion closes off a portion of the oil hole, restricting the supply. The spring under its lower extension is used to return it to position. Its shape is such that the oil has no tendency to act upon it, either to open or close it. In this system the pressure varies from 12 to 60 pounds.

Oil Pumps. The expedient of feeding the oil by individual pumps, independently driven and capable of individual adjustment

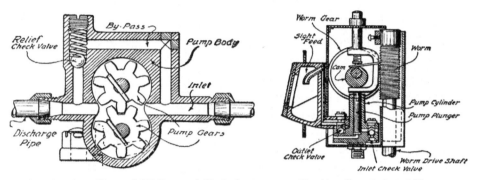

Fig. 10. Gear Type of Oil Pump of Marked Simplicity   Fig. 11.   Cam-Actuated Plunger Form of Oil Pump

which enables them to feed any desired amount of oil to any particular bearing regardless of the amount that may be fed to any other bearing, has been widely applied. In such a system, if obstruction of any one of the leads should occur, it is almost certain to be forced out by the action of the pump, which, in all lubricating systems of established type, is made capable of working against enormous pressure.

There are but three or four types of oil pumps now in use, these being the gear, plunger, plunger operated by a cam, and in a few cases the vane pump. While essentially the same as the forms used for pumping water, they are smaller in actual size and have some different details. In the gear form, Fig. 10, one gear is driven directly from the engine and, in turn, drives the other, their rotation forcing the oil along in the direction of rotation. Usually a by-pass with a check valve is provided, and when the pipe is obstructed or the pressure rises for any other reason, this opens and the oil passes around the pump at low pressure, equalizing the system.

The cam-operated plunger form, Fig. 11, is the method of drive adopted for mechanical lubricators, but few engines have an individually constructed pump of this type. It is simple, easy to regulate, seldom gets out of order, and can be arranged to give a different supply at each plunger should the system warrant or necessitate this. A good example of the plunger form is the oil pump on the Reo engine, Fig. 12, which works as follows: When the pump plunger A is moved upward by the curved eccentric B, it draws oil through the ports C and the screen D, as the entire lower part is submerged in the oil. When the maximum amount of oil is drawn into the pump chamber in this way, the plunger descends, the ball E rises, and the oil flows up inside the hollow plunger to the top ports F, through these to the surrounding chamber G, and thence to the outlet H and into the oil pipes. This form is very accurate and reliable.

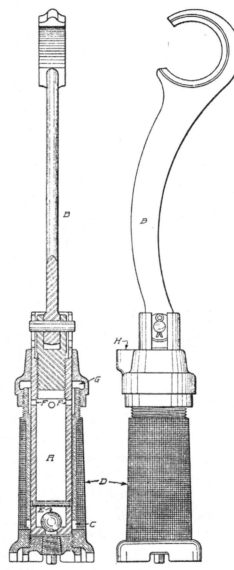

Fig. 12. Typical Plunger Pump
Courtesy of Reo Motor Car Company, Lansing, Michigan

Methods of Driving Pumps. Another point of considerable importance to the repair man is the method of driving the pump,

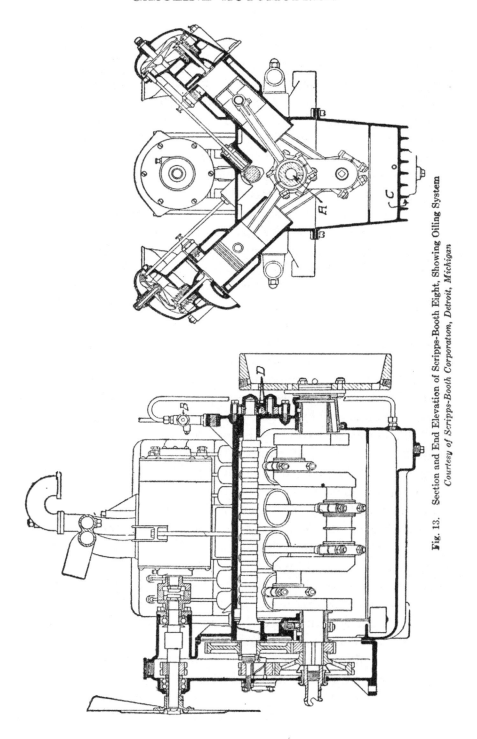

Fig. 13. Section and End Elevation of Scripps-Booth Eight, Showing Oiling System

Courtesy of Scripps-Booth Corporation, Detroit, Michigan

since this influences its location and its accessibility. There are but two general methods of driving. One is by means of a special oil-pump shaft, in which the pump will generally be found in the bottom of the oil sump or very close to it; the other is from some part of a shaft used for other purposes, in which case the position may vary widely. Examples of the first, or special-shaft method, will be seen in the Overland, Fig. 5, and Cadillac, Fig. 6. Examples of the second method are seen in the Stearns, Fig. 7, and the Marmon, Fig. 8, in both of which the camshaft is used.

In Fig. 13, a gear is placed directly upon the rear end of the camshaft meshing, with another immediately below it which forms the pump. This is the Scripps-Booth eight. Attention is called to these additional points, the hollow crankshaft for oil circulation at A, the method of carrying the oil leads and regulator up to a handy point on top of the motor at B, and the air cooling flanges on the bottom of the oil pan at C. The purpose of the latter is to reduce the temperature of the oil after it has been used and returned to the oil-supply reservoir and before it has been used a second time. The oil pump on the end of the camshaft is marked D.

In Fig. 14, the oil pump is a simple plunger operated by a cam on the camshaft. It projects out at right angles on the side between the second and third cylinders. It is possible to arrange a system of this kind so that an extra cam is not needed, one of the regular valve cams doing the work of pumping the oil. The oil suction pipe is marked B and the pipe carrying the supply to the bearings is marked C. Attention is called to the connecting-rod oil scoops D, the feed adjustment E, the pressure-relief valve F, and to the main oil lead G.

Lubricating the Whole Car. It is best for both the private owner and the repair man to have a definite regular system for going over the grease and oil cups on the chassis. As shown in Fig. 15, there are a number of cups varying from 30 to 32 and upward, as well as oil holes, which need to be looked after occasionally. The worker should get an oiling chart and fix firmly in his mind the requirements of the various parts to be oiled or greased and should regulate his oil and grease cups by hand from day to day and week to week so as to produce the desired results.

External Lubrication. In the lubrication of the external parts of the motor, such as the pump shaft, magneto shaft, oiler shaft, fan

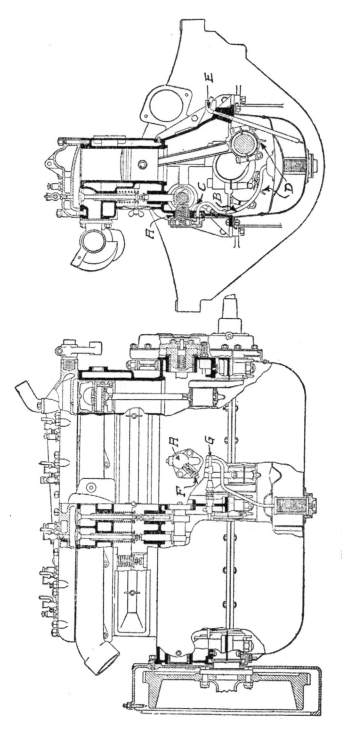

Fig. 14.   Side and End Sections of Engine with Horizontal Plunger Type of Oil Pump

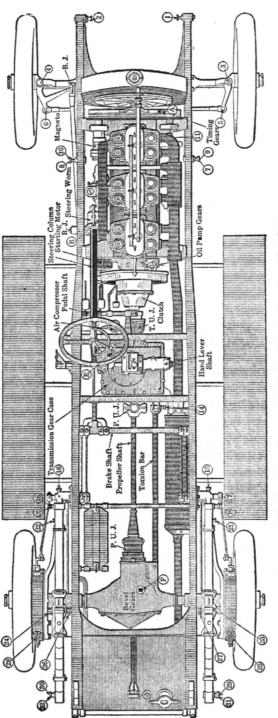

Fig. 15. View of Locomobile Chassis, Showing Complete Oiling System

Instructions as follows: Spring Grease Cups 1, 2, 7 to 10, 17 to 20, and 29 to 32 should be given full turn every day, and kept filled; Distance Rod Grease Cups 15, 16, 21, 22, 23, 24, 26 and 27 should be given a full turn every other day or once in 500 miles and kept filled; Steering Tie Rod and Steering Pivot Grease Cups 3 to 6 should be given full turn every day, and kept filled; Water Pump Grease Cup 11 should be turned down every day—special heavy mineral grease or beef or mutton tallow should be used in these: Torsion Bar Pivot Grease Cup 14 should be turned down once a week or every 1000 miles; Brake Shoe Supporting Bracket Oil Cups 25 and 28 should be turned down once a week; Engine Oiling System should be drained every 2000 miles and refilled through plug A; Steering Worm Gear Case should be filled with grease every 2000 miles through plug B: Oil-Pump Gear Housing should be packed with grease once a season through plug C; Transmission Case should have grease added, through plug E, every 2000 miles to bring supply up to proper level; Rear Axle Housing should be drained every 5000 miles and refilled with grease through plug F; Clutch Universal T. U. J. and Universal Joints P. U. J. should be packed with grease once a season; Generator, Starting Motor, Spark and Throttle Levers, Steering Column, Carburetor Regulating Collar, and Brake Shaft Equalizers should be oiled every 1000 miles; Magneto and Air Compressor should be oiled, Transmission, Steering Worm-Gear Case, and Ball and Socket Universals in Steering Connections should be greased every 2000 miles; Foot Pedal Shafts and Hand Lever Shafts should be oiled every 5000 miles or once a season; Fan Bearings, Clutch Brake Ball Bearing, and Steering Column Screw and Nut should be greased every 5000 miles or once a season.

shaft, generator shaft, air pump shaft, etc., an entirely different method of lubrication is necessary—one that is more simple in every respect, allows the use of more simple lubricating devices, and does not require anything like the care and adjustment previously pointed out for the internal parts.

Oil and Grease Cups. Chief among the devices used for lubricating these outside parts are oil and grease cups, the oil cups being used in decreasing quantities and the grease cups in increasing quantities. Formerly, oil cups were much used, but they gave poor satisfaction, collected dirt, and were unsatisfactory generally. In the use of

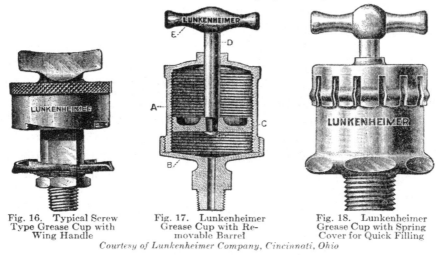

Fig. 16. Typical Screw Type Grease Cup with Wing Handle

Fig. 17. Lunkenheimer Grease Cup with Removable Barrel

Fig. 18. Lunkenheimer Grease Cup with Spring Cover for Quick Filling

Courtesy of Lunkenheimer Company, Cincinnati, Ohio

grease cups, there are but three things to observe: They should be large enough, accessible, and easy to fill.

For application to spring eye-bolts there is a particular type of grease cup. This grease cup is of the type that feeds by being occasionally screwed up a small distance as the bearing uses up the lubricant, and its positive action is rendered more certain by the use of a detent that holds the cover in any position in which it may be left. The grease is contained in the entire cap which, when unscrewed from the lower portion, is readily and conveniently filled by scooping up the grease.

A form quite generally used is the simple cup shown in Fig. 16. This is a screw-compression cup from which the lubricant is forced out by screwing down on the reservoir. This form is prevented from coming loose by the compression spring, here shown very much compressed below the ratchet, which governs the screwing down of the reservoir. To fill the reservoir, the ratchet portion is held down and the top screwed off, turning in the reverse of the usual direction. Although fitted with a wing handle, it is not easy to refill.

Another widely used form is seen in section in Fig. 17. This has a larger handle and, in this respect, may be considered easier to fill. A type which is rapidly coming into use and has all the advantages of the other two, and more, is shown in Fig. 18. This is a plain screw type with a large handle, but the cap is of sheet brass and is sprung into place. As this is sprung off by the plunger inside when screwed away out, filling is reduced to a matter of seconds. The plunger screws all the way in and affords pressure all the way.

The simplest form of oil cup has a hole in one side, which is covered with a spring-held cover. To use it, the cover is lifted with the fingers until the hole is uncovered, then the point of the oil can is inserted and the oil forced in.

Automatic Lubrication. There are signs at present that the lubrication of the motor may be controlled through the medium of a thermostat in order to conserve every unit of heat needed in the vaporization of the fuel and thus increase the efficiency of the engine as a whole. There would be a double advantage in this, for lubrication would be placed on a more economical basis. In using the thermostat, smoking and carbonization would be reduced, and their heat utilized. This process, carried out to a logical conclusion, might result in forced lubrication of all points on the chassis by means of the oil-pump system. A system of forced lubrication somewhat like the above has been produced in the Fergus car, but here the idea was to reduce the amount of work in connection with lubrication. The number of points outside of the automatic oiling system which required oil or grease application by hand has been reduced in this car from 80 to 11. Some 18 points in the springing system have been eliminated entirely by enclosing the springs in leather boots, grooving and drilling them, and forcing oil in under pressure from the main pump. It is questionable, however, whether the results as obtained in this case are worth the cost in money and complication, for this system gives a freak appearance to the car.

One of the more recent improvements in chassis lubrication is the Alemite system. In this system a grease gun is used to force the grease into the spring bolts, bearings in wheels, differential housing, bearings of breakshafts, and other places where lubrication could not be given in any other way. Fig. 19 shows the Alemite gun. It consists of a cylinder in which the grease is placed, the top of the cylinder is threaded to take a cap and in the cap is a thread for the operation of the plunger. As the handle is turned it moves the plunger down into the cylinder, forcing the grease into the bearing being lubricated. The attachment to the part being lubricated is by a flexible tube fastened to a nipple screwed into the part. The

Fig. 19.   Alemite Gun

Fig. 20.   Alemite Gun in Use

nipple has a small ball in the end which prevents the grease from coming out after it has been forced in. The ball also keeps dirt and water away from the bearing. Fig. 20 shows this device being used to grease the bearing in the front of a drive pinion on a rear axle.

Another form of automatic lubrication is the one-shot system. In this type all working parts in the chassis such as the spring bolt, knuckle, and steering gear are lubricated from one central point by a plunger. When the plunger is pressed down the oil is forced to every working part through small tubes laid along the inside of the chassis and leading to the different points. The only care that is necessary is to keep the tank full of oil. The advantage of this system is that oil will not harden as will grease, lubrication can be given at any time or place, even when the car is being driven, and oil penetrates much easier than grease.

Characteristics of Good Oils. The variety of oils and greases recommended for automobile use is so extensive, and there are so many cheap and worthless lubricating compounds on the market, that it is almost impossible for the purchaser without technical knowledge to discriminate between them. The various tests from time to time recommended, whereby the user may ascertain for himself the quality of the lubricant he is using, are rarely of positive value, since the compounders of the shoddy oils and greases are usually sufficiently expert chemists to concoct admixtures that will successfully pass such simple tests as are available to the average layman, and will fail only under the more critical analysis of a competent chemist, or under the severe and more risky practical demonstration that results from long use, in the course of which the worthlessness of the lubricant is likely to be found out only at the cost of serious injury to the mechanism. The only really safe policy to follow is the purchase of the highest grades of oils and greases, marketed by concerns of established reputation.

The oils generally found best for gasoline-engine cylinder lubrication are the mineral oils derived from petroleum, though castor oil is found to possess peculiar merits for the lubrication of air-cooled motors working at high temperatures in which the friction of steel surfaces working over steel surfaces is often involved. This oil is exclusively employed in aviation motors, such as the Gnome, which is built with steel cylinders and pistons, and it is often utilized in racing automobile motors. Its chief merit seems to be that instead of withstanding the high temperatures, which is the result sought in the use of mineral oils of high fire test, it burns up clean without leaving any deposit upon the cylinder walls. It has to be fed in excessive quantities, which makes its use a rather expensive method of lubrication. But for the peculiar services for which it is adapted, it certainly proves most satisfactory.

In greases and oils used for the lubrication of parts not exposed to such high temperatures as prevail in gasoline-engine cylinders, the admixture of vegetable and animal greases and oils with mineral oils and greases is not objectionable and often may be of considerable benefit.

Graphite is a solid lubricant and is very advantageous to employ in many parts of an automobile. In the deflocculated form, admixed in very small percentages with cylinder oils, gearbox greases, etc., there is no question but what it greatly conduces to smooth running and to long life of bearings. Its resistance to the very highest temperatures makes it constitute a considerable safeguard against immediate injury in case of neglect to replenish the lubricants as often as is properly required.

Oil Tests. *Heat Test.* The reaction known as the heat test is very easily made with any lubricating oil. There is perhaps no other test which indicates so decisively and so quickly the purity, the durability, and the degree of refinement of an oil.

This test consists of heating a sample of oil to a temperature of between 300° F. and 500° F.—depending upon the flash point—and holding it at this temperature for a period of from ten to fifteen minutes. A good quality of oil will show a slight change in color, turning to a darker shade, but the oil will remain clear.

A poorly refined and impure oil will show an immediate alteration in color and will change to a dense black. As the heat is maintained, a black precipitate settles, the quantity of the precipitation depending upon the impurity of the oil.

Oil will act in just the same way when subjected to the heat of the explosions in the internal-combustion motor, and thus there is a continuous precipitation of black sediment if the oil is poor. This is what causes the costly wear of all parts in moving contact within a short time.

Emulsion Test. The emulsion test shows the quality of lubricating oils about as accurately as does the heat test on straight or blended hydrocarbon oils, but it is not reliable when animal or vegetable oils are present.

Reclaiming Oil. It is now authentically stated by some scientists that oil does not wear out and can be reclaimed for motor use if the proper equipment and method are used. A number of manufacturers and service stations are now reclaiming this oil with wonderful success. The government reclaimed cylinder oil used in aeroplanes, and it is authentically stated that 40 per cent of the oil used in the motors was returned to the reclaiming station and that from 50 to 90 per cent of this oil was treated in such a manner that it was as good, if not better, than the original oil. The cost of the reclaiming was less than 10 cents a gallon. The most generally used process of reclaiming this oil is by heating it after it has been emulsified with soda ash and water. When this is done, the impurities separate from the oil with the ash. After the oil is thus treated it is dumped into the reclaimer. Live steam is passed into the oil and a violent agitation is set up. This is done to distill off the gasoline that had collected in the oil when it was in use.

Testing Oils for Acid, Etc. Oils must be purchased with much care. Once an oil is found which does the work satisfactorily, it should be adhered to consistently. No two oils are exactly alike, and for that reason, no two will do the same work under the same conditions in the same way. So, it is advisable to experiment only until an oil is found which will do the work. Thereafter, stick to that brand. As an instance of the impurities which may be found in oils, acids may be mentioned. These are fatal to delicate and closely machined parts, such as ball bearings, cylinder walls, pistons, etc., and consequently they should be watched for.

Pure mineral oils contain little acid, and what they do contain is readily determined. Vegetable and animal oils, on the other hand, all have acid content and under the action of heat this may be liberated. A simple home test may be practiced as follows: Secure from a druggist a solution of sodium carbonate in an equal weight of water. Place this in a small glass bottle or vial. To test an oil, take a small quantity of the lubricant and an equal amount of the sodium solution. Put both in another bottle, agitate thoroughly, and then allow it to stand. If any acid is present, a precipitate will settle to the bottom, the amount of the precipitation being a measure of the amount of acid present.

Another method is to allow the acid, if there is any, to attack some metal. To do this proceed as follows: Soak a piece of cloth or, preferably, wicking in the oil suspected of containing acid. Select a piece of steel at random and polish it to a bright surface. Wrap the steel in the soaked rag or wicking, and place in the sunlight but protect it from wind or weather. Allow it to stand several days, and if there is no sign of etching of the surface, repeat with a freshly soaked rag, being careful to use the same oil as before. After two trials, if no sign of the etching appears, you may consider it free from acid.

Principles of Effective Lubrication. To render lubrication positive and effective there are certain conditions regarding the design of bearings and the feeding of lubricants that must be scrupulously observed.

The proper application of a lubricant to a revolving shaft passing through a bearing requires that definite space be provided between shaft and bearing for the lubricating material. The amount of this space varies with the size of the shaft, the speed of rotation, and other conditions, but in a general way it can be specified that the space must be greater as the shaft diameter increases, and

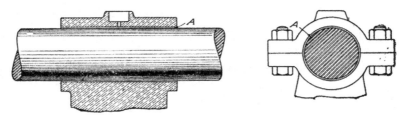

Fig. 21. Condition of Bearing for Proper Lubrication

greater for heavy oils and low speeds than for light oils and high speeds. For the crankshafts of automobile engines, to take a specific example, it is rarely desirable to have the bearing smaller than from .0005 to .0015 inch larger than the shaft. The annular space thus provided, as suggested at A in the end and sectional views in Fig. 21, is occupied by the lubricant, which, contrary to another general impression, will not be squeezed out unless the shaft is loaded above its capacity; this is more likely to occur because the bearing area is too small than from any other condition likely to be encountered.

With the bearing area large enough—which means that the specific pressure on its projected area must not be excessive—the tendency of the oil to remain in its place by capillary attraction, perhaps helped by the pressure under which it is fed into the bearing, is much greater than the tendency of the load upon the shaft to force it out.

From the foregoing, it is evident that the condition of effective lubrication is that in which the shaft literally floats in an oil film of microscopic thickness, this film completely surrounding it and so protecting it from any contact whatever, under normal conditions, with the bearing surface. The necessity for the accurate fitting of bearings is to provide an oil film of uniform thickness.

Lubrication Troubles. After a period of service, the oil pressure, as shown on the pressure gage, drops off considerably and it is a sure indication that something in the engine needs attention.

Worn bearings will cause a drop in pressure because the resistance to the flow of the oil is less than when the bearings are a good fit. This is due to the fact that the oil escapes at the sides of the bearing very easily. The remedy is to take up the play in both main and connecting rods where force feed lubrication is used.

Worn gears will cause a drop in pressure in a system that uses a gear pump for circulating the oil. When the gears are in good order, the oil is carried around with the teeth of the gear and is forced out of the supply opening to the engine. When the gears are worn, the oil travels around but the pressure is so great when it gets to the outlet that some of the oil passes back through the teeth and less pressure is shown on the gage. New gears should be installed. If new gears are put in, care should be taken when replacing the cover of the pump. The cover should be close to the top of the gears so that if a new gasket is fitted it will not be very thick. If too thick, the gears in the pump will not be able to function correctly. See that the shafts are a good fit in their bearings in the pump.

In systems where a ball check is used, as in the plunger type of pump, dirt will sometimes get on the ball seat and allow the oil to pass back by the relief side of the pump. The balls will also stick at times so that when the suction stroke of the pump comes there is no suction and no oil is drawn into the pump. Therefore, there is no pressure or circulation of oil.

Every condition may be correct in the engine and if this is the case, a drop in pressure may mean that the oil needs renewing. It does not pay to put new oil into the crankcase with the old oil for the old will dilute the new and the virtue of the latter is destroyed. Remember that oil is cheaper than repairs.

When changing oil, kerosene should not be used to flush the crankcase because all of the kerosene will not be drained out of the case. When the new oil is put in, it will be diluted at once by the kerosene, and a certain amount of the lubricating quality of the oil is lost.

Care of Lubricant in Cold Weather. Nearly everyone realizes the amount of care necessary with cooling water in freezing weather, but few realize that extreme cold has practically the same effect upon lubricants. In the coldest weather, a lighter grade of oil specially made to withstand low temperatures should be used. If a special oil cannot be obtained, the lighter thinner quality will suffice, as even when thickened up by the low temperatures this oil will flow more readily than the thick oils. Sometimes the slow circulation of the oil in cold weather allows the motor bearings to run dry and heat. This trouble can be remedied by changing to a lighter oil. The same is true of the clutch oil which is in the multiple disc running in oil. Thick oil in this in cold weather will often thicken up and stick so the clutch will not work well.

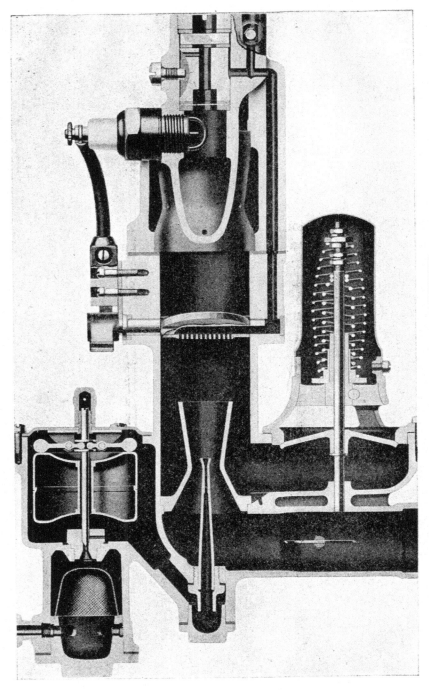

PACKARD CARBURETOR FUELIZER

CARBURETORS

PART I

The change in the design and the operation of the carburetor has been rapid, as with every other part of the automobile. The aim of the manufacturer throughout has been to make the carburetor as simple, as economical, and with as few adjustments as possible.

Function of the Carburetor. As has been pointed out in the general outline of the motor car, the first and most important thing in the engine cycle is to get the fuel into the cylinders. This is done through the medium of the carburetion system, the principal unit in which is the carburetor. The function of this is to convert a liquid (gasoline) into gas (gasoline vapor) measure this, and add to it the right quantity of air to give proper and complete combustion. If this be not done, power is lost, either through the use of too much or too little air. In the latter case, not all the fuel is vaporized, hence some of it is wasted.

This sounds like a simple proposition, yet its very simplicity has been the undoing of many automobile experts. The vaporizer becomes more and more complex each year, constant additions and changes are being made in the other parts of the system, and in other ways the carburetion system shows a constant change. Despite all this, few fundamental laws have been found to be in error, and few new ones have been discovered or developed.

Effect of Heavier Fuels. For some years past there has been under way a subtle change in the character of the fuel—the gasoline used for the propulsion of automobiles. The small production and the increasing demand have combined to render almost unpurchasable, except at high prices and then from large dealers, the lighter and more volatile gasolines of some years ago. In the place of them there have been quietly introduced much heavier petroleum distillates, which evaporate less readily—though they are actually of higher value in terms of power units. This condition has compelled several changes in the carburetor problem.

In addition to the foregoing, in some parts of the world there have been serious efforts made to utilize in automobile motors alcohol and benzene (not benzine), which, with proper provision for their carburetion, constitute excellent fuels.

The most important of the changes dictated by this development in the fuel situation is the now general practice of heating the float chambers of carburetors, either by water from the circulating system or by exhaust gases. An alternative scheme is that of drawing of the air for the carburetor from a point adjacent to the exhaust piping, so that this air is sufficiently warmed to readily take up the gasoline necessary to constitute a proper explosive mixture.

Jacketed Manifolds. A subsequent and very successful method of handling the heavier fuels is that of jacketing the upper portion of the inlet manifold, and the circulating of the hot water in the cylinder-cooling system through this. By having this jacket close to the point where the gaseous mixture enters the cylinder, any remaining particles of liquid fuel are vaporized before entering the cylinders. In a few instances, the same effect is obtained by incorporating the carburetor in the cylinder water-jacket casting. In still others, where the carburetor is placed on one side and the inlet valves on the other, there is a cored inlet passage through the cylinder block between the cylinders which heats the mixture, with the same result as stated above.

Fuel Injection. Systems of fuel feeding by direct injection of minute quantities of the combustible liquid into the cylinders or into the intake piping have been advocated or experimented with for many years, and have found very successful application in stationary and flight engineering, though as yet not one of these sytems has successfully competed with the carburetor in automobile service, where the conditions of power variation are such that fuel injection has not seemed readily applicable.

Nevertheless, there are many engineers who adhere to the view that sooner or later fuel injection will supplant present systems of carburetion, and progress made recently with aviation motors of fuel-injection types may seem in some measure to justify this view.

Despite the success of this system on aeroplane and stationary engines—notably on the Antoinette and the Diesel, respectively—there is not, to the writer's knowledge, a single American motor-car manufacturer now using or experimenting with fuel injection. A few years ago a motor car brought out in the Middle West used it, but this was short-lived. Since then, nothing has been done.

More Valves vs. Forced Induction. The present-day tendency toward the use of many valves, four per cylinder, seems to indicate a necessity for getting more gas into the cylinders in order to get more power and speed from the same size of motor. This would seem to lead back to the subject, agitated a few years ago and dropped for lack of interest, of the need for forced induction. This will introduce a greater quantity of gas into the cylinders without resorting to the complications and trouble-breeding possibilities of four valves per cylinder. It differs widely from fuel injection, consisting in its simplest form of a special form of fan or blower to drive the vaporized fuel into the cylinders.

Classification of Carburetors. Carburetors, as a whole, may be divided into three classes: the surface form, in which the air passing over the surface of the fuel picks up some of it, mixes with it, and produces an explosive vapor; the ebullition, or filtering, type, in which air is forced through a body of fuel from below, absorbing small particles so that when it reaches the top and is drawn off, it is suitable for use in the cylinders; and the float-feed, or spraying, type, under which head nearly all modern devices come. The others have gone out of use, as fuels today are too heavy for them to be practicable.

The original float-feed carburetor consisted of one part besides the fuel pipe, float chamber, and passage to cylinder, which made it remarkable for its simplicity. It had no adjustments, nor was there any way of securing an even and continuous flow of fuel or of air, except as the engine suction produced these. The need for these qualities brought out, one by one, the modifications of the original; and through continuous modifications and recombinations of these, all the modern devices have been developed.

Defects in the Original Are Not Found in Modern Types. The original carburetor had no adjustment; the opening in the casting measured the amount of air, while the size of the nozzle measured the amount of the fuel and the fineness of the spray. There was no means of regrinding the float valve, and thus no way of assuring an even and continuous flow of fuel. The modern adjuncts of the original Maybach device consist of remedies for these defects, and, in addition, a proper means of balancing and adjusting the float.

To pick out a modern carburetor at random, take the one shown in Fig. 1. Like its ancestor, it has a gasoline chamber into which

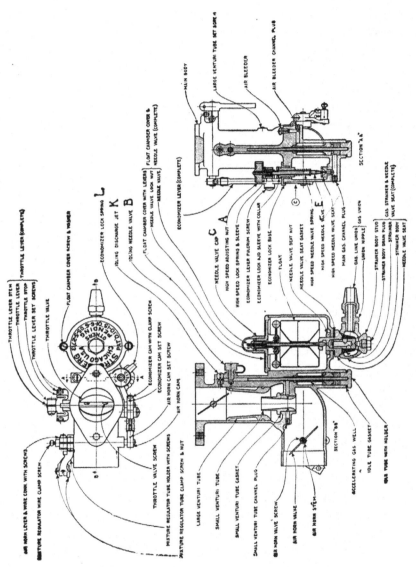

Fig. 1. Stromberg Model "L" Carburetor
Courtesy Stromberg Carburetor Company, Chicago

the fuel is admitted by the action of a float, when it first passes through a strainer. From the float chamber the liquid passes up to and through the spraying nozzle. The weight of the float is so calculated that the level in the final nozzle is just 1 millimeter (0.04 inch) below the top. This insures that there will always be fuel there for the air suction to draw off. As the physical action of changing a substance from a liquid to a gas is usually accompanied by the absorption of heat, it is advisable to supply a reasonable amount of this, and thus assist the change of form. In the older Maybach, this was inadvertently done by placing the whole apparatus in close contact with the hot cylinder. In the modern carburetor, placed some distance from the heated portions of the engine, this additional heat is supplied by the jacket water. An alternate scheme is to pre-heat the air supply by a special pipe from the exhaust manifold.

From this mixing chamber the mixture of air and gasoline vapor passes upward into a secondary mixing chamber. This communicates with the inlet pipe through the medium of the throttle valve. The auxiliary air supply, when used, has access into the secondary chamber through the auxiliary air valve. This comes into action on very high speeds when the engine is pulling very strongly. At this time the proportion of gasoline to air is likely to be too large, so the auxiliary opens, admits more air, and thus dilutes the mixture.

Throttle Valves. *Butterfly Type.* Whatever the nature of the mixture in the carburetor, it is admitted to the cylinder by the throttle valve, which may take the form known as the butterfly. This is a flat piece of sheet metal, preferably brass, attached to a suitable shaft with an operating lever on the external end.

Piston Type. Besides the butterfly type there are fully as many of the piston type. The sliding form is a cylindrical ring or shell of metal, which is free to slide in a corresponding cylindrical chamber. In the walls of the latter are a number of apertures or ports which the longitudinal movement of the piston either uncovers or covers as the case may be. Sometimes, to facilitate this action, the sides of the piston are grooved or notched, but this does not alter the principle of sliding a cylinder within another cylinder to cover or uncover certain ports in the cylinder walls.

In addition to the sliding piston, there is the rotating piston, working in practically the same manner, that is, its rotation connects openings in the piston walls with the interior of the vaporizing chamber on one side and with the inlet manifold on the other, the amount of the opening depending upon the distance the piston is rotated.

Needle Valves. Needle valves—or spray nozzles as they are sometimes called because of the function they perform—constitute an important part of every carburetor, or liquid-vaporizing device. It might be thought that so long as there is a hole by which the fuel can enter the vaporizing chamber that is sufficient; yet such is far from the case. In addition to the function of an entering hole, the needle has the additional duty of breaking the fuel up into a fine spray or mist, the particles of which are easily picked up by the inrushing air, and as easily converted into a vapor. Therefore, that shape, form, or arrangement which will divide the entering liquid up into the finest particles will be the most efficient. The difference of opinion on this latter point has

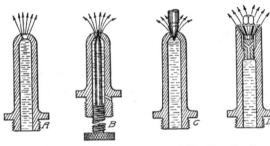

Fig. 2. The Four Usual Shapes of Gasoline Needle Valves and Spray Nozzles

produced the large number of shapes of nozzle and needle which are now in use.

Simple Vertical Tube. In general, practically all these can be divided into four groups, illustrated in Fig. 2. The one at *A* is a simple round vertical tube with an opening in the top, through which the liquid may pass out. It does not alter the type if the sides of the opening converge, diverge, or are straight, but it will influence the resulting spray somewhat. Of the twelve makes shown with this type, practically all indicate the opening as straight, but this may be due to the small size of the drawing which does not make the taper apparent.

Internal Needle Type. Type *B*, Fig. 2, is similar to the first, except that an adjustable pointed needle is added on the inside. This occupies most of the center space, forcing the liquid to pass out in a smaller circular sheet or stream than would be the case with Type *A*, considering equal-sized holes. In addition, the fact that the internal needle valve may be raised or lowered allows this stream to vary greatly, both as to quantity of fuel flowing, and the extent to which it is spread out. When the needle is down very low, only its point enters the hole, so that practically the full area of the latter is available, the central needle influencing the column of fuel passing out only to make it hollow in the center.

With the needle raised to nearly its maximum height, however, the point projects clear through, and the needle shaft almost fills the lower part of the hole. This reduces the flow to a very fine hollow column of spray, as the shape of the needle and of the lower edge of the hole is such as to force it inward and then outward so that as it leaves the top of the hole it is diverging widely. Thus, the effect of the addition of the needle is to allow the use of much smaller quantities of liquid with the same-sized hole, of diffusing it more widely, and of making it adjustable to varying needs. Despite all its advantages, only three of the carburetors and vaporizers shown use this type; and of these, one is a combination of this with *A*.

External Needle Type. The third type shown at *C*, Fig. 2, is an inversion of *B* in that the needle is made external and descends from above into the hole in the nozzle. In this form, the shape of the needle point produces the desired diffusion and spraying effect, which accounts for its popularity. Of the models shown herewith, nine are of this kind, one being a modified combination of this form and *A*.

External Sectional Needle Type. The fourth form, shown at *D*, is like *C*, except that instead of a needle resting upon the upper surface of the hole and allowing a continuous hollow stream of fuel to flow, a series of holes break up the column into a number of very much smaller columns, each with its own opening. In this form the central member may be movable or not, while the holes may be set at any angle. Of the examples of this form shown in this article, three in all, every one has the holes placed horizontally instead of inclined to a vertical, as shown in Fig. 2. Of these, two show a combination of *B* and *D*. This is an effective combination.

Floats. Another feature of the earlier forms of carburetors, which was soon found to be in need of a change, was the arrangement of the float. In Maybach's original vaporizer, there was no means of balancing the float; consequently, there was no way of preventing wrenching and breaking of the needle-valve spindle. As this disarranged the gasoline supply, it made a change very important;

and this problem received early attention. There was also the necessity for reliable devices to regulate the supply of air and of gasoline spray from the nozzle, either by original adjustment, by means of a governor, or by effecting a constant variation by hand to meet constantly varying conditions of engine demands.

These additions to the original form caused some trouble. The ordinary way of managing the balancing of the float, while it may be the cause of trouble at times, is a very simple one. The float is of exceeding lightness, whether made of cork or metal. With the inflow of gasoline in liquid form this float rises, and in so doing it strikes against a pair of small pivoted levers near the top of the float chamber. The other ends of the pivoted levers rest upon a form of shifting collar on the needle-valve stem. So, when the float rises above a certain level, it automatically shuts off the flow of gasoline by pressing against the pivoted levers, which, in turn, act against the stem and press it down until the flow is cut off. The float will stay up until the suction of the engine has lowered the gasoline level so that the dropping of the float releases the levers which raise the needle valve off its seat. The gasoline flow is thus automatically regulated by this balanced-float arrangement.

ADJUSTMENT OF AIR AND GASOLINE SUPPLY

Methods of Handling Fuel Spray. Probably no one detail of the whole list of carburetor parts has caused, and still does cause, more difference of opinion than the source of and adjustment of the air supply, and its companion, the adjustment of the gasoline spray. The latter drew attention long before the former; in fact, the former is more of a modern appliance. The fuel spray was investigated long ago; for the gasoline spray had no adjustment, but the size and the location of the level of the nozzle were fixed. The spray itself, however, received special treatment. It was projected against a conical spray deflector which served to break up the column into finer and more diffused particles. In this way, greater vaporizing action was gained.

Water=Jacketing. Longuemare was among the first to use a water jacket around the vaporizing chamber. The conversion of a liquid into a gas is an endothermic reaction and requires heat for its completion. If this is not supplied by external means, it will be extracted from surrounding objects. This accounts for the frost which gathers on the outside of the mixing chambers of carburetors which do not have a water jacket or other source of heat supply. The heat is abstracted from the air so rapidly that the moisture in the air is frozen, appearing as frost on the outside of the carburetor.

Auxiliary Air Valve. The auxiliary air valve has always caused discussion, its opponents claiming that it means extra parts, and therefore more adjustments and more sources of trouble; while those favoring it say that without some additional means of this sort for diluting the mixture at high speeds, it is impossible to run the engine fast, as high speed will then mean an over-rich charge. Be that as it may, the fact remains that the weight of opinion lies with the auxiliary valve.

Necessity with Heavy Fuels. Practically all the more modern vaporizers use an auxiliary air valve, as this is a partial necessity with the heavier fuels. That is, it has been found that the heavier fuels require more air to vaporize them than can be supplied by the primary air inlet. Moreover, these heavy fuels require considerable additional heat in order to vaporize, and the auxiliary air inlet has been made the vehicle for conveying this. As will be explained in detail later on, this is generally connected with the exhaust manifold in such a way that the air entering through it is heated to a high temperature. Adding this after the fuel has been split up by the spraying nozzle and the primary air has proved very successful.

Usual Forms of Auxiliary Air=Inlet Valve. The auxiliary air inlet usually consists of a simple valve, opening inward, held in its place by a spring of a certain known tension. The strength of the spring is carefully determined so that at the proper moment—when the motor requires more air in proportion to the amount of gasoline used—the valve will open just enough to allow the required amount of air to enter. It will be seen that the time and the amount of opening will be controlled by the speed of the engine, i.e., by the amount of suction produced by the movement of the piston in the cylinder. Of course, as the engine speeds up, there is a greater piston displacement to be filled per minute, and therefore it is necessary to supply a greater amount of mixture. Upon changing speed suddenly from, say, 500 revolutions to 900 or 1000, the carburetor which does not have this device will *not* give a uniform mixture immediately; in fact, it might require a new adjustment of the gasoline flow in order to supply the right amount of fuel. What the auxiliary air inlet actually does, then, is to control automatically, above a certain point, the amount of air admitted, thereby always maintaining a homogeneous mixture. In order to prevent any chattering of the valve or rapid changes in the air supply, a diaphragm or a dashpot is sometimes used in connection with the valve.

As a substitute for an auxiliary air valve, a number of makers have tried the use of steel balls, resting in holes about two-thirds the diameter of the ball. By varying the size and weight of the balls, a truly progressive action is obtained, for light suction lifts the light balls, and strong suction all balls.

Venturi=Tube Mixing Chamber. Like every other carburetor part, the spraying action and the shape or size of the chamber in which it takes place have been the subject of much debate. Originally, the chamber took any convenient shape and varied all the way from a perfectly plain cylindrical shape to an equally perfect square, with all the possible variations in between. A few years ago, however, scientists began to look into the vaporizing and equally important measuring action of carburetors, with the result that a new shape came into use, which was based upon a scientific principle.

This is the principle of the Venturi meter used for measuring the flow of water, and from its use the tube, or chamber, having this shape has come to be known as a Venturi tube. In form, this consists of two cone-shaped tubes diverging in opposite directions from a common point, which in the water meter is the *point of measurement* and in the carburetor is the *point of location* of the spray nozzle. The principle is that if these two frustrums of cones are of the proper shape, i.e., include the proper angle and are correctly set with relation to one another, the flow of air and gas will be in correct proportions to each other at all speeds, assuming first that the air enters at the bottom of the tube having the greater angle.

As a proof of the soundness of the principle of this type of vaporizing chamber, it might be said that the majority of carburetors in use today have it incorporated in one form or another. Many make the upper tube conical for a very short distance, beyond which it assumes a cylindrical form. In the true Venturi shape, the usual angle at the bottom is 30 degrees, while that at the top is 5 degrees

In water meters the contracted area is made one-ninth that of the pipe. This same relation, although not exact, holds in the case of the carburetor. Since the area varies as the square of the diameter, this is equivalent to saying that the diameter of the contraction should be one-third the diameter of the full-sized pipe.

Double=Nozzle Type. A distinctive design of two connections leading into the vaporization chamber is the Zenith (French) car-

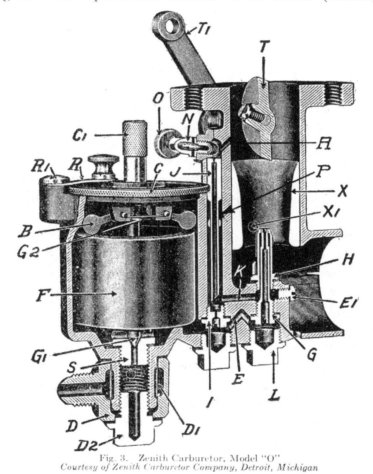

Fig. 3. Zenith Carburetor, Model "O"
Courtesy of Zenith Carburetor Company, Detroit, Michigan

buretor, a diagrammatic sketch being shown in Fig. 3. This is but a modification, in a way, of the Venturi plan, for the latter shape is actually used for the vaporizing chamber. The new idea consists in leading into this mixing chamber, two tubes. Of these, one is the ordinary spray nozzle and does not differ from that used on hundreds of other devices. The second, however, is very different. While it leads into the same mixing chamber, it does so through the medium of a secondary chamber, or standpipe, to which the suction of the engine has access. If this suction is strong, more gasoline is drawn into the secondary chamber, from which it may enter the spraying zone.

The ordinary nozzle is of an exact size and, consequently, can pass only a certain amount of fuel, always at the same speed. With the additional nozzle, this does not hold; and being of large diameter (comparatively), the flow through it depends wholly upon the engine suction, which varies at all speeds, often at the same speed upon different occasions.

Use of By=Pass. This matter of two standpipes has a parallel in the use of a by-pass, so-called, around the usual mixing chamber. On some carburetors this is made so as to allow easy starting, the idea being that when suction is applied to the carburetor by cranking, with the throttle closed, practically pure gasoline vapor will be drawn through the by-pass. This will start the engine after which, as the throttle is opened gradually, its movement cuts off the by-pass, until at medium speeds it is out of use entirely. The same thing applies to the use of a secondary tube or standpipe for low-speed running.

A by-pass of a separate nature is made use of for starting and priming purposes; this consists of a small separate tank of gasoline attached to the dashboard under the hood, with a valve running through to the driver's side for turning on the supply. This is connected into the inlet manifold above the carburetor by means of a special pipe tapped into the manifold. When it is desired to start the motor, it is primed with this device by simply turning on the supply. Some gasoline flows into the manifold, and after a few seconds it vaporizes. The motor is than cranked over sharply, and a start is almost certain. This has the advantage of simplicity, accessibility, and low cost. In addition, it is economical of time as compared with lifting the hood to prime each cylinder separately.

Nature of New Developments. *Horizontal Carburetor Outlets.* Among the newest carburetor features are some which have worked themselves out naturally, and others which have been forced by changes in engine design, in fuel quality, etc. Thus the tendency toward block motors, and with it the tendency toward neat lines and simplicity, has brought forth a general simplification, or elimination of inlet pipes, and a fairly wide use of horizontal carburetor outlets. The latter has affected carburetors by requiring a shorter and more compact instrument, with a side outlet and a vaporizing arrangement which will produce tolerably complete vaporization in a comparatively short distance. To a certain extent, this horizontal-carburetor tendency has modified existing practice in nozzles, Venturi tubes, interior areas and arrangements, etc.

Effect of Heavier Fuels. The growing realization by carburetor manufacturers that the increased use of heavier fuels is inevitable has brought forth much worthy effort in the way of vaporizing them. This has temporarily set aside the kerosene and other heavy-fuel vaporizers. However, as the fuel is bound to become heavier and heavier, on account of the excessive demands for gasoline, it is only a question of a year or so before kerosene and distillate vaporizers will be agitated again.

Effect of Vacuum Feeds. The wide use of vacuum feeding devices, combined with the tendency mentioned above to clean and simplify, has caused a much higher mounting of carburetors. This has always been desirable, but hitherto it has not been possible. The vacuum feed for the gasoline supply has made this change possible, while the cleaning process and simplification actually forced it.

Effect of Motor Changes. The high-speed form of motor now so generally being adopted has had a big influence, as have also the multi-cylinder forms, both creating a demand for greater acceleration. Similarly, starting devices have forced the use of a carburetor modification by which instant starting is possible. These requirements have called for new designs, smaller and lighter parts, more nearly complete automatic actions to uncover large air ports, as well as other improvements.

Double Carburetors for Multi=Cylinder Motors. While many eight- and twelve-cylinder motors have but a larger-sized plain carburetor, the better forms have a double device, each half supplying a group of cylinders, and the halves are entirely separate and distinct from the other, except for a common fuel-supply pipe. Each set of cylinders has its own suction-actuated nozzle and its own independent nozzle. This form has shown its worth in actual use, having been very successful in aeroplane work on eight-cylinder and twelve-cylinder motors, and also on a number of the better eight- and twelve-cylinder motor cars.

Multiple=Nozzle Carburetors. Another development brought about by this demand for rapid acceleration, coupled with great maximum capacity, has been the swing toward multiple nozzles. As has been pointed out on previous pages, there are a number of carburetors now with two nozzles.

Stromberg Carburetors. Fig. 1 shows a cross-section of the Stromberg Model "L." Except that Model "LB," which is shown in Fig. 4, has a horizontal outlet which necessitates the air entering from the top and downward, instead of the side and upward, these two are almost identical, and the general instructions which follow will cover both. In general, all the Stromberg carburetors are of the so-called plain tube type, that is, the air and gasoline openings are plain tubes and thus fixed in size. This construction automatically meters the fuel by the suction of air velocity past the jets, and in addition does away with the auxiliary air valve, all the air supply being taken in through a single pipe which is heated. Thus, the entire air supply is heated, this making for more efficient operation with the present heavier fuels.

The Model "M" is a vertical, and "MB" horizontal form which are similar to the "L" and "LB" models except that they are made without the economizer attachment. This alters their outward appearance, cross sections, and eliminates one adjustment. That is, the "L" and "LB" have three adjustments, high, low, and economizer, while the "M" and "MB" have but two adjustments, high and low. To make these points plain in the subsequent adjustment instructions, Model "MB" is shown in Fig. 5.

General Instructions. The high speed is controlled by the knurled nut "A," which locates the position of the needle "E," past whose point all the gasoline is taken at all speeds. Turning nut "A" to the right or clockwise raises the needle "E" and gives more fuel; turning it to the left or counterclockwise gives less fuel on the "L" and "LB" models. On the "M" and "MB" the instructions are the same except that turning to the left or counterclockwise gives more fuel and to the right less.

If an entirely new setting becomes necessary, put the economizer "L" in the fifth notch (farthest from the float chamber)

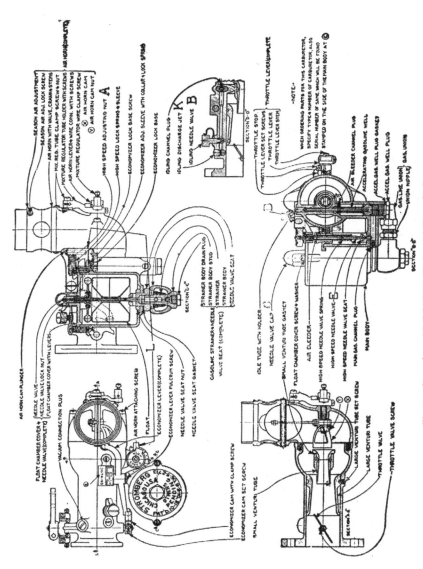

Fig. 4. Stromberg Model "LB" Horizontal Type Carburetor
Courtesy Stromberg Carburetor Company, Chicago

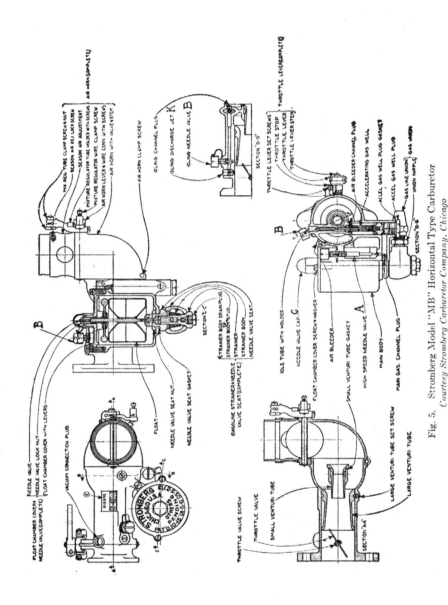

Fig. 5. Stromberg Model "MB" Horizontal Type Carburetor
Courtesy Stromberg Carburetor Company, Chicago

as an indicator, then turn the nut "A" to the left until the needle "E" reaches its seat as shown by the nut not moving when the throttle is opened and closed. When the needle "E" is in its seat it can be felt to stick slightly when nut "A" is lifted with the fingers. Find the adjustment of "A" where it just begins to move with the throttle opening, then give it 24 notches to the right or clockwise. In this turning the notches can be felt. Then move the economizer pointer "L" back to the zero (0) notch, toward the float chamber which will give a rich adjustment. Warm the motor thoroughly, then thin down the mixture by turning "A" counterclockwise until the motor shows the best power with a quick opening of the throttle. This will be the desired adjustment.

The low speed adjustment is made by means of the adjusting screw "B," which controls the jet "K." The latter passes the gasoline in above the throttle and the movement of "B" provides the necessary air dilution. Screwing "B" in clockwise gives more fuel on all models; outward, less. The best adjustment is usually $\frac{1}{2}$ to 3 turns outward from a seated position. This, it should be noted, is only an idling adjustment and does not affect the mixture above a car speed of 8 miles per hour. When the motor is idling properly, there should be a steady hiss in the carburetor; if there is a leak anywhere, or one cylinder leaks, or if the adjustment is entirely too rich, the hissing sound will be unsteady. The adjustment process should be continued until a steady hissing sound is produced, for best all-around results.

As pointed out previously, Models "L" and "LB," Figs. 1 and 4, have an additional adjustment called the economizer. This tends to the use of a leaner mixture, that is, economy of fuel, hence its name. To give this desired result, high speed needle "E" and nut "A" are raised slightly, the amount of movement being regulated by the pointer "L." After making the high speed adjustment for best power with "L" in the zero (0) notch, as described previously, place the throttle lever on the steering wheel in a position giving about 20 m.p.h. road speed. Then move the pointer "L" clockwise or away from the float chamber, slowly and one notch at a time, until the motor begins to slow down. At this point turn back one notch, that is, the adjustment should be one notch before the point of slowing down.

The amount of this economizer action depends upon the quality of fuel, which differs in different parts of the country, and also varies with the temperature. Thus, in the Middle West the best economizer adjustment will be the third or fourth notch, usually. With Pennsylvania gasolines and throughout the South, the second notch will prove the best adjustment, while on the Pacific Coast no economizer action will be necessary unless distillate is used. Fewer notches of economizer action will be needed in summer than in winter.

Model "LS." A sectional view of the Stromberg Model "LS" carburetor is shown in Fig. 6. It is of the plain-tube type because, having no air valve or metering needles, both the air passage and the gasoline jet are of fixed size for all engine speeds. It has several

interesting features, such as a gasoline feed above the throttle with idling adjustment, an accelerating well, which gives an extra supply of fuel the moment the throttle is opened, and an economizer, which permits the carburetor to operate on a very lean and economical mixture at the closed-throttle, or average driving, position. This economizer automatically shifts to the richer setting when the full power of the

Fig. 6. Stromberg Carburetor, Model "LS"

motor is called for and operates on the thinner setting when maximum power from the motor is unnecessary.

Adjustments. The idling mixture is controlled by the turning of the idle adjustment screw *A*. This regulates the amount of air; screwing it in gives a richer mixture, and screwing it out a leaner one. Turn screw *A* out, anti-clockwise, until the motor slows down. Then turn in, or clockwise, notch by notch until the motor runs at its greatest speed without missing or "loping." When the motor is idling properly, there should be a steady hiss in the carburetor. If there is a weak cylinder or a manifold leak, the hiss may be unsteady and the motor is likely to miss if this unsteady hiss is allowed to continue.

After adjusting the low speed, if the motor runs too fast, the throttle stop screw M should be turned to the left, or counter-clockwise, until the motor runs at the desired speed. If, however, the motor idles too slowly and stops, the screw M should be turned to the right, or clockwise, until the proper speed is reached. Before adjusting the screw M, it will be necessary to loosen the lock screw O.

The high-speed adjustment is regulated by the high-speed needle B. This needle regulates the opening through which the fuel flows to the jet. Turning B to the left, or counter-clockwise, gives more gasoline; turning it to the right, or clockwise, gives less gasoline. In order to make the proper high-speed adjustment, the spark lever should be advanced. Set the throttle lever on the steering wheel at a position that will give about 25 miles an hour car speed on a smooth road. Then adjust the high-speed needle to the minimum opening that will give the greatest engine speed for that throttle opening. This will give a good average adjustment, although two or three notches lean will give best economy for continuous driving, or touring; two or three notches rich may be best for short runs in cold weather, when the motor is not operating at the proper temperature. To secure greater economy as thin a mixture as possible should be used.

To prevent the wrong high-speed adjustment from giving a harmful rich mixture, the gasoline nozzle reducer is inserted beyond the high-speed needle in the base of the discharge jet above the plug K. To secure a richer mixture the reducer placed in the carburetor at the factory will permit about 20 per cent more gas to pass than may be needed. The economizer device D operates to automatically thin out the mixture at speeds from 10 to 45 miles per hour.

In all cases adjustments should be made when the motor is warm and the motometer shows a temperature higher than 140 degrees.

This carburetor is manufactured in sizes suitable for both the vertical and horizontal style. It is now used on a large number of truck and pleasure car manufacturers, as it is simple and has a very wide range of adjustment. There is a dirt trap in this carburetor which collects dirt and sediment, thereby preventing this dirt from clogging up the nozzles and causing the motor to miss. This strainer is provided in practically all modern carburetors. The float is adjusted at the factory and should not be changed only in rare instances.

Zenith Carburetors. The Zenith Model "O" carburetor, shown in Fig. 3, enjoys wide use in this country because of its simplicity. It has fewer ordinary adjustments than any other carburetor This is so constructed that but one adjustment, that for slow speed, is provided. However, its makers realize that sometimes changes and adjustments are necessary to secure proper results. They provide for these by the removal of three internal parts and their replacement with simpler parts, but with different working orifices, or holes.

Zenith Adjustments. The three parts mentioned are: choke tube, main jet, and compensator. In Fig. 3, the choke tube is marked X. This is really an air nozzle of such a stream-line shape (approximating the Venturi) as to allow the maximum flow of air without eddies and with the least resistance. When the pick-up, or acceleration, is defective and slow-speed running is not smooth, the choke tube is too large. In this case, it will be found that a larger compensator I does not better the situation. Then a smaller choke tube is needed. This is held in place by a screw X_1 in the choke itself with a lock washer to prevent its jarring loose. To remove the choke, the butterfly T must first be removed. In the horizontal types, the body is in two pieces, which are held together by an assembling nut. When this is removed and the two pieces taken apart (the bowl from the barrel), the choke can easily be slipped out of the barrel. When the motor will not take a full charge, that is, when it cannot, with the throttle fully opened, this indicates the need for a larger choke tube. It will be noted that although the pick-up is good, the car will not make all the speed of which it is capable. In this case, take out the choke tube X, as explained above, and replace with a larger one.

Changing the Main Jet. The main jet *G*, Fig. 3, shows its influence mostly at high speeds. When running at high speed on a level road, if the indications show a rich mixture, irregular running, characteristic smell of over-rich mixture from the exhaust, firing in the muffler, sooting up of the spark plugs, and low mileage, the main jet is too large and should be replaced by a smaller one. On the other hand, when running at high speed, if the indications are that the mixture is too lean, if the car will not attain its maximum speed, if there is occasional back firing at high speed, then the main jet is too small and should be replaced by a larger one. In respect to back firing, however, care should be used, as this is more often due to large air leaks in the intake or valves or to defects in the gasoline line.

To Replace Main Jet. When it is necessary to change the main jet *G*, Fig. 3, to a larger or smaller size, the lower plug *L* is removed first. This has a square head and is removed with a wrench. Then the main jet is unscrewed from below by means of a screwdriver, a notch being cut into its lower part for this purpose. In reassembling care should be taken to see that the fiber joint packing is on the jet and that the jet is screwed up far enough to compress this. Otherwise gasoline may leak around the threads. But one fiber washer should be used. Then the lower plug *L* is replaced, and this also must be screwed up tight.

Changing the Compensator. The third change which can be made is in the compensator *I*, Fig. 3. The opening in this supplies the fuel to the secondary well and, if too large or too small, will have a corresponding influence upon the running of the car. The makers call attention to the fact that its influence is most marked at low speeds and suggest that when this is suspected, the car should be tried out on a hill, regular but long, and of such a slope that the motor will labor rather hard to make it on high gear. Under such a test, if the indications are of too rich a mixture, that is, the same as for a rich mixture at high speed on the level, as previously explained, the compensator is too large, and must be replaced with a smaller one. If the indications are of a lean mixture, with the motor liable to miss and give a jerky action, the compensator is too small and must be replaced with a larger one. This is easily removed in the same manner as the main jet *G*, by removing the bottom plug beneath it and then removing *I* with a screwdriver, through the medium of slots for this purpose in its lower surface. In connection with this last method of adjustment, the makers recommend that the workman should start with the setting provided, then proceed to determine first the main jet, then the compensator, then the choke. In a sense, this method makes double work, for any change in the choke calls for a corresponding change in the main jet, but it gives superior results.

Slow-Speed Adjustment. The one adjustment in the Zenith device which is really an adjustment and not a change is that for slow speed. This is preferably made on the garage floor, with the motor properly warmed up. When this has been done and it has been throttled down to idling speed, any irregularity, such as the lack of ability to throttle down to a really slow speed (say 350 or less r.p.m.), calls for a change in the adjustment. When the throttle T, Fig. 3, is nearly closed, there is considerable suction at the edge, and the tube J in the top of the secondary well P terminates in a hole A near the edge of the butterfly at which gasoline is picked up. If the motor will not throttle down as slowly as it should, the supply of gasoline can be reduced by means of the external milled screw O. When this is turned in, the air entrance N is restricted, and consequently a richer mixture is drawn in. When it is unscrewed, or turned out, a larger air opening is uncovered, and consequently a leaner mixture is drawn in.

In this connection, many factors other than the correct slow-speed adjustment of the carburetor may prevent good idling. Some of these are: too light a flywheel, too much spark advance, and air leaks created by (1) poor gaskets, (2) loose valve stems, (3) pitted or scored valves, (4) leaky valve caps, (5) spark or valve plugs, (6) leaky priming cups, and others. Obviously, if any of these faults exist, no amount of adjustment of the slow-speed device on the carburetor will give good idling.

Horizontal Type Adjustments and Changes. Everything that has been said thus far applies equally well to the horizontal type shown in Fig. 7, except for the adjustment of the idling jet. In this form, the idling jet P_2 is supported by the knurled nut O which governs the air opening for this jet, and replaces the horizontal milled screw O. If a leaner mixture is desired, this is turned to the right, or clockwise; this lowers the jet and increases the size of the available air passage. For a rich mixture it is turned the other way, or counter-clockwise, reducing the air opening.

Float Removal. In both models, it will be noted that the float cover is held on by the spring catch. This is lifted by means of its handle, and swung around out of the way. The float cover can then be lifted readily by means of the knurled edge. When this is removed it should be lifted up straight. The float is then exposed

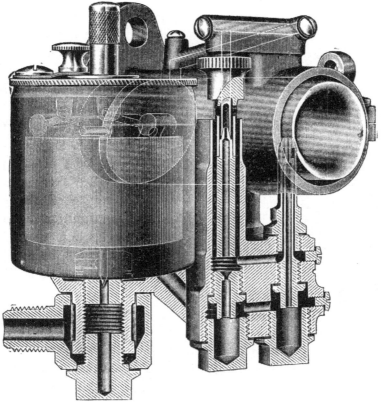

Fig. 7. Zenith Carburetor, Model "HP"
Courtesy of Zenith Carburetor Company, Detroit, Michigan

and can be removed easily with a piece of wire bent at the end or with a match inserted in the center hole.

Model "T4." One of the latest developments of the Zenith Carburetor Company is the Model "T4" carburetor, which is similar in principle to the other Zenith products, the main difference being in the refinements and adjusting features. A sectional view of this carburetor is shown in Fig. 8.

Operation. The gasoline from the tank enters the strainer body *D*, passes through filter screw *D1* and enters the float chamber bowl through the needle-valve seat S. As soon as the fuel reaches a predetermined height—shown by the horizontal level line—in the bowl, the float automatically rises, which forces the needle down by lifting the needle arms B. The gasoline is then fed from this bowl through the nozzles in different quantities, which are always in relation to the speed of the engine.

Adjustments. The sizes of the nozzles have been determined at the factory and should not be changed. The only adjustment which might be useful is the idling adjustment. When the butterfly throttle valve T is nearly closed and the motor is turned off, a strong suction is produced at the edge of the butterfly where the idling is located. Under this condition, little or no fuel is supplied at the main jet G or cap jet H. Gasoline from compensating jet I flows into the atmospheric well W, the suction then lifting it through idling jet P, which has a calibrated measuring hole at its upper end. From this point, it is carried into

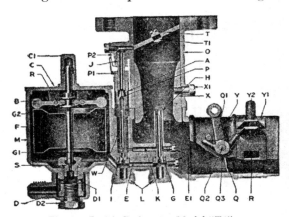

Fig. 8.   Zenith Carburetor Model "T4"

its idling port J, where it is mixed with the air measured past the conical end of the idling jet. It then passes through the idling hole into the carburetor manifold and to the motor. Idling tube J is screwed into the bottom of the barrel and its position is thus fixed. Idling adjusting tube $P1$, which is permanently assembled to idling jet P, screws into the idling tube and is screwed up or down to secure the proper adjustment for idling the motor.

Screwing down increases the air passage left between the conical upper end of idling jet P and the flared-out lower end of idling tube J, thus admitting more air and thinning the mixture. Screwing up reduces the air passage and thus enriches the mixture. The adjustment is locked by the idling spring $P2$, which engages the knurled surface of the idling adjustment 2. As the throttle is opened, the idling jet ceases to function and the gas vapor is supplied through the main jet H as in other previous Zenith models. The choke $Q1$ is supplied for easy starting. This choke cuts off the air supply and is operated from the dash. $Y1$ is a revolving air shutter which controls the hot or cold air supplied to the carburetor.

As the adjustment is changed, a difference in the idling should be noticed. If the motor begins to run evenly or speeds up, it shows that the mixture becomes right in proportion, but that there is too much of it. This is remedied by changing the butterfly throttle position slightly, closing it by screwing out the stop screw which regulates the closed position for idling. Care should be taken to have the butterfly held firmly against this stop at all times when idling the motor. The single thing which is radically different and must be remembered in this connection is that multi-cylinder engines have very light flywheels and reciprocating parts, so the motor is extremely sensitive at low speeds to unequal conditions of ignition, compression, and air leaks. This makes it more necessary than with a plain four- or six-cylinder form to have the motor in the best possible condition before changing the carburetor idling adjustment.

The Zenith Model "L" is a refinement of Model "O," just described, but all adjustments are made in the way described for "O."

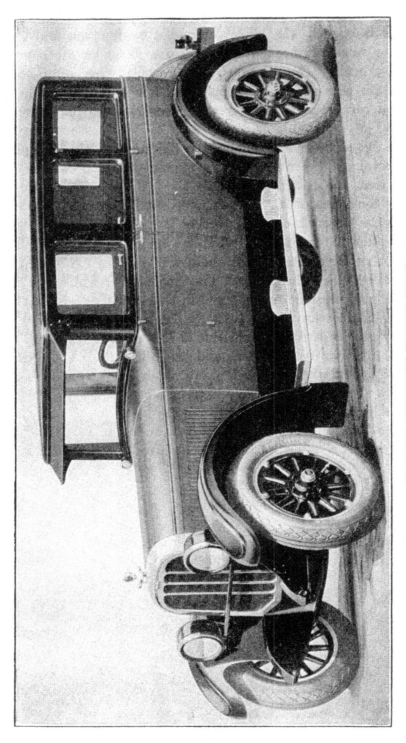

CHANDLER TWENTIETH CENTURY SEDAN

CARBURETORS

PART II

Carburetor adjustment is an essential part of the operation of the engine. When adjustments are made, the maker's instructions should be followed as closely as possible so that the engine will get a correct mixture. If the mixture is too rich, that is, too much gasoline in proportion to air, there will be considerable carbon formed inside the cylinder. This carbon is flint hard and dry in appearance. A large deposit of carbon is not desirable because it becomes red hot and causes preignition. Gas carbon can be distinguished from oil carbon. the latter being wet and sticky, while the former is dry, hard, and black in color. Too lean a mixture, or one that has too much air in proportion to the amount of gas taken into the cylinders, will burn very slowly and will continue to burn when the intake valve opens again for the next intake stroke. It fires the incoming charge and causes the "spit back" through the carburetor. It must be remembered that carburetor adjustments are not the cure for all troubles found in the automobile engine and if the engine has been operating correctly previously, other conditions should be examined before making new adjustments.

Holley Carburetors. The Model "K" carburetor, Fig. 9, is very similar to the Model "G", Fig. 16, the biggest differences being the vertical outlet in place of a horizontal and the placing of the needle valve at the bottom because of this. In Model "K", fuel enters by the gasoline pipe through the strainer A, past the float valve B, into the float chamber D, the level being regulated by the movements of the cork float C. From there, it passes through the opening F into the nozzle well E, through the hole H past the needle to a level in its cup-shaped upper end which just submerges the bottom of a small tube J, with its outlet at the edge of the throttle disc K. When the engine is cranked with the throttle nearly closed an energetic flow of air past this point draws liquid fuel which is atomized upon its exit from the small opening at the throttle edge.

As the engine rotates, considerable air is forced to move through the conical passage outside of the strangling tube *L*. The shape of the passage around the lower end of this is such that the entering air attains its highest velocity, and thus lowest pressure, near the upper end of the standpipe *M*. Consequently, there is a difference in pressure between the top and bottom of this pipe, and the air flows downward through the series of holes *N*. At the bottom it turns sharply upward, picks up the fuel spray there and passes into

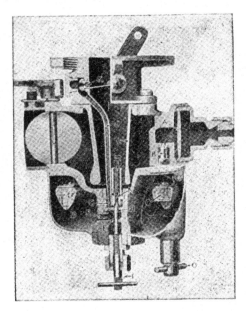

Fig. 9. Holley Carburetor, Model "K"
Courtesy of Holley Brothers Company,
Detroit, Michigan

the main vaporizing chamber above *O*, and thence past the opened throttle to the inlet manifold at *P*.

Model "K" Adjustment. There is but one adjustment and that is provided by the movement of the needle valve *I*. When this is screwed to the right, or clockwise, the valve moves upward and reduces the size of the fuel opening. When turned backward to the left, or counter-clockwise, it increases the opening and admits more fuel. The effect of these changes in its setting are claimed by the maker to be manifest equally over the whole range of the motor. According to the maker, this desirable feature is the result of utilizing in the nozzle action the pressure drop due to velocity of flow rather than the pressure drop causing the air to flow. There are other Holley models which are used for motorcycles and small cars and are smaller in size.

Fig. 10 shows a new Holley carburetor which has a hot spot incorporated in it to help vaporize the fuel. The adjustment in this type of carburetor is the same as in the other Holley devices.

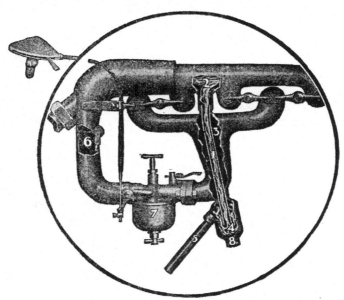

Fig. 10. Holley Carburetor "Hot-Spot"
Courtesy of Holley Carburetor Company

Temperature Regulator. The Holley Company recommends a temperature regulator for use with its own and other carburetors. It is admitted by all that the heat is necessary in cold months, but that it is less necessary, although advisable, in warm months. This necessitates a means of varying it. There is no better source of heat than the handy exhaust pipe where heat is going to waste, so the Holley device, Fig. 11, utilizes the exhaust pipe as a source of heat and leads the same to the carburetor through a flexible tube with a regulating valve at the lower, or carburetor, end. This is regulated by a simple rod connection with a small handle which projects through the dash and has a dial behind it. This can also be used as a strangling valve to assist starting, as shown at *A*, for hot-air supply in winter, and as shown at *B*, for half cold air in the spring and fall months and for all cold air in the summer months.

Kingston Carburetors. *Enclosed Type.* In the Kingston enclosed type, Fig. 12, the auxiliary air valves in the form of various sizes of steel balls are used. These are normally seated, but they

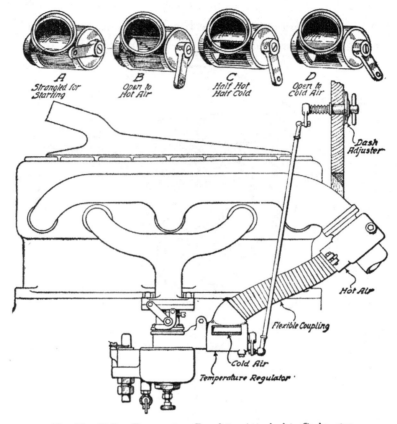

Fig. 11.   Holley Temperature Regulator Attached to Carburetor

are lifted from their seats by increased suction. The passage of air through the primary air valve is vertical rather than at an angle. When the suction lifts the ball valves, more air is admitted. This joins the partially vaporized mixture at the top of the vaporizing chamber and completes the vaporization and dilution before passing the throttle valve on its way to the inlet manifold. The carburetor has the cup-shaped needle recess, so that when the motor is shut off a pool of fuel collects in the recess. This makes starting easy, for this fuel is drawn directly in, almost without dilution.

Adjustments. If the float is found to be too high or too low, it can be adjusted readily by bending the float lever to which it is attached. The only other adjustments are the setting of the throttle which governs the lowest speed—this being accomplished by the screw shown in the throttle-lever arm projection at the left—and the setting of the needle valve for satisfactory high speeds—this being accomplished by unscrewing the cap to which the needle is attached and allowing more fuel to flow. It should be continued until the highest speed is reached and passed, then turned back until the maximum speed is reached.

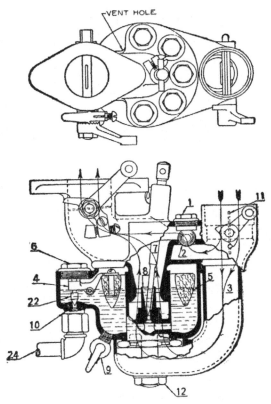

Fig. 12. Plan and Section of Kingston Enclosed
Carburetor
Courtesy of Byrne, Kingston and Company
Kokomo, Indiana

Dual Form. This form, Fig. 13, is really two of the enclosed models, Fig. 12, attached to a common outlet and with a single throttle valve. It is intended for use with heavy fuels; one side is connected up for gasoline, which is used in starting and for exceptionally slow speeds long continued, while the other side is set for heavy fuel, such as kerosene, distillate, etc., and is used as soon as the engine running on gasoline has heated up sufficiently. It will be noted that one-half of this device is fitted with a water valve, which is placed on the heavy fuel side. It is a gravity valve seated by its own weight at low speeds and lifted progressively at higher speeds until wide open. In continuous running on heavy fuels, it has been

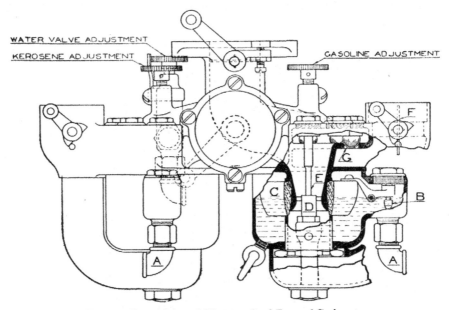

Fig. 13. Part Section of Kingston Dual Form of Carburetor
Courtesy of Byrne, Kingston and Company, Kokomo, Indiana

found that after a certain time the engine begins to pound, but that if cooling water be introduced with the mixture, the engine will run cooler, and this pound will disappear. To remedy this is the function of the water valve.

Model "L." The Kingston carburetor, Fig. 14, is very similar to the Ford model, Fig. 15, except that it is formed with a vertical outlet, and the air valve *B* added in the vaporizing chamber so formed. This is hinged at the side so as to be swung upward by the suction of the motor, thus uncovering a larger and larger orifice. It is weighted and acts automatically. It will be noted also that the shape of the nozzle has been altered slightly, that on the Ford model being perfectly straight. Near its lower end, it passes through the low-speed tube *C*, which has a series of holes around the bottom and an annular space around the body of the needle. Through this space the fuel and a very little air are drawn

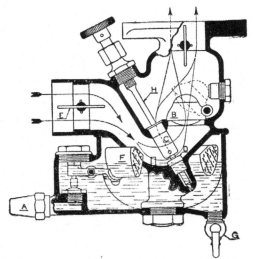

Fig. 14. Section of Kingston Model "L" Carburetor
Courtesy of Byrne, Kingston and Company
Kokomo, Indiana

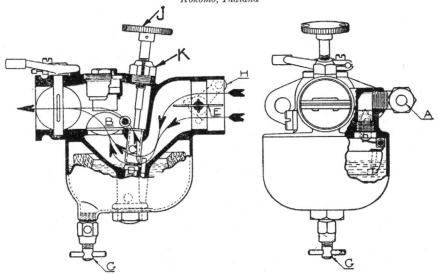

Fig. 15. Drawings Showing Construction of Kingston Model "L2" Carburetor
Courtesy Byrne, Kingston and Company, Kokomo, Indiana

for starting, as, at that low suction, the valve *B* would be entirely seated.

Adjustments. After retarding the spark, opening the throttle, loosening the needle, and starting the motor, let it run at a fair speed long enough to warm up. Then adjust the needle valve. Close the throttle by adjusting the stop screw in the throttle lever until the motor runs at the desired idling speed. Adjust the needle valve towards the seat slowly until the motor begins to lose speed, which indicates a weak mixture. Now adjust the needle valve away from its seat until the motor attains its best and most positive speed. This should complete the adjustment. Close the throttle and let the motor idle, then jerk it open rapidly. The motor should respond readily. If it does not respond, a slight further adjustment may be necessary. When the adjustment has been made, lock it. Float troubles may be remedied in the same way as for the enclosed model.

Carburetors on Ford Cars. On the Model "T" Ford car there are two very simple forms of carburetor used. They are very much alike in general design and construction. The Kingston is shown in Fig. 15 and the Holley, Model "G", is shown in Fig. 16. Both forms have been used in about equal quantities by the Ford Company from 1909 to date.

In the Kingston, A is the fuel connection, B the air valve, C the low speed tube, D the spray nozzle, E the choke throttle, G the drain cock, H the lever operating the choke throttle, J the needle valve, and K the needle valve binder nut. To adjust, warm up the motor, retard the spark fully, open the throttle five or six notches on the steering post quadrant, then loosen the binder nut K so the needle valve J turns easily. Turn this valve down with the dash adjustment until it seats lightly but do not force it. Then turn back, away from the seat, one complete turn. Let the motor run a little while, then make the final adjustment. Close the throttle until the motor runs at idling speed, which can be controlled by adjusting the stop screw in the throttle lever. Adjust the needle valve J towards its seat slowly until the motor begins to lose speed. Stop and adjust the needle valve away from its seat very slowly until the motor attains its best and most positive speed. Close the throttle until the motor runs slowly, then pull it open quickly. The motor should respond strongly. If sluggish, a further adjustment may be necessary. Tighten the binder nut.

In the Holley, A is the thumbscrew with an extension to the dash, by means of which the needle valve B is raised or lowered. The lower end of this projects down into the spray nozzle C, where fuel enters from the float chamber D, reaching it through the gaso-line intake E. To draw off sediment and water use the cock F.

From the nozzle, the fuel passes up through the strangling tube G, where it is met by the entering air from the air inlet H, which has been deflected downward and towards the center of this circular

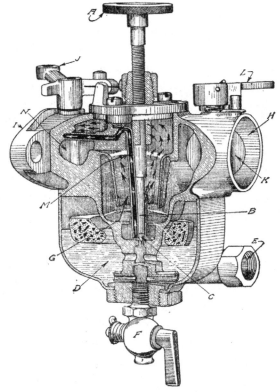

Fig. 16. Section of Holley Carburetor for Ford Cars
Courtesy of Holley Brothers Company, Detroit, Michigan

space so as to pick up the spray of fuel at the nozzle and carry it upward in the strangling tube. Then it passes into the mixing tube N, thence out to the motor by way of the mixture outlet I. In this, its quantity is governed by the throttle, the lever of which may be seen at J. In the air intake there is a throttle plate K, which deflects a large part of the entering air so that it passes to the right (straight in) and is added to the mixture in the mixer chamber. This forms the auxiliary air valve. The position of this plate, governed by the auxiliary throttle lever L, determines the quantity of both the primary and auxiliary air, since by its position it splits the entering air into two parts, one of which becomes the primary air, and the other the auxiliary air. For low speeds and idling, the low-speed tube M carries the very rich mixture up direct to the mixing chamber and thus into the engine.

Ford Adjustment. The Holley, Model "G", like the Kingston, has but one adjustment. The needle valve B, which has a projecting knurled head A for turning it, has a conical point C which

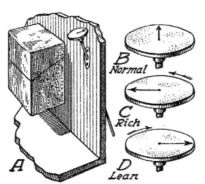

Fig. 17. Dash Adjustment of Ford Carburetor
*Courtesy of Ford Motor Company,
Detroit, Michigan*

seats into the fuel opening. If this is seated, no gasoline can enter, but as it is screwed out or up an opening is created and increased, which allows fuel to flow. The amount of this determines the amount of mixture entering the cylinder combustion chambers. Consequently, the primary adjustment with this screw is that of the fuel flow. Air enters through the opening H, passes the throttle K, and then mixes with the fuel spray, diluting it and carrying it up into the cylinders. The amount of the air is governed by the air lever L, its position being adjusted at the factory.

The usual method of regulating the carburetor is to start the motor, advance the throttle lever (on the steering wheel) to about the sixth notch, with the spark lever (also on the steering wheel) retarded to about the fourth notch. The flow of gasoline should now be cut off by screwing the needle valve down (to the right) until the engine begins to misfire; then gradually increase the gasoline feed by opening the needle valve until the motor picks up and reaches its highest speed and until no trace of black smoke comes from the exhaust. Having determined the point where the motor runs at its maximum speed, the adjustment should not be changed except as indicated below. For average results, a lean mixture will give better results than a rich one.

The gasoline adjustment is placed on the dash, Fig. 17, the milled head shown being fastened to a long rod whose lower end is attached to the needle valve head A, Fig. 16. Any movement of the milled head moves the needle valve and gives more or less gasoline. After the car has been worked in so that it runs satisfactorily, a file mark should be made on the face of this milled head

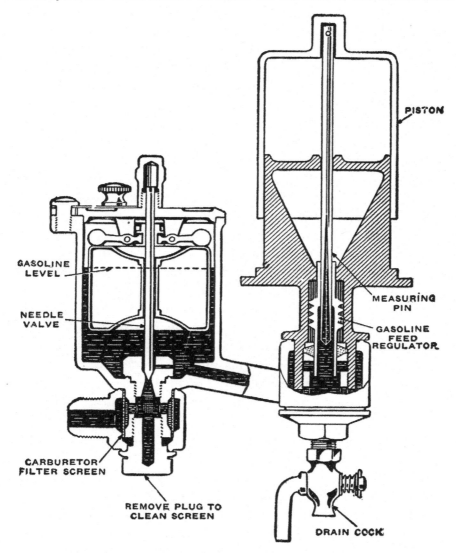

Fig. 18. End View of the Hudson and Essex Carburetor

to indicate the point at which the engine runs most satisfactorily. This is indicated by Fig. 17, in which *A* shows the milled head rod projecting through the dash, and *B* the mark for satisfactory normal running. In cold weather it will probably be found necessary to turn the finger wheel one-quarter turn to the left, or counter-clockwise, as shown at *C*, particularly in starting a cold engine. This movement increases the amount of gasoline and makes the mixture richer. In warm weather, gasoline vaporizes more readily, and it will be found advisable to give the milled head a one-quarter turn to the right, or clockwise, about as shown at *D*. This admits less gasoline and gives a leaner mixture, which is particularly advisable when taking long rides at high speed for it increases the mileage per gallon of fuel.

Carburetors on Hudson and Essex Cars. The carburetors used on the Hudson and the Essex are identical in principle but a little different in detail construction. The gasoline level, Fig. 18, is somewhat lower than the top of the gasoline feed regulator. This regulator, which is adjustable from the dash, determines the amount of gasoline fed at a given altitude or temperature. For high altitudes where the pressure of the air is lower than at sea level, less gasoline is needed, and the sleeve is moved upward.

Principle of Operation. When the throttle is open, the air is drawn out of the air chamber, Fig. 19, through the pneumatic control passage, thus creating a vacuum in the air chamber which allows the piston to be lifted up. As the measuring pin is connected to the piston, it will also be lifted and will expose a deeper portion of the tapered slot on this pin, thus increasing the amount of gasoline as the air is increased. The piston also acts as the air cutoff and returns to its position slowly after the throttle has been closed.

This action is necessary as a greater amount of air must be provided with the greater amount of gasoline in order to obtain the same ratio in the result of mixture. A peculiar air intake construction is provided on both the Hudson and Essex carburetors, and the inquisitive mechanic often wonders why this construction is used. This air inlet is made in the form of an inverted funnel, having the large end toward the carburetor. A butterfly valve is located at the small end to shut off the air side when it is necessary to supply the motor with a rich mixture in starting. This style of motor inlet manifold was not used on the first Hudson cars, and it was found that a hiss was constantly present when the motor was in operation. While this noise was not detrimental, it was

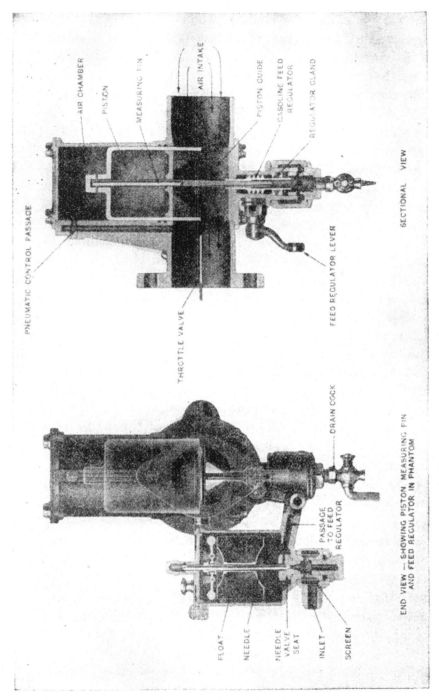

PNEUMATIC CONTROL PASSAGE

AIR CHAMBER

PISTON

MEASURING PIN

AIR INTAKE

PISTON GUIDE

GASOLINE FEED REGULATOR

REGULATOR GLAND

THROTTLE VALVE

FEED REGULATOR LEVER

SECTIONAL VIEW

FLOAT

NEEDLE

NEEDLE VALVE SEAT

INLET

SCREEN

PASSAGE TO FEED REGULATOR

DRAIN COCK

END VIEW — SHOWING PISTON, MEASURING PIN AND FEED REGULATOR IN PHANTOM

Fig. 19. Front and Side View of the Hudson and Essex Carburetor

rather annoying, and the Hudson people found that if the air inlet was constructed in the form of an inverted funnel that this undesirable hiss would be done away with, the manifold acting as a muffler just as the muffler that is attached to the exhaust of the motor, so that the noise resulting from the escaping gases may be deadened.

Master Carburetor. The Master is called a "carburetor without an adjustment." It was originally developed in Los Angeles for the purpose of using the heavy oil, called distillate, which is available there. This, as shown in Fig. 20, is a design of remarkable individuality. Except for the float chamber, it does not resemble any other carburetor. In design it consists of a float chamber to which the fuel enters from below through a round pan-like screen which filters it. From the float chamber the fuel passes through another cylinder-like screen which filters it again. Then it passes to one end of a long fuel passage, from which lead a series of vertical passages, each ending in a nozzle. These passages discharge the fuel into a cylindrical throttle chamber within which is placed a rotary throttle valve. This has a peculiar spiral-shaped edge, so that one tube—the end one shown on the right-hand edge slightly separated from the others—alone communicates with the vaporizing space. This is the starting and idling tube, or nozzle. As the throttle is revolved, the spiral edge brings the other tubes into play, one at a time, until the whole number is engaged. When the throttle is revolved to the full opening, its central portion, as shown in the left-hand figure, is seen to be somewhat restricted at the center and flared at the ends to produce a slightly modified Venturi shape. The passage above the throttle leading to the inlet manifold and the shape of the passage below it through which the air enters, both contribute to this effect.

The air enters from the right, Fig. 20, and the shape of this passage, to match the general shape of the carburetor, is low but wide. This has led to the development of a variable method of furnishing the air—a division in the end of the passage allows of having all cold air, half cold and half hot, or all hot, as desired. For the heavy fuel conditions under which the device was developed, the all-hot air arrangement was used. Except in the hot summer months this would be most desirable, but there are conditions under which the semi-hot air arrangement would be best.

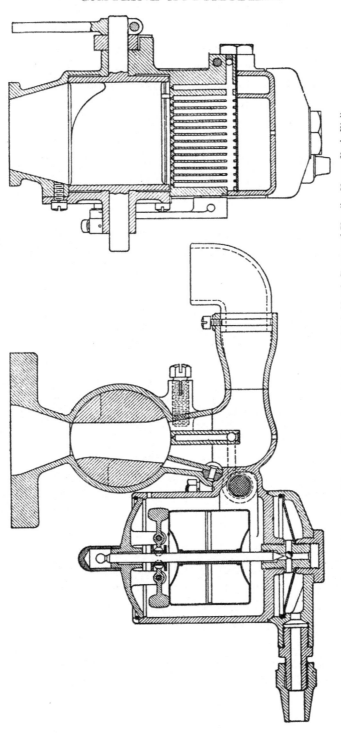

Fig. 20.   Section through the Master Carburetor, which is a Multiple-Nozzle Form and Handles Heavy Fuels Well

Courtesy of Master Carburetor Company, Detroit, Michigan

Adjustment. While it is said not to have any adjustment, there is a variation which corresponds to the adjustment in many carburetors. This is the air damper, which is a long, rigid, flat plate extending across the incoming air passage parallel to the distributor and is connected by means of a Bowden wire mechanism to an operating lever on the steering post in the position where the usual carburetor adjustment is located. When this is moved, the air damper is swung over toward, or away from, the distributor. This movement restricts or increases the air passage at the jets. When the damper is moved so as to restrict the passage of air, its velocity is increased, and the greater suction carries up more fuel from the jets, and thereby produces a richer mixture. On the other hand, when the damper is moved to enlarge the area, there is less suction; consequently less fuel is drawn up, and the mixture is leaner. In the sense that the operator can change nozzles or modify the maximum or minimum amount of air or fuel entering the carburetor, this device has no adjustments. The nozzle cannot be changed and the amount of air can be varied only in a wholesale way—by changing from lean to rich through the whole range between these two. This device has been used four years as regular equipment on Moreland trucks which are built to use distillate selling at 6 cents a gallon, in barrel lots. This fuel has a specific gravity of 51 at 60° F.

When made for Ford cars, this device has only 11 nozzles. On the larger sizes, from 14 to 19 are employed. The use of this device, with its vertical opening, necessitates a special inlet manifold to replace that on the Ford, which provides for a horizontal carburetor outlet.

Miller Racing Carburetor. A device very similar to the Master is the Miller carburetor, Fig. 21. Proof of its efficiency is shown by its wide use on the highest powered engines, such as the King-Bugatti 16-cylinder aeronautic engine, the Duesenberg line of racing and airplane engines, and on the majority of recent racing cars.

In Fig. 21, which shows the carburetor as used on the King-Bugatti 400-horsepower engine, seven screwed-in jets are used, while the number of carburetors used is four, one for each four cylinders. In ordinary racing practice one or two of the seven-jet carburetors are used.

GASOLINE AUTOMOBILES

Gasoline is drawn into each one of the jets through the small hole in the bottom of the threaded end, mixing with a certain

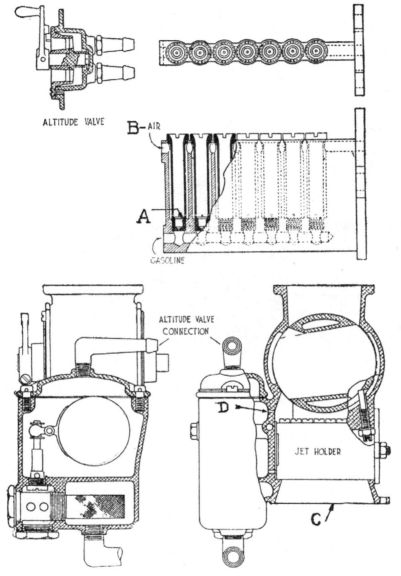

Fig. 21.   Miller Multi-Jet Carburetor and Altitude Valve Details
Courtesy H. A. Miller Manufacturing Company, Los Angeles, California

amount of air sucked in through the four small holes at *A*, drilled in the barrel of the jet just above the threaded portion. This air is taken from the outside through the upper $\frac{3}{16}$-inch hole B in the jet holder, and passes down around the outside of the jet to the four small holes mentioned. The major portion of the air enters the carburetor through the lower end C of the Venturi, which is 3 inches in diameter, passes up around the jet bar holder, combining above this with the rich mixture from the seven jets to form the proper mixture for combustion.

This particular instrument being for airplane use, an altitude adjustment is necessary, the details of which are shown in the

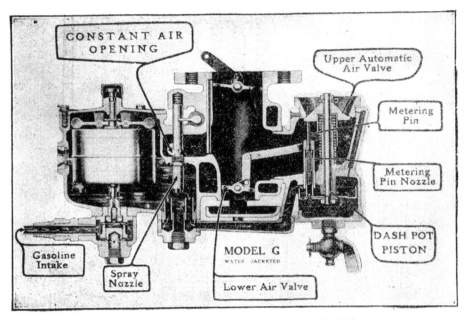

Fig. 22. Section of Rayfield Carburetor, Model "G"
Courtesy of Findeisen and Kropf Manufacturing Company, Chicago

illustration. It operates by turning the lever and has two openings in its seat which, when open, register with similar holes in the cover, giving the free passages to the atmosphere. The float chamber is in direct connection with the Venturi through the drilled hole D, $\frac{5}{64}$ inch in diameter, this being well above the fuel level. When the altitude control valve is opened, the vacuum in the float chamber is decreased, thus increasing the flow of fuel through jets.

Like the Master, this has no adjustment, changes in performance being produced by replacing the jets with different ones.

Rayfield Carburetors. *Model "G"*. The Rayfield carburetor, Model "G", Fig. 22, is of the double-needle type, with three air-inlet openings and an eccentric float chamber. The latter is shown at the left, with fuel entering from below through a strainer. Communicating directly with this float chamber is the passage in which the low-speed nozzle (marked spray nozzle) is situated. This consists of a hollow member with the actual needle point coming down vertically from outside and above, similar to *C*, Fig. 2, Part I. Communicating with the float chamber is a passage, or well, through which fuel flows across to the bottom of the high-speed well. In this passage is located a hollow metering-pin nozzle in the upper part of which is the metering-pin. The upper end, through which the fuel flows, is located in one end of the elongated vaporizing chamber, while the upper automatic air valve has access to the top of it and furnishes the air supply.

At the other end of the vaporizing chamber the idling needle is located, and directly beyond it is the constant air opening, a simple round hole communicating with the atmosphere. This end is short and close to the central portion of the chamber, which is approximately cylindrical. The lower air valve is at the bottom, while the vertical connection to the inlet manifold and the butterfly throttle are at the top. The lower air valve and the upper automatic air valve are linked together so as to operate simultaneously. The movement of the upper automatic air valve downward actuates the metering-pin, moving it downward. This tends to allow fuel to flow out around the pin. At the same time the stem of this valve is connected at the bottom with a piston working in the dashpot which is filled with fuel, so that any sudden tendency for the air valve to open is checked by this dashpot. At the same time this piston communicates with the hollow metering-pin nozzle, so that the downward movement of the piston forces an extra supply of fuel into the nozzle and enriches the mixture. Thus, the opening of the throttle automatically produces a rich mixture for starting, as the slow movement of the air valve in opening against the drag of the dashpot causes a relatively stronger suction on the nozzles. This arrangement eliminates the necessity for an air-valve adjustment, that is, an adjustment which owner or repair man is supposed to use. As a matter of fact the carburetor is made with an adjusting ring, which, after setting at the factory, is locked by means of a set screw and is not supposed to be touched.

Adjustments. There are two simple adjustments on the Rayfield and both are made by means of external milled head screws, Fig. 23. Before making any adjustments, be sure there are no obstructions in the gasoline line, that all manifold connections are tight and free from air leaks, that valves and ignition are correctly timed, and that there is good compression and hot spark in all cylinders.

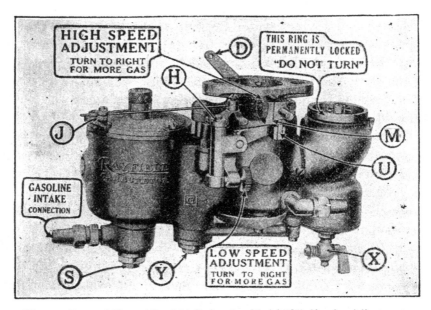

Fig. 23. External View of Rayfield Carburetor, Model "G", Showing Adjustments

These carburetors are generally fitted with dash control. Always adjust the carburetor with this dash control down.

Low-Speed Adjustment. This should be made first. To do this, close the throttle and let the dash control down, then close the nozzle needle by turning the low-speed adjustment to the left until the block *U* leaves contact with the cam *M* slightly. Then turn to the right about three full turns. Start the motor and allow it to run until warmed up, then push the dash control all the way down, retard the spark, close the throttle until the motor runs slowly without stopping. Now make the final adjustment by turning the low-speed screw to the left until the motor slows down. Next, turn to the right, one notch at a time, until the motor idles smoothly.

If the motor does not throttle low enough, turn the stop-arm screw on the main throttle-valve shaft to the left until the motor does run at the minimum speed desired.

High-Speed Adjustment. Advance the spark about one-quarter with the motor running, then open the throttle quickly. Should the motor back-fire, it indicates a lean mixture. Correct this by turning the high-speed adjusting screw, Fig. 23, to the right, about one notch at a time, until the throttle can be opened quickly without back-firing. If loading, or choking, is experienced when the motor is running under heavy load with the throttle wide open, it indicates too rich a mixture. This can be overcome by turning the high-speed adjustment to the left. Adjustments made for high speed will not affect low speed. Low-speed adjustments must not be used to get a correct mixture at high speed. Both adjustments are positively locked.

Model "L". The Model "L" is the same as Model "G" without the water jacket. It is adjusted in the same manner.

Changing Nozzles. "Never, under any circumstances, change nozzles in the Models "G" and "L" carburetors." Neither should the float level be changed, as this is correctly set at the factory and should not be touched. For use with a pressure system, two pounds pressure is advised. The plugs S, Y, and X are for cleaning and draining purposes. In the bottom of the float chamber there is a strainer strap, which can be cleaned by shutting off the gasoline supply and removing the nut S. The dashpot is drained by opening the drain cock X. It is advisable to do this occasionally to remove any sediment that may have accumulated there. The float chamber should also be drained occasionally by removing the plug Y. When this is replaced, it should be tightened very carefully; and when the strainer trap is removed and cleaned, care should be taken in replacing it to put the gaskets back in place as well as to tighten the nut adequately.

Model "M". The Rayfield firm makes another model, known as Model "M", which is similar to Model "L", except that it has a side, or horizontal, outlet. It has the same two adjustments, made in the same way, but the shape of the carburetor locates these in a different place. The low-speed adjusting screw is on the extreme top of the carburetor, and the high-speed adjusting screw is also on the top, but it is made accessible by removing the hot-air elbow from the main air valve. This model is fitted with a starting primer incorporated in the device itself and operated through the medium of a dash lever. The construction and operation of this are shown in Fig. 24. When pressure feed is used, not more than one pound is recommended for Model "M". When the starting primer is to be attached, locate the position on the dash desired for the push button and drill a $\frac{5}{8}$-inch hole at the proper angle.

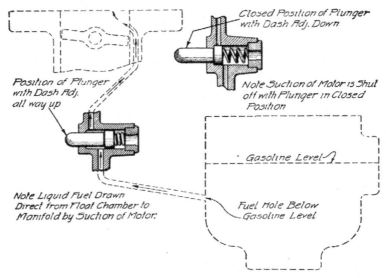

Fig. 24.   Sketch of Starting Primer Attached to Model "M" Rayfield Carburetor

Attach the adjustment and run the tubing to the bracket on the carburetor, avoiding sharp bends. Cut off the tubing so it will extend beyond the bracket not more than $\frac{1}{4}$ inch. Remove the temporary wire from the carburetor, insert the tubing and secure permanently by tightening the clamp screw. Run the dash adjustment wire through the hole in the binding post on the eccentric lever. Then, with the push button down, place the eccentric arm in position so that the line on the eccentric just comes in contact with the adjusting screw. Tighten the screw in the binding post, cut off the surplus wire, and, without changing the position of the push button, make the carburetor adjustment.

Model "S.T." This carburetor is quite different to the other types of Rayfield carburetors both in appearance and in operation. The operation can be followed by referring to Fig. 25. There is a

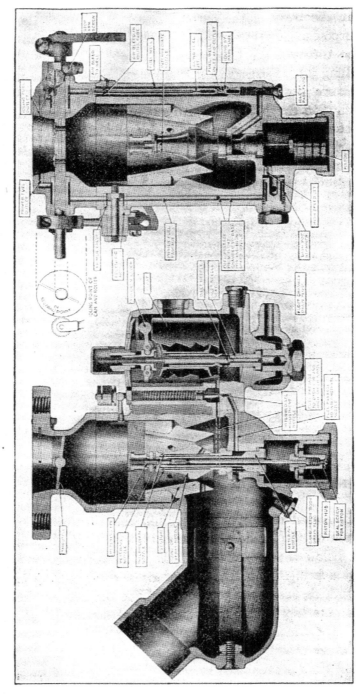

Fig. 25. Model S.T. Rayfield Carburetor

311

passage in the body of the carburetor which supplies the fuel for idling purposes. An idling tube carries the fuel to an opening above the throttle, the strength of the mixture being controlled by the idling jet. With the throttle almost closed, as in the idling position, there is a high vacuum in the carburetor above the throttle and the suction draws the mixture out of the tube into the manifold. When the throttle is opened wider, the suction increases and the Venturi tube is raised off of its seat. At the point of the smallest diameter of the Venturi the spray nozzle is cone shaped on the outside. As the space increases or as the Venturi rises, the supply

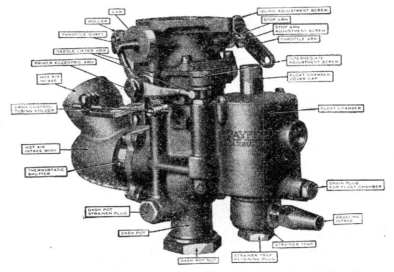

Fig. 26. Model S.T. Rayfield Carburetor, Showing Names of Parts

of air is increased in proportion around the Venturi. There is a metering pin on the inside of the spray nozzle which tapers from a point just below the top of the nozzle. It is also attached to the Venturi by a bridge. As the Venturi rises, the metering pin must also rise and, as the taper gets smaller, the opening in the top of the nozzle gets larger and consequently the supply of gasoline is increased. There is a dashpot and piston incorporated in the bottom of the Venturi chamber which tend to retard the raising of the Venturi and thus prevent too much air being supplied at the time of acceleration. This action causes a greater amount of gas to be supplied at the time of acceleration.

In adjusting this carburetor, the idling adjustment should be open two full turns and allowed to remain until the intermediate adjustment has been made. The engine should be started and allowed to thoroughly warm up. The throttle lever should then be opened about one-eighth of a turn, Fig. 26. While making this adjustment be sure that the adjustment on the dash of the car is down the entire distance. The intermediate adjustment screw

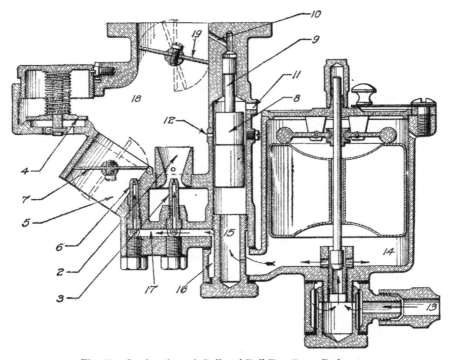

Fig. 27.   Section through Ball and Ball Two-Stage Carburetor
Courtesy of Penberthy Injector Company, Detroit, Michigan

should then be turned to the right a few notches at a time until the engine starts to slow down or until the mixture becomes very thin. Then turn to the left until the engine runs evenly.

To adjust the idling, move the throttle lever to the idling position. The screw should be turned to the right until the mixture gets too thin and then to the left until the engine idles smoothly.

Ball and Ball Carburetor. The Ball and Ball device has been developed by Frank H. Ball and Frederick O. Ball and is named after them, but it is manufactured and sold by the Penberthy

Injector Company. In all its forms, whether single or double, horizontal or vertical, it is a two-stage instrument. These two stages are called the primary and the secondary, the primary stage corresponding to the usual simple air-valve carburetor, Fig. 27. This consists of nozzle, or jet, 3, located in the fixed air passage, or Venturi, 2. In the space above this, the air for complete vaporization is received through the valve 4. Some air is, of course, admitted around the nozzle 3 below the Venturi 2, otherwise the fuel would not be drawn up. This nozzle receives its fuel from the float chamber 14, which is supplied through a strainer in the usual manner from the gasoline pipe 13. The connection from the float chamber to the jet extends first to the well 16, thence across the horizontal passage 17, from which the nozzle 3 draws its supply.

Now, to this simple carburetor add another which consists of the nozzle 6 and of the air supply 5, which is normally closed by the butterfly throttle 7; this latter, when closed by a spring, covers the top of the jet 6 so that it cannot function. It is obvious that the primary stage is constructed for low speed, idling, and for the lower range of driving, and is very economical. As this lower range covers perhaps 85 to 90 per cent of ordinary driving, this would be a desirable feature.

As the drawing shows, the opening of the second throttle valve 7 allows additional air to enter and, at the same time, uncovers the second jet 6, so that this starts to function by drawing its gasoline from the same horizontal passage 17 as does the primary jet. If this throttle were connected up to the other throttle in such a way that, when approaching the maximum opening of the main throttle, the secondary throttle would begin to open, we would have, in effect, two carburetors, one working over the lower range, which gives good idling and splendid economy, and the other high-speed and high-power device adding its total effect to that of the primary. The two contradictory and opposed qualities of highest power and highest economy are thus produced by what is, in effect, a double carburetor. This, with variations for various sizes and types of cars, constitutes the Ball and Ball device, Fig. 27.

Pick-Up Device. This carburetor has a pick-up device which produces remarkable acceleration. This consists of the plunger 8 having a smaller sized upper end 9. It is loosely fitted in the chamber *15*, the bottom of which communicates with the float chamber, and is thus kept full of gasoline. At the top, a small hole *10* communicates with the manifold above the throttle, while *11* is an opening to the atmosphere, and *12* is an opening to the mixing chamber. When the throttle is nearly closed, the vacuum in the manifold raises the plunger, and the space below it fills with gasoline. In this position it is ready to act. When the throttle is opened suddenly, the vacuum is broken, and the plunger drops of its own weight, forcing the gasoline up where it is swept into the mixing chamber by the air entering through the passages *11* and *12*. This is repeated as often as the throttle is suddenly opened from a nearly closed position.

Adjustments. The primary stage must be adjusted as a whole to give the best idling and slow speeds; this consists of the adjustment of the air-valve spring, the arrangement of the hot-air passage leading to it, or, if these prove insufficient, the changing of the primary nozzle. The last change is opposed by the makers.

Beyond this, the only adjustment possible lies in the hot-air choke valve which can be moved or altered from the dash to give more or less hot air. The partial closing of this valve makes starting easier and helps the running of the motor until it gets warmed up, but in normal running its manipulation has little effect. In going farther than this, the only possibility lies in altering the design by varying the connection between the two throttles, so the second stage cuts in sooner or later, but this might impair the usefulness of the instrument. The same is true if the secondary nozzle is changed. The device, then, is really lacking in adjustments in the ordinary sense, except for the initial setting of the primary-stage air valve.

Marvel Carburetor. The Marvel carburetor, Model "E", Fig. 28, is notable for using the exhaust gases directly for heating the vaporizing chamber as well as for pre-heating the air used for vaporizing the fuel. The latter is common enough, but in the usual case where heating is thought necessary, hot water from the motor's water-circulating system is used. Another novelty in this design is the inclined hinged form of air valve set across the lower part of the vaporizing chamber. The float chamber *A* is eccentric to the central vaporizing chamber *B*, but is set very close to it. so the ends of the cylindrical float *C* have to be cut off for clearance. Fuel enters from below. It enters the gasoline passage from above, as this is horizontal. The primary, or low-speed, nozzle *D*, which is adjustable, takes off from this about midway of its length, and the high-speed nozzle *E* from the end. The former operates within a Venturi tube which is supplied with air from below. Above this, the chamber broadens out through the zone in which the high-speed

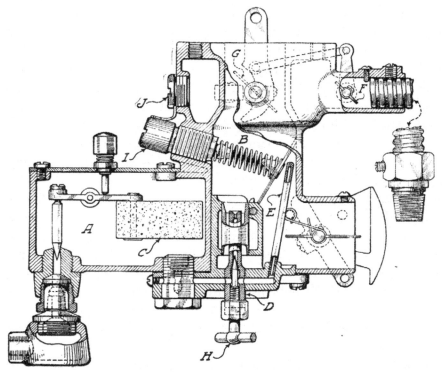

Fig. 28. Section through Marvel Carburetor, Model "E"
Courtesy of Marvel Carburetor Company, Flint, Michigan

nozzle contributes, but above that it narrows down again before meeting the outlet, the last few inches having exhaust heat applied around it.

These exhaust gases pass downward through an external cylindrical passage and, after warming the Venturi and primary nozzle region, escape to the atmosphere. This gas is obtained by tapping into the exhaust manifold within a few inches of the last cylinder outlet (4 inches are recommended). As the motor demand rises beyond the ability of the primary nozzle, the inclined air valve is drawn toward the vertical position, and, as soon as it leaves the cylinder wall, the high-speed nozzle is uncovered and starts to contribute. The air is supplied from the same air inlet, but it rises more directly. A throttle is placed in the air inlet to facilitate starting; closing this cuts off the air, so that a richer mixture is supplied. There is a damper, or throttle, F, in the exhaust gas-inlet passage. It is interconnected with the main throttle G in such a way that it is opened when the latter is closed and closed when the latter is opened. The idea is to furnish a great quantity of heat when the throttle is nearly closed, and to gradually diminish the supply as the throttle is opened and the motor warms up.

Adjustments. There are two adjustments: the gasoline adjustent H, so-called by the maker, and the air adjustment I. The gasoline adjustment operates the primary nozzle. These primary adjustments can be made on the instrument as received by closing the gasoline needle valve H by turning it gently to the right until seated, then opening it by turning to the left a three-quarter turn. The air-adjusting screw I should be turned until the end of the screw is about even with the edge of the spring ratchet J provided to hold it when set. After starting, close the throttle to produce a moderate speed. Then close the gasoline needle H a very little at a time until the motor runs smoothly. It is necessary to allow the motor to get thoroughly warmed up, though, before making the final adjustment.

Next, adjust the air valve. Turn the adjusting screw I to the left to back it out and release the air spring about one-eighth of a turn at a time until the motor begins to slow down. This indicates that the screw is too loose, so turn back slowly, one-eighth of a turn at a time, until it runs smoothly again. Next, advance the spark two-thirds of its travel and open the throttle quickly. The motor should speed up promptly and quickly. If it hesitates or pops back, a little more gasoline should be released at the needle valve H by turning it to the left a very little at a time. It may also be necessary to tighten the air screw I a little more. Now, wait for the motor to settle down to this new adjustment, then open the throttle again quickly. Continue this sudden throttle opening and subsequent adjustment until the point is reached where the motor will respond in a satisfactory manner to a sudden throttle opening. The highest economy is obtained by turning the air screw to the left and the gasoline needle *H* to the right, closing it as nearly as possible and still obtain the desired results.

Fuel Supply. When the carburetor is fed by gravity, the bottom of the bowl should be at least eight inches below the bottom of the gasoline tank. When it is fed by pressure, one pound is sufficient, and two pounds should never be exceeded.

The Marvel Carburetor Company also makes a Model "N", designed for Ford cars to which it can be attached without change of manifold, levers, or other fittings. It is built on the same general plan as the Model "E".

CARBURETORS

PART III

If a new carburetor is to be installed on an engine, care should be taken that it is of the correct size. There should be no restriction to the flow of gas from the carburetor, therefore the opening in the carburetor body should be the same size as that of the intake manifold. When ordering a new carburetor give full particulars as to the size of the intake manifold—inside measurement, and model of engine that it is to be installed upon. The gasket between the carburetor body and the manifold should be in good condition so that there will be no air leaks as this would upset the mixture and cause trouble in the operation of the engine.

Schebler Carburetors. The Schebler carburetor is one of the simplest complete carburetors made. In general, all Scheblers have a concentric float; a single needle valve—the position of which can be adjusted to suit varying needs; and an auxiliary air valve which is also adjustable. In all these models, too, there is a primary air orifice of unvarying section.

In the later models, the needle valve, or metering pin, as it is more correctly called, is interconnected with the air valve so that operation of the latter varies the former. Many models are made and all are still in use.

Adjustment of Model "R." Model "R," Fig. 29, has a vertical setting of the needle valve E. Its movement is adjusted by an internal lever connected to the air-valve cap A. The air inlet group has been raised to correspond with the longer Venturi, and its main opening is on top, with the adjusting screw F on the bottom. To adjust this model, see that lever B is attached to the steering-column control or dash control in such a way that the boss D is against the stop C when the lever on the steering column or dash registers lean, or air. This is the proper running position. To adjust, turn the air-valve cap A clockwise, or to the right, until it stops, then turn to the left, or counter-clockwise, one full turn. Open the throttle one-eighth to one-quarter, start the motor, let it warm up, then turn the air-valve cap A to left, or counter-clockwise, until the engine hits perfectly. Advance the spark three-quarters, and if the engine back-fires on quick acceleration, turn the adjusting screw F up until acceleration is satisfactory. This increases the tension on the air-valve spring. Turning the air-valve cap to the right, or clockwise, lifts the needle valve E out of the nozzle and enriches the mixture. Turning it counter-clockwise lowers it and makes the mixture lean. When the motor is cold or the car has been stand-

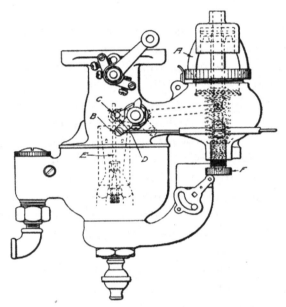

Fig. 29. Schebler Carburetor, Model "R"
Courtesy of Wheeler and Schebler, Indianapolis, Indiana

ing, move the steering-column or dash-control lever towards the gas, or rich, position. This lifts the needle E out of the nozzle and makes a rich mixture for starting. As the motor warms up, move the lever back to obtain the best running position.

Adjustments of Model "A." The newest form, Model "A," is made in both the vertical and horizontal forms. Only the former will be illustrated here, this being shown in Fig. 30, which presents a vertical section. This is built around the principle of the "Pitot" tube, utilizing the differential head created by an up-stream and down-stream pitot tube to control the fuel delivery into the Venturi-shaped vaporizing chamber, to which the air has access from below. This arrangement gives a fuel flow exactly proportioned and controlled by the air. In the figure, E indicates the up-stream opening and F the down-stream nozzle of this arrangement, with air entering at the lower left through the passage there, which is controlled by the starting shutter C. The high speed adjustment is simple, and is made through the needle B. The low speed or idling device delivers fuel and air at the low edge of the throttle disc in its closed position, this being adjusted through

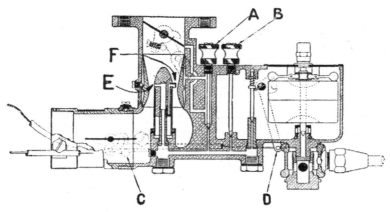

Fig. 30. Schebler Model "A" Carburetor, a Single Tube Device
Courtesy Wheeler and Schebler Company, Indianapolis, Indiana

needle A and the passages in the body of the carburetor, shown adjacent to A.

With the lever D set to give a rich mixture and air choker C set to cut off all the air, both fuel nozzles A and B are opened three or four complete turns from the closed or seated position. Open throttle, start motor and let it warm up. Then with warming-up lever D fully retarded adjust A to correct mixture for idling. Open throttle one-quarter and adjust high speed mixture with needle B.

Adjustment of Model "S." There are three adjustments on the Model "S" Schebler. The idling for low speed; a range adjustment, which is effective only at speeds between from twenty to forty miles an hour; and the power adjustment, which is effective only with throttle in the wide open position. The idle adjustment is made by turning the adjustment *A*, Fig. 31. If turned to the right, a lean mixture will be obtained, and if turned to the left, a rich mixture is obtained. This adjustment is not very sensitive and consequently care should be taken with this adjustment to insure against too rich a mixture at idling speed. Care should be taken not to turn screw *A* to the left too far, as by so doing it will

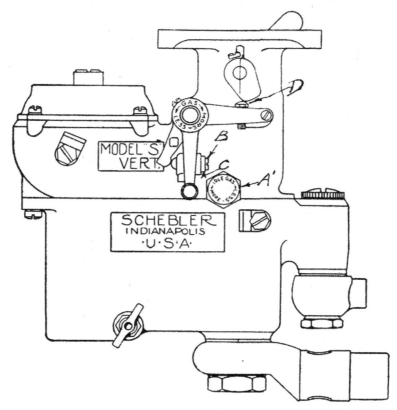

Fig. 31. Schebler Model "S" Carburetor
Courtesy of Wheeler and Schebler Company, Indianapolis, Indiana

screw the needle valve seat out of its thread and hold the air valve open, upsetting the idle adjustment.

To start the engine, open the throttle one-quarter way. The dash control should be pulled out but just as soon as the engine starts push the plunger in half way, and continue to push it in as the engine warms up until the plunger is all the way in. The idle adjustment can then be made.

The *idle adjustment*, as set at the factory, is almost correct and a test can be made in the following manner before the final idle adjustment is made. Close the throttle or set the throttle adjustment screw with the spark in the full retard position so that the engine runs at the desired speed. Depress the air valve $\frac{1}{32}$ to $\frac{1}{16}$ of an inch. If the engine starts to miss, the mixture is about correct. If the mixture is too lean, the engine will stop immediately, and the adjustment A should be turned slightly to the left to enrich the mixture. If the mixture is too rich, the engine will speed up with the air valve depressed as stated, and then the adjustments should be turned to the right to lean out the mixture. In this manner a correct idling adjustment can be made.

The *range adjustment* is made by turning the screw B to the left for a lean mixture and to the right for a rich mixture. This adjustment, as made at the factory, is usually found to be correct, but should it be altered in any way the following method can be used to get the factory adjustment. Screw the adjustment screw in or out until the head of the screw B is level with the bushing B through which the screw passes.

The *power adjustment*, as made at the factory, is also usually found to be correct, but should there be need for adjustment, the cam tappet screw D should be turned clockwise for leaner mixture and in the other direction for rich mixture. The direction is given as if the screw was looked at from above. This adjustment should be kept as lean as possible.

Stewart Carburetor. The predominating feature of the Stewart Model "25" is the automatic metering valve by which the air admitted measures the gasoline used. This valve, which is the only moving part, is drawn upward by the suction of the motor and comes back down onto its seat through its own weight when the suction is lessened. In Fig. 32, the complete carburetor with the throttle open is shown at the right, and the vaporizing chamber only and with throttle closed is shown at the left; the float chamber is the same in both cases. Gasoline flows in through the strainer to the float chamber, thence to the dashpot, filling this and continuing to rise to a point about on a line with the top of the tapered metering pin, which corresponds to the usual needle valve.

With the engine at rest, as shown by the left-hand figure, the upper end of the metering valve, which has a conical lower surface, rests upon the valve seat, thus closing the main air passage. Its lower end extends down into the gasoline in the dashpot. Through its center is an opening, known as the aspirating tube, into the lower end of which extends (from below) the tapered metering pin. As soon as the motor starts, or is turned over, so that a partial vacuum is created in the mixing chamber, the metering valve is lifted to admit air past the valve seat, as shown in the right-hand part of the figure. This vacuum is also communicated to the fuel chamber through the aspirating tube, drawing gasoline through it and up

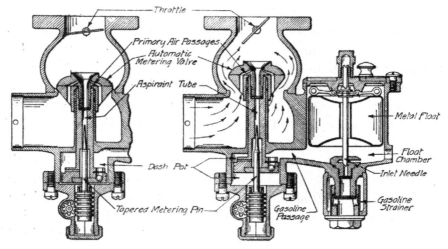

Fig. 32.   Sections Showing Construction of Stewart Carburetor
Courtesy of Detroit Lubricator Company, Detroit, Michigan

the central passage; the latter is expanded in diameter near the top and is then flared out to a large size at the point where the air entering through the vertical holes in the metering valve meets the gasoline and picks it up. The purpose of this flare is to spread the fuel out into a thin film, which the high velocity primary air picks up readily in minute particles, producing thorough atomization. The high velocity of the air is due to the constant vacuum, this vacuum being determined by the weight of the valve which is always the same. Obviously, atomization is equally good at all speeds.

Starting. This arrangement also makes for easy starting, but this is further facilitated by means of a dash control, which is attached to the metering pin in such a way that, when the plunger (on the dash) is pulled out, the metering pin is lowered away from the metering valve above. This permits more gasoline to be drawn up through the aspirating tube and results in a richer mixture. The dashpot arrangement prevents rapid fluctuations and also makes the metering valve slower to respond than the fuel valve; in this way it produces a gasoline lead over the air which gives good acceleration.

Fig. 33. Exterior of Stewart Carburetor, Showing Adjustments
Courtesy of Detroit Lubricator Company, Detroit, Michigan

The higher the metering valve lifts in response to engine suction, the greater will be the opening around the metering pin, which permits more gasoline to be drawn up; therefore, as the suction varies and the metering valve moves up and down, the volume of air and amount of gasoline must always increase or decrease in the right ratio, automatically giving the right proportions in the mixture at all speeds.

Adjustment. The Stewart has but one adjustment. This consists of the lowering or raising of the tapered metering pin, thereby increasing or decreasing the relative amount of gasoline admitted to the mixing chamber in response to the movement of the metering valve. This movement is produced by the rotation of the small gear A, which engages with a rack on the lower end of the tapered metering pin. This gear is rotated by means of a flexible-wire (Bowden) connection to the dash control. The limit of this motion, as well as the normal position of the gear, is governed by the setting of the adjusting, or stop, screw B, shown in the external view, Fig. 33.

This screw can be turned either way; turning it to the right lowers the position of the metering pin, admitting more gasoline; and turning it to the left raises it so that less fuel is admitted. A wider range of adjustment than this stop screw affords can be had by releasing the clamp C of the pinion-shaft lever D and moving it around to a new position on the shaft. This adjustment, however, is not recommended except for expert repair men.

With the motor idling the adjustment should be made by moving the screw up and down, that is, out and in until the motor runs smoothly. This adjustment must be made with the dash control pushed all the way in. When this simple adjustment is made correctly, the device is practically automatic from that time on. A stop screw E on the throttle lever is movable and affords the equivalent of a limited adjustment, for it can be set to give a smaller and smaller opening and thus slower and slower idling. It also has an influence on the maximum opening which influences the highest speed.

Johnson Carburetor. The Johnson carburetor, of which a section through Model "D" is shown in Fig. 34, is one of the newer designs to be placed on the market. It is a simple form, with a concentric type of float chamber A, above which is a simple cylindrical mixing chamber B containing the air-regulating device. It is surrounded by a hot-air jacket C, which warms the mixing chamber and furnishes the primary air supply. This is composed of the strangle tube D and air controlling sleeve E, with a lift plate F suspended from this sleeve in the strangle tube.

Operation. Gasoline enters the float chamber from above, in the usual way. It enters the spray nozzle through the cross-hole G, then rises inside this and passes the tip of the needle H, where it continues out through the nozzle point into the lower part of the mixing chamber. The fuel issues as a fine spray into the strangle tube D, which is conical in shape. In the mixing chamber is a sliding brass sleeve E, which moves up and down according to the engine suction and carries the lift plate F which is just above the outlet from the spraying nozzle. Warm air enters the air inlet I and finds its way

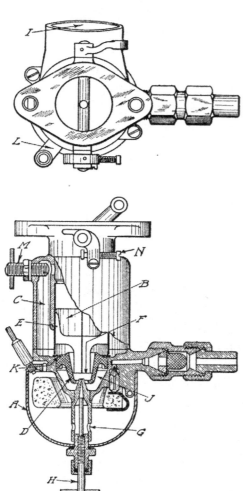

Fig. 34. Top View and Section of Johnson Carburetor, Model "D"

around the chamber C, some of it reaching the passage J below the lift plate and strangle tube. Here it picks up the fuel from the nozzle and impinges it against the lift plate to break it up into finer particles. In addition, the rising air and fuel raise the plate and with it the sleeve E, allowing more air to enter around the bottom of the sleeve. By this arrangement, the current of air is divided and forms both the primary and the auxiliary currents. The latter current is varied to suit the engine demands by the rising and falling of the sleeve. This movement of the sleeve automatically proportions the air and gas to the demand, for, in rising, the lift plate is drawn away from the nozzle tip, and more fuel is allowed to flow out.

On top of the strangle tube rests a flat choker plate K, which is capable of being turned around. There are holes in this to correspond with the holes in the strangle tube through which the primary air passes down to the lower side. In rising again, it picks up the fuel spray. A lever L extends through the outside of the carburetor and is connected up to the dash control. This lever controls the choker plate which can be moved around to cover or uncover the air holes and give more or less primary air as the device needs it. Thus, the low-speed screw M, the needle valve, and the stop screw N on the throttle shaft constitute the adjustments.

Adjusting the Johnson. The function of the low-speed screw is to admit or to cut off the small amount of air supply to the upper part of the mixing chamber as the motor demands; this screw is to be adjusted only with a closed throttle, retarded spark, and the motor idling. The motor should be hot. This is an idling adjustment, designed to supply additional air through the opening O, the need for which is caused by the sleeve E being in its bottom position and thus cutting off the supply, which is available later when the sleeve has risen and in so doing has formed the annular air passage.

The spray needle H, adjusted by the external handle, takes care of all other throttle positions and speeds by admitting more or less fuel. To adjust it, turn the low-speed screw and spray needle to their seats and set the throttle-lever stop screw to approximate the correct closed position. Open the spray needle one and one-half turns. Start the motor, and when it has warmed up, place the spark lever in the fully retarded position; then open the throttle quickly, and if the motor does not back-fire, the mixture is slightly rich and the spray needle should be closed by turning to the right about one-eighth of a turn.· Again open the throttle quickly and repeat until the motor does back-fire; this will determine a lean mixture. Open the needle slightly to correct the mixture, which will give the correct adjustment on high and intermediate speed. Adjust the throttle stop screw until the desired idling speed, or about 240 r.p.m., is secured. If the motor does not fire continuously and run smoothly, the low-speed mixture is too rich and is corrected by backing out the low-speed screw M until sufficient air is admitted for smooth even firing. Then lock it with the lock nut. If this last adjustment has increased the speed of the motor, restore the idling speed by unscrewing the throttle stop screw N slightly. If necessary, reset the low-speed screw, as both of these have to be adjusted in combination.

Dash Control. This controls the choker plate, which acts as a choke to the nozzle by reducing the supply of primary air. After the motor has been warmed up, this should be in the wide-open position. The position for a cold motor, approximating the closed position, will be determined by experience. It is recommended that the motor be choked, that is, the dash control set in the closed position, when stopping. This provides a rich charge for starting. As will be seen from this, the choker plate, with its dash control, is primarily a starting device.

Other Models. This carburetor is made in other models, notably a small one for the Ford car; the essential difference in this being the location of the low-speed screw on top, as it has a horizontal outlet on one side and the warm air inlet on the other. Another large size for eight-cylinder models has a special accelerating device consisting of a fuel plunger operated from the throttle. Still another model is a fixed-needle type in which the nozzle is calibrated for the motor. The adjustment is practically the same for all these.

Carter Carburetor. The Carter carburetor is a multiple-jet device in which, at slow or idling speed, but one jet is furnishing fuel, while at extreme high speed eighteen are operating. These are not jets in the sense that the ordinary carburetor has separate vertical or horizontal jets, as in the Master carburetor, for instance, but they consist of a series of holes set spirally around a central standpipe of fairly large diameter. The action of the device is such that only one is working at low speed, while at high speed the great suction is drawing the fuel up so high in the standpipe that it is issuing from the entire group of 18 holes.

A vertical section through the center of this carburetor is shown in Fig. 35. As will be noted, the bottom of this rests in a tube, or open standpipe, which communicates with the float chamber and is kept filled to the float level with fuel. Just at the top of this tube is the main air inlet. The air enters around the sides of the standpipe

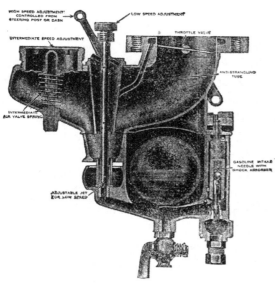

Fig. 35. Section of Carter Multiple-Jet Carburetor
Courtesy of Carter Carburetor Company,
St. Louis, Missouri

and rises vertically along it. Around the upper part of the standpipe is a flaring conical tube, the top of which is closed by a damper. Air enters here and is drawn downward, its amount being controlled by the damper. At the left will be seen the supplementary air valve, a third source of air; this air is also drawn downward, and the amount is adjustable. From this it can be seen that the primary air and the fuel from the first few jets come upward, while the secondary air and the fuel from the additional jets go downward, and that the supplementary air rushes in at an angle where these two meet at the bottom of the U-shaped vaporizing chamber. This produces a constant state of turbulence around the standpipe, which facilitates breaking up and vaporizing the fuel. The fuel passes a butterfly throttle in its passage to the inlet manifold.

For easy starting, a tube (marked anti-strangling tube in the cut) is by-passed around the vaporizing chamber, taking its fuel directly from the well at the left of the float chamber and furnishing it directly into the outlet pipe above the throttle. In starting and idling on the lowest jet, or hole, of the standpipe, the fuel is drawn almost directly from the float chamber. For this reason an unusually accurate float arrangement is necessary, and this is provided by the metal ball float and the needle arrangement with its ball and spring shock absorber. The latter eliminates any possibility of jamming and gives accurate control of the fuel level. The action of the device is very simple, the engine suction drawing the fuel higher and higher in the standpipe as the suction increases, while the same suction draws open the intermediate air valve as soon as the required supply exceeds the capacity of the main air intake. The high-speed air inlet, operated by the damper, is thrown into action from the steering post or dash at the will of the operator.

Adjusting the Carter. By reference to Fig. 35, the adjusting will be made plain. First set the high-speed adjustment with the lever in a vertical position; then turn the knurled button marked low-speed adjustment down, or to the right as far as it will go; next back it off and turn it to the left three-quarters of a turn. Turn the knurled valve ring marked intermediate-speed adjustment to the point where the valve seats lightly, then turn the valve down, or to the right, from eight to ten notches to increase the spring tension. Pull the easy-starting lever, connected with the dash, forward to the position shown in Fig. **38**, advance the spark a very little, close the throttle, and start the engine.

Through the medium of the anti-strangling tube, this will furnish rich mixture (almost pure fuel) to the inlet manifold and result in instantaneous starting. Immediately reverse the easy-starting lever which controls the flow of fuel and open the main throttle slightly. By means of the two screws AA on either side of the throttle lever, set the throttle valve where it gives the desired engine speed when idling. Move the low-speed adjustment to the left, one notch at a time, until the engine slows down, noting each setting. Now move it in the opposite direction, one notch at a time, until the engine again slows down. Then move the adjustment to a point midway between the two, and the low-speed setting will have been finally fixed. This should not be changed on account of weather or temperature variations.

Set the throttle about one-third open and turn the intermediate adjustment to the left until the engine slows down. Move to the right until a similar decrease in speed is noted, then set midway between the two. This adjustment, when once properly made, should not be changed for weather or temperature changes. After this adjustment has been made, connect the high-speed adjusting lever to the dash or steering-post control so that in the center of its movement the lever on the carburetor is vertical. Drive the car over a level road at about 20 miles an hour, then move the control lever to the point where the engine gives the best results at this speed. At low temperatures, or when the engine is cold, this control should be moved toward the closed position, so as to cut off air and make a richer mixture. At high temperatures and with a warm engine, the best results are obtained with the control wide open. This is the only adjustment which should be varied for weather or temperature variations.

Newer Carter Models. In addition, this company has two newer models, "H" and "L," the principal difference being in the outlets, "H" having a vertical and "L" a horizontal outlet. The former is shown in Fig. 36, which shows both a vertical section and end view. It will be noted that the fuel passes through a strainer into the float chamber, then entering below passes through the high speed jet if the throttle is open and through the small hole in it, and thence through the low speed jet, up the vertical fuel passage, and part passes out into the vaporizing chamber, while part continues on up into the inlet manifold above or beyond the throttle. The action of these two jets is evident from their construction and this description.

Adjustment of Carter "H" and "L" Models. The adjustment of these two models is similar, this being controlled ordinarily by setting the throw of the throttle lever in the proper position for idle engine speed. This is done by means of an adjusting screw,

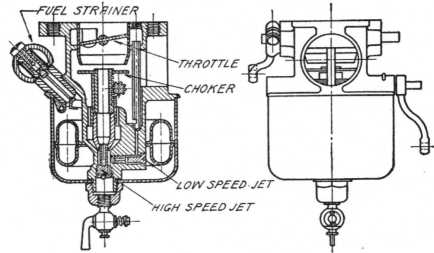

Fig. 36. Carter Model "H" Carburetor with Vertical Outlet
Courtesy Carter Carburetor Company, St. Louis, Missouri

which is provided with a lock screw to hold it when adjusted. This lever should be so set that with steering wheel quadrant lever and accelerator closed, engine will turn over at normal idling speed of 250 to 300 r.p.m. Model "L" has an additional idling adjustment, consisting of a small screw which controls the amount of fuel passing out into the manifold beyond the throttle. The only other normal adjustment is the connection of the dash control wire to the carburetor choker lever; shortening this will cause the air shutter to close more tightly, lengthening it, not as tightly.

Carter Truck Carburetor. A Carter carburetor especially designed for truck use is made with extra large bearings for the working parts. The throttle and choke shaft are larger than those employed in common practice, and the bearings for these shafts are longer. Bronze bushings are used on the throttle shaft where the wear is greatest; if these bearings become worn, however, they may be replaced. The upper part of the float is reinforced, which

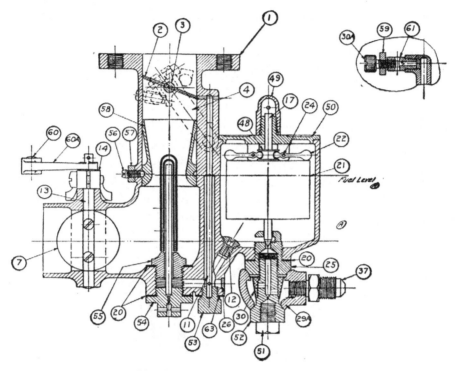

Fig. 37. Model "M" Carter Carburetor

List of Parts—Description: 1, body; 2, throttle valve; 3, throttle shaft; 4, throttle lever; 7, choker valve; 11, idle well tube; 12, fuel metering jet; 13, choker shaft; 14, choker lever; 17, needle; 20, main jet and float needle seat plug gasket; 21, float; 22, float lever; 24, float lever pin; 25, float needle seat plug; 29A, strainer cap; 30, strainer gauze; 30A, idle adjustment screw; 37, gasoline connection; 48, float needle adjusting collar; 49, float cover dust cap; 50, float cover; 51, drain plug; 52, strainer trap screw; 53, idle well plug; 54, jet body plug; 55, nozzle assembly; 59, idle adjustment screw lock nut; 60, wire clamp; 60A, lower lever; 61, idle adjustment screw body; 63, idle well plug gasket.

eliminates the wearing of holes, for the float is in continuous contact with the float weights. It will be noted that the idling adjusting screw and lock nut are shown in detail in the upper half of Fig. 37.

A sectional view of this carburetor is shown in Fig. 37. This is a standard, plain-tube carburetor, idling through the by-pass at the throttle and having but one main gasoline passage, through which a metered supply of fuel is admitted to the main nozzle from the float chamber.

The main nozzle is of the air-bleed type, composed of a combination of passages and ports which admit both air and fuel to the mixing chamber. This nozzle, being entirely self-contained, is automatic in action, supplying the proper mixture at all speeds.

There is but one main nonadjustable supply jet, although this jet can be changed to a different sized jet when it becomes necessary to make another adjustment.

Tillotson Carburetor. In a general way the Tillotson carburetor resembles a long U-shaped tube laid upon its side, with the air entering the upper branch, passing around the curve and out to the motor at the end of the lower branch. In the latter near the delivery end, are placed the two jets, first the secondary, next the primary. A pair of flexible reeds are arranged within the passage in such a way that they entirely enclose and shut off the secondary when they are closed, but do not interfere with the primary. The reeds are opened by the suction of the engine, so

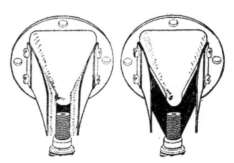

Fig. 38. Tillotson Model "C" Carburetor, Showing Steel Reeds
Courtesy Tillotson Manufacturing Company, Toledo, Ohio

that the primary nozzle furnishes fuel at all engine speeds but is the *only* one in operation at the slower speeds, and is the only one that is adjustable. The secondary nozzle gives the added fuel for high engine speeds and is in operation at these higher speeds only.

Not all the Tillotson models have this exact shape, many being more of an L shape. The float chamber location varies with the different models in some being below the U (or L) tube, in others at one side.

GASOLINE AUTOMOBILES

Adjustment of the Tillotson Carburetor. As has been stated the primary nozzle only is adjustable. The company recommends that this be done with unusual care, and very slowly. With the motor running and well warmed up, turn the adjusting handle up to the right until the motor commences to slow down from lack of fuel, then turn it back about one-eighth of a turn. Avoid getting the mixture too rich. Fig. 38 shows Model "C" 85-6 in partial section and the reed action.

Pierce=Arrow Carburetor. This carburetor utilizes a little different principle in the introduction of auxiliary air from most other carburetors as the air passes through reeds in somewhat the same manner as in the Tillotson carburetor. Fig. 39 shows the construction of this carburetor. The gasoline level should be $\frac{5}{16}$ inch below the top of the spray nozzle K. The opening of the spray nozzle is regulated by a valve II when the throttle is practically closed. The air entering the carburetor at R is thoroughly mixed with gasoline regulated by the nozzle S. The amount of mixture entering the cylinder is regulated by the adjusting screw E, which is really a throttle for the small passage R. The three auxiliary air reed valves are closed. As the throttle B opens, the suction is greater through R than through the main passage for a short period and then becomes the same in both. As the motor speeds up, the light, intermediate, and heavy reeds open in succession, admitting more air. In setting the reeds, the distance between the reed valves and the supplementary springs should be $\frac{1}{8}$ inch for the light reed and $\frac{5}{32}$ inch for the intermediate and heavy reeds. There is a supplementary spray nozzle L, provided with the adjustment needle valve J. This spray nozzle comes into action when the motor is operating at high speeds and the reed valves are open.

Adjustments. Disconnect the throttle rod from the lever and close the main throttle B tight by backing off on screw C. Adjust this screw until it touches the lever A. Then screw in from $\frac{1}{2}$ to $\frac{3}{4}$ of a turn more and turn lock nut D. Connect the throttle rod, adjusting the length so that the throttle just begins to open. Turn idle screw E into the shoulder until the head of the screw seats, then back out about $1\frac{1}{2}$ turns. Loosen screw F on lever G and turn needle II to the left until it is seated, then turn to the

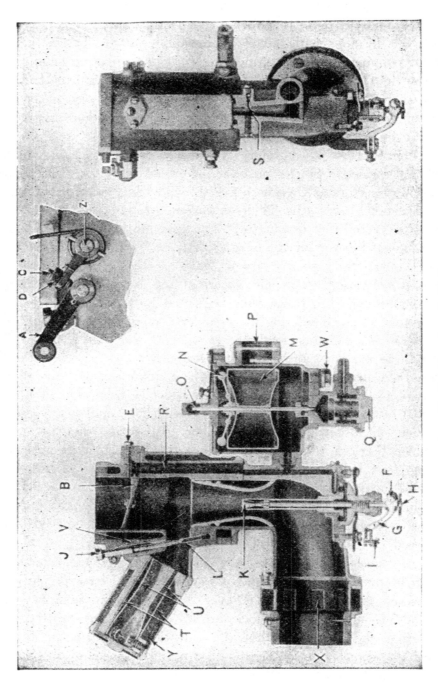

Fig. 39. Pierce-Arrow Carburetor

right to open $\frac{3}{4}$ of a turn. Start the motor by priming and allow it to run until warm—run on battery with the lever advanced $\frac{1}{2}$ inch on the quadrant—and then open the throttle so that a motor speed of 20 to 30 miles per hour is obtained. Next adjust needle H until the motor runs best, set lever G at right angles to center line, and tighten screw F. Set the regulator on the steering column in center, put the wire in lever G, and tighten screw I. This should give equal travel to each side of center. Loosen the high-speed screw on high-speed needle J and, with the finger, screw down until closed, and then turn back or up from $\frac{3}{8}$ to $\frac{5}{8}$ of a turn. The car should then be tested on the road and should not be adjusted to run slower than 5 or 6 miles. Always keep throttle screw E closed as much as possible. If the car works best at a speed of 20 to 30 miles per hour with the regulator in center adjustment on needle H, it can be considered O.K. If it will run better at 50 miles with the regulator at the heavy position, the high-speed needle must be open more; the reverse is true if it runs better with the regulator on the light side. If properly adjusted, the motor should run the entire range of speed with the regulator in one position. No change is necessary except to take care of climatic conditions.

Packard Carburetor. The carburetor used on the Packard twin-six (twelve-cylinder) cars is shown in section in Fig. 40. The inlet manifold, or rather the pipe which leads in both directions to the manifold proper, is seen at the top at A. It will be noted that this is water-jacketed, the water space being at the top. The float arrangement is of the usual type, with a metal float which supplies fuel to a small well B at the base of the single-spray tube C. This has a flared end located in the center of the Venturi. When the air from the air horn D passes the air shutter E, it picks up the fuel and carries it up into the vaporizing chamber F. The primary air shutter is normally open but not in use. It is operated by a hand wheel on the control board which also operates the auxiliary air valve G. By turning this clear over to the position marked choke, the air intake is closed, and a rich mixture is drawn in for starting. After that, the hand wheel should be set back toward the position marked **AIR** which opens the air intake.

The auxiliary air valve is controlled by the springs *H* and *I*. These are adjusted so that the valve opens very slightly at low speed, but more and more as the speed, and consequently the suction, increases. The air enters around the outside of the Venturi, communicating with the mixture only above the top of the latter where the real vaporizing chamber commences. The tension of the springs

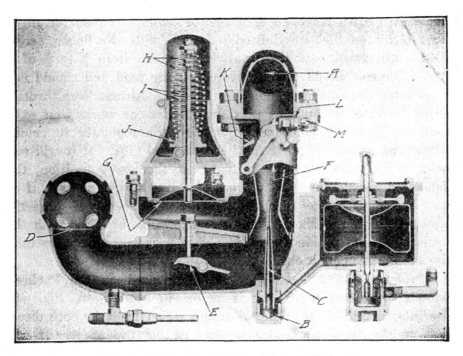

Fig. 40.   Section through Packard Twin-Six Carburetor
Courtesy of Packard Motor Car Company, Detroit, Michigan

is varied by means of the adjusting nuts at the top and by the adjusting cams *J*. The cams are connected up to the air-valve hand wheel which is turned toward gas to provide a richer mixture and toward air for a leaner mixture. If the wheel is turned too far toward air, spitting back may result; and if it is turned too far toward gas, the result may be irregular running and overheating. The throttle *K* is of the butterfly type and regulates the quantity of mixture allowed to pass out, not its quality. An adjustable stop holds this valve open slightly and allows a small amount of mixture to pass, even when the hand throttle is entirely closed. This minimum amount is for slowest running, or idling, only. To increase it, loosen the check nut *L* and screw the stop *M* forward. To decrease the minimum speed, screw the stop backward.

The Packard carburetor is difficult to adjust and it should be done only by men who have had extended experience in adjusting the Packard motor and carburetor combinations.

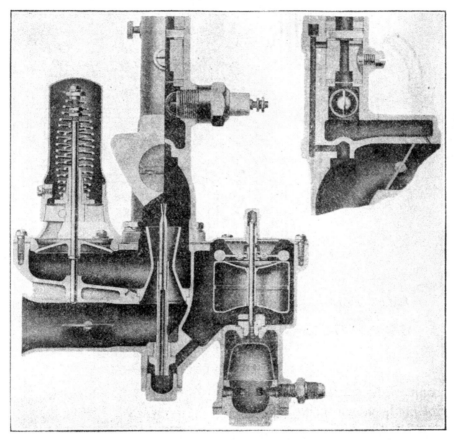

Fig. 41. Packard Straight-Eight Fuelizer
Courtesy of Packard Motor Company

Packard Fuelizer. The Packard fuelizer is an auxiliary carburetor operated by motor suction. This fuelizer, Fig. 41, is connected to a combustion chamber located on the carburetor body, the combustion chamber having an ordinary spark plug igniting the incoming gas, which is under atmospheric pressure. As this carbureted gas burns, the products of combustion, which are composed of hot gases, mix through small openings with the cold incoming gas vapor from the carburetor, shown in cross-section. This heat thoroughly vaporizes the mixture, making it dry—it does not condense and does not pass the piston rings into the crank-case. The fuelizer also does away with a great deal of carbon on

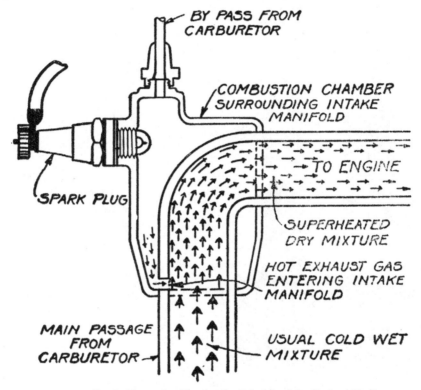

Fig. 42. Simple Illustration Showing the Principle of the Packard Fuelizer

account of better vaporization and of better fuel combustion. The principle is shown in Fig. 42.

With the fuelizer installed and in proper operating condition, it is possible, even in cold weather, to operate the car with the choke set in normal position after the motor has been running for from twenty to thirty seconds. The acceleration, or pick-up, of the car is thus greatly improved. On account of the fuel being thoroughly vaporized, better combustion takes place, carbon for-mation is practically eliminated, and a great deal of spark-plug trouble is overcome. Gasoline economy is not effected to a great extent, although in cold weather more mileage is obtained.

GASOLINE AUTOMOBILES

A certain number of sparks per revolution of the engine are used at the fuelizer plug. There are two methods of obtaining the spark. On new cars an auxiliary breaker is provided, operating from the same cam which works the main breakers, this breaker being supplied with its own condenser and resistance. An additional spark coil located on the dash receives current from the ignition current in the same manner as the standard ignition coils. A somewhat simpler construction applied to cars in service consists of the same coil, the primary of which is wired in series with the

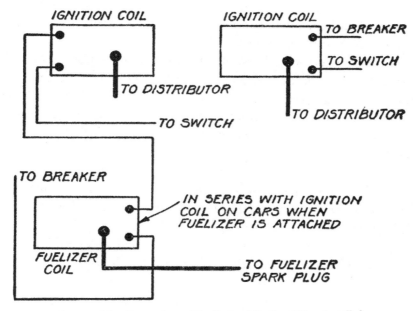

Fig. 43. Wire Connections of the Packard Fuelizer When Installed After the Car Leaves the Factory

primary of one of the main coils, Fig. 43. The extra resistance and self-induction of the extra coil in series do not perceptibly have any effect on the regular ignition at engine speeds under 2600 r.p.m.

Special Suggestions and Precautions. If the inspection glass is dirty, it should be cleaned through the spark-plug opening instead of removing the glass from the container. If the nut is removed, air leaks may be caused in replacing, as the nut may be drawn up too tight, which will cause the glass to break when at running temperature. If the glass becomes sooted rapidly, it is a sign that the mixture is too rich; this should be corrected by raising the vaporizer choke and inserting a gasket. The glass may foul up if oil or some other substance is mixed with the gasoline.

If there is no gas passing through the burner, the spark appears purple and stringy. This is due to some obstruction which prevents the gasoline vapor from reaching the burner. The entire vaporizer equipment may be easily removed.

To check the gasoline level and to make sure that the gasoline is reaching the vaporizer in proper condition, it is simply necessary to remove the vaporizer and measure the distance from the top of the float chamber down to the gasoline level while the motor is running. This dimension should be $1\frac{7}{16}$ inches.

Cadillac Thermostatic Control Carburetor Adjustment. The adjustment as made at the factory is considered to be correct and should not be tampered with unless absolutely necessary. As this carburetor is thermostatically controlled, atmospherical changes should not make any change in the adjustment when once it is correctly made. Before making an adjustment in the carburetor be sure that it is not some other condition which is causing the trouble. When changes in carburetor adjustment are necessary select a quiet spot so that any changes in the engine speed may be noticed immediately.

There are several adjustments on this carburetor and they are rather complicated so that the directions should be carefully read over before doing the work.

Fuel Level Adjustment. This adjustment is correctly made at the factory and should not need adjustment, but the position of the float can be checked to see if the correct gas level is obtained.

To make this adjustment the carburetor must be removed from the manifold and the float bowl removed and the carburetor inverted. Remove the gasket, against which the bowl presses to form a tight fit, and measure the distance from the point K on the flange to the cork float as shown in Fig. 44.

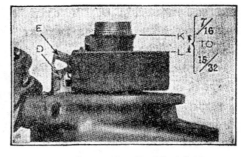

Fig. 44. Correct Gasoline Float Setting
Courtesy of Cadillac Motor Car Company, Detroit

This distance between K and L should be $\frac{7}{16}$ to $\frac{15}{32}$ of an inch. A variation can be obtained by slightly bending the cork float hinge bracket.

Enriching Device Adjustment. This adjustment should be made when the engine is not in operation. To make this adjustment correctly the atmosphere should be at room temperature or between 65° to 85° F. The tip of the air valve S, Fig. 45-a, should be open $\frac{1}{16}$ to $\frac{1}{8}$ of an inch when held up lightly with the lever B, Fig. 45-b, pressed against the stop on the carburetor body. When testing the air valve do not use a heavy pressure as it will spring the thermostatic member to which the end of the air valve spring is attached. If the gap at the tip of the air valve is more or less than the limits given, it can be readjusted after removing the cover H, Fig. 45-a, and loosening the two screws which hold the bracket which carries the thermostatic member. Be sure to tighten the screws after making the change.

CAUTION. When removing the cover be careful not to twist or stretch the spring on the air valve as this will ruin it. Lift the cover sufficiently to disconnect the spring and then take the cover away altogether.

The tongue A, Fig. 45-b, should line up with the center of the slot in lever B when the enriching button on dashboard is pushed as far forward as possible. If the position of A is not correct in relation to B, it can be corrected by increasing or decreasing the length of the control rod attached to lever B.

Auxiliary Air Valve Adjustment. Before making any adjustment at this point the enriching adjustment must be correct, also be certain that the cover H, which is over the air valve, seats correctly, otherwise the air leaks at this point will prevent proper air valve adjustment.

The thermostatic member to which the air valve is attached automatically adjusts the tension on the air valve spring to take care of changes in temperature, and therefore adjustments at this point are comparatively rare. Should there be need of an adjustment it is made by screw C, Fig. 45-b. Screwing down on C increases the tension on the spring T, Fig. 45-a, and prevents the opening of the air valve and reduces the amount of air taken in. Before making this adjustment be sure that the engine is warmed

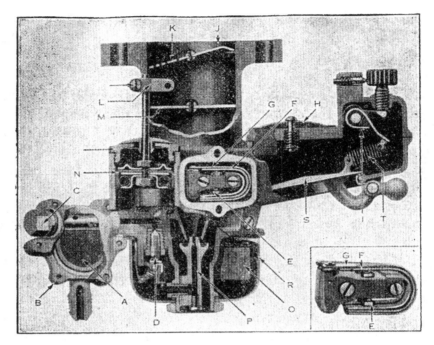

Fig. 45-a. Enriching Device Adjustment
Courtesy of Cadillac Motor Car Company, Detroit

Fig. 45-b. Auxiliary Air Valve Adjustment
Courtesy of Cadillac Motor Car Company, Detroit

up to the normal driving temperature. Place the spark lever in full retard position. The engine should then be running at about 300 revolutions per minute, but if the speed is faster or slower, then it must be regulated by the throttle stop screw D, Fig. 45-b.

The following is an indicative test as to the direction in which the screw C should be turned. Press down lightly on the ball-shaped counterweight attached to the air valve S, Fig. 45-a, and note whether the engine immediately increases or decreases its speed, then release the weight and allow the engine to regain its normal operation. Next press up lightly on the counterweight and note its effect on the engine speed. If the mixture is correct, there should be a slight decrease in engine speed whichever way the counterweight is pressed.

If the upward pressure on the counterweight gives a slight decrease in speed and the downward pressure gives a slight increase in speed, the mixture is too rich, and the screw should be turned to the left to decrease the spring pressure and allow more air to flow in. If the upward pressure gives an increase of speed and the downward pressure gives a decrease in speed, then the mixture is too lean and the screw C should be turned to the right to cut down the amount of air by increasing the spring tension, thereby making the mixture richer. When making this adjustment do not move the adjustment screw C in more than two notches in either direction at one time. When the adjustment is correct, the engine should run at the 300 revolutions a minute speed with the throttle in the closed position.

Thermostatic Throttle Pump Control. At the side of the carburetor is a piston-like arrangement N, Fig. 45-a, which increases the supply of gas at time of acceleration. When the engine is warmed up thoroughly, better acceleration is obtained by a slightly leaner mixture than that required for acceleration with a colder engine. A thermostatic control is attached to decrease the amount of gas supplied at acceleration when the engine is warm. The operation of the piston is as follows. When the accelerator pedal is pressed down, the piston N, Fig. 45-a, forces compressed air into the float bowl above the gasoline, forcing an extra supply of gas up into the jet or spray nozzle. Thermostatic controls are located on the side of the carburetor at G and E, Fig. 45-a, covered by cap

F, Fig. 45-b. These controls uncover a vent hole, which allows a portion of the compressed air to escape from under the piston when the carburetor reaches a predetermined temperature, thereby reducing the amount of gasoline forced up into the spray nozzle. These thermostatic controls* are adjustable in the following manner but they should not be tampered with unless absolutely necessary, as the adjustment is correct when the car leaves the factory.

Throttle Pump Thermostatic Adjustment. To make this adjustment, the thermostat, shown at *G* and *F*, Fig. 45-a, must be removed from the body of the carburetor, by removing the left-hand screw in the face of the thermostat block. When removing this unit be careful not to injure the gasket. The thermostat adjustment screw *E* should be so adjusted that the relief vent hole is just closed at a temperature of 75° F. and just open at the temperature of 77° F. To test this use two dishes of water, one at the temperature of 75° and the other at 77°. The thermostat and block should be immersed in the 75° water, which should cause the thermostat to just close the vent hole. If it does not do this, the screw *E* should be adjusted until it does close the hole. After this test, the block and thermostat should be immersed in the 77° water and the vent hole should be just open. Care should be used to get the water at the exact temperature and to leave the block in the water long enough so that it becomes heated to the same temperature as the water. As the efficient operation of the carburetor depends on the adjustment of the thermostatic controls, the adjustments should be very carefully and accurately made.

Vent Control Thermostatic Adjustment. The object of the outer thermostat *G*, Fig. 45-a, is to control the opening and closing of a large vent hole from the float bowl of the carburetor and comes into use at higher temperatures during hot weather, this being especially desirable with high test gasoline.

The same method of testing is used as in adjusting the throttle pump thermostat but this large vent should close at 130° F. and open at 135° F. If the temperature is very hot, such as in tropical countries, and the gasoline is very high test, it may be desirable to change the setting so that the thermostat will close this vent at 112° F. and open at 120° F.

Throttle Pump Adjustment Screw. On the gasoline intake side of the carburetor there is an adjustment screw which opens a bypass in the passage between the throttle pump and the throttle pump control thermostat. At all temperatures with carburetors having the throttle pump control thermostat only, and at ordinary temperatures with carburetors having the vent control thermostat, the pressure of the air above the gasoline in the carburetor bowl is lessened at the moment of acceleration and less gasoline is forced through the spray nozzle as a result. On carburetors with the dash control, pressure is relieved at high temperature by the operation of the high temperature thermostat.

Seven turns of this adjusting screw in a counter-clockwise direction fully opens the bypass. The amount of opening required depends upon the quality of the gasoline and the atmospheric temperature. Ordinarily it is necessary to unscrew the adjustment not more than two or three turns when adjustment is required at all. Be sure to lock the nut S after the adjustment is made.

As with all other carburetors the adjustment should be made with the engine thoroughly warmed up to operating temperature because the temperature has a great deal to do with the operating of the thermostatic control.

Oxygen=Adding Devices. There are now upon the market a number of devices for assisting carburetion by furnishing an additional source of oxygen. These are not carburetors in themselves, in that they do not handle any fuel, consequently they must be used in addition to some standard carburetor, furnished with fuel in the regular way. The desired result is obtained in a number of different ways, as, for instance, the direct injection of water which the heat of combustion is supposed to break up into its components, hydrogen and oxygen. The hydrogen is a fuel itself, and the oxygen assists the vaporized gasoline fuel to burn better and more completely. Steam is but a variation of this, the exhaust heat being used to create this from water furnished by a special tank. When equipped with valves to control water passage or steam emission, these constitute the only adjustment.

Scoe Carburetors. This carburetor has a variable Venturi which operates under the suction of the engine. The Venturi is formed by the air shutter and the floor of the carburetor. The metering pin is attached to the air shutter and is raised or lowered by the action of the shutter. At the bottom of the metering pin is a dashpot arrangement which prevents the fluctuations of the air shutter in acceleration. The jet arrangement in this carburetor is different in that the jet openings are horizontal instead of vertical

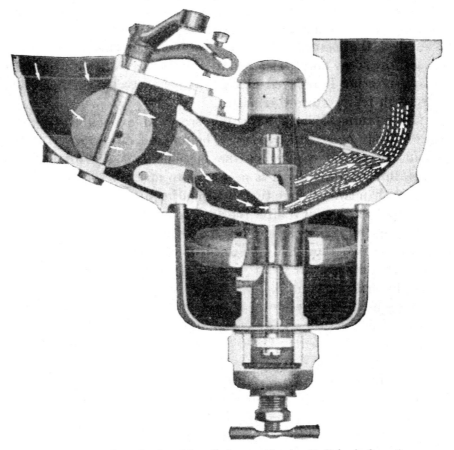

Fig. 46. Cross-Section of Scoe Carburetor Showing Air Valve in Operation
Courtesy of Scoe Carburetor Company

as in most other carburetors. The jets are brought into action as the metering pin rises. The air suction around the metering pin, caused by the air shutter and the floor of the carburetor, draws gasoline out of the jets, Fig. 46. The idling jet is at the top of the metering pin and is fed by two lateral holes and is adjustable by a screw at the top of the pin, Fig. 47. This idling jet has a small Venturi of its own and the adjustment screw restricts the amount of fuel drawn out of the idling jet by the action of this Venturi. The next jet is a flat one, milled on the front side of the metering pin, and is formed by the space between the flat and the guide in which the pin works or operates.

The action of the metering pin and air shutter can be divided into four phases which clearly explain the carburetor action under all conditions.

First Phase. When the engine is running at idling speed, the flat jet is not in full operation and the suction is not sufficient to raise the air shutter. Fuel is fed almost entirely through the central jet, Fig. 48.

Second Phase. At a car speed of about 16 miles per hour, the air shutter is raised from its seat and the flat jet comes into operation. Fuel is drawn through the central jet as well as through the flat jet, Fig. 49.

Third Phase. In this phase, the mixture is made much leaner. As the air shutter rises higher, the upper lateral hole, which is a large one, enters the guide and is prevented from supplying any fuel. The amount of fuel is governed by the lower feed hole, which is smaller, and the amount of gas supplied by the central jet is less. The mixture is thinned out because this phase controls the mixture for car speeds between 18 and 35 miles per hour, which is the usual car speed, and economy of fuel must be considered. This is shown in Fig. 50.

Fig. 47. Idling Adjustment
Courtesy of Scoe Carburetor Company

Fourth Phase. This is the action for car speeds above 35 miles per hour. The central jet is still being supplied by the restricted lower jet, but the space between the flat jet and the metering-pin guide has been increased by the taper and consequently a greater amount of fuel is supplied by the flat jet, Fig. 51. There is only one adjustment, that of the idling speed. This is so sensitive in its action that the least movement of the screw makes a great deal of difference in operation. Moving the screw to the left enriches the mixture, while turning the screw to the right leans or thins out the mixture.

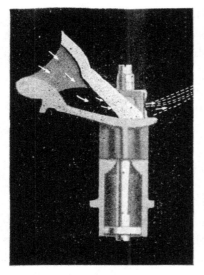

Fig. 48. Idling Jet in Operation
First Phase.
Courtesy of Scoe Carburetor Company

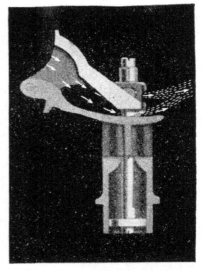

Fig. 49. First Lateral Hole in Operation. Second Phase.
Courtesy of Scoe Carburetor Company

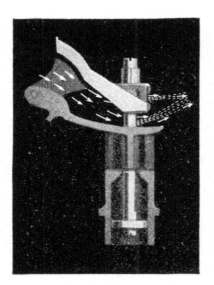

Fig. 50. Second Lateral Hole in Operation. Third Phase.
Courtesy of Scoe Carburetor Company

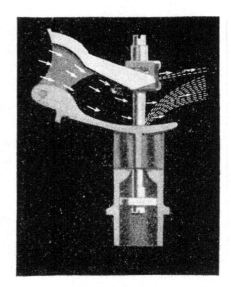

Fig. 51. Flat Jet in Operation. Fourth
Phase.
Courtesy of Scoe Carburetor Company

CARBURETORS

PART IV

KEROSENE AND HEAVY FUEL CARBURETORS

Need for Heavy Fuel Carburetors. The lighter more volatile grades of gasoline are not available in sufficient quantities to supply the present demand. Consequently, the fuel now carries a considerable quantity of what was formerly sold as kerosene and also under other names. At that, the fuel sold is still much lighter than kerosene—of which tremendous quantities are available—as well as other heavy fuels, notably benzol in England, where kerosene is called paraffin. To develop a carburetor which would handle these cheaper but heavier and more available fuels has been the aim of many inventors and a vexing problem for carburetor manufacturers.

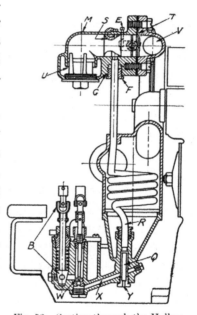

Fig. 52. Section through the Holley Kerosene Carburetor

Holley Type. The Holley Company has devoted much time and study to this problem and has developed a device which is not offered as perfect, even by its maker, who is still working on this problem. However, it has been found to do these things: cut the fuel cost over 50 per cent; increase the power 5 to 8 per cent; save almost one-half of the engine lubricant; give less spark-plug trouble and less carbonizing; and give a greater mileage to the gallon. It also has these deficiencies: requires the use of gasoline for starting and necessitates a material reduction in compression pressures.

This device as shown in Fig. 52 has two float chambers, one for gasoline used in starting, the other for the kerosene or heavier fuel. The shifter valve B determines which fuel flows to the adjusting needle valve W and through a jet where a minute quantity of the total air needed in the form of an air blast atomizes it. Then it is carried up through the tube R situated in the exhaust manifold and heated by it. Then it enters the main mixing chamber M, where the main air supply enters through U, this opening being governed by the suction of the motor and the throttle valve opening. From here it is drawn in through the intake manifold I in the usual way.

Adjustment Holley Kerosene Device. In general, the motor is always started on gasoline, which is used purely for starting and warming up the motor, when the change over to kerosene is made. The adjustments should be made on the basis of kerosene, even though it seems somewhat rich when running on gasoline. Set screw E, which limits the throw of the throttle lever, should be adjusted so the motor runs at proper idling speed when the hand throttle lever is in the closed position.

Holley All=Fuel Carburetor. Another Holley device, Fig. 53, is intended for the use of all kinds of fuel, heavier than our so-called gasoline. This carburetor consists of a simple spraying device with an air valve which sprays the heavy fuel, adds a very small amount of air to it, and then forces this mixture through a vapor tube, consisting of coils of thin-walled pipe surrounding the exhaust pipe. The exhaust heats the walls enough to completely vaporize any fuel that will evaporate below 600° F. This heated, rich, dry gas mixture is then returned to the main body of the carburetor where additional cold air is admitted to convert it into a perfectly combustible mixture. It then passes through the throttle and inlet manifold to the engine. Like the Holley kerosene carburetor, this starts on gasoline, and is switched to the heavier fuel as soon as the motor is well warmed up and the exhaust heat begins to be available. Aside from the usual throttle and air valve limit stops there really is but one adjustment.

Adjusting the All-Fuel Carburetor. The principal adjustment on this device is the idling. It consists of a valve with a milled outside head which controls the inflow of air. Sufficient air is drawn past this for idling and it lifts to admit more air for higher motor speeds. The valve is regulated so that in its lowest position just enough air passes to give a satisfactory idling speed. An arrow on the top indicates this. When the valve is entirely closed, as indicated by the arrow, the air is practically shut off and the mixture is richest.

The air intake is fitted with a choke throttle and the tightness of closing this can be regulated by a stop screw. Similarly, the main throttle can be regulated by means of a stop screw, to vary

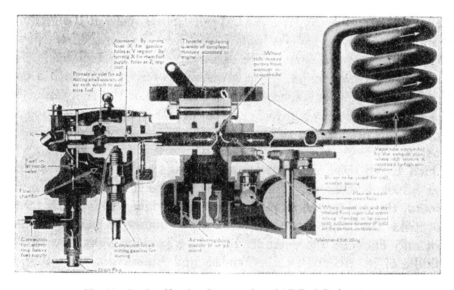

Fig. 53. Section Showing Construction of All-Fuel Carburetor
Courtesy Holley Brothers Company, Detroit, Michigan

its tightness in the closed position. The only other changes or adjustments would be to change the atomizer for one with different sized jet holes at *Y* and *Z* as well as the primary air inlet.

Foreign Kerosene Carburetors. A large number of firms in different parts of the world have worked on this problem of kerosene vaporization. In Germany, the following have done so, and in solving this each has been obliged to develop his own vaporizer: Daimler; Swiderski; Maurer; Adler; Sleipner (boats mostly); Deutz; Banki; Neckarsulmer (motorcycle); Koerting (fuel injection); Kämper; Diesel (fuel injection); Capitaine (boats mostly); Gardner; Dufaux (Swiss motorcycle); and others. Space prevents a description of these, the list being given simply to show that kerosene as a fuel has attracted wide attention.

GASOLINE AUTOMOBILES

In France the same is true; the Aster device, for instance, having been so very successful that it is now made under license in both England and Germany.

In England, the Binks, with two jets, is designed to use 20 per cent gasoline and 80 per cent kerosene after starting. The Hamilton Bi-fuel has two float chambers, two nozzles, and other duplicate features. This is designed for a 44 gasoline (petrol) and 56 kerosene (paraffin) mixture; on such a mixture, a test of a bus engine showed equal (rated) power at 890 r.p.m.; 1 horsepower more at 1050; almost 3 more at 1275; and at its highest speed, 1375 r.p.m., 3 horsepower more, maximum output. The Kellaway has two fuel leads, but these use a common jet. The Morris uses forced feed with a constant air pressure of 4 pounds per square inch on the fuel tank; this is supposed to minimize variations in fuel flow, and thus, as pointed out in the description of the Browne, minimize variations in the output. The Southey ignites part of the fuel to create heat with which to vaporize the balance, delivering to the cylinders a fixed gas which is heated. The Edwards has been described. In the Notax, the fuel spray, as it enters the vaporizing chamber, is forced to strike the lower hot surface of the exhaust-gas passage, which not only encircles the chamber but has a passage right through the middle of it. In the G. C. (English and American), the vaporizer complete replaces both carburetor and muffler. It is constructed to utilize all the heat in the exhaust gases for vaporizing the kerosene, which then is led up to the engine, and auxiliary air added just before it enters the manifold. This has a separate small gasoline carburetor for starting and a special float chamber for the kerosene. In America, the Knox employs an arrangement in which a gasoline by-pass around the entire carburetor is used for starting, while the exhaust heating concerns the fuel at the bottom of the device only. The Secor type is used on the Rumely tractors. The Hart-Parr Tractor Company and a number of other builders of tractor, marine, and stationary engines have been more or less successful in vaporizing kerosene so as to use it advantageously.

Master Carburetor. The Master device was designed primarily for the extra heavy fuels, or the residuum in the distilling process called distillate, which is heavier than kerosene and has heretofore been considered a waste product. The Master has utilized this successfully in actual service for more than four years. In addition, it will handle kerosene, alcohol, and other heavy fuels, as well as mixtures of all these with one another and with gasoline.

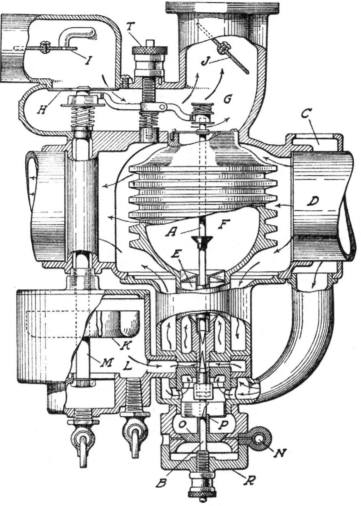

Fig. 54. Section through Bennett Double-Jet Kerosene Carburetor
Courtesy of Wilcox-Bennett Carburetor Company,
Minneapolis, Minnesota

Like the Master, the Miller also was designed originally for the extra heavy fuels of the coast, so that it must be considered as a heavy fuel carburetor. This is partly true of the "H and N," which was designed originally for heavy fuels, the present form embodying the most successful details of the heavy-fuel device.

Bennett Carburetor. The Bennett device, Type "C," Fig. 54, is intended for kerosene, alcohol, distillates, or other heavy fuels, but by a simple change of the adjustments it can be used for gasoline. For alcohol, however, the makers provide a special float, the carburetor remaining the same otherwise. It has two needle valves: one projecting downward from the top of the device A, called the slow-speed needle; and the other, projecting upward from the bottom B, called the high-speed needle. The primary air for both enters at C, passes around the exhaust heating pipe D, and enters from below. It rises around the lower needle and fuel passage into the chamber E, where the fuel is picked up and carried up into the main vaporizing chamber F. From here it passes up into the passage G, where additional air comes in from the air valve H, after passing the air throttle I. This dilutes the mixture and completes vaporization, and the mixture passes the main throttle J into the manifold, or engine.

The fuel enters the float chamber K, in which the float is indicated, and passes from this through the horizontal opening L to the needles. As there is hot air in the passage just below the opening, and exhaust gases in the passage just above it, it is subjected to a considerable warming effect. In the center at the bottom, a recess forms a dashpot for the lower end of the shaft M, which is connected to the air valve H at its upper end; this prevents rapid fluctuation, or fluttering, of this valve when there is a sudden opening of the throttle after running at slow speed. The extra suction created by the sudden opening of the throttle tends to jerk the auxiliary air valve open quickly to its maximum area. Another feature of the device is the feeding of small quantities of hot water from the motor circulating system through the pipe N; this has an adjustable valve (not shown) connected to the dash. The water is sprayed in through the medium of the valve O attached to the bottom of the small dashpot and the plunger P which surrounds the bottom of the high-speed needle B. An additional feature of the device is an air cleaner Q, which is shown at the left in the diagram, Fig. 55. Its function is to clean all dust out of the entering air when the carburetor is used on a tractor or other unit which must work in the midst of considerable dust. This dust is known to filter slowly but surely through the carburetor and, in time, mixes with the oil and reaches the pistons, valves, rings, and bearings, where it does considerable damage. The utility of this simple auxiliary device, which has no moving parts, is evident.

Installation. Whenever it is possible to use the air cleaner, install the carburetor with the hood of the air intake facing away from the fan so as to prevent dirt from being blown into it. Connect the exhaust manifold to the carburetor, using the three-way valve or damper in such a way that the amount of gas can be regulated. Whenever possible the exhaust connection should enter the

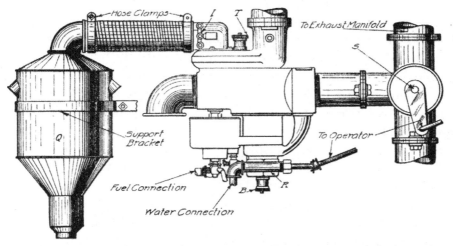

Fig. 55. Diagram Showing Method of Connecting and Adjusting Bennett Carburetor

larger end, because the cored passage for heating the primary air is there. Screw an elbow in at the other end, and, if required, a short piece of pipe, to carry the used exhaust gases away from the carburetor. Connect the water jet near the bottom with the water jacket or a small auxiliary water tank. This water jet and its regulating needle can be moved to any desired position by means of the large nut *R*. The needle is connected to the dash so as to be operated by the driver. Two fuel tanks are needed, one for gasoline to be used for starting, and the other for kerosene to be used in regular running; they should be connected to the float chamber at the bottom by means of a three-way valve or a siamesed pipe, with a shut-off cock in each line above the T-connection.

Adjustment. There are but two adjustments, so-called: the high-speed fuel needle for full load; and the slow-speed fuel needle for slow speeds and idling. Both are made by knurled nuts, which are turned clockwise to close and counter-clockwise to open. In the process of adjusting, close the exhaust damper S, so as to throw the exhaust gases through the carburetor and furnish the needed heat. Then close the air-choke valve I, to make a rich mixture for starting purposes. Before turning on the gasoline, open the high-speed needle B about two turns. Then start the motor and immediately open the air choke valve I. If it fires unevenly after running a little while, close the slow-speed needle A by turning the knurled nut T to the right, one notch at a time, until the motor fires and runs evenly when throttled down to the slowest speed. If the motor hesitates and stops when the air choke valve is opened, open the slow-speed adjustment, one notch at a time, until the point is reached at which the motor will just run and fire evenly when throttled down.

Regulate the high-speed needle until the motor will respond when the throttle is opened quickly, by speeding it up to its maximum number of revolutions without missing. If the motor misses when the throttle is jerked open, close the needle slowly, one notch at a time, until the missing ceases and the motor responds to the quick opening smoothly. On the other hand, if the motor backfires when the throttle is suddenly opened wide, open the needle slowly until it will speed up without missing or popping back. As soon as motor and carburetor have become thoroughly heated, turn on the kerosene and shut off the gasoline.

Kerosene Modified Adjustments. The use of the kerosene may change the adjustments slightly. Thus the slow-speed needle adjustment may have to be opened one or two notches more for kerosene than for gasoline. Similarly, the high-speed needle adjustment will have to be opened two or three notches more. If the motor becomes so hot when running on kerosene that pre-ignition occurs—and this is likely because the whole device is designed to use the maximum possible amount of heat—the water-needle connection to the operator should be opened. This pre-ignition can be detected as a sharp metallic knock in the cylinder. Only enough water should be used to stop the knock; the carburetor should not be flooded with it. The cap at the bottom, or inlet, of the air cleaner Q should be kept tight. The air cleaner should be emptied once a day, but it should not be removed while the engine is running.

Bennett Air Washer. The wider use of tractors and also of cars and trucks in the country, over dusty roads, and in the dust-laden fields which are being plowed, harrowed or otherwise worked, has forced the use of devices for removing the dust from the entering air. The device indicated at Q is one of these and is shown in detail in Fig. 56. Its interior consists of a series of spiral passages. The air enters one of these at A and is forced to pass through the water. Then it passes upward and out along the other spirals C, C. The air is doubly purified, first, by passing through the water, and second, in the removal of dirt by centrifugal action.

Air Cleaners. The use of air cleaners is rapidly becoming standard on both the tractor and automobile. From the analysis of

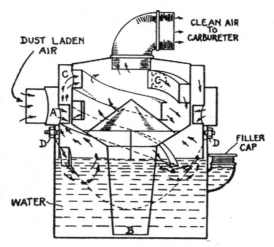

Fig. 56. Bennett Air Washer, Indicating Operation
Courtesy Wilcox-Bennett Company, Minneapolis, Minnesota

the carbon found in the cylinder of an automobile, it was found that it consisted of from 20% to 75% road dirt. It proved beyond doubt that if the dirt could get into the combustion chamber it could also get into the crankcase. An air cleaner keeps the supply of air to the carburetor free of dirt and is especially valuable where a great deal of country driving is done on roads that are not paved. The dirt that finds its way into an engine is an abrasive and causes wear on bearings as well as on cylinder and piston walls. An air cleaner used on the Franklin car with great success is shown in Fig. 57. The stream of air enters the top of the cleaner and comes in contact with the centrifugal fan. The dirt and dust is forced to the outside shell where it passes to the outside and is prevented from entering the carburetor. There are other types of cleaners which contain water or oil through which the air must pass before reaching the carburetor which filters out the dust and dirt. In this type the solution must be changed occasionally.

Parrett Air Cleaner. A device similar to the air washer but working on a different principle is the Parrett air cleaner, Fig. 58.

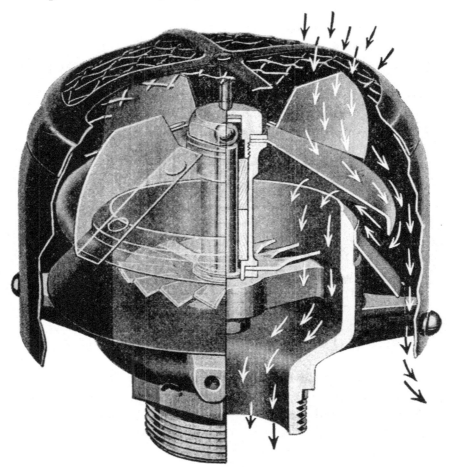

Fig. 57.   Air Cleaner used on Franklin Car—Ejector Type
Courtesy of United Manufacturing Company, Chicago

Air enters at the top and is drawn downward through the central tube, the lower part of which is flared out and is supported on a metal float smaller than the bottom of the bell. The air passes between the two, through a very narrow opening, at high velocity. Large air bubbles can not form, and because of the high velocity all heavy dust particles are thrown directly into the water. The rising

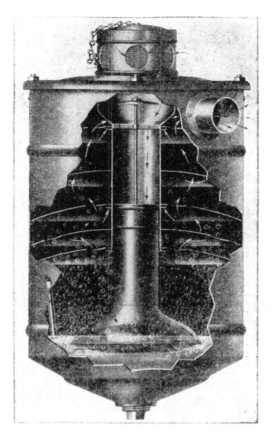

Fig. 58. Parrett Air Cleaner for Removing
Dust and Dirt
Courtesy Ross-Wortham Company, Chicago

purified air and moisture are separated by a series of baffle plates, so the air finally passing to the carburetor is completely cleaned of dirt or dust.

Deppé Gas Generator. Although not called a carburetor by its maker, the Deppé gas generator replaces the ordinary carburetor for the purpose of vaporizing kerosene. In appearance and in sectional drawing, as shown in Fig. 59, it is not unlike an ordinary carburetor with an extra-special somewhat globular chamber above it, and below it the ordinary inlet manifold, which is exhaust heated.

Some of the things claimed for it, when it is attached to ordinary cars with no change except in the vaporizer, are: perfect gas at all speeds; superior acceleration; no loading; increased high speed; lower slow speed on high gear; much greater fuel efficiency expressed

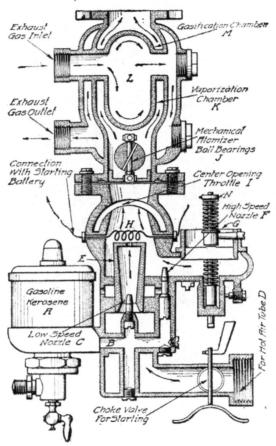

Fig. 59. Section of Deppé Gas Generator, Showing Construction
Courtesy of W. P. Deppé, New York City

in miles per gallon; handles all ordinary hydrocarbon liquids— gasoline, kerosene, naphtha, etc., and mixtures of these; fixed metering adjustment which is not affected by altitude, temperature, or location; easy starting; less vibration of engine; and others.

In Fig. 59, the fuel enters the float chamber A from below and passes through a horizontal passage B from which the two nozzles lead upward. The low-speed nozzle C draws its heated air through the primary intake D and mingles with this in the modified Venturi E. When the engine demands more fuel, it is supplied by the high-speed nozzle F, which gets its air from the auxiliary air valve G; this air and fuel mixture combine with the other in the chamber H, just above the Venturi and just below the center-opening throttle I. Up to this point it is not radically different from the average two-jet carburetor with the auxiliary air valve.

However, in the chamber just above this a mechanical atomizer, or rotating mixer on ball bearings J, is inserted. The idea is to combine the air and fuel particles more intimately through the rotation of this mixer within the zone of vaporization. The actual vaporizing chamber K is next above this. It is an annular passage around the highly heated exhaust gas chamber L, but inside of the outer exhaust chamber. This insures the absolute completion of the gasification started in other chambers, so that the mixture passing into the gasification chamber M at the top and thence into the inlet manifolds and cylinders is sure to be a pure dry gas.

Starting. To assist in starting, the primary-air passage is fitted with a choke valve of the butterfly type, which closes off this passage entirely so as to produce a rich mixture. Across the middle of the lower vaporizing chamber H, an electric resistance wire or heating coil is strung. The coil is connected to the starting battery. The connection is made so that the current passes through this heating coil as soon as it is turned on. This supplies the cold carburetor with the equivalent of the exhaust gas heat, which is available shortly after the engine has been started.

Adjustments. As will be seen from the illustration, the low-speed nozzle and air opening are fixed, the only possible adjustment, setting, or change being in the alteration of the nozzle or in the quantity of primary air admitted. The high-speed nozzle is fixed similarly so that it cannot be adjusted, the high-speed air valve G furnishing the only adjustment. The adjustment of this is very simple; with the engine running, advance the spark pretty well to the limit, open the throttle lever to its maximum, and then vary the position of the nut N which governs the tension of the spring O to the point where the maximum speed of rotation is obtained. This setting should be checked against actual high-speed running on the road, as there is usually a difference between the best road

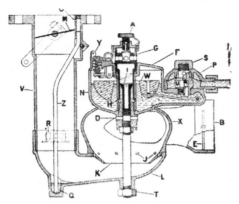

Fig. 60. Ensign Carburetor, Model "G"
Courtesy Ensign Carburetor Company
Los Angeles, California

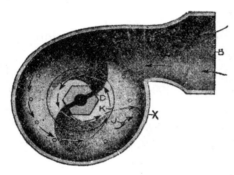

Fig. 61. Horizontal Section of Ensign Carburetor Showing Vortex Mixing Chamber

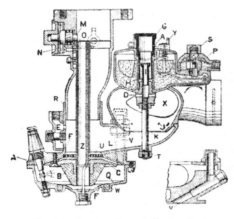

Fig. 62. Section through Ensign Fuel
Converter

high-speed setting and the best engine-speed setting, with the car standing on the garage floor.

Ensign Heavy Fuel Car=buretors. A section through a new device recently perfected on the Pacific Coast, the Ensign carburetor, is shown in Fig. 60, while Fig. 61 is a horizontal section of the vortex mixing chamber which forms an important part of this. This device was designed to handle heavy fuels, but that shown in Fig. 60 can be used for gasoline. As the figure shows, the fuel enters a float chamber, thence into the bottom of a standpipe, *H*, within which a suction tube *A* is set with its top opening slightly above the fuel level so that fuel must be drawn up by the air suction. This air enters at *B* and passing around the vortex, of which 61 shows a better view, acquires a high velocity. Thus a considerable suction is exerted on the fuel which passes out through holes *D* into the whirling air stream, which vaporizes it. Should any fuel moisture remain, centrifugal action of the air stream throws it against the walls whence it drips down through holes *J* into the mixture which passes through the narrowed throat *K*, thence makes a sharp bend to a horizontal direction, and another to a vertical flow entering the inlet pipe V on its way past the throttle M to the cylinders. The nature of this vortex chamber thins the mixture as it is produced at D, and with increasing demands, and thus increasing air velocity, continues to thin it, so the vortex chamber automatically delivers a thinner and thinner mixture as the engine speeds up.

Adjusting the Ensign Type G. This model has two adjustments, air at A and fuel at G. Screw both of these clockwise to a closed position; then open G one and a half turns, and A one-fourth turn for four-cylinder motors, one-eighth turn for six or more cylinders. Start the motor and warm it up. Open the throttle to high speed and use G as a needle valve, adjusting to get the highest motor speed. Then refine this by adjusting A, one notch at a time. To start cold, open throttle M to slightly more than an idling position, and pull primer Y heavily before cranking.

Ensign Fuel Converter. This company's Model "N" device is intended to handle the very heaviest fuels, up to a dry boiling point of 600° F. It consists of three elements: the carburetor proper, the gas producer, and the temperature regulator. Fig. 62 shows that the carburetor is almost identical with the carburetor, Fig. 60. The gas producer consists of the fire screen U to which the heavy unvaporized fuel flows, the combustion chamber Q, and the sparking element A which ignites it. This heats up screen U and the plate C below it so that these subsequently vaporize a larger portion of the fuel, and less of it passes down into chamber Q to be ignited and thus vaporized. That is, this part of the device is self-regulating as to temperature. The idling temperature is controlled by thermostat capsule N which operates temperature control plug M. This is half full of alcohol, and its chamber is provided with means for circulating the hot mixture. As the mixture approaches 210° F., the capsule pushes the plug outward and closes the port O, reducing the draft and thus controlling the temperature.

Adjustment. Adjustment of this device is the same as for the carburetor, except for starting and with the addition of the spark plug care. In starting G is opened one turn, then E is filled with gasoline to fill the fire bowl up to the overflow F. If motor and converter are hot, prime very little; if motor has stopped but a few minutes, prime with Y on top of the flat bowl and start directly on the heavy fuel. With spark retarded adjust G to maximum engine speed. After engine has been running some time check this adjustment.

GENERAL TROUBLES AND REPAIRS

Operation Troubles. The basis of good engine operation has been given as good compression. The basis for economical operation is good carburetion, and it cannot be obtained unless the symptoms of incorrect carburetion, carburetor troubles, and their effect on engine operation, are known and understood. The following is a summary of troubles due to carburetors and their action on engine operation and their cures:

(1) *Spitting Back through the Carburetor on Sudden Acceleration.* This may be caused by two things. (a) Weak mixture, due to incorrect adjustment of the carburetor. The cure is to readjust the carburetor. (b) Air leaks in the intake manifold or stoppage in the gasoline supply. Air leaks in the intake system can be in two or three places. One, at the intake-manifold joint, can be tested in the following manner. Take an oil can and fill it with gasoline and squirt the gasoline around the joints. If the engine runs better after this treatment, the trouble is at these joints. Air will also leak in at the intake valves if they are worn, which will necessitate new guides being installed. If the mixture must be made very rich to have the engine run smoothly, it will often indicate worn intake-valve guides. If the carburetor butterfly-valve shaft is badly worn in the bushing, a great deal of air will be drawn in that will upset any kind of adjustment that may be made with the carburetor adjustments, and the only cure is the fitting of new shaft and bushings to the carburetor. If on trying the adjustments no change can be noticed, it is a good plan to examine the butterfly shaft and bushings. Stoppage of the gasoline supply can be caused by the strainer being clogged up with dirt or lint. To cure this trouble it will be necessary to take the instrument apart and clean every part thoroughly.

(2) *Uneven Running at High Speeds with Black Smoke Coming from the Exhaust.* This indicates too rich a mixture and the engine will tend to run in the following manner: There will be a series of explosions followed by a period of rest. These periods follow each other quickly with every cylinder firing during the time the

explosions are taking place. It is termed "galloping." If more air makes the engine run evenly, readjust the carburetor. In systems where vacuum tanks are used it often happens that the valves inside the vacuum tank will fail to operate correctly so that the tank will fill up and raw gasoline will be drawn through the suction pipe into the intake manifold and a very rich mixture will result. In testing, disconnect the suction pipe and place a finger over the opening in the intake manifold. If the engine runs better, then the vacuum tank must be overhauled. In the case of the cork float type of carburetor, the float may be soaked with gasoline and is too heavy to shut off the gasoline at the correct level, causing too rich a mixture. Dry the float and give it a thin coating of shellac, being careful not to make the float too heavy. A metal float may be punctured and filled with gasoline. This will make it too heavy to function correctly, causing the carburetor to flood. It is best to install a new float in this case. A temporary repair may be made by immersing the float in very hot water. This will vaporize the gasoline inside the float and the hole can be found. The hole can then be covered with a very thin layer of solder. Care should be taken that the float is not thrown out of balance or it will stick in the float chamber. Too rich a mixture can also be caused by the choke valve sticking or not working correctly due to some mechanical trouble such as a broken choke wire, which should be renewed.

(3) *Missing at Low Speeds.* This trouble is usually caused by air leaks.

Another cause of missing at low engine or idling speed is the dilution of the charge by exhaust or burnt gases. If the exhaust valve leaks some of the exhaust gases will be drawn back into the cylinder, as the piston goes down on the suction stroke. The low speed or idling speed fuel charge is very small, and a very small quantity of burnt gas drawn back into the cylinder will dilute the charge and cause missing at low speeds. The dilution of this charge will often cause missing even up to a speed of 30 miles per hour. The trouble is not exactly a miss but rather a weak explosion, which makes it seem like a miss and causes the engine to run unevenly.

(4) *Missing at High Speeds.* This trouble may be caused by stoppage in the gasoline supply or by valves holding open. Water in the gasoline may also be a cause. The supply system should be

cleaned out and the valve clearance checked. If there is water in the gasoline, the carburetor should be drained and the presence of water will be shown by little bubbles separating themselves from the gasoline. The gasoline should be poured back into the tank through a chamois skin.

(5) *No Power on a Hill Climb.* When a car runs well on the level but will not pull on coming to a hill, it is an indication of a stoppage in the gasoline supply. The cure for this has been given. In high altitudes an engine seems to lose power due to the compression volume being less than in low altitudes.

(6) *Engine Overheats.* Too rich a mixture may be the cause and the cure for this has also been given. In high altitudes an engine will heat because of the lower boiling point of water as well as because the air is less dense which causes the mixture to be richer.

(7) *Engine Starts and Then Stops.* This may be caused by dirt in the jet. The engine will start but as quick as the suction comes particles of dirt will be drawn into the jet opening and gasoline will be prevented from passing through the opening. The carburetor should be cleaned out. This same trouble may be caused by the gasoline level being too low.

(8) *Engine Will Not Start.* See that the gasoline is getting through to the carburetor—if there is any in the tank—by raising the needle valve and seeing if the carburetor floods or the gasoline runs over the top of the float bowl. If there is gasoline in the carburetor, the trouble must be in the ignition system, unless the adjustment of the carburetor is entirely out of order. When starting the engine, excessive use of the choke should be avoided because it floods the engine with raw gasoline and makes it still harder to start. It also causes a great deal of carbon to form as well as causing crankcase dilution. It will also wash the oil off of the cylinder

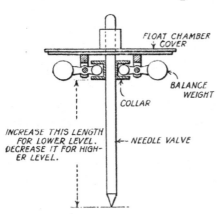

Fig. 63.   Gasoline Level Control

walls and gives a chance for the cylinders to score. In very hot weather the engine will lack pep or operate sluggishly. If the heater pipe is disconnected or some of the heat shut off from the carburetor, the operation of the engine will be greatly improved. It is a good plan to crank the engine in cold weather with the switch in the "off" position so that a charge of gas can be drawn into the cylinder before the switch is turned on. The clutch pedal should also be pushed down because the starter will not have to pull against the heavy oil in the transmission and it will give the spark a better chance to fire the cold gasoline. After the engine has started, the mixture should be set so that the engine will run evenly. The engine should be allowed to warm up before the car is driven. This not only prevents the intake of raw gasoline, but also gives the oil a chance to warm up and start circulating.

(9) *Mis-firing or Back-firing in Muffler When Descending a Hill.* When coasting down a hill with the gears in mesh the trouble of back-firing in the muffler is often experienced. This trouble is also caused by charge dilution. If the exhaust valves do not seat properly some of the exhaust or burnt gases will be drawn back into the cylinder and dilute the charge. The throttle being closed the charge is very small and the least little dilution upsets the explosion and makes it a very slow burning mixture. A weak spark will also cause this firing in the muffler.

Mechanical Troubles and Cures. The height of the gasoline is an important item in the operation of the carburetor. The correct level for the gasoline in the jet is on a level with the top or with a bead of gasoline on the top of the jet. The level is controlled by the length of the needle above or below the collar on the needle valve, Fig. 63. If the length of the needle is increased below the collar, the valve will shut off earlier and the level will be lower. If the length of the needle is decreased below the collar, the valve will shut later and the level will be higher. The result of too high a level will be flooding, while too low will cause hard starting or no starting at all. Fig. 64 shows how the level of the gasoline can be tested. In most carburetors the body of the device can be removed and the jet exposed to view. Take a small tank and place it up high so that there will be a good deal of pressure behind the gasoline. Clamp the carburetor in a vice so that it is level. Connect the tank with the carburetor and allow the liquid to flow into the float bowl. If the gasoline runs over, the level is too high and the length of the needle below the collar should be increased. If the liquid cannot be seen in the top of the jet, the level is too low

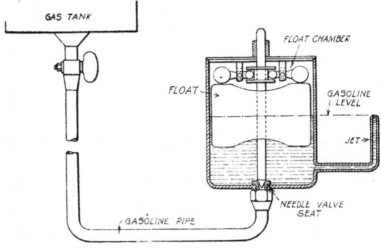

Fig. 64. Testing the Level of Gasoline

and the length of the needle below the collar should be decreased. In decreasing the length of the needle the point of the valve should not be damaged or the needle will never seat. In the cork or hinged-type of float, the hinge of the float must be bent or altered to correct the gasoline level.

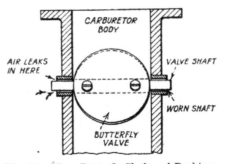

Fig. 65. Worn Butterfly Shaft and Bushings

Another cause of flooding is a worn needle valve and seat. If the needle is not badly grooved, it can be lightly ground to fit the seat again by the use of ground glass and oil. The best and cheapest plan is to install a new valve and seat. The needle valve seat is screwed into the carburetor body at the bottom of the float bowl. Particles of dirt will lodge on the valve seat and prevent the proper closing of the valve, causing a gasoline leak. If the body of the carburetor is wet, it does not always indicate that there is a leak because with the heavy fuel in use today, there is always dampness around the body which dries when the engine is started. The body remains dry as long as the engine is warm.

Worn Butterfly Shaft and Bushings. Fig. 65 shows this condition and the only cure is to install new shaft and bushings. This trouble will upset any adjustment that is made on the carburetor because a great deal of air can be drawn into the manifold above the point at which the gasoline and air are mixed. Therefore the mixture is thinned out considerably.

Butterfly Valve Loose On Its Shaft. This trouble would cause a fluttering action when the engine is accelerated and the action of the engine would be uneven. It will also cause the throttle to remain open and the engine would race even after the throttle lever or accelerator pedal had been returned to the closed position.

Choke Valve Loose On the Shaft. This would either cause too rich a mixture because it failed to open after the choke lever had been moved to the open position or the engine would be very hard to start because the choke valve could not be closed to give the rich mixture necessary for starting. Examine the choke wire and the screws that hold the valve on its shaft. Replace them if they are lost or tighten them if they are loose.

Cleaning the Carburetor. Cleaning the carburetor should be done very carefully, until one becomes quite familiar with it and with the influence which movement of the various parts will have. First, the gasoline supply should be shut off between the tank and the carburetor so that the supply of gasoline may be saved; second, disconnect the priming arrangement; third, the top part of the float chamber should then be removed. In taking off the top, the cover should be loosened and then lifted straight up until clear of all remaining parts. With the cover off, the float may readily be removed in the same way, the only care being in starting it. As the amount, or length, of the needle point within the tapered seat is small, the float need be raised but a small amount.

Fuel Supply. There are two general ways of getting the fuel from the gas tank to the carburetor—gravity pressure and vacuum pressure. In the gravity system, the gasoline tank is placed higher than the carburetor and gravity pressure carries the fuel to the carburetor. In the cap of the gasoline tank there should be a vent hole so that air can enter the tank and give a constant supply. If there is a poor flow of gasoline from the tank to the carburetor, see that the vent hole is clear. The vacuum system is the type mostly in use today and is very efficient.

Gravity. With the tanks placed high, the gasoline can be depended upon to run down to the float chamber by gravity. In mountainous districts it is sometimes found, in climbing very steep hills, that the angle becomes such that the fuel will not flow, especially when the tanks are under or back of the rear seat, or when they are nearly empty.

A means of getting around this difficulty is to place an auxiliary tank of one or two gallons capacity on the front of the dashboard behind the engine and under the bonnet, and run a pipe direct from it to the carburetor. When the car is in a level position, this auxiliary tank fills automatically from the main tank, but a simple valve prevents the contents of the auxiliary tank from running back when the machine is tilted up. In this way a sufficient supply for 15 or 20 miles running is placed in a position to reach the carburetor under any possible road condition.

Vacuum Feed Device. The many troubles incident to the use of the rear tank location with pressure feed have brought about the production of a new device, which is called the Stewart vacuum feed. This is a small compact circular unit, which is placed on the dash under the hood for use with a rear tank and, when so used eliminates the pressure feed. In the sectional drawing, Fig. 66, there are two connections shown at the top: one to the gasoline tank, and one to the intake manifold. Through the medium of the intake manifold connection, the motor suction is communicated to the tank, for that is what the device amounts to. This produces a vacuum and opens the valve connecting with the gasoline tank. That, as well as the connecting-pipe line, being air tight, gasoline is drawn in to fill the vacuum, flowing into the upper chamber with which the gasoline tank communicates.

This has a valve connection to the lower chamber, operated by means of a float; it, in turn, is controlled by the intake manifold suction, through the medium of the system of levers. By it the lower chamber is kept filled to a fairly high level, whence feed to the carburetor is by gravity. This method thus does away with all the troubles of the pressure system, at the same time allowing the accessible and advantageous rear-tank location. It is placed as

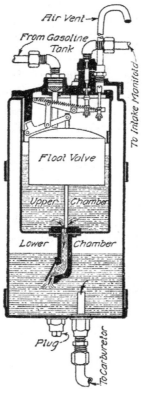

Fig. 66. Section through the Stewart Vacuum Gasoline Feed Device

high as possible on the inside of the dash under the hood, hence there is never any trouble with the gravity feed even on the steepest hill. In one test, this vacuum-feed device increased the mileage of the car per gallon of fuel by more than 22 per cent.

After a period of service, the valves in the tank wear and fail in their action and allow the tank to become so full of gasoline that raw gasoline is drawn into the intake manifold giving a very rich mixture. The tank should be drained frequently to get rid of any sediment that may be in the tank. The vent hole in the tank should be kept free of dirt. Sometimes no suction can be obtained to draw in the gasoline. Examine all connections, especially soldered joints, for cracks or breaks in the pipe. Sometimes the swedging or flange at the end of the suction pipe will break off and destroy the vacuum set up by the suction of the engine which operates the vacuum system and since no gasoline will flow into the vacuum tank none will reach the carburetor.

G & G Vacuum Tank. A similar vacuum feed system to that of the Stewart is the G & G, and its operation is the same. About the only difference is in the shape of the outside tank, which is circular instead of long and round. Suction is taken from the intake manifold to draw the gasoline from the main supply tank. As the inner tank fills, the float rises and closes the suction valve and then atmospheric pressure is obtained in the inner tank. The weight of the gasoline in the inner tank opens the flapper valve and allows the gasoline to flow into the outer chamber; from there it passes into the carburetor float bowl.

The strainer at the top of the tank should be cleaned occasionally and about every three months the inside of the main tank should be cleaned out. To gain access to the outer tank to remove the sediment which may accumulate there remove the inner tank. The main vent hole at the top of the tank should be kept clean at all times so that atmospheric pressure will always be present in the outer tank.

COOLING SYSTEMS

The cooling system plays an important part in the automobile, for without efficient cooling, lubrication between the cylinder and the piston will not be satisfactory. There will also be preignition of the fresh charge coming into the cylinders. To aid lubrication and prevent preignition, the heat absorbed from the cylinder walls and from the burning gases must be dispersed as quickly as possible.

There are two general methods of cooling the engine: (1) by the direct application of water to the outside of the cylinder walls through a water jacket and (2) by air cooling. There are variations in these two general methods. For instance, there is the use of a pump to circulate the water around the cylinders and cooling system, and the thermosyphon, in which the natural circulation of heated water is used to advantage in the water-cooled engine. In the air-cooled engine there is the use of the blower which gives a constant stream of air under pressure to the cylinder walls, and the natural circulation of cold air carries away the heat as the air becomes heated when in contact with the cylinder walls. In the thermosyphon system, the water passages must be large and all obstructions and sharp corners must be eliminated. Large hose connections must be used and the cooling surface of the radiator must be large. The disadvantage of this system is that water will freeze very easily because there is nothing to keep it in motion until the water becomes hot. In the pump system, the water is made to circulate, is cooled quickly, and is less likely to freeze during the warming-up period.

WATER COOLING

Though nearly all successful automobile engines, as well as other internal combustion engines, are water cooled, there is so much obvious fault with this system of securing a result—involving first the generation of heat and its waste by a complicated refrigerating system, instead of its utilization by converting more of the heat units into useful work—that it is surprising that water cooling persists.

Water=Jacketing. The first essential in water-cooling a motor is to provide the cylinders with water jackets, through which the cooling water is circulated in contact with the outside of the walls within which the heat is liberated.

Water jackets are of two types, integral and built-on. The latter system of construction, though adding to complications and conducive to leakage, permits of lighter construction, besides diminishing the likelihood of hidden flaws in the cylinder castings, which, with cored jackets, are not likely to reveal themselves until they cause a breakdown, perhaps after the engine has been long in use.

Integral Jackets. With integral jackets, the usual system is to form the jackets by cores, in the founding, so that there are no

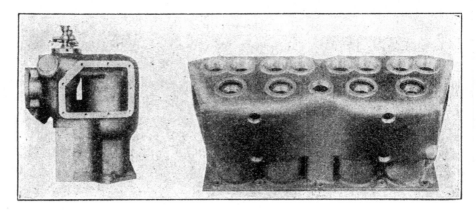

Fig. 1. Detailed View of Cadillac Cylinder Chassis

openings in the jackets except those for removing the core, sand, and wires, and for connecting the pipes of the circulating system. In the best examples of design the core openings are very large with plane faces, and are closed by screwed-on or clamped-on plates, thus making the construction practically a compromise between the completely integral and the completely built-on jackets.

For example, in such modern construction as that shown in Fig. 1, a large plate will be noted on the ends of the cylinders. This covers a tremendous core hole, by the use of which the internal construction of the water jackets is made practically perfect in the foundry. This also allows easy inspection and cleaning, the removal of the two end plates enabling a person to see right through the water jacket from end to end. This latter-day construction overcomes all objections previously raised against troubles with complicated water-jacket cores. A detail of this cylinder block, showing clearly the arrangement of the end plates, the water passages around the cylinder bores, and other points, is presented in Fig. 1. The designers of large block castings for cylinders were forced to provide for easy inspection of this kind for self-protection, although in this connection, it is no more than fair to state that foundry men have made just as rapid advances in the art of casting automobile-engine cylinders and other complicated parts as the designers of machines have made in every other way.

Built-On Jackets. There are a number of forms of built-on water jackets, but few of these are in use at present. The best was the old Cadillac jacket, a cylindrical one-piece member with a junk ring, top and bottom, to hold tightly against water leakage. The form more often used is the applied plate, or sheet, which must be held by screws, flanges, or clamps. As these are not really successful in holding the water continuously, particularly against the combination of hot water, internal pressure, twisting, and racking action which comes from traveling over bad roads at high speeds, they are giving way to the older form of jacket.

An important advantage of applied jackets of the type just described is their freedom to yield in case the water freezes in them. The danger of cracked cylinders, which not infrequently results from exposure to cold weather in ordinary automobile motors having jackets integral with the cylinder, is eliminated.

Welded Applied Jackets. The method of welding by the oxy-acetylene process promises to produce a cylinder with a cast-iron center and a sheet-metal water-jacket exterior made of pressed steel or of flat plates. The designers who consider this combination the best—in that the thin sheet metal of copper or steel is lighter, radiates more heat, and will yield under freezing strains—will now be able to obtain such a combination at a reasonable cost. It has been used on racing cars and is, at the present time, in use on Liberty airplane engines, in which the lightest possible weight is obtained regardless of cost. In a car to sell at an ordinary price, the cost might be prohibitive.

Radiators and Piping. It has often been pointed out that all cooling of automobile engines is, in reality, air cooling; the water-cooled motor is simply one in which the heat units to be disposed of are conveyed from the cylinders to the radiator by the circulating water, to be dissipated in the air that passes through it, instead of directly lost in air passing over thin flanges cast on the cylinders. A water-cooling system therefore constitutes a sort of indirect-air cooling. This being the case, the chief justification for water cooling consists in the margin it allows for much greater cooling areas in

Fig. 2. Fin-Type Radiator

contact with air than it is possible to provide by mere extensions of the cylinder surfaces themselves.

A typical pleasure-car radiator of the fin type is shown in Fig. 2. The flanges which have a continuous horizontal appearance simply serve as a heat-radiating surface. The vertical tubes which actually carry the water can be seen in the background. This type is rapidly increasing in popularity for pleasure cars of medium and low price, at the expense of all others.

The total cooling area of the radiators employed in automobiles will range all the way from ten to ninety square feet; the latter

Fig. 3. Honeycomb Radiator

surface is not unusual in the best type of honeycomb radiators with hexagonal openings and very thin water spaces.

The smaller areas are found in the cheaper types of radiators built up of straight, round, or flat tubes, and provided with fins to increase the area exposed to the air. Radiators of these types, unless very large, are often inadequate to cool a motor when it is laboring under continued heavy usage, as in pulling on the low gear through deep sand or mud or up long heavy grades. Under such conditions, a motor that may have run for months without any cooling trouble whatever in level country will often boil all the water out of the cooling system within a few minutes.

Types of Cells. In the cellular, or honeycomb, radiator, Fig. 3, there are three forms of tubing in general use. These forms are: the square, with its flat sides set horizontally and vertically; the round, with the tubes staggered so as to make the number as large as possible; and the hexagon, which is also set staggered so as to use the maximum number. The square and hexagon are more used

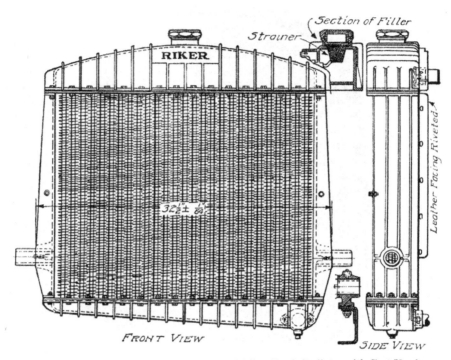

Fig. 4. Vertical Tubular Spiral Fin Type of Riker Truck Radiator with Cast Headers
Courtesy of Locomobile Company of America, Bridgeport, Connecticut

on pleasure cars, while the round form has been used on higher-priced motor trucks. A modification of the round-tube form is found in the radiator which utilizes the plain copper tubes, bunched and fitted into a header, or water tank, at the end, but which are not formed into a composite unit. This is used on both pleasure cars and trucks.

Types of Tubes. In the tubular form, there are two well-known types: the round vertical tube with spiral fin, or flange, welded or sweated on; and the so-called tube-and-plate construction, shown in Fig. 2, in which a set of horizontal plates is pierced with a number of holes, tubes set into these, and the whole dip-soldered into a unit. The former type is gaining rapidly for truck use on account of its freedom from leakage under the severe racking conditions.

An example of this type is to be found in Fig. 4, which shows a welded tubular radiator. It is of interest to note that the welded type replaced a soldered honeycomb unit of the highest quality which could not be kept water-tight in war service.

Modifications of Cellular and Tubular Forms. In addition to the types shown in Figs. 2 and 4, there are a number of forms which partake somewhat of their characteristics but which show a marked individuality. The Renault form is placed back of the engine at the dash instead of at the front. It has a tank at the top and small tanks at the bottom and sides, the central bottom space being taken up by the fan. The tubes are of pure copper and are not fastened together as in the cellular radiator, but merely connected at the

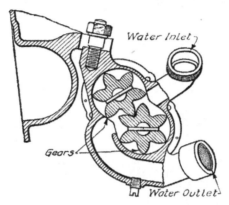

Fig. 5. Gear Type of Water Pump of Very Simple Construction

two ends. As compared with the average radiator of the cellular type of equal cooling capacity, this form requires greater height, width, and depth. Its dash position has the disadvantage of keeping the driver's compartment uncomfortably hot in the summer months.

The piping of automobile cooling systems in a great many cars is made too small to afford free circulation, and this mistake in design, common in the earlier days of automobile engineering, is one that cannot be too carefully avoided.

In the experience of most automobile designers, the most satisfactory method of connecting up the piping of a circulating system is found in the use of ordinary steam hose, which is clamped around the ends of the pipe by small metal straps.

Circulation. An unobstructed and vigorous circulation of the water in a cooling system is a great factor in reducing the size of radiator required and in preventing overheating.

Pumps. The usual method of circulating the cooling water is to use one type or another of small pumps, driven by suitable gearing from the engine itself.

Gear pumps are often used for this purpose because of their extreme simplicity, but it is difficult to make them large enough to handle as great volumes of water as most designers now regard desirable.

A good example of the gear form of water pump is shown in Fig. 5. This is simply a pair of gears which mesh rather closely; the movement of the flat side of the teeth carries or forces the water

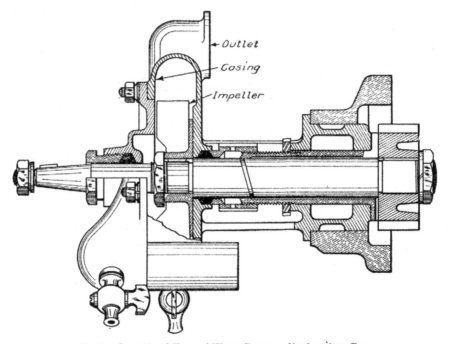

Fig. 6. Centrifugal Type of Water Pump as Used on Reo Cars

forward. In general, the gears are made of small diameter but wide face to take advantage of this action. The result is a very compact pump. The vane type of pump is really a modification of the gear pump in that a rotating member is placed in an eccentric chamber with a sliding arm on either side, which is held out into contact

382

with the sides of the chamber by a central spring. This double sliding arm simulates the effect of the teeth of the gear form. This has small capacity and is not widely used on that account.

The consequence is that the centrifugal pump is now the type most preferred. In their best forms, centrifugal pumps consist of simple multi-bladed "impellers" revolving with close clearances in a housing.

One advantage of the centrifugal pump is that if any small object, such as a stick or pebble, should by any chance get into the

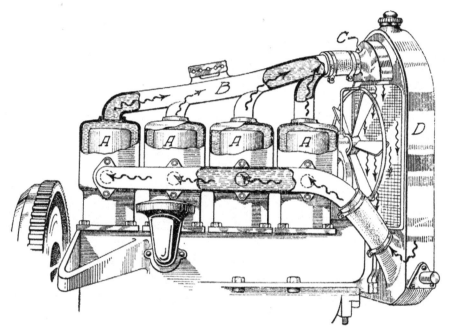

Fig. 7. Thermosyphon System of Cooling as Used on Overland Cars

circulating system—though strainers always should be provided to prevent this contingency—no serious harm is likely to result, whereas with a gear pump breakage is almost certain to ensue.

The construction of the centrifugal pump is shown in Fig. 6. The impeller is sectioned at the water-outlet space. The impeller fits the casing very closely except at the water outlet where the water is thrown off by the centrifugal force generated in rotation.

Reciprocating plunger pumps are used chiefly in motor-boat motors of the two-cycle types to circulate the cooling water. The volume of water handled by pumps of this type, of dimensions that can be conveniently employed, is not very large, however, and it is only the fact that the water is not re-used and is, therefore, cooler and of a consequently greater effectiveness that makes possible the use of plunger pumps in motor boats.

Thermosyphon. Circulation of the cooling water by the thermosyphon action, owing to the heated water in the jackets rising and the cooled water in the radiator descending, is the practice of an

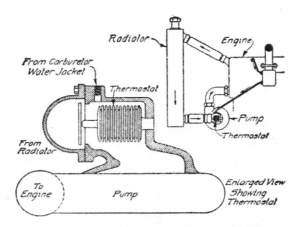

Fig. 8. Thermostatic Device in Latest Cadillac Water-Cooling System to Preserve Equilibrium and Even Temperature

increasing number of designers, and has been demonstrated to be very effective with liberal jacket spaces and large-diameter piping.

The pioneer and still the most prominent exponent of thermosyphon cooling is the Renault Company, France. Such cars as the Ford and Stearns-Knight use the thermosyphon system.

The thermosyphon system, Fig. 7, shows the large open pipes with few bends—and those few very easy so as to reduce water friction to a minimum—also the small difference in level between the top and bottom of the system. The difference in temperature causes the movement of the water. It is said that the pressure which the temperature variation produces is seldom more than a small fraction of a pound; for this reason it is necessary to reduce surface friction and losses at bends and at other similar points.

Cadillac System. An entirely new idea in the control of the temperature of the cooling water is that used on the new eight-cylinder Cadillac motors. Here, each block of four cylinders has its own circulating system, with pump and piping, entirely distinct from the other. In each one, a thermostat, like that shown in Fig. 8, is located on top of the pump housing. This controls the movement of a valve, which, when shut off, prevents the flow of water to the radiator, that is, when the temperature of the water falls below a certain figure at which the thermostat is set, it comes into action and

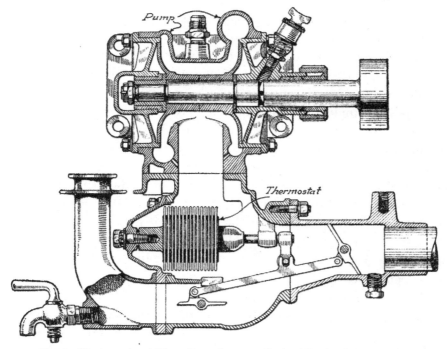

Fig. 9. Thermostat and Water-Pump Group on Packard Twelve-Cylinder Motor
Courtesy of Packard Motor Car Company, Detroit, Michigan

cuts off the flow of water from the radiator to the pump. The result is that the pump can circulate only that part which comes through the very small pipe to the inlet manifold and carburetor and from there back to the pump. This continues until the water becomes heated; the raising of the temperature operates the thermostat which opens the valve, and the system is again complete. In the upper right-hand part of Fig. 8 the circulating system of one block of cylinders is shown in outline.

The method of controlling the temperature of the engine with an automatic check valve is receiving much attention; there is even talk of extending the same system of control to the exhaust gases and all sources of heat, interconnecting them with the fuel vaporizer so as to vaporize the maximum amount of fuel in the minimum time with the least heat-loss. The thermostat and pump combination used on the Packard twelve-cylinder motor is shown in Fig. 9. Two centrifugal pumps are placed on the pump shaft, one at each end so that the thrust of each one balances the other. In the Cadillac, the two cylinder groups are separate, each having all the units shown in Fig. 8, except the radiator. In both the Cadillac and Packard systems, the thermostat is placed at the bottom of the system. It has been advocated by engineers for other companies that this would do the most good if placed at the top of the system.

The value of a thermostat may be gained from these figures. One particular make of thermostat, as used on a popular make of car, was tested out with the following results: Without it, the car did $14\frac{1}{2}$ miles on a gallon of fuel at 15 m.p.h. and $13\frac{1}{2}$ miles at 30 m.p.h. At the same speeds and with the thermostat set at 160 degrees, the same car under the same circumstances did $16\frac{1}{2}$ miles at almost 15 m.p.h. With everything the same but with the device set to work at 180 degrees, the car did $19\frac{1}{4}$ and $16\frac{1}{4}$ miles, respectively. The gain at the lowest speed of 15 miles an hour from $14\frac{1}{2}$ to $16\frac{1}{2}$ and then to $19\frac{1}{4}$ miles per gallon represents gains of almost 14 and 38 per cent in economy.

Fans. In the earlier days of automobile designing it was deemed sufficient to secure circulation of air through the radiators by the movement of the car alone. This was soon found inadequate, however, for often when most cooling was needed, as in hill climbing or hard pulling on the level, the car would be moving at its lowest speed on low gear, with the result that the air draft through the radiator was not sufficient to cool the water.

This condition was remedied by the use of a fan behind the radiator, driven by a belt or gearing from the motor so as to draw a constant draft through the radiator in proportion to the speed of the engine rather than of the car.

Nowadays, practically all automobile power plants are provided with fans, the only exceptions being a few very small motors in which the difficulty of cooling is not so great as with the higher powers.

In some cases, instead of a separate fan, fan blades are placed on the flywheel, and so made to induce a draft through the bonnet that covers the engine, thus avoiding the necessity for the addition to the moving parts involved in the usual fan system. Such a flywheel fan is used with the Renault engine.

A later plan of even greater effectiveness is the housing-in of the whole rear end of the radiator, so that what air passes through must pass through the center where the fan is located. This is but another way of saying that all air must pass through at a high velocity, which insures efficiency. This plan fulfills one requirement of air cooling, that is, the large quantity of air which must be used.

Where this system is used now, the entire engine in front of the fan is made air-tight. The hood, which has no openings anywhere, is set into carefully fitted rubber strips to cut off any possible leakage. The same precautions of drawing all the air through the radiator, and through that alone, are observed elsewhere. While this method is effective, it is a disadvantage in another way, for some direct cooling is effected through the cylinder walls, exhaust pipes, etc., in the ordinary system by the cold air passing over the radiator, particularly the air which comes in from around the hood top and sides.

Anti=Freezing Solutions. In using automobiles in very cold climates during the winter months there is great danger of the water in the cooling system freezing when the car is standing still, or even with the motor running slowly if the temperature is very low. The result of such freezing is almost certain injury to the cylinders, through cracking of the water jackets, as well as the probability of bursting out radiator seams, with consequent leakage.

To avoid these difficulties it is not uncommon to use, instead of pure water, one kind or another of anti-freezing solution, usually compounded by the mixture of some chemical with water to lower its freezing point. Thus, glycerine or alcohol mixed with water will keep it from freezing at all ordinary winter temperatures. Glycerine is somewhat objected to because of its sticky, gummy nature, and also because of its deleterious effects upon the rubber hose of the piping system. Alcohol, if not replenished from time to time, will evaporate out of the water and thus permit it to freeze, or, if mixed in too great a quantity, it may introduce a fire risk otherwise avoidable.

A much favored anti-freezing solution consists of calcium chloride dissolved in water, in a quantity proportioned to the temperatures that it is desired to guard against.

All anti-freezing solutions are more or less objectionable in that they are more likely than pure water to corrode and clog up the circulating system, and there is no doubt that the elimination of the necessity for them by the substitution of air cooling for water cooling will mark a great advance in automobile development.

Non=Freezing Solutions. To prevent the water from freezing when it is not desirable to drain it out, either wood alcohol, denatured alcohol, or glycerine may be mixed with the water. The alcohol mixture is as follows:

Wood Alcohol and Water

10° above zero; 80% water, 20% alcohol
Zero; 75% water, 25% alcohol; sp. gr. .969
7° below zero; 79% water, 30% alcohol; sp. gr. .963
22° below zero; 60% water, 40% alcohol; sp. gr. .951

If denatured alcohol is used, increase the above percentage by approximately 15.

For evaporation, use 75 per cent alcohol to 25 per cent water, as the alcohol evaporates quicker. This does not apply to loss by leaks or boiling over.

A hydrometer can be used for mixing and maintaining correct solution, by first testing the original and keeping it up to a standard of 1250 gravity.

Glycerine and Alcohol

30 to 15 above zero:	Per Cent
Alcohol	10
Glycerine	10
Water	80

Not lower than 5 below:	
Alcohol	15
Glycerine	15
Water	70

Not lower than 15 below:	
Alcohol	17
Glycerine	17
Water	66

STEAM COOLING

An entirely new system of cooling which is now coming into use is the Rushmore System of steam cooling. In this system the radiator is not full of water, as in the conventional type, the only water being present in the radiator is in the tank at the bottom of the radiator. A small pump is used to draw the water from the tank at the bottom of the radiator and force it into the cylinder water jacket. As this water strikes the cylinder it is converted into steam and the steam passes out at the top of the cylinder water jacket and is conducted by pipe to the bottom of the radiator.

The steam passes up through the radiator and is condensed. The condensed steam in the form of water drops down into the water tank at the bottom of the radiator where it is passed into the

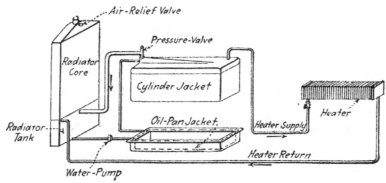

Fig. 10. Steam-Cooling Connections
Courtesy of Rushmore Laboratory, Plainfield

cylinder to go through the same cycle again. Many advantages are claimed for this system, such as reduced crankcase dilution, because of better vaporization of the particle of gasoline in the combustion chamber, quicker warming up, and more uniform operating temperature, no loss of water or cooling medium by evaporation, which is invaluable in winter when alcohol is used.

A steam pipe can be attached to the inside of the crankcase to heat the case whereby any water accumulation in the case can be vaporized and thus prevent damage by freezing with its consequent loss of lubrication.

A steam heating unit for the inside of the car can be utilized whereby a heat of 70° can be maintained, making winter driving very enjoyable as far as warmth is concerned.

The pump as used in this system is very small and is of the gear type, which materially reduces the power which is taken from the engine to operate the ordinary centrifugal pump used on the average car.

The greatest benefit of all is that it reduces gasoline consumption. It has been proved that with this system an increase of 20% more miles per gallon of gasoline has been obtained. Fig. 10 is a sketch showing how the system is linked up with small pipes. It will be noticed that a safety pressure valve is used to prevent a heavy discharge of steam.

AIR COOLING

Air cooling is not considered by most engineers to be successfully applicable to the average automobile, though successfully employed in one or two automobiles and remarkably developed in some of its applications to aviation motors. That it will become more practical in the future, however, is the opinion of many.

Unfortunately, this is an instance where the better and simpler method does not meet with popular approval, that is, the cooling of automobile cylinders is one of those cases in which the best in theory is not by any means accepted practice.

Flanges, or Fins. The usual method of air cooling, successfully employed in aviation and motorcycle motors and in a few automobiles, is to provide the cylinders with fins, or flanges, for increasing the area of the surface, supplementing this with means for blowing large volumes of air over the surfaces thus provided.

Air Jackets. Several of the most practical examples of air-cooled motors in aviation construction are those which have, in addition to the flanges, or fins, on the cylinders, air jackets to concentrate the drafts of air that effect the cooling.

Blowers and Fans. The most successful air cooling has been accomplished by types of blowers capable of inducing much more vigorous air currents than are drawn through the radiators of water-cooled automobiles by the types of fans commonly used in power plants of that character.

Franklin Cooling. In the Franklin, the most successful of air-cooled cars, the cooling is a combination of the blower and the fin system. The cylinders are made of gray iron with the fins cast into the walls in a vertical position. In the front of the engine is a blower or fan, enclosed in a housing, which directs the air into the upper and lower air hoods, forces it down through the fins, cooling the engine. The fins should be cleaned occasionally so that they

Fig. 11. Diagrammatic Illustration Showing System of Air Cooling on Franklin Cars
Courtesy of H. H. Franklin Manufacturing Company, Syracuse, New York

will conduct the heat away from the cylinder walls efficiently. When replacing the air hoods, see that they are fastened tight so that none of the air from the fan escapes. Fig. 11 shows the position of the fan with the air hoods cut away to show the direction of air travel.

Internal Cooling and Scavenging. Perhaps more promising as a road to final and universal use of air cooling are the systems of pumping air through the interiors of the cylinders instead of blowing it over the exteriors of the cylinders. Such internal cooling, in addition to directing the maximum cooling effect where it is most needed on the oil-coated surfaces that are exposed to the heat of combustion, has a further advantage in that it may be made to scavenge out all residual exhaust gases, which, besides helping to accumulate heat, also act so detrimentally upon the functioning of ordinary motors. This is a direct result of the admixture of retained exhaust gases with incoming fresh charges.

Methods of internal cooling and scavenging that appear of definite promise are those proposed in various recent schemes for pumping air first into the crankcase—either by using the under side of the piston as a pump, as in common two-cycle constructions, or by applying special pumps to the crankcase for this particular purpose—then into the cylinders by means of by-passes, with the result that it exerts a positive cooling effect inside the cylinder.

In England, some interesting experiments have been made on a theory of internal cooling in which water is introduced into the cylinders in the form of a spray, at certain points in the cycle. This is said to add power in addition to helping the cooling.

COOLING TROUBLES, ADJUSTMENTS, AND CURES

Dirty Cooling System. It is highly important that the cooling system be entirely cleaned out at least once, and preferably twice, a year. When this is done, the water jackets and radiator should be flushed out with a strong current of water, preferably a hot soda solution. This should be forced through in a direction opposite to the usual course of the water. Thus, a hose can be put in the radiator filler cap and city pressure applied to force the water through; in this radiator, it will be made to go from bottom to top instead of the usual top to bottom. If this method, which is the usual and easy one, does not remove all dirt, sediment, and foreign matter, the radiator can be removed and boiled, or at least submerged, in a strong soda solution which will clean it out thoroughly. The radiator is the most important member of the system.

Oil in Cooling System. The leakage of oil into the cooling system will cause a loss of cooling. The oil will accumulate on the inside of the radiator tubes and prevent the water from coming in contact with the cooling surfaces. When this trouble is found, usually in the detachable head type of cylinder, it can be traced to a leaky head gasket. If the head is not bolted down tight, the oil will be forced into the cooling system by the action of the piston. When replacing the head gasket be sure that there are no particles of carbon under the gasket or the latter will not be held away from the metal. It is a good plan to smear white lead on both sides of the gasket before bolting the head gasket in place. It should be allowed to cool before running the engine. If this trouble has occurred, the cooling system should be washed out with a strong soda solution.

Water Hose Connection Troubles. These troubles are caused by the inside of the hose swelling and stopping the circulation. If long hose connections are used, the pump action will be so strong that the hose will collapse or be drawn together, preventing the circulation and causing overheating. Another cause for overheating is the formation of air pockets that prevent circulation.

Replacements. When replacements are made, it is advisable also to look over all hose and hose connections. Many times the hose will have become worn or frayed through and cut or otherwise damaged from the outside, or the water may have attacked it from the inside, particularly if it has been through a winter when an anti-freezing solution was used. It is well, when cleaning the system, to replace all hose with new. The clamps are important as they determine the water tightness of the hose, so they should be looked over for missing nuts, broken screws, broken clamp ends, as well as to note if each one is applied straight and true over the hose and the end of the pipe on which it is placed.

Dirty Radiators. If the radiator is splashed with mud or dirt, the washing should be done from the rear, with the hood removed. This method allows free use of the hose, and at the same time it insures against getting any water in the ignition system where it would cause trouble.

Loose Fan Belt. Usually the fan is hung on an eccentric bushing held in a clamp. It is important that the fan belt be tight enough so that there is no slippage, otherwise the engine will heat up. To tighten a belt, loosen the clamping bolt on the fan eccentric, and then turn this eccentric so as to move the fan shaft center away from the crankshaft-pulley center. The eccentric may be moved with the hands, in some cases; in others, a wrench is provided, and the fan eccentric made with surfaces on which the wrench fits; in other cases the application of a pointed tool and hammer is needed to turn it. In the latter case, do this very carefully so as not to chip off any metal. Occasionally, the fan bearings need adjustment or lubrication. When they are of the plain type, a grease cup is generally provided and, after the engine is stopped, a couple of turns of this will be sufficient; if of the ball or roller type, they will be packed in grease, and if they show signs of running dry, the fan should be taken apart and a good grade of grease used.

Leaky Pump Packing Nuts. Generally, the pump is made so as to need no adjustment. However, a leak may occur at one of the packing nuts. To remedy it, tighten the nut as far as possible, but if this does no good, remove the nut and add packing under it. Special packing is provided for this purpose, but if no other is available, a thick heavy piece of string can be well coated with graphite or a graphite grease and wound on as packing. In putting on packing of this kind it should be wound on right handed, or in the same direction as the packing nut turns to tighten. Otherwise, tightening the nut will loosen the packing.

Engine Heats, Loses Power, and Knocks. These are all symptoms of lack of water circulation. To see if this is the case, look into the opening in the top of the radiator and see whether water is flowing in from the engine. If not, either the water-piping system is stopped up, which can be checked by disconnecting, or else the circulating pump is not working properly. All modern engines are so proportioned that, in this event, the water continues to circulate by thermosyphon action. Taking off the pump will verify this.

Water Pump Impeller Loose on Its Shaft. One of the causes of poor or no circulation in the cooling system is the pump impeller being loose on the shaft so that it does not move and the water is not circulated. The passages in a pump cooling system are not large enough to give efficient cooling by the thermosyphon method so that the impeller should be repaired as soon as possible.

MANIFOLD DESIGN AND CONSTRUCTION

INLET MANIFOLDS

The design of the manifold has a great deal to do with the efficient operation of the internal combustion machine. For smooth and even running the charges taken into the cylinder should be of the same strength and quality. In other words, the charge taken into one cylinder should not be richer or in a better state of vaporization than the charge taken into another cylinder. The distribution of the fuel to the cylinder should, therefore, be as even as possible, which depends greatly on the design of the intake manifold. The ideal form of charge is one that consists of dry gas, but the present-day fuel prevents such a charge unless the mixture is subjected to a high temperature. If the charge is too highly heated, the volumetric efficiency is destroyed and the power output of the engine drops off. A compromise between these two mixtures is used and the charge is introduced into the cylinder in the form of a gas fog. Even this has its disadvantages as some of the fuel will be deposited on the walls of the cylinder and manifold. The manifold should, therefore, be designed so that wall condensation is reduced as much as possible. If condensation does occur, each cylinder will then receive its equal share of the wet mixture which is taken up by the incoming charge.

Four=Cylinder Manifolds. The firing order and the valve timing also have something to do with the design of the manifold. When two cylinders in the same block next to each other fire one after the other and the intake valve opens a little before the previous intake valve closes, there is a possibility of a supply of gas to the first cylinder being cut off by the suction of the second cylinder. In Fig. 1 is shown a manifold for a four-cylinder engine which is suitable for a firing order of 1-3-4-2, and will give good distribution, but is not as suitable for the 1-2-4-3 order. In the first order, number 4 fires after number 3 and the suction of 4 will tend to add to the amount in 3 without stopping its own suction. Both will benefit if there should be any wet gasoline on the walls of the manifold. In the second order, 2 firing after 1 will tend to draw some of the mixture from 1 or at least cut off the supply to that cylinder, while in the other pair number 4 will get the benefit of the wet gas that has accumulated on the walls of the manifold between cylinders 3 and 4, and will be richer than the mixture supplied to number 3.

The inside of the intake manifold should be smooth and the passages should be large enough so that there is no obstruction to the flow of gases. The bends in the manifold should be so designed

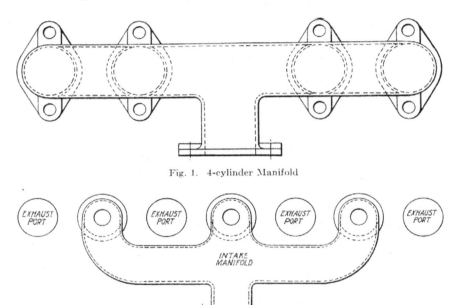

Fig. 1. 4-cylinder Manifold

Fig. 2. 6-cylinder Manifold

that the movement of the gases will prevent, or pick up, any fuel accumulating on the walls of the manifold through condensation. The flat-bottom manifold is well adapted for heat application and quick vaporization of condensed fuel moisture on its walls, as the drops of moisture fall to the floor at once. This applies to all manifolds whether for four, six, or more cylinders.

Six=Cylinder Manifolds. The design of a manifold for a six-cylinder engine is governed by the firing order of the engine and, of course, that is governed by the placing of the cranks. In most six-cylinder engines the intake valves and ports are so laid out that two intake valves draw their charge for the same manifold connection. The most desirable arrangement for the six-cylinder engine is to have the suction in the intake manifold come from opposite ends of the engine. This prevents any one branch accumulating more moisture than another. There are two firing orders which allow this and they are the orders in use at the present time—1-5-3-6-2-4 and 1-4-2-6-3-5. A manifold that is suitable for these is shown in Fig. 2.

In most manifolds the bends have been made with radii because it was thought that abrupt turns prevented the easy flow of the

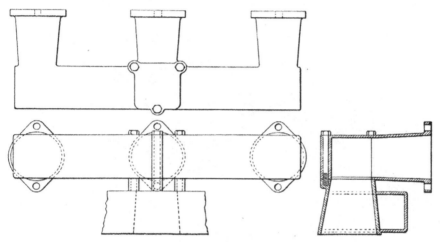

Fig. 3. Square-Type Manifold

gas mixture. A recent design of manifold that is proving successful is one of square cross-section, Fig. 3. This manifold has the flat floor and all gas passages are exactly alike in shape. It is claimed that the abrupt turns tend to keep the particles of gasoline in the stream flow of the gases and direct them in a straight line. The turbulence set up by the abrupt turns helps to keep the particles in suspension at all times. Any particles of gasoline that may accumulate on the roof of the manifold and drop down must fall into the gas stream, while the square section gives the greatest floor area for the evaporation of the condensed fuel that might accumulate there.

Eight= and Twelve=Cylinder Manifolds. The coming of the V-type motors, both eights and twelves, has had another influence for they came at the time when fuel was getting heavier and heavier. Designers were beginning to recognize the difficulty of vaporizing all the heavy fuel before it reached the cylinders and, to assist in this, they began utilizing the manifold. Consequently, the majority, if not all, the eight- and twelve-cylinder engines have manifolds of the loop type, Fig. 4. This is a typical eight- and twelve-cylinder manifold, except that some have a pair of pet cocks for priming or cylinder testing purposes. The unusual diameter is due to the

Fig. 4. View of National Twelve-Cylinder Motor from Above, Showing Inlet Manifold
Courtesy of National Motor Vehicle Company, Indianapolis, Indiana

water jacket around it. The unusual height is due to two things: (1) the necessity of getting the carburetor between it and the cylinders, yet not too close for accessibility; and (2) the necessity of having a sufficient volume to act as a storage reservoir, since each side of this (each half of the loop) serves six cylinders (four in the case of the eight-cylinder engine).

Heating the Charge. The method of heating the charge has taken a number of forms. In a simple four-cylinder motor of the L=head type, like the Ford, it has been possible to develop a combination inlet and exhaust manifold (a single casting which would replace both of the former manifolds) which would give the heating effect desired in the inlet portion. Fig. 5 shows one way in which this is done and shows the central plate, or rib, between the two manifolds, which is heated to a high temperature by the exhaust gases, and thus has a large influence on the final vaporization of the inflowing gases on the other side of it. It is claimed for this form that it will save from 25 to 40 per cent of the fuel used and even though this claim is not borne out in all cases, the fact that there is a saving shows that this is a correct method. Many of the more modern motors are not only incorporating this as a method of saving fuel and increasing the motor's efficiency but also of reducing the number of parts in the machine, the opportunities for trouble, and possibly of reducing weight.

Changes in Construction of Manifold. The construction of inlet manifolds has shown marked improvement. A manifold of

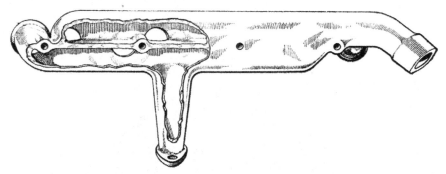

Fig. 5. Type of Combination Inlet and Exhaust Manifold Which Improves Vaporization

aluminum, iron, or other cast metal is usually quite different from what a manifold for the same engine would be if made from copper or steel tubing. In addition to the limitations of the process of production, there would be the changes which the surface produced would have. Thus, a casting would have a more or less rough surface, while a drawn tube would be perfectly smooth, which allows the use of a slightly smaller diameter and more abrupt bends.

On a number of block-cast motors, the manifolds have been cast integral with the cylinders, thus taking further advantage of the heat generated within the motor for fuel vaporizing purposes. It is for this type of motor that the horizontal-outlet type of carburetor has been developed. In this type the volume of vaporizing space beyond the spray nozzle is at a minimum, that is, the carburetor has been designed simply to mix the fuel spray and air, while the highly heated inlet passages do the actual vaporizing.

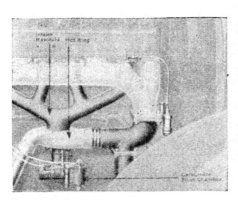

Fig. 6. Marmon "Hot-Spot" Ring Form
Courtesy of Marmon Motor Car Company

Fig. 8. Stove Heater

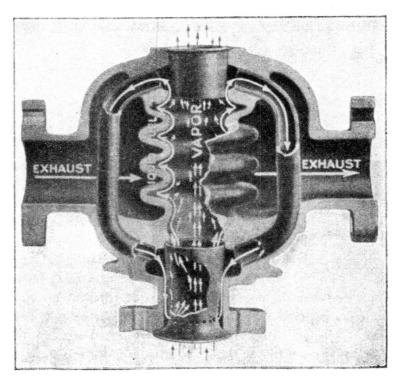

Fig. 7. Franklin Fuelizer
Courtesy of Franklin Motor Car Company

Hot=Spot Manifolds. It is very desirable to place the carburetor close to the cylinders so that there will not be a great deal of condensation in the lower part of the intake manifold. In a system

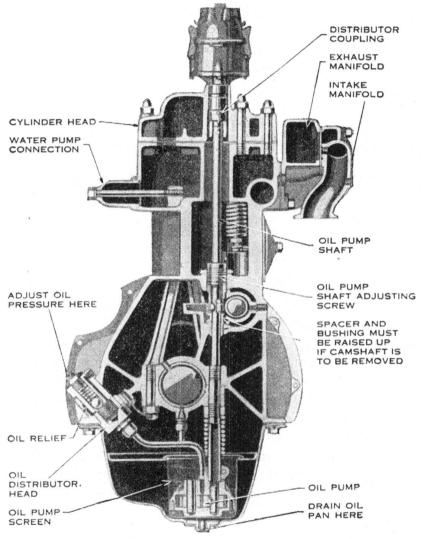

Fig. 9. Cross-Section of an Engine
Rickenbacker Motor Company

where a long riser pipe was used a great deal of the condensed gasoline would drain back into the carburetor and cause loading and a means had to be devised to vaporize this fuel. The hot-spot manifold was the outcome. It is so constructed that a portion of it, consisting of solid metal, is in constant contact with the exhaust manifold so that in continuous running this solid metal in the intake manifold becomes heated, perhaps to a high degree. Furthermore, this "hot-spot" is so located in the inlet passages that all fuel must pass over it before passing to the cylinders, with the result that any unvaporized particles remaining in the fuel gas are thrown against this highly heated spot and vaporized instead of being carried into the cylinders as liquid particles, as would be the case without this heated spot.

Even today there are some engines in which the carburetor is not very close to the cylinders. A good example is the Marmon

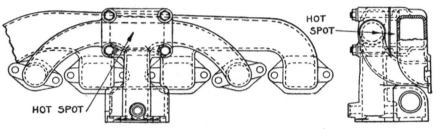

Fig. 10. Hot-Spot Manifold Arrangement on Hinkley Truck Engine
Courtesy Hinkley Motors Corporation, Detroit, Michigan

installation, Fig. 6, which is also a good illustration of the up-to-date hot-spot manifold. Any gasoline that drains back into the carburetor falls onto this "hot-spot" and is vaporized, passing back into the engine with the other fuel. Another type of fuelizer, used on the Franklin car, is shown in Fig. 7. It has proved very efficient in operation.

Another method used to vaporize the fuel is the stove in which the intake passages pass through the exhaust manifold as shown in Fig. 8. A cutaway section of the heating arrangement on the Ricken-backer engine is shown in Fig. 9. It will be noticed that the intake and exhaust manifold are bolted together.

Since heavy fuel is available on the Pacific Coast at low prices, considerable effort has been expended on using these cheaper but heavier fuels. A modification of the hot-spot arrangement, de-signed to be used on a Hinkley truck engine is shown in Fig. 10, and on Ford cars in Fig. 11. Here the hot spot projecting into the exhaust manifold is not alone made very large but the outer or heating surface is increased by the addition of fins similar to an air-cooled engine. This adds metal to heat up and hold the heat, which is what the heavier fuels like distillate must have. In addition, the carburetor is so constructed as to spray all the fuel oil directly into the interior of this highly heated mass of metal, the gasified parts coming down into the intake manifold. This heated mass of metal is thus the entire dependence for vaporization in this case, the actual carburetor part of the device having been

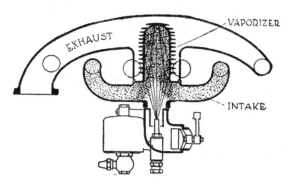

Fig. 11. Far-Western Carburetor Which Is All Hot Spot

eliminated. It would seem that this carries the hot-spot or hot surface plan almost too far, its original intention having been for use as an auxiliary, the hot surface vaporizing only those heavy globules of the liquid which the spraying and atomizing and air mixing did not or could not break up and vaporize. In short it was intended originally only as a clean-up device, following and wholly dependent upon the carburetor. The device in Fig. 11 aims to make the hot surface become hot surface, vaporizer, and clean-up device all in one.

Another version of the heated manifold surface is shown in Fig. 12, the manifolds of the Velie tractor. Here the first part of the inlet manifold is highly heated by constructing the two manifolds as one, the inlet consisting of a straight vertical passage through the center of the exhaust passages, just as the detail at the left shows. This would give the high heat necessary for the original vaporization or cracking up of all the fuel, but to insure continuation of this condition, that is, to prevent any of the mixture condensing out into liquid again, the second portion across the top of the cylinders is water cooled. In this condition, the gas would be too hot to enter the cylinders, hence it is cooled by means of air-cooling fins or ribs along the last portion of its length. As a permanent gas has been produced by the previous steps, this carries with it small possibility of any condensation.

The real flaw in the hot-surface method is that it is of no help whatever in starting, since it does not begin to work until after the engine has run for some time and heated up. Poor starting is really a greater drawback than running on heavier fuels.

Inlet Manifold Troubles. The principal inlet manifold troubles are air leaks, which dilute the mixture beyond the carburetor, making

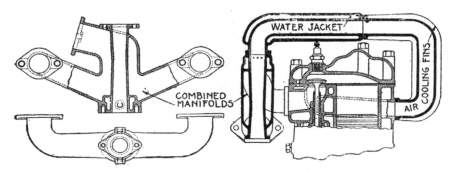

Fig. 12. Combined Inlet and Exhaust Manifold of Velie Tractor
Courtesy Velie Motors Corporation, Moline, Illinois

it and its many elaborate adjustments more or less useless. These leaks may be due to leaks around joints, connections, or gaskets, or to porous castings. If the inlet manifold is of copper or steel tubing, the idea of a leak can be dismissed. On the other hand, a porous pipe can be discovered at idling speeds by squirting gasoline upon the suspected surface of the manifold and noting if the motor speeds up. If it does, it is a sign that some of the gasoline has been drawn through the holes in the manifold, enriching the mixture.

The leaks around joints, connections, or gaskets can be found in much the same way. When the leak is found, the joint should be tightened if possible, or a new gasket should be put in, or both. In the case of the porous manifold casting, it can be painted with a fairly heavy paint while hot so that the pores of the metal are well opened. Then, after this has dried in thoroughly, another coat will probably finish the job. If this is not satisfactory, special cement for filling porous castings can be purchased and applied. If the case is a bad one, an entirely new manifold should be put in.

EXHAUST MANIFOLDS

Importance of Handling Exhaust Gases Properly. The matter of handling exhaust gases in the past has been done with the smallest possible amount of time, trouble, and thought. They had to be gotten rid of, so it was done as easily and quickly as possible. As engines became larger, and as speeds increased, there was more and more gas to handle. The growing cry for a quiet or noiseless car necessitated giving the problem more thought, for the simple application of a muffler did not entirely eliminate the noise. As fuels grew heavier, heat was required to assist in the process of vaporizing. In order to apply heat, many designers began to see possible uses for some of the gas pouring out at the rear end of the car. Today, the handling of the exhaust gases is probably being given as much thought as any part or unit on the entire car.

The design of the exhaust pipe should be such that it excludes any chance of back pressure. It must be remembered that in multiple-cylinder engines, the strokes overlap. Consequently, at certain parts of the cycle there are two cylinders exhausting at the same time and the exhaust pipe should be large enough to take care of both. The exhaust pipe should gradually increase in size toward its outlet so that there will be no restriction. When a curved exhaust pipe is used, care should be taken in the layout of the curves so that a cylinder that is exhausting at high pressure does not blow over into a cylinder in which the pressure is low and in which the valve is open.

Forms of Exhaust Manifolds. Ordinarily, the exhaust gases emerge from the cylinders into the exhaust manifold. This is generally a cast-iron member of fairly large size held in position by bolts. At its rear end, which is round, it is threaded or flanged for the attachment of the exhaust pipe. This is shown rather well in the National engine, Fig. 13. Although this is a twelve-cylinder motor, it has the outside valves, so the exhaust manifold is located there. It is a typical cast-iron manifold, differing from the ordinary manifold only in having the outlet at the center instead of the rear end. Six bolts hold it in place—four on the upper edge and two on the lower. Its interior structure is evidently the same throughout, and no special provision has been made for reducing gas friction. It has no attachments of any kind.

Many exhaust manifolds have been cast integral with the cylinder block. This method is quite popular among small car makers, as

Fig. 13. View of National Twelve-Cylinder Motor, Showing Particularly Exhaust Manifold
Courtesy of National Motor Vehicle Company, Indianapolis, Indiana

it is used as much to save the expense of machining and fitting and to reduce the weight and number of parts as for any other reason. In the larger sizes it probably never will become popular, because of the difficult core work in the foundry which makes cylinder-casting cost prohibitive, and thus more than offsets any other saving.

A number of manifolds have been cast with cooling fins, or flanges on the outside, the effect being to reduce the exhaust heat immediately by dissipation; a secondary idea is that of making the casting stiffer and stronger and less liable to loss by breakage. A flanged manifold is shown in Fig. 14, which illustrates the Peerless eight-cylinder motor; the exhaust manifold is marked at *A* and *B*. The section taken at A shows the full exterior size; the boss, through which a

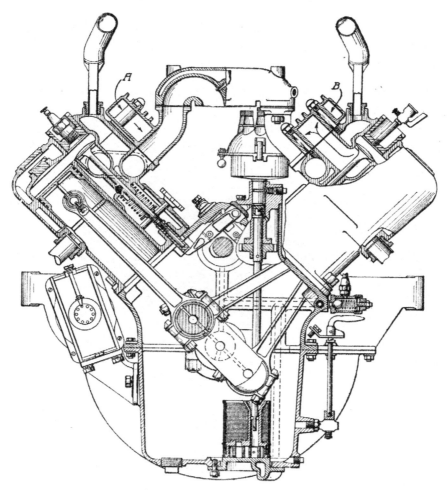

Fig. 14. Section through Peerless Eight, Showing Ribbed Exhaust Manifold
Courtesy of Peerless Motor Car and Truck Corporation, Cleveland, Ohio

holding bolt passes, is seen in elevation. At *B*, however, the section is taken through a pair of bolts, so the section appears smaller than it actually is.

In the usual eight- and twelve-cylinder motor and in some sixes, a pair of manifolds, each with its own exhaust pipe and muffler, are used. It has been found by experience that the tremendous volume of gas to be handled, the speed at which it had to be handled, and the necessity for silence called for a separate exhausting system for each group of cylinders. These were problems, aside from the fact that it was more simple structurally to handle the exhaust in two manifolds. A double-manifold construction is shown in the Cadillac, Fig. 15, which is a view of the rear end of the engine. The two manifolds

Fig. 15. Three-Quarter Rear View of Cadillac Motor in Chassis, Showing Exhaust Manifold and Pipes in Duplicate

for the two sides can be seen readily; also the two separate exhaust pipes, wrapped with asbestos where they pass the dash and other wooden parts. A further view of this car is shown in Fig. 16, the chassis from above, in which the two separate systems can be followed back to the mufflers just forward of the rear axle on either side.

Muffler. The purpose of the muffler is to reduce the pressure of the gases by expansion to a point where they will emerge into the atmosphere without noise. This is generally done by providing a number of concentric chambers. The gas is allowed to expand from

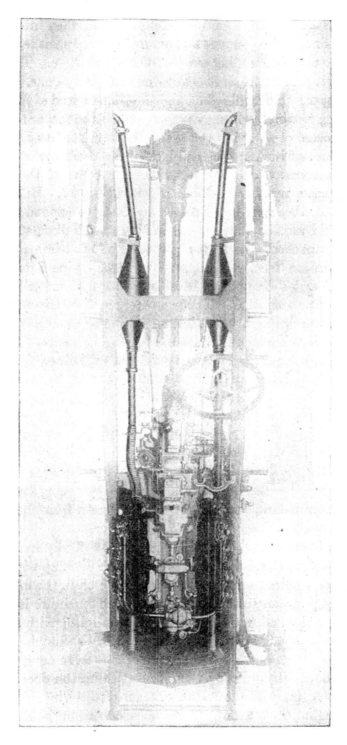

Fig. 16. Cadillac Chassis from Above, Showing Double System of Exhausting with Twin Mufflers

the first passage into the much larger second one, then into the still larger third one, and so on, to the final and largest passage, which is connected to the pipe leading out into the atmosphere. This is not as simple as it sounds, for, if it is not well and wisely done, there will be back pressure which will reduce the power and speed of the engine, cause heating troubles, and may possibly cause the motor to stop.

The process of spraying water into the muffler has been tried, but on account of its first cost and lack of positive beneficial results it has been abandoned. The actual construction of the muffler, however, takes a number of different forms, Fig. 17. Baffle plates are used in A, the gases being forced by them to expand from one chamber to the next so all the speed and pressure is dissipated before the outlet is reached. In B, the gases are allowed immediate and sudden expansion from a comparatively small pipe into a large chamber. A series of annular chambers of large diameter but small depth forms the basis of C. The gas enters each of these chambers from the center through small holes, thence exhausting outwards, each chamber having an outlet around its circumference. In D, the gases enter the central small pipe, escape through holes at its far end, which is blocked off, into the first concentric chamber where they travel to the front end where holes allow it to pass out into the second concentric chamber and out into the atmosphere. This is a widely used type. Cone-shaped baffles which force the gases to expand and then pass through very small apertures and expand again form the basis of E. This is the so-called ejector type, the passage of the gases from the large to the small end of the various cones being supposed to create a suction behind it which draws the gas out from the exhaust pipe continuously.

Muffler Troubles. When the engine mysteriously loses power, it is well to look at the muffler. A dirty muffler filled up with oil and carbon, which results from the use of too much oil in the motor, will choke up the passages so that considerable back pressure is created. When this is suspected, tap the muffler all over lightly with a wooden mallet, and the exhaust gases will blow the sooty accumulations out.

Cut=Outs. Formerly, the majority of cars were equipped with muffler cut-outs. By pressing the foot on the button operating the cut-out, the engine was allowed to exhaust directly into the atmosphere, cutting out the muffler. It served as a warning signal; it gave

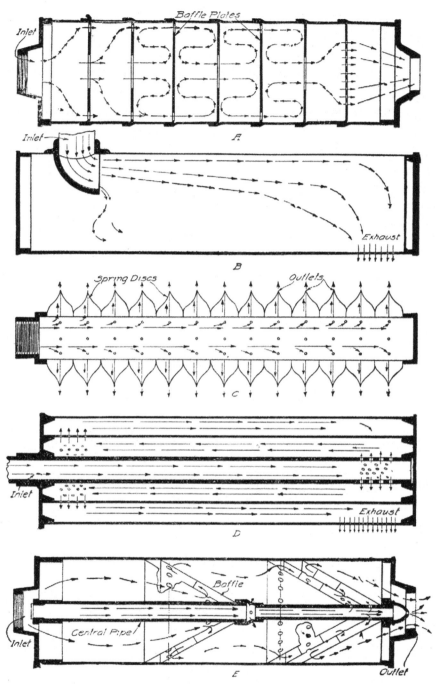

Fig. 17. Five of the Many Different Types of Mufflers
Courtesy of N. W. Henley Publishing Company, New York City

a good means of checking up the firing of the various cylinders; and several years ago, it was supposed to give greater power. Since its use was overdone, many cities and states prohibited such an arrangement on a car. Furthermore, the power loss has been proved a fallacy; consequently, the cut-out has gradually gone out of use.

On six-cylinder motors, and particularly motors with more than six cylinders, the sound of the exhaust is not an accurate guide to the firing of the cylinders, except for the expert mechanic with unusually keen hearing. The explosions of the six-, eight-, and twelve-cylinder engine overlap to such an extent that the weak explosion between two healthy ones cannot be detected. A missing cylinder can be found in this way, but not one that is simply getting a poor or weak spark.

JORDAN LINE-EIGHT SEDAN

413

CLUTCHES

TYPES OF CLUTCHES

Classification. Principal among the indispensable parts intervening between engine and road wheels is the clutch. There are three forms into which clutches may be divided, all of which are in general use in the automobile. These different forms are: cone clutches; disc clutches; and plate clutches.

The necessity for a clutch lies in the fact that the best results are obtained in an automobile engine when run at constant speed. Inasmuch as the speed of the car cannot from the nature of its use be constant, it requires some form of speed variator. This is the usual gear box, or transmission. Then there is the necessity of disconnecting it from the motor upon starting, since the engine cannot start under a load. There is also the necessity for disconnecting the two when it is desired to change from one speed to another either by way of an increase or a decrease. Also, when one wishes to stop the car, there must be some form of disconnection. There are, then, three real and weighty reasons for having a clutch.

Requirements Applying to All Clutches. In a serviceable clutch there are two general requirements which are applicable to all forms. These are gradual engagement and large contact surfaces, although the latter requirement may be made to lose much of its force by making the surfaces very efficient. In the cone clutch, gradual engaging qualities are secured by placing a series of flat springs under the leather or clutch lining. By means of these springs, acting against the main clutch spring, the clutch does not grab, since the large spring must have time in which to overcome the numerous small springs. In this way, the engagement is gradual and the progress of the car is easy as well as continuous.

The specific necessity in a cone clutch is a two-fold one—sufficient friction surface and proper angularity. The latter, in a way, affects the former. The angularity varies in practice from 8 to 18 degrees.

Cone Clutch. The cone clutch consists of two members, one fixed on the flywheel or other rotating part of the engine and the other fixed to the transmission shaft. The latter usually slides upon the shaft so as to allow engagement and disengagement, a spring holding the two together. When the smaller-diameter member

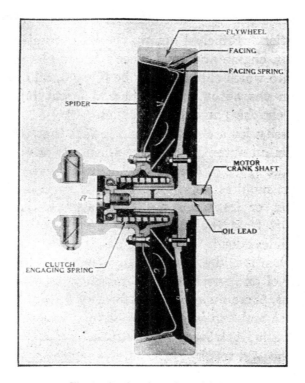

Fig. 1. Section through Studebaker
Direct Cone Clutch
Courtesy of Studebaker Corporation, Detroit, Michigan

is spoken of, it is usually called the male member, while the part of larger size is spoken of as the female member.

An excellent example of the direct cone clutch is shown in Fig. 1. The noticeable point about this clutch is its simplicity. It will be noted that the spring is entirely enclosed, so that when it needs adjusting the repair man must open the universal joint and operate the bolt A, which regulates the tension of the spring.

Another good example of the simplicity of the cone clutch is shown in Fig. 2, which is an aluminum member with bosses cast for cork inserts. Between the inserts may be seen the flat heads of the copper rivets which hold the clutch facing in place. Obviously this has the same disadvantage of internal, and thus inaccessible, spring.

In the cone type of clutch, Fig. 3, the inaccessible spring is avoided. In addition, a number of small springs are used in place of one very large and very stiff one. The ease of adjustment and

Fig. 2. Direct Cone Clutch with Cork Inserts

the greater ease in handling the springs make this clutch a much better design for average use from the repair man's point of view.

Disc Clutch. With its advent in 1904, the multiple-disc clutch has steadily grown in popularity, until today it is looked upon as the most satisfactory solution of the difficult clutch problem. Designers who have once adopted it, seldom, if ever, go back to another form, while of the new cars coming out from time to time nearly three-fourths are equipped with some form of disc clutch.

There are several improvements in the design of the disc type of clutch which are worthy of mention—use of self-aligning parts which take up the wear and the inaccuracies of machine work in manufacture; easy means of adjustment; use of better construction to prevent warping of the plates by overheating; ease of lubrication; elimination of surfaces that require lubrication; and means for getting a more uniform pressure on the friction surfaces of the plates.

Interchangeable Use of Cone and Disc. The relative advantages of the cone clutch and the disc clutch are presented in a very strik-

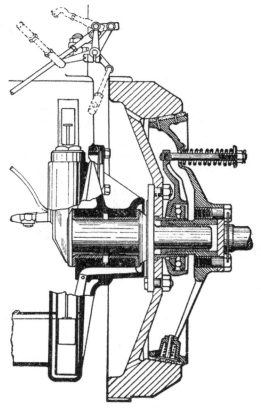

Fig. 3. Direct Cone Clutch with Small Springs and
External Adjustment
Courtesy of Willys-Overland Company, Toledo, Ohio

ing manner in Figs. 4 and 5. These clutches are designed to be interchangeable, consequently the general layout is the same. It will be noted that the cone is somewhat simpler than the disc, as it has fewer parts which take up room. The design is such that the terminal spring of the cone can be adjusted from the outside, as can the outside spring of the disc. An interesting point in this connection is that the transmissions also are interchangeable.

Simple Types of Disc. These types differ in number and shape, method of clutching, material, and lubrication; but in principle all are alike. This clutch is one in which the flat surfaces properly pressed together will transmit more power with less trouble than any

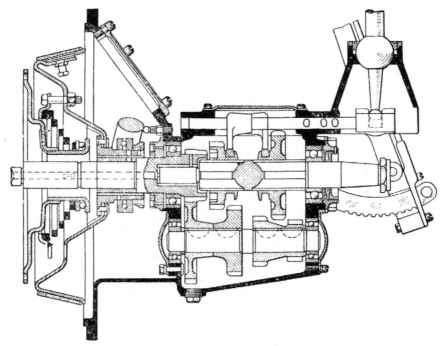

Fig. 4. Typical Three-Speed Gearset with Cone Clutch for Unit Power Plant
Courtesy of Warner Gear Company, Toledo, Ohio

other form. By multiplying the number of surfaces and making them infinitely thin, the power transmitted may be increased indefinitely. The discs should not be made too large. The greater the distance from the center on a revolving disc, the faster the movement and this tends to make the clutch action harsh with a tendency to grab. The smaller the disc, the softer the action when the clutch engages. That this is not idle fancy is shown by a number of very successful installations of 1000 horsepower and over in marine service.

The minimum number of plates in use is said to be three, but very often the construction of a three-plate clutch is such that one or two surfaces of other parts are utilized, making it a two- or even one-plate clutch in reality. In the Warner clutch, Fig. 5, there are really but two clutching surfaces, the face of the inner plate against the flywheel and the outer face against the engaging disc. Both plates are faced with suitable friction surface but it really is a one-disc clutch.

Multiple-Disc Clutches. The modern tendency in disc clutches, however, is away from those of few plates requiring a very high spring pressure—since the friction area is necessarily limited— toward the multiple-disc variety, in which a very large area is obtained. The large area needs a very light spring pressure, and

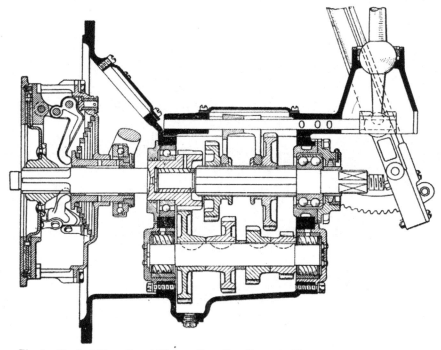

Fig. 5. Typical Three-Speed Warner Gear Box Shown in Fig. 4, but with Disc Clutch

consequently it is easier to engage and disengage the clutch. For this reason, the multiple disc is becoming more popular with owners and drivers than the variety requiring the extra-heavy effort. The construction of the three-plate disc clutch does not differ radically from one maker to another. Three fingers are used to clutch and declutch generally, the amount of movement being adjustable. A single spring of large diameter and large-size wire is generally used, and sheet steel is used for one-half the clutch plates. Between the three-plate and multiple-disc are many gradations.

In the true multiple-plate clutch, there are three general varieties met with in practice: the metal-to-metal with straight faces; the metal-to-metal with angular or other shaped faces designed to increase the holding power; and the straight-face kind in which metal does not contact with metal, one member either being lined with a removable lining or fitted with cork inserts.

Metal-to-Metal Dry-Disc Type. The metal-to-metal method has the additional advantage of having the central part within which the clutch is housed very small in diameter, so that the portion of the flywheel between the rim and the clutch housing may be made in the

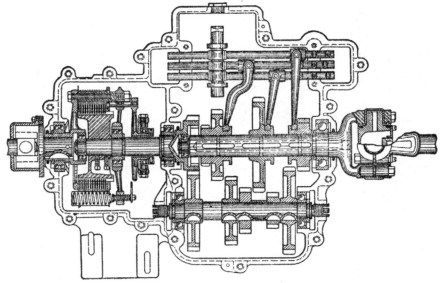

Fig. 6. Multiple-Disc Clutch and Transmission of Winton Cars
Courtesy of Winton Motor Car Company, Cleveland, Ohio

form of fan spokes that convert it into a fan which serves to cool the motor better.

As the various examples of disc clutch shown would indicate, the designer has had his choice between a few large discs and a large number of small ones. If he chose the former, the clutch could be housed within the flywheel, but that would make it inaccessible. If he chose the latter, the clutch could not be kept within the flywheel length. A separate clutch housing would be a necessity, but the clutch could be made accessible and flywheel fan blades could be used.

Another example of the plain metal-to-metal disc clutch is shown in Fig. 6. In this case also the clutch is not housed in the flywheel, as in most of the preceding examples of this form of clutch, but in the forward end of the transmission case, that is, instead of motor and clutch forming a unit, the clutch is a unit with the transmission. It is claimed that this position makes it more accessible, since it brings the clutch directly under the floor boards of the driver's compartment where it can be lubricated better. The lubrication is effected through communication with the gear part of the case, which is always filled with lubricant.

In the figure it will be noted that there are 13 driven discs, with keyways, which hold them to the driven drum. Note that the drum is held to its shaft by means of a pair of large set screws. The clutching springs are of small diameter and size, spaced equally around the periphery of the discs; each disc is enclosed in a small and thin metal casing. Attention is called also to the universal joint shown. This joint forms the rear end of the driving connection with the flywheel, which will be referred to later. These discs are flat-stamped out of sheet steel with the proper keyways for internal or external holdings.

Use of Facings. The more modern disc clutch has two sets of sheet metal discs, one of which is faced on one or both sides with a special material. Without a single exception, all the disc clutches shown have had plain discs against plain discs. This makes a simple and fairly inexpensive construction, but one that is not very efficient. The most recent tests have shown that metal against metal gives a coefficient of friction of but .15, which is reduced to .07 when the surfaces become oily or greasy. With one of these contacting faces lined with leather, the coefficient rises to .23 when dry and to .15 when oiled. Again if fiber is used for the facing, the coefficient becomes, respectively, .27 and .10, while with cork or with cork and leather, it becomes, respectively, .35 and .32. Here is a very apparent reason for (1) facing the clutch discs, and (2) running them dry.

By going over these figures, it will be noted that discs with almost any form of facing will show an increase in efficiency over the same discs without facing, varying from 60 up to almost 300 per cent. Again, any form of disc clutch, faced or otherwise, will show a much higher coefficient when dry than when oiled and thus a greater efficiency. These two facts point out the obvious reasons for the modern tendency toward the multiple-disc clutch, faced and running dry.

To present an example of the faced type, Fig. 7 shows the multiple-disc clutch of the eight-cylinder V-type Cadillac. In this illustration the eight driving discs can be seen with the facing on each side of each one. This facing is of wire-mesh asbestos, and between each pair of discs comes a plain driven disc, so that it has a facing of the asbestos against each side of the metal which it grips. The keys holding the inner discs to the shaft can be seen on the

Fig. 7.   1917 Cadillac Clutch and Transmission, Showing New Clutch Drive
Courtesy of Cadillac Motor Car Company, Detroit, Michigan

end of the housing, while the slots into which the keys project can be seen on the discs. By examining the group closely, the driven plain discs can be seen between each pair of the drivers. The method of driving these discs through a multiplicity of keys and grooves is unusual, but it is a good example of Cadillac thoroughness. Fig. 7 also shows the pedals and the exterior of the clutch case where it bolts up to the engine. This indicates how a unit power plant simplifies the control group and eliminates parts.

Floating Discs a Novelty. The clutch on Locomobile cars, shown in section in Fig. 8, is very much like the Cadillac just shown, except for the novel feature that the fabric facings are not attached either to the driving or to the driven discs but float between them. This fabric, usually a woven asbestos material with a central core of interwoven metal wires, instead of being attached to both sides of every other disc or to one side of every disc, is not attached at all. The rings for the fabric discs are made up in the form of annular rings. They have the same inner diameter as the inside of the

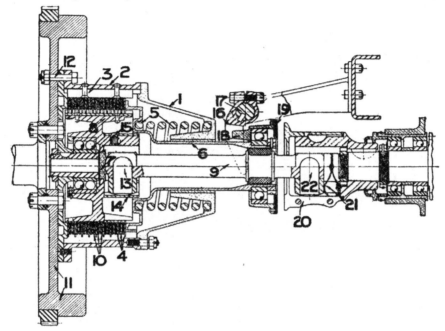

Fig. 8.   Floating Dry-Disc Clutch Used on Locomobile Cars

driving discs and the same outside size as the driven discs; consequently, assembling one of these clutches is simply a question of piling first a driven disc, then a fabric, then a driving disc, and so on.

The fact that the fabric rings are not united to either of the metal discs allows them to free themselves with remarkable rapidity so that either on engagement or on declutching the action is very quick.

Greater Power Transmitted by Surfaces Not Plane. To increase the power transmitted by a clutch of given size, either the number of plates must be increased or the form of the surface changed. The latter method was followed on the clutch of the French car "Ours."

The discs of this unusual clutch had a perfectly flat outer portion and a conical inner portion, only the latter taking part in the transmission of power. In this disc form, then, we have the advantage of the disc economy of space, together with the advantages of the cone clutch and the additive gain of running in a bath of oil.

Another form utilizing this principle, and one that is more widely used, is that known as the "Hele-Shaw" so named from its inventor, the famous English scientist, Dr. H. S. Hele-Shaw. This is essentially a flat disc, as shown at A, Fig. 9, with a ridge B at about the middle of the friction surface; this ridge consists of a portion

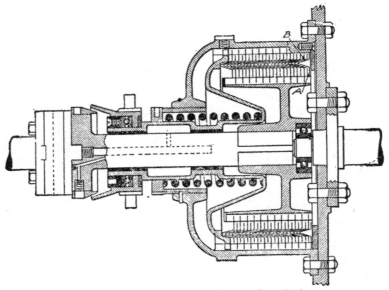

Fig. 9.   Hele-Shaw Disc Clutch, Showing Cone Surfaces

of the surface, which has been obtruded during the stamping process in such a way as to leave the surface of the ridge in the form of an angle of small height. The angle used is 35 degrees, and this value has been determined upon experimentally as the best. Fig. 9 shows a cross-section through an assembled clutch, which reveals the clutch angle very plainly. In use, the ridges nest one on top of the other: and in the extreme act of clutching, not only the flat surfaces but both sides of the ridge are in contact with the next plate. Thus, not only is the surface for a given diameter increased, but the wedge shape is also taken advantage of.

Hydraulic Clutches. All the methods of engaging and disengaging the engine at will, as discussed before, have been of a mechanical nature. The hydraulic clutch, on the other hand, partakes more of the fluid nature, although it is operated by mechanical means. Ordinarily, it is in the nature of a pump with a by-pass, the pump working at ordinary speeds to force the heavy liquid, usually glycerine, through the by-pass. To clutch up tightly, however, the by-pass is closed and, the liquid being unable to circulate while the pump continues to operate, the whole device is rotated as a unit. In this case it operates just as any other clutch, but, due to the sluggish action of the fluid, it is slower to respond. Then, too, the grave question of leakage is always present, and the smallest leak puts the clutch entirely out of use. These disadvantages, together with the necessary complications, have retarded the development of the hydraulic form so that there are few of that type in use today.

Borg & Beck Clutch. To adjust the Borg & Beck clutch, first release it with the foot lever. Loosen both slot-bolts A, Fig. 10, and shift either of them clockwise about $\frac{1}{2}$ inch. Let in the clutch, and if the opening at B is less than required, throw out the clutch and move either slot-bolt back far enough to open the space at B to the proper distance. This space varies from $1\frac{1}{2}$ to $4\frac{7}{16}$ inches according to the installation.

The adjustment A also adjusts the foot pedal, and when the clutch slips, this is usually owing to the clutch pedal striking against the under side of the foot board. When adjusting the clutch, be sure that at least $\frac{1}{2}$ inch clearance is left between the pedal and the foot board to allow for wear-in.

If the pedal touches the under side of the foot board, use the clutch adjustment only for obtaining the necessary clearance, as the single clutch adjustment automatically adjusts the pedal. When the clutch is adjusted, the clutch pedal automatically moves forward, giving the necessary clearance for wear-in.

Should it be necessary to adjust the pedal at any time, set the clutch at proper position first, and then set the pedal according to the location of the clutch throw-out collar.

The adjustment A must be used to increase or decrease the B space. If the proper space is not between these faces when the clutch is in, the throw-out movement will be too short.

When bolts *A* reach the end of the cover slots, owing to repeated adjustments, take them out of their mounting holes and set them back into the repeat holes exposed near the first end of the slots, thus doubling the range of adjustment.

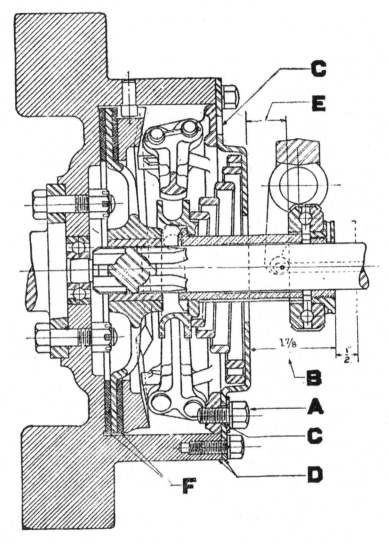

Fig. 10. Cross-Section of Borg & Beck Clutch

If, for any reason, the clutch is to be taken apart, first punch remounting line-up marks on the cover and the casing, as the clutch will not work properly if the cover is shifted in remounting.

In taking the clutch apart, first throw it out and lock out the spring by placing a space-block $1\frac{3}{8}$ inches high and 4 inches long between the cover and the throw-out yoke at E.

The two asbestos rings should be loose in their seats. When assembling, these rings should be coated on all sides with a thin layer of non-acid grease or cylinder oil. About every thousand miles, remove the adjusting screw and squirt a little oil into the clutch to moisten the asbestos mats. Too much oil will cause the clutch to slip until the oil is burned out.

The incline thrust ring should slide freely on the three drive pins in the flywheel.

It is good practice to block out the clutch to prevent it from becoming set, if the car is stored for any long period.

If the clutch needs cleaning, remove the adjusting screw and pour $\frac{1}{2}$ pint of kerosene into the clutch; let the motor run for fifteen minutes and then drain the clutch by letting the car stand over night with the front wheels at a higher position than the rear wheels.

Magnetic Clutches. A great deal of experimental work has been done with clutches operating on the magnetic principle. A magnet of large size and strength has a great pulling power that can be applied to an iron or steel member. In the electric clutch the main purpose was to devise some means of controlling the strength of these magnets so that they could be strengthened or weakened and cause the clutch to hold, slip, or disengage entirely. The strength of an electromagnet depends upon the amount of current flowing through the coils; and this principle was used to vary the magnetic strength. None of these clutches, however, were placed on the market as they were both expensive and complicated. Magnetic clutches, however, are used a great deal in machine shops to hold small parts on lathes, grinding machines, etc., where there is no method of holding the work with a mechanical clutch. One form of magnetic clutch is used on the Owen magnetic car. Both the gear box and clutch function by electricity or magnetism.

DETAILS OF CLUTCH OPERATION

Methods of Operation. Practically all modern clutches are operated by means of a special pedal moved by the left foot. The pedal is connected to the internal member by means of rods and levers, which compresses the clutch spring or springs and allows the clutch members to separate. This throws the clutch out. To throw it back in, remove the foot pressure from the pedal, and the springs again exert pressure and force the parts together. This action causes them to take hold. There was a time when a considerable number of cars had the clutch so constructed that the pedal held it in and the springs threw it out, just the reverse of the present plan. This method is no longer used, as it necessitated a constant pressure on the pedal while driving—a very fatiguing process.

Gradual Clutch Release. The Dorris clutch, made by the Dorris Motor Car Company, St. Louis, Missouri, Fig. 11, is a new arrangement of the clutch pedal, and its operation is such that the clutch is released or thrown out with very light pressure on the pedal. Pressure on the pedal *A* is transmitted by the shorter lever arm *B*, thus greatly increasing the leverage. This pressure is transmitted to lever *C* and through it to lever *D*, these two being hung on the frame cross member *E*. As *C* is much longer than *D*, there is another multiplying action here. This does not act directly upon the clutch but upon the upper end of the clutch shifter

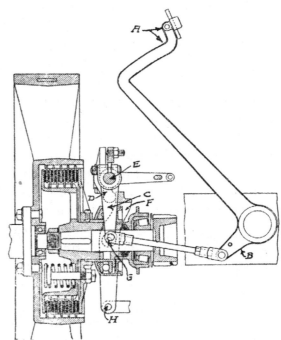

Fig. 11. Multiplying Lever of Dorris Clutch to Make Pedal Pressure Light

Courtesy of Dorris Motor Car Company, St. Louis, Missouri

F, which is attached to the clutch at *G* and pivoted at its lower end *H*—here again in a multiplying action. The net result of these three multiplications is a combination which will release the strongest and stiffest clutch with a very slight pressure of the foot.

Clutch Pedals. It has been the general practice in the past to have the clutch pedals separate and distinct, with the service-brake pedal on a concentric shaft occasionally. Now, however, the rapidly growing practice of simplification, combined with the wide use of the unit power plant, is to eliminate the so-called clutch shaft with its bearings and fastenings to the frame, to the clutch operating yoke, and to many other parts. As the Cadillac illustration, Fig. 7, shows and as the Templar unit, Fig. 12, shows even better, all these shafts, rods, and fastenings can be eliminated and the pedals and levers mounted directly on or in the power unit. In the Templar illustration, the foot brake has a simple rod connection from the ear on the pedal to the brake-operating system, while the hand

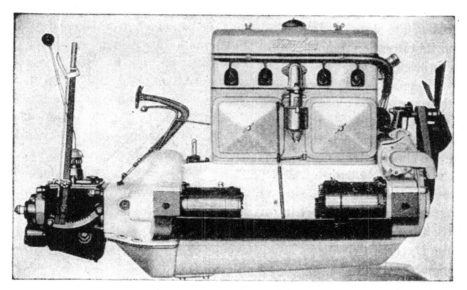

Fig. 12   Unit Power Plant of the Templar Four

brake has a similar connection from the extended lower end of the rod to the brake-operating system. In this simple way, perhaps 40 or more pieces are eliminated and their weight saved.

Clutch Lubrication. As has been previously pointed out, some clutches run in oil, while others run dry. The former type must be kept filled with lubricant at all times. The general plan in such a case is to provide a lead from the engine oiler when the clutch case is separated from the engine case or a connecting means when the two are in one case. In addition to the actual clutching members, there is practically always a sliding member, which must have lubricant of some form, while the thrust bearings to take the thrust of the clutch springs must be cared for. Generally these two cases are cared for by a pair of grease cups, which are clearly shown in Fig. 2. The operating rods are lubricated usually by means of small oil holes, either drilled directly into the part or covered with a small oil cup. In those cases in which the clutch runs in oil, it will be noted that a filling plug is provided, by means of which additional lubricant can be poured into the casing, Fig. 9.

Clutch-bearing lubrication is highly important, particularly with clutches like the cone which must be kept free from lubricant and the dry disc in which lubricant is not used. Where the clutch itself runs in oil, it is a simple matter to lubricate the bearings, but in the other cases, oil or grease must be provided from one of three places: from a prolongation of the engine oiling system, as shown in Figs. 1 and 4; from the outside—generally by means of grease cups—as just discussed; or from the transmission end. The last form is used only in unit power plants; combinations of clutch and transmission, as shown in Fig. 6; and in cases, Fig. 9, where the construction allows a grease or an oil cup attachment at the transmission end, the transmission itself being some distance away.

Clutch Bearings. The need for bearings in a clutch depends somewhat upon its nature and location, but regardless of these a thrust bearing is needed for the clutch spring. To explain this briefly, it is known that action and reaction are equal, and opposite in direction. For this reason, when a clutch spring presses the discs or parts together with a force of, say, 100 pounds, there is exerted in the opposite direction this same force of 100 pounds. In order to have something for this to work against, a bearing is used, and since it takes up this spring thrust, it is called a thrust bearing. Not all bearings are fitted to take thrust, as the majority are designed for radial loads only. For this reason a special design is needed.

When the clutch is incorporated in the flywheel, two additional bearings — one for the end of the crankshaft and another for the transmission or driven shaft—are generally needed. The bearings will be noted in Figs. 1 and 3, although the transmission-shaft bearing does not have the clutch combined with the engine but rather with the transmission. In the majority of cases, it will be found that a means of fastening the end of one shaft has been worked out so as to eliminate one bearing. This accounts for the large number which show but two—the thrust and one other. In looking back over the clutches, it will be noticed also that nearly all the bearings are of the plain ball form. This is due in large part to the fact that the plain ball bearings take up the least room for the load carried, both in diameter and width—a contributing reason being the fact that in many cases one of the shafts or parts can be formed to take the place of either the inner or outer ball race.

Clutch Adjustment. Adjusting a clutch, as a rule, is not a difficult task as there are but two possible sources of adjustment—the throw or movement of the operating pedal or lever and the tension of the spring. An adjustment is generally provided for each. When the fullest possible throw of the pedal does not disengage the clutch, an adjustment is required to give a greater throw. If the throw is correct, but the clutch takes hold too quickly and vigorously, the spring pressure can be lessened somewhat to soften down this action. On the other hand, when dropped in quickly, if it takes hold slowly, more spring pressure is needed, and it should be tightened.

Clutch Accessibility. Clutches are made accessible in two ways: by their location on the car and by the relative ease with which they can be removed. Accessibility as to location is less in the various combinations, such as in the unit power plant, housed within the flywheel, or combined with the transmission. Ease of removal is determined by the number and location of the joints (usually universal) used with the clutch.

CLUTCH TROUBLES AND REMEDIES

The very fact that the clutch is a more or less flexible, or rather, variable, connection between engine and road wheels makes it necessary that it be kept in the best of shape. It is rather surprising to the novice with his first clutch trouble to have his motor racing at the highest possible speed and to find his car barely moving, but to the experienced driver it is humiliating.

Slipping Clutch. Slipping is the most common of clutch troubles. This is brought about in a cone clutch by oil, grease, or other slippery matter on the surface of the clutch and can often be cured temporarily by throwing sand, dirt, or other matter on the clutch surface, although this is not recommended. Many times, the clutch leather, or facing, becomes so glazed that it slips without any oil or grease on it. In that case it is desirable to roughen the surface. This may be done by taking the clutch out, cleaning the surface with kerosene and gasoline, and then roughing-up the surface with a file or other similar tool.

In case it is not desired to take the clutch out, or when it is very inaccessible, the clutch surface may be roughened by fastening the clutch pedal in its extreme out position with some kind of a stick, cord, or wire, and then roughing the surface, as far in as it can be reached, with the end of a small saw, preferably of the keyhole type,

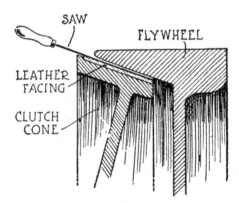

Fig. 13. Method of Roughing-Up
Clutch Leather with Saw

as shown in Fig. 13. Before starting this repair, it is well to soak the leather with neat's-foot oil. This softens the leather and makes the roughening task lighter.

Many drivers make the mistake of driving with the foot constantly on the clutch pedal. This wears the leather surface and helps it to glaze quickly. The constant rubbing from frequent slipping makes the leather hard and dry.

When a metal-to-metal oiled clutch slips, the trouble usually is in the clutch spring, which is too weak to hold the plates together. To remedy slipping with this type, it is necessary to tighten up the clutch-spring adjustment.

There is one cause for a slipping clutch which is often overlooked but which should be looked for before any adjustment is made on the clutch itself. The trouble is caused by the clutch-pedal arm touching the floor boards. Fig. 14 shows this condition and a typical method for adjustment. This trouble also occurs in the disc type of clutch. There should be at least one-half inch play between the floor boards and the pedal arm, as shown in Fig. 14.

Other causes of slipping clutches are the misalignment of shafts —either in manufacture or by the parts becoming worn—and the different units held loosely on their supports. This is often taken care of by the use of a self-aligning hub or some compensating device

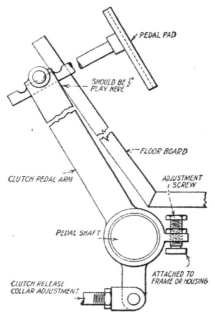

Fig. 14. Pedal-Arm and Foot-Board
Clearance

incorporated in the toggals or levers used to give the necessary pressure to the driving plates.

Clutch troubles are not always so obvious. In one instance, the clutch slipped on a new car. In the shop, the clutch spider seemed perfect and properly adjusted, also the spring, but to make sure, a new clutch was put in. Still the clutch slipped. To test it out still farther, the linkage was disconnected right at the clutch and then it held perfectly, showing that the trouble was in the linkage. On examination one bushing was found to be such a tight fit that it would not allow the pedal to move freely enough to release the clutch fully. When this was relieved a little, the clutch acted all right.

Replacing Clutch Leathers. Clutches offer many chances for trouble. The most frequent causes are the wear of leather facings, with the attendant loss of power, and weak springs. Weak springs may be cured by screwing up on the adjusting nut or bolt provided. Slippery leather may also be corrected by washing first with gasoline and then with water, finally roughing the surface with a coarse rasp and replacing only after the leather is thoroughly clean. Dry leather is fixed by soaking in water or neat's-foot oil. It should be replaced while still moist, and copious lubrication will keep it soft.

The greatest problem in replacing a worn, charred, or otherwise defective leather lies in getting the right layout for the form of the new leather the first time. It must be remembered that the surface is a portion of a cone and, therefore, its development is not easy. Prepare the cone by removing the old leather and all rivets, cleaning out the rivet holes, and providing new rivets. Measure the cone, taking the diameters at both the large

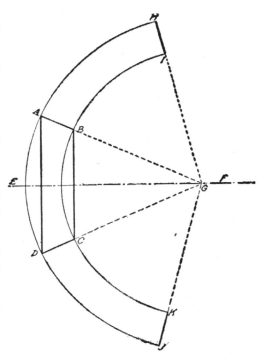

Fig. 15.   Diagram Showing How to Cut Clutch Leathers

and small ends and also the width. Take a large sheet of paper and lay off upon it a figure similar to *ABCD*, Fig. 15, drawn to exact scale and having for its dimensions the three measurements just obtained, viz, the large and small diameters and the width of the cone measured horizontally. This figure represents the **projection** of the cone in a flat plane. Bisect the line *AD* and draw the **center** line *EF* at right angles to *AD*. Prolong the two tapered lines *AB* and *DC* until they meet the center line as at *G*.

The point *G* represents the apex of the cone if it were complete, and hence any circular arc with the correct radius, drawn from this point as a center, will be a correct projection of the development of that portion of the conical surface. With *GA* and *GB* as radii, draw the two circular arcs *HADJ* and *IBCK*, also draw the radial lines *HI* and *JK* to pass through *G*. The enclosed figure *HIBCKJDAH* may then be cut out and used as a pattern from which to cut out clutch leathers. If the distances *AH* and *DJ* be made approximately equal to or slightly more than *AD*, the pattern will a little more than encircle the cone clutch.

After the leather has been cut out, it should be prepared by soaking in water or oil, according as its surface is fairly soft or rather harsh. In either case it must be well soaked so as to stretch easily.

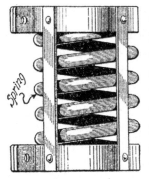

Fig. 16. Type of Clutch Spring Holder Which Works by Friction
Courtesy of "Motor World"

In putting it on the cone, one end is cut to a diagonal, laid down on the cone, and riveted in place. Next, the leather is drawn down tightly past the next pair of rivet holes, which are then driven into place. This is continued until the strip is secured. The leather is now wetted again for, if allowed to dry off immediately, the shrinking action will break it out at most of the rivet holes and render it useless. By drying it out gradually, a taut condition may be arrived at without this danger.

Handling Clutch Springs. Clutch springs are mean to handle and compress. The best way is to compress and hold them compressed until needed. For this purpose, a rig similar to that described for valve springs should be made but of stiffer, stronger stock. A very good one can be made from two round plates, one small, and the other of larger diameter with a pair of L-shaped bolts through it. The spring is placed between the two, with the ends of the L's looped over the smaller plate, and then, by tightening the nuts on the bolts, the spring is gradually compressed.

An excellent device for holding clutch springs consists of a simple pair of metal clamps which are joined together by three or more short metal bars, Fig. 16. If one particular clutch spring is handled continuously, the length can be made to fit this best, otherwise it will have to be made of any convenient length. The inside diameter of the clamps when fully open is greater than the outside diameter of the spring. The clamp is set in a vise or on a drill press and the spring set inside of it. Then the spring is compressed by working the vise handle or by lowering the drill-press spindle. When compressed down to the length used in the car, the ends of the clamp are tightened and the spring is held by friction. Then the spring can be handled readily, using one of the metal bars as a handle. It is put into place, and then the retaining screws can be loosened and the clamp removed.

Fierce Clutch. A fierce clutch is one that does not take hold gradually but grabs the moment the clutch pedal is released. In a metal-disc clutch this is caused by roughened plate surfaces and insufficient lubricant, so that, instead of the plates twisting gradually across each other as the lubricant is squeezed out from between them, they catch at once and the car starts with a jerk. The pins or keys on which the plates slide become worn by the action of the plates until there are small grooves worn in them. The plates have a tendency to stick in these grooves, allowing a few of the plates to engage easily. When the full pressure of the spring is exerted on the plates, they quickly slip out of the grooves causing a sudden engagement of the clutch, and the car jumps forward. A warped plate in the clutch will also cause a disc or plate clutch to be fierce and grab. The cure for the first is to install new keys in drum and spider; in the second, it is best to install new plates.

On a cone clutch, this fierceness is produced by too strong a spring, too large a clutching surface in combination with a very strong spring, or a hard or burned clutch surface or both. If the leather facing of the clutch becomes worn, a rivet will stick up above the facing and the clutch will take hold at that point and cause it to grab. Rerivet the facing and see that the rivets are well below the surface of the leather. If the clutch facing is not put on the cone correctly, it may touch the flywheel and the clutch will grab, because there is a sudden application of the power to the cone instead of gradual engagement. It will be necessary in this case to install a new facing of the correct size and it should not overhang the cone. If the facing is a little too wide it may overhang the cone on the end that enters the cone last and not the front end.

Ford Clutch Troubles. There are now so many Fords in use that the average repair man feels justified in making special apparatus or tools to save time or work in Ford repairs. For one thing, the clutch-disc drum frequently needs removal and this is a difficult job. It can be taken off in a few minutes and with little trouble, however, by means of a simple rigging which consists of a $\frac{1}{4}$-inch plate of steel with three holes drilled in it for three bolts, Fig. 17. The two outside ones have T-head ends and have to be specially made, and made carefully, as this T-head must slip through either one of the oval holes in the web of the drum. When this is done, it is straightened up so as to stand at right angles to the drum and

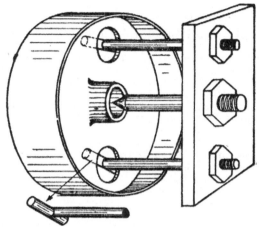

Fig. 17. Simple Rigging for Removing Ford Clutch Disc

is thus in a position to press firmly against the drum from the inside. There are nuts on the center bolt on both sides of the plate, but the drawing shows only that on the outer end. When the T-bolts are in place, the center bolt, which is slightly pointed and preferably hardened on the end, is screwed down so as to come into contact with the end of the clutch shaft. After tightening the center bolt, the T-head bolts are tightened until they pull the drum off the shaft.

Clutch Spinning. A trouble which is bothersome but not dangerous is clutch spinning. This is the name applied to the action of the male clutch member when it continues to rotate, or spin, after the clutch spring pressure has been released. With the male member connected up to the principal transmission shaft and gear, as is often the case, these members continue to rotate with it. This gives trouble mainly in gear shifting, for the member which is out of engagement is considered to be at rest or rapidly approaching that condition. When at rest, it is an easy matter to mesh another gear with this one; but when this one is rotating or spinning, it is not so easy, particularly for the novice.

In any case, the best and quickest remedy is a form of clutch spinning brake. This may consist simply of a small pad of leather or of metal covered with leather so located on the frame members that the male drum touches against it when fully released. Or it may be something more elaborate as to size or construction or both. On many modern cars, in fact on practically all good cars, some form of clutch spinning brake is fitted.

The principal causes of clutch spinning are as follows:

(1) A defect in the manufacture or design which is hard to cure unless the units concerned are taken apart, thoroughly examined, faults corrected, and the units reassembled. Parts that are out of balance can be put in perfect balance and the trouble eliminated.

(2) Insufficient lubrication causes the operating parts to bind and prevents the clutch from being released properly. To cure this trouble the parts should be disassembled and polished and reinstalled after a thorough lubrication.

(3) Where plates or discs are used a dust, which will wear off the lining or rings, accumulates in the clutch housing and mixes with the oil that finds its way into the clutch. This becomes a thick gummy substance, causing the plates to stick and preventing the clutch from being released. The clutch should be taken apart and all the parts cleaned. If the clutch has been standing for a long time, the plates will stick together and it will be impossible to separate them.

(4) Plates that have been overheated will warp and cause spinning and this can only be corrected by the installation of new plates. In some clutches, the plates are prevented from warping by slotting the plates radially.

(5) The grooves that are worn in the keys or pins used to take the drive in the multiple disc type of clutch will also cause this trouble because the plates tend to stick in these grooves. The keys should be renewed.

The tendency toward the use of lighter materials in the manufacture of clutches is doing away with the trouble of spinning. Because of the heavy parts that have been used in the past it was difficult to stop the clutch from spinning, owing to the speed developed by the centrifugal force set up by the revolving mass, but there is a good deal to be said in favor of the heavy parts, such as heavy plates which do not warp very easily and give less tendency to rattle when disengaged.

Cork Inserts. When cork inserts are used in a clutch, the insertion of new corks is not an easy job. A cork is a difficult and unhandy thing to work with, and above all to hold straight and true while applying longitudinal force to it. By making up a special tool with a tubular member having an inner taper, into which the corks are forced by means of a special plunger which forms the other part of the tool, this is simplified considerably. This tool is shown

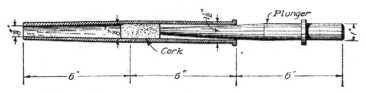

Fig. 18. Simple Device for Inserting Corks in Clutches

in Fig. 18, with such dimensions as would be needed for a $\frac{7}{8}$-inch cork. It is advisable to make the small end of the tube $\frac{1}{8}$ inch smaller than the cork, as this amount pro-

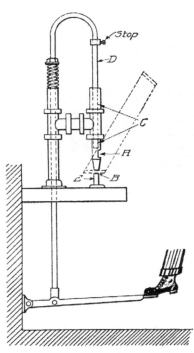

Fig. 19. Machine for Handling Cork Inserts Quickly
Courtesy of "Motor World"

vides the proper compression. After being soaked in water for 10 or 15 minutes, the cork is dropped into the large end of the tube, and, with the small end in place against the cork opening in the clutch, a single stroke of the plunger will force the cork through the tool, incidentally compressing it into the hole in the clutch. With a few handlings any clever mechanic can soon become expert in the use of this tool.

A more elaborate device and one which works more quickly is shown in Fig. 19. This is not an expensive machine. The framework is made of standard pipe fittings, the spring is a valve spring, and the rods are cold rolled steel. Only a few pieces, such as the working member C, were specially made. The working member is made with a slot at A into which the corks are inserted. When the pedal attached to the rod D is pressed, it brings the rod down and forces out the cork at B. At point B, the clutch resting on the anvil E is held ready. The stop limits the downward movement, so a strong stroke of the foot will just push **the cork** into the hole flush and no more. The lower end of the working member is made with a taper so as to compress the corks about $\frac{1}{8}$ inch. They should be soaked in water just the same as when using the hand tool.

In Fig. 20, several other common clutch troubles **and** their remedies are suggested; the parts shown in the illustration, however, are in excellent condition, in fact, new.

When the right kind of clutch discs for a multiple-disc form are not on hand, new discs can be cut from leather by means of the

Fig. 20. Clutch Troubles Illustrated

gasket cutter, Fig. 21. This cutter consists of a pair of steel **L**-shaped arms, preferably forged, with points sharpened enough to cut the leather or the gasket material. The clamp has a point for the center of the circle on its under side, while the actual clamping is done by the bolt or screw with wing head. To use for clutch discs, set the inner, or shorter, member to the radius of the inside of the outer discs and the outer, or longer, arm to the radius of the outside of the inner discs. By pressing down hard on the arms and rotating them at the same time, an annular ring will be cut out which will fit exactly. One hand should be held on or near the center, while the other hand supplies the pressure and rotating motion on the cutting ends. It should not be expected that the points will cut through in one revolution; on the contrary, the first time around will just mark out the section and it will need from 6 to 10 revolutions, with heavy pressure, to cut a leather disc. In

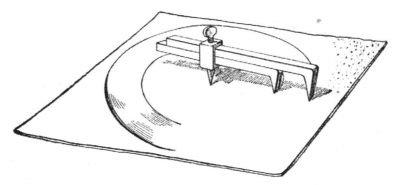

Fig. 21. Method of Cutting Facing for Disc Clutches in an Emergency
Courtesy of "Motor World"

time, the workman will become skilled in the use of this cutter and have a knowledge of its limits, as well as of the method of keeping it in good cutting order.

Adjusting Clutch Pedals. Some cars are made with adjustable clutch pedals so the long- or short-legged driver can set the length of these to suit, but when no adjustment is provided and it is desired to change the length, some figuring must be done. To shorten a non-adjustable pedal, the best way is to take it out of the car and bend it somewhat on the order of the dotted lines in Fig. 22. The idea is to make the same amount of metal take a roundabout and longer path. In doing this, the workman must be governed largely by what the floor boards and the other parts of the mechanism in the immediate vicinity will allow. The bend must be made so as to allow the pedal to work in the same slot. If necessary, cut the slot a little longer, but first consider the result before bending the pedal.

On the other hand, when the pedal is too short, the pad can be removed from where it is bolted on at A and a pair of steel strips cut so as to fit into the two sides of the pedal shank and brought together at the other end. These are bolted in at A, where the pad was formerly, and the pad moved out to the new end at *B*. In some such cases, where the sides of the pedal shank offer no groove to help hold the steel strips, it is necessary to put another bolt through them, as at *C*, to prevent the whole addition swinging about *A* as a center.

Clutch Troubles Outside of Clutch. Frequently, there is trouble in the clutch when the basic reason for it is outside of the clutch entirely. Thus, failure of a clutch to engage or disengage properly is often the fault of the connecting rods and levers; wear in the clutch collar or in other parts; or the emergency-brake interlock may have been fitted so close that as soon as the rods are shortened once or twice to compensate for wear, it stands in such a position as to throw the clutch out slightly although the latter appears to be fully engaged.

Another clutch trouble outside of the clutch is apparent

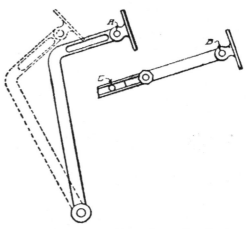

Fig. 22. Schemes for Shortening or Lengthening Clutch Pedals to Fit Driver

slipping at corners, especially at turns on grades. On a turn—the road being cambered—the frame is distorted, especially with the combination of curve and grade. This may be sufficient to throw the clutch and driving shaft out of alignment just enough so the clutch face will not make full contact. This is most noticeable on cars with a single universal joint, in which case the distortion of the frame has more effect on the driving shaft. Similarly, a car with an unusually light or flexible frame will show this trouble very often, as the combination of curve and grade is too much for the light frame.

Grinding Noises in Clutch. This trouble is usually caused by insufficient lubrication in the bearing on the clutch release collar or between the sliding parts of the clutch. The pilot bearing, which supports the front end of the clutch shaft often becomes dry, causing a grinding noise and, if badly worn, allows the shaft to drop down slightly. This causes the plates to bind as well as grind when the clutch is released.

Continued in Volume 2

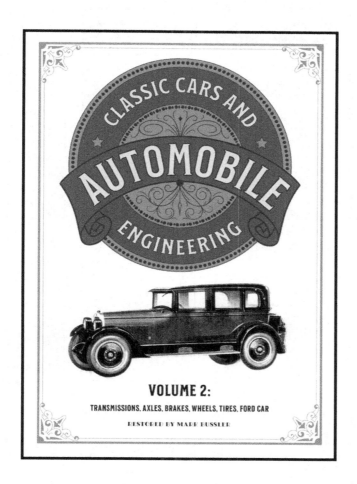

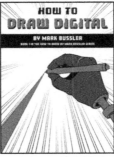

OTHER BOOKS FROM CGR PUBLISHING AT CGRPUBLISHING.COM

Ultra Massive Video Game Console Guide Volume 1

Ultra Massive Video Game Console Guide Volume 2

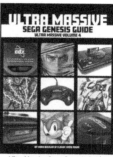

Ultra Massive Video Game Console Guide Volume 3

Ultra Massive Sega Genesis Guide

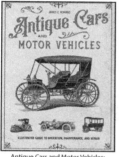

Antique Cars and Motor Vehicles: Illustrated Guide to Operation...

Chicago's White City Cookbook

The Clock Book: A Detailed Illustrated Collection of Classic Clocks

The Complete Book of Birds: Illustrated Enlarged Special Edition

1901 Buffalo World's Fair: The Pan-American Exposition in Photographs

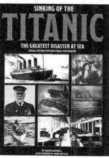

Sinking of the Titanic: The Greatest Disaster at Sea

Gustave Doré's London: A Pilgrimage: Retro Restored Special Edition

Milton's Paradise Lost: Gustave Doré Retro Restored Edition

The Art of World War 1

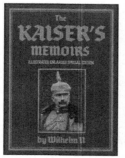

The Kaiser's Memoirs: Illustrated Enlarged Special Edition

Captain William Kidd and the Pirates and Buccaneers Who Ravaged the Seas

The Complete Butterfly Book: Enlarged Illustrated Special Edition

445

Made in the USA
Coppell, TX
25 January 2022

72245063R00247